Understanding Intergovernmental Relations

The Duxbury Press Series on Public Policy

Charles O. Jones, *University of Pittsburgh*
General Editor

An Introduction to the Study of Public Policy, Second Edition
Charles O. Jones

The Domestic Presidency: Decision-Making in the White House
John H. Kessel, *Ohio State University*

Public Policy and Politics in America
James E. Anderson, David W. Brady, *University of Houston* and Charles L. Bullock, III, *University of Georgia*

Understanding Intergovernmental Relations
Deil Wright, *University of North Carolina*

Introduction to Budgeting
John Wanat, *University of Kentucky*

FORTHCOMING

Policy Analysis: An Interdisciplinary Approach
Duncan MacRae, Jr. and James Wilde, *University of North Carolina*

Bureaucracy and Public Policy
Kenneth Meier, *University of Oklahoma*

OF RELATED INTEREST

A Logic of Public Policy: Aspects of Political Economy
L. L. Wade, *University of California, Davis* and Robert L. Curry, Jr., *California State University, Sacramento*

Democracy in America: A Public Choice Perspective
L. L. Wade, *University of California, Davis* and R. L. Meek, *Colorado State University*

Politics, Change, and the Urban Crisis
Bryan Downes, *University of Oregon*

Understanding Intergovernmental Relations

Public Policy and Participants' Perspectives in Local, State, and National Governments

Deil S. Wright
University of North Carolina, Chapel Hill

Duxbury Press
North Scituate, Massachusetts

Duxbury Press
A Division of Wadsworth Publishing Company, Inc.

© 1978 by Wadsworth Publishing Company, Inc., Belmont, California 94002. All rights reserved. No part of this book may be reproduced, stored in a retrieval system, or transcribed, in
any form or by any means, electronic, mechanical, photocopying, recording, or otherwise,
without the prior written permission of the publisher, Duxbury Press, a division of Wadsworth
Publishing Company, Inc., Belmont, California.

Understanding Intergovernmental Relations was edited and prepared for composition by
Kevin Gleason. Interior design was provided by Amato Prudente and the cover was designed
by Garrow Throop.

Library of Congress Cataloging in Publication Data

Wright, Deil Spencer, 1930–
  Understanding intergovernmental relations.

  Includes index.
  1. Intergovernmental fiscal relations—United States. I. Title.
HJ275.W72   350'.725'0973   77-26967
ISBN 0-87872-152-5

Printed in the United States of America

2 3 4 5 6 7 8 9   82 81 80 79

To
David, Mark, Matthew, Lois
and Pat
for their understanding

Contents

Foreword

The problems and prospects of national-state relations have been central concerns of the Republic since its very inception. The writers of the U.S. Constitution were at their work in Philadelphia in large part because the first effort to establish a workable distribution of authority failed miserably. James Madison, among others, understood above all that questions about federalism had to be resolved in Philadelphia and urged his colleagues to consider a strong nationalist option.

These questions are even more important today than they were then. For however vital it was to define and establish intergovernmental spheres in 1789, the growth of functions at all levels of government now demands almost hourly attention to such matters. No longer merely an issue to debate in the classroom or the courts, national-state-local distribution of functions, authority, revenues, and administration has to be untangled for every domestic program. The allocations of twenty years ago no longer apply, in particular because of the virtual explosion of national-level domestic programs enacted in the 1960s. If no day can pass in government without treating these matters, then surely no course in American government and politics can afford to ignore the topic.

Deil S. Wright has been monitoring our complex intergovernmental operations for many years and thus was the natural choice to write a basic text on the subject. Happily he came to us with his plans already well-formed. We think that the book that has resulted will serve both the needs of the classroom and the interests of the scholar. Professor Wright offers a detailed and readable description and analysis of all the major issues associated with intergovernmental relations. He provides important trend data, relevant illustrations, and imaginative charts and diagrams. *Understanding Intergovernmental Relations* is well titled: It is a book designed to promote awareness and understanding of future domestic policy making and implementation in the American federal system.

Charles O. Jones
University of Pittsburgh

Preface

One of Murphy's several "laws" asserts that "before you can do the one thing you want to do, something else must be done first." This book represents a "thing" I have wanted to do for several years, but "something else" always seemed to claim prior attention.

For more than two decades, at four universities I have annually taught a course titled Intergovernmental Relations. The courses and my own thinking on intergovernmental relations (IGR) have changed through the years. These shifts reflect not only the changing character of IGR but also my own intellectual development, research interests, consulting-advising activities, professional exchanges, and students' curiosity and responses. This book is a blend of these experiences and relationships.

Three interrelated themes have guided my selection and organization of the material in this book. Those themes are: change, concepts, and description. Change is inherent in all contemporary political systems and the multi-jurisdictional system-of-systems in the United States is no exception to this general rule. The intelligent reader, the interested student, and the active practitioner of IGR may differ sharply on the degree and direction of change in the United States. But all would concede that our political systems, public policies, and governmental officials are markedly different in the 1970s from those operating in earlier decades of the twentieth century. This small volume attempts to capture some of the more significant changes in these systems, policies, and officials.

The second theme is an emphasis on concepts. I have attempted to provide the reader with verbal handles for grasping the overall character of relationships among governments and officials. The conceptual components of this book furnish a framework for generalizing about issues, policies, and events affecting governments and about the attitudes and actions of public officials pursuing goals that bring them together in an IGR context. The cornerstone of this conceptual structure is the term *intergovernmental relations*. The book is an effort to promote better and more widespread understanding of this fundamental concept, which is relatively recent in origin and not extensively understood but of major and increasing significance.

Description is the third theme. The description of IGR draws on two traditions of political science/public administration research: the historical/institutional and the quantitative/empirical. The former tradition looks at legal powers (or cases), formal roles, and governmental structures. The second relies on behavioral data, survey results, and fiscal regularities. A large and largely unmined body of data exists on IGR interactions, preferences, and perceptions. This book does little more than scratch the surface of that large empirical mass. It may encourage and suggest avenues for further exploration. Simply stated the aim of the description is to show how governments and officials operate in practice as well as in theory. The reader should obtain a feel for the way things work in IGR. The materials included in the appendices are designed to supplement the real-world descriptive focus.

In writing this book I have attempted to keep three audiences in mind: students, the practitioner of IGR, and the interested, intelligent citizen. The practitioner and the citizen are secondary audiences, but they are not exempt from the central value premise of this volume: citizens, officials, and students alike can benefit from a better understanding of IGR. My primary audience is students in three types of college-level courses: federalism or intergovernmental relations, state and local government, and public administration. The first of these three needs no comment or explanation. I have melded my research interests and value biases toward state and local governments with an intent to reach students enrolled in these courses. Nearly all practitioners and academics emphasize that it is not possible to study state and/or local government today without knowing a great deal about IGR. My interest and bias toward public administration prompted me to keep another audience in mind: students enrolled in introductory public administration courses. One focus of many public administration courses is how things get done in government—how money is used and how officials, especially administrators, relate to each other. The attention and analysis devoted to these aspects of governmental operations reflects my effort to meet these student and course concerns more than halfway.

How well I have reached these audiences is problematic. I solicit and welcome all feedback. I have already had the benefit of substantial feedback from reviewers of various portions of the manuscript. I have not always followed their comments, criticisms, and suggestions, but their reactions have been exceptionally constructive and have added notably to whatever merit there is in the product. Those who gave me the benefit of their views include: Thad Beyle, Kenneth Howard, Charles Jones, Richard Leach, Mary Lepper, Donald Liner, Michael Regan, Robert Thomas, and Gordon Whitaker. One other person who contributed significantly to the overall improvement of the original manuscript was Kevin Gleason, my copy editor. His insistence on clarity, precision, and logic in the use of words and expression of ideas are hereby acknowledged and appreciated.

Others also aided in the development and completion of this book. My associates on the general revenue sharing research staff deserve special mention for helping to formulate and analyze research questions from the state administrators data. These included David Kovenock, Dan Silver, Mike Karpinski, Fred Light and Mary Wagner. Greg Feller was helpful in pulling together data from the diverse surveys of federal, state, and local officials. Charlotte Mansfield did an excellent job of translating my original drafts and tables into neat and accurate typescript. My wife, Pat, functioned as a constructive critic and a spot typist in emergency situations.

I would also like to add my thanks to the staff at Duxbury Press for their interest, cooperation, assistance, and patience. I refer to Robert Gormley, Patrick Fitzgerald, Katharine Gregg, and Margaret Kearney.

Finally, I should acknowledge my ultimate responsibility for the book's contents and my own capacity to at least modify, if not repeal one of Murphy's laws. I was at last able to do this "thing" before something else!

Intergovernmental Relations:

Who? Where? When? What?

1

CITIZENS, OFFICIALS, AND INTERGOVERNMENTAL RELATIONS

On an unpaved street in a southern town lives Amanda Jones in a small, dilapidated 40-year-old house on which she is paying off the mortgage. With the help of the town housing authority, Ms. Jones recently qualified for a modest, 2 percent interest loan from the town's Housing Loan Revolving Fund to install much-needed new plumbing and heating equipment. The half-million dollars in the Revolving Fund came from General Revenue Sharing funds earmarked by the Town Council for repair loans. The street in front of Ms. Jones's house will soon be paved as part of a neighborhood renewal program financed, in part, with funds from the Department of Housing and Urban Development.

In a medium-sized city in the upper Midwest, Bill West owns and lives in the 100-year-old house where he was born over 80 years ago. He

ekes out a spare but comfortable existence on his monthly social security check of $250. Bill's possessiveness about his home makes un-
derstandable the near-apoplexy he used to experience when city,
county, and school property tax bills, totaling over $350, would arrive
in the mail. His mental (and fiscal) health have improved considerably
since 1973, when the state legislature adopted a so-called circuit breaker
property tax relief program. This legislation was designed to pick up
the property tax overload on low-income, elderly persons. The state
government now pays over $200 of Bill's annual property tax bills.

David S. Anderson is the "metro manager" for the adjoining
central-Illinois cities of Bloomington and Normal, with a combined
population of 75,000. In July 1975 each appointed Anderson its city
manager. This unique experiment capped a decade of cooperation and
conflict between the two communities, including two consolidation
referenda that were defeated substantially in both jurisdictions. Anderson spends half of each day in each city, and each pays half his
salary and benefits. Despite his experimental, even tenuous, fence-
straddling role, Anderson has been actively exploring ways to reduce
costs by such measures as consolidating departments of the two cities.[1]

Few people envied Mayor Abraham Beame of New York City
during the latter months of 1975, when he was castigated as the cus-
todian of the "Big Apple with a rotten core." Besides cutting thousands
of workers from the city payroll he spent dozens of hours pleading in
Albany and Washington for fiscal assistance that might keep the city
from defaulting on its debt obligations. State and national assistance
were forthcoming only after the city had several times teetered on the
brink of bankruptcy. Federal support, which many argued was tardy
and niggardly, came in the form of $2.3 billion in short-term loans to
ease the city's catastrophic cash flow and massive debt problems. The
December 1975 "bail-out" was not without significant costs which
were not incurred by Mayor Beame alone. To secure the assistance the
mayor was forced not only to pledge draconian fiscal measures but also
to concede oversight and decision-making authority to state and national officials. The "cost" to the federal government seemed slim,
since the funds were repayable loans, not grants. One unanticipated
consequence of the national, state, and local actions took some time to
surface. About two months later (February 19, 1976) the *Wall Street
Journal* reported that the U.S. dollar slipped on the European money
market "against all major currencies based on fresh concern abroad

---

1. "Metro-Manager Experiment," *Public Management,* 58 (June 1976): 20–23.

over New York State and City finances." These worries, acknowledged the *Journal*, "were reawakened on reports that the federal government has assigned inspectors to look over state [and city] budget proposals."

Don Jackson had been superintendent for less than a year in a suburban southern California school district, but it had taken him only a few weeks to realize that the district was far too dependent on the local property tax. He had called a meeting of his administrative staff with two items on the agenda: (1) What are the prospects for getting a more favorable break under the state formula for aid to local schools? (2) How could the district get more federal money? Don was chiefly searching for ideas from his staff, but on the second question he had one specific proposal to make: He suggested that one staff member be assigned to visit six to eight similar districts around the state and learn firsthand how to play the "federal grantsmanship game." He thought the idea would go over well with his staff.

Ms. Bonnie Brown, Assistant Director of the Department of Administration for the city of Durham, North Carolina, is also Director of Intergovernmental Programs, where her central responsibility lies. In the latter capacity she and her staff deal with virtually all aspects of the city's relationships with the state and national governments, with special emphasis on getting money—that is, grantsmanship. Activities include researching grant availability, reviewing all grant proposals developed by any city agency, writing applications, informally promoting grant applications submitted to state and federal agencies, and monitoring the administration of grants received. Twenty-seven active grants are now channeled through her office, producing more than $4 million annually. She has become thoroughly familiar with the "bible" of federal grantsmanship, the *Catalog of Federal Domestic Assistance* describing the 1026 aid programs administered by 54 different federal departments, independent agencies, commissions, and councils.

From 1960 to 1964 Terry Sanford was governor of North Carolina. Subsequently he directed a two-year "Study of American States." This research, combined with his gubernatorial experience, resulted in a landmark book, *Storm over the States*. Among the several significant ideas he set forth is a set of propositions:

1. The national government cannot effectively reach its goals without the power of the states.
2. The states cannot serve all their people without the power of the national government.

3. The city cannot overcome its problems without the power of the national government plus the power of the state.
4. The national and state governments cannot do their duty by the city residents without the power of the city government.[2]

Less than two years after Sanford's book was published, the interrelatedness of federal, state, and local governments came prominently, even dramatically, to the nation's attention. On August 8, 1969, in an evening address on nationwide television, President Richard M. Nixon outlined four major planks in his "New Federalism" program. He highlighted features of proposals dealing with family assistance (welfare), economic opportunity, manpower, and revenue sharing. The president enunciated a recurrent theme in governmental affairs affecting our everyday lives—and one that will be treated in this book. Emphasizing interdependency, he observed: "We can no longer have effective government at any level unless we have it at all levels. There is too much to be done for the cities to do it alone, or for Washington to do it alone, or for the States to do it alone."[3]

The experiences, actions, and ideas of Jones, West, Anderson, Beame, Jackson, Brown, Sanford, and Nixon all reflect the theme of governmental interdependence. All of these citizens and officials share in a process or set of activities that have come to be known as "intergovernmental relations," or IGR. We can now give brief, partial answers to the questions posed in the title of this chapter, but this book will be devoted to expanding upon and elaborating these answers.

- Who? IGR involve both citizens and public officials as well as governmental entities of all sizes and types.
- Where? IGR are everywhere in our political and administrative systems. Like yeast in bread, IGR penetrate and leaven the whole governmental loaf.
- When? IGR are current, focusing as they do on critical issues of public policy. But IGR also have substantial roots in the past and will have important consequences for how we cope with the future on such issues as education, energy, environment, transportation, etc.

---

2. Terry Sanford, *Storm over the States* (New York: McGraw-Hill, 1967), p. 97.
3. Text of president's speech, August 8, 1969, *Congressional Quarterly Almanac*, Vol. 25, 91st Congress, 1st Session, 1969 (Washington, D.C.: Congressional Quarterly, Inc., 1970), p. 77–A.

- What? That is, how can IGR be systematically defined? Professor William Anderson defines IGR as "an important body of activities or interactions occurring between governmental units of all types and levels within the [U.S.] federal system."[4]

One of the more expansive statements about IGR came in 1962, from a public official then about to become deeply immersed in the subject. At the initial hearings held by the newly formed Senate Subcommittee on Intergovernmental Relations, chairman Edmund Muskie asserted that:

> The field of intergovernmental relations might be categorized as the "hidden dimension of government."
>
> Performing as almost a fourth branch of government in meeting the needs of our people, it nonetheless has no direct electorate, operates from no set perspective, is under no special control, and moves in no particular direction.
>
> Programs in this field make an unpredictable impact on our society and our economy. The world of intergovernmental relations is represented by no policymaking body—there is no executive, no legislative, and no judiciary. The Advisory Commission on Intergovernmental Relations serves as its major meeting ground, but this organization functions only in an advisory capacity.
>
> What we hope to do in the work of this subcommittee is to give this so-called hidden dimension of government definition and identity—to understand what it is and what its potential is, and in what directions it is moving.
>
> Evidence that this field makes a major impact on the lives of all Americans can be found in its involvement in such matters as highways, housing, public assistance, hospitals, airports, public health, unemployment compensation, education, agricultural extension, and waste treatment facilities.[5]

How did this "hidden dimension" of government come about? That is, what features of our political system do IGR reflect that tradition and prior terminology failed to? And what central concerns have motivated IGR participants in their activities?

---

4. William Anderson, *Intergovernmental Relations in Review* (Minneapolis: University of Minnesota Press, 1960), p. 3.
5. *Problems of Federal-State-Local Relations,* hearing before the Subcommittee on Intergovernmental Relations of the Committee on Government Operations, U.S. Senate, 87th Congress, 2nd Session, September 18, 1962, p. 4.

THE ORIGINS OF IGR

IGR originated in the 1930s with the advent of the New Deal, the federal government's massive effort to combat the Great Depression and its economic and social havoc. IGR were thus concerned with policy —that is, with choosing courses of action and assessing their practical effects. Franklin D. Roosevelt's skirmishes with the U.S. Supreme Court over various of his social welfare programs, and his pragmatically oriented techniques for circumventing the Court's legalistic resistance, typify the policy essence of IGR.

Hence from their beginnings to the present day IGR have been motivated by a strong concern for the effective delivery of public services to clients, be they particular groups in the society or the entire citizenry. As a result, since the 1930s the distributive and re-distributive activities of the "service," or welfare state, have far sur-passed the government's function of social control. From the social welfare legislation of the New Deal IGR then progressed to such issues as federal aid to education, urban development, and civil rights. Still more recent issues of concern have been citizen participation in social institutions affecting them, and formulating effective service delivery systems.

Use of the term *intergovernmental relations* is longstanding and widespread among public officials and scholars. Yet its origins defy discovery and it continues to lack a formal definition. One of the term's earliest appearances in print was in a 1937 article by Professor Clyde F. Snider, on county and township government.[6] Another scholar who used the term in the 1930s is Professor William Anderson, acknowledged to have contributed immensely to the development of the concept. Neither Snider nor Anderson takes credit for creating the term—or indeed can say where it came from.[7]

One of Anderson's chief contemporaries in studying IGR was W. Brooke Graves. Graves was editor in 1940 of a special *Annals* issue that was straightforwardly titled: "Intergovernmental Relations in the United States."[8] Twenty-five articles covered federal-state, federal-

---

6. Clyde F. Snider, "County and Township Government in 1935-36," *American Political Science Review,* 31 (October 1937): 909.
7. Letters to the author, from Clyde F. Snider, August 5, 1969; and from William Anderson, May 20, 1970.
8. *The Annals,* 207 (January 1940). The subtitle of the issue was: "A broad survey of recent developments in the fields of American government at all levels."

local, interstate, regional, and interlocal relationships. Curiously, however, neither the editor nor any of the authors felt the need to define IGR or to distinguish it from *federalism, new federalism, cooperative federalism,* and similar terms used in the articles. A quarter-century later Graves produced the magnum opus of the field, *American Intergovernmental Relations.*[9]

The avenue to wider usage was paved in the 1950s when the Congress twice employed the term in statutory language. In 1953 it created the temporary (1953–1955) Commission on Intergovernmental Relations (P.L. 83–109). Commonly known as the Kestnbaum Commission, it conducted the first official broad-ranging review of national-state-local relationships since the adoption of the Constitution. In 1959 the Congress created the permanent Advisory Commission on Intergovernmental Relations (P.L. 86–390). This agency, with a small but excellent staff, has produced dozens of research studies and hundreds of policy recommendations on IGR.

During the 1960s and 70s formal use of the concept of IGR has been widespread and is growing, on national, state, and local levels. For example, in 1968 the Congress passed the Intergovernmental Cooperation Act (P.L. 90–577). Among other requirements, this act mandated regional and state review of most federal grant applications initiated by any local governmental unit. The Intergovernmental Personnel Act of 1970 (P.L. 91–648), in addition to providing federal funds for professional training of state and local officials, allowed and encouraged the temporary transfer of career officials between the federal government and state and local governments.

By 1970 nearly all states had established an executive agency or official to deal exclusively with IGR. Most of these tended to emphasize state-federal relationships, but several states created separate community-affairs departments to handle state-local relationships. Among city governments a 1969 survey reported that 16 percent of the cities with populations over 10,000 had a full-time intergovernmental relations coordinator (like Bonnie Brown of Durham, North Carolina); 52 percent of the cities of over 100,000 had one.[10] By 1975 the proportions had risen to 39 percent and 76 percent respectively. In addi-

---

9. W. Brooke Graves, *American Intergovernmental Relations: Their Origins, Historical Development, and Current Status* (New York: Scribner's Sons, 1964).

10. "Local Intergovernmental Coordinators," *Urban Data Service* (International City Management Association), 2 (August 1970): 3.

tion, 69 percent of the counties with populations above 50,000 had IGR coordinators in 1975.[11]

THE DISTINCTIVE FEATURES OF IGR

From Professor Anderson's definition of IGR as (again) "an important body of activities or interactions occurring between governmental units of all types and levels within the [U.S.] federal system" we can elaborate the distinctive features of IGR, which are identified in table 1-1. These features at once describe IGR and suggest the increased complexity and interdependency in the U.S. political system. The hallmarks of this more complex and interdependent system are: the number and growth of governmental units; the number and variety of public officials involved in IGR; the intensity and regularity of contacts among those officials; the importance of officials' actions and attitudes; and the preoccupation with financial policy issues.

First, although IGR occur within our federal system they encompass more than the term *federalism* usually conveys. Federalism has been a commonplace term of great political significance across the nineteen decades of the U.S. constitutional history; the same cannot be said for intergovernmental relations. Yet whereas federalism emphasizes national-state relationships with occasional attention to interstate relations, the concept of IGR recognizes not only national-state and interstate relations, but also national-local, state-local, national-state-local, and interlocal relations. In short, IGR encompasses all the permutations and combinations of relations among the units of government in our system.

Trends in the number and types of governmental units reveal the jurisdictional diversity and complexity of IGR. Table 1-2 provides figures for each major type of jurisdiction for the past thirty years. Although the units have been halved in number, nearly 525,000 popularly elected officials govern these 78,000 units. The drastic reduction in the number of units indicates to most observers not that IGR have become simpler and more straightforward but on the contrary far more complex.

---

11. Advisory Commission on Intergovernmental Relations, *The Intergovernmental Grant System as Seen by Local, State, and Federal Officials* (Washington, D.C., March 1977, A-54), p. 45.

Table 1–1. *Illustrative Features of Intergovernmental Relations*

1. *All Governmental Units*

| Federal | Counties | School districts | Townships |
| States | Municipalities | Special districts | |

2. *Officials' Actions and Attitudes*
   Purposeful behavior
   Perceptions of other participants

3. *Regular Interactions among Officials*
   Day-to-day contacts
   Practical working relationships

4. *All Public Officials*
   Elected officials: legislators, executives
   Appointed officials: administrators,
     managers, department heads,
     staff personnel

5. *Policy Issues Centered on Finances*
   Loans
   Grants-in-aid
   Revenue sharing

Table 1–2 bears this out: First, most of the units lost were school districts, down from over 100,000 to about 15,000; second, the number of cities or municipalities increased by more than 2000; third, the number of special districts (e.g., fire, sanitation, parks, etc.) nearly tripled. Moreover, the data in table 1–2, being solely numbers of units, do not reflect increases in populations, employment, services, finances, etc., that have occurred in more than three decades.

The second feature of IGR is the human dimension—the activities and attitudes of the persons occupying official positions in the units of government under consideration. As Anderson says: "It is human beings clothed with office who are the real determiners of what the relations between units of government will be. Consequently the concept of intergovernmental relations necessarily has to be formulated largely in terms of human relations and human behavior."[12] Strictly speaking, then, there are no intergovernmental relations; there are only relations among officials who govern different units. The individual actions and attitudes of public officials are at the core of IGR. Their behavior is purposeful—for example, to obtain a grant or provide a program.

---

12. Anderson, *Intergovernmental Relations*, p. 4.

Table 1-2. *Governmental Units in the United States, 1942-1972*

Level of Government	1942	1952	1957	1962	1967	1972
Federal	1	1	1	1	1	1
State	48	48	48	50	50	50
County	3,050	3,049	3,047	3,043	3,049	3,044
Municipal (town)	16,220	16,778	17,183	18,000	18,048	18,516
Township	18,919	17,202	17,198	17,142	17,105	16,991
Special district	8,299	12,319	14,405	18,323	21,264	23,886
School district	108,579	67,346	50,446	34,678	21,782	15,780
Total	155,116	116,743	102,328	91,237	81,299	78,268

Sources: U.S. Bureau of the Census, *Governments in the United States,* Vol. 1, No. 1, 1957 Census of Governments; *Governmental Units in 1972,* Preliminary No. 1, 1972 Census of Governments (Washington, D.C.).

And their actions are heavily influenced by how they perceive other participant's actions and attitudes.

Figure 1-1 provides data on the numbers and growth patterns of "human beings clothed with office" from 1951 to 1976 by type of governmental unit. The ratio scale on the vertical axis allows comparison of rate changes among the jurisdictions according to the slope of the lines (because of the logarithmic spacing of integers on the vertical scale). At the same time the absolute levels of employment can be roughly identified. Employment figures are "full-time equivalent"; that is, part-time employees are fractionally counted.

Table 1-3 gives precise figures on government employment levels for twenty-five years through 1976. Figure 1-1 and table 1-3 provide the basis for several observations:

- Local government is the largest public employer (table 1-3);
- school employment makes up a major share (nearly half) of local employment (table 1-3);
- national employment has grown only slightly (figure 1-1);
- national- and state-government trends have converged, with the latter now exceeding the former (figure 1-1);
- the steep rates of annual increase in state, county, and special district employment from 1966-1976 (figure 1-1 and table 1-3).

Although these data and observations hardly convey the growth and complexity of IGR, they alert us to secular shifts in the roles and

IN MILLIONS
(full time equivalent)

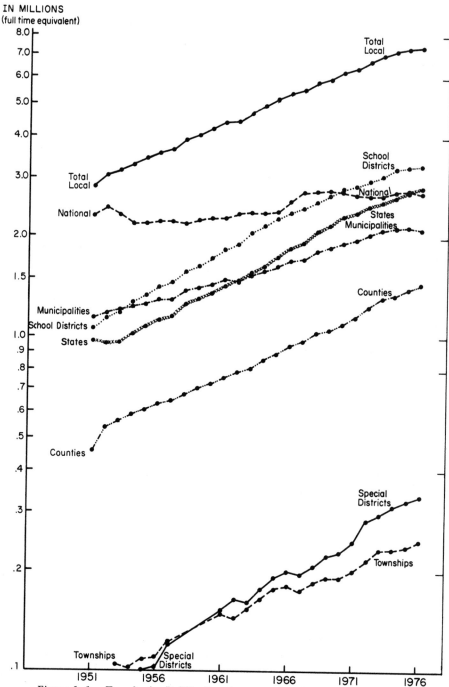

Figure 1-1. *Trends in Public Employment in National, State, and Local
Governments, 1951-1976 (Ratio Scale)*

Sources: Bureau of the Census, *Public Employment in 1976* (Series GE 76, No. 1);
Economic Report of the President (February, 1977).

Table 1-3. *Full-Time Equivalent Governmental Employment by Jurisdiction, Selected Years, 1952–1976*

Type of Government	1952	1962	1972	1976	(Average Annual % Increase, 1966–1976)
		(in millions)			
National	2.5	2.4	2.8	2.7	(1.1)
State	1.0	1.5	2.5	2.8	(4.2)
Total local	3.1	4.5	6.7	7.4	(3.2)
Counties	.5	.8	1.2	1.4	(4.3)
Municipalities	1.2	1.5	2.0	2.1	(2.2)
Townships	.1	.1	.2	.2	(3.0)
Special districts	.1	.2	.3	.3	(5.3)
School districts	1.1	1.9	3.0	3.3	(3.3)

Source: U.S. Bureau of the Census, *Public Employment in 1976*, Series GE 76, No. 1 (Washington, D.C.) pp. 2, 8.

jurisdictional functions of public officials. For example, over the past decade the growth rate of county employment substantially exceeded the rate for municipalities (4.3 percent to 2.2 percent). If we are "a nation of cities," why does a unit of local government commonly associated with rural areas show such rapid growth? The facts are, of course, that 300 to 400 of the 3000-odd counties are anything but rural. Escalating county employment reflects accelerated suburban growth and the accompanying role of counties in Standard Metropolitan Statistical Areas (SMSAs) as they respond to demands for urban services.

The third feature implicit in IGR is that relations among officials are not one-time or occasional occurrences, formally ratified in agreements or rigidly fixed by statutes or court decisions. Rather, IGR includes the officials' continuous, day-to-day patterns of contact and exchanges of information and views. The participants in IGR are centrally concerned with "getting things done"—that is, with the informal, practical, goal-oriented arrangements that can be realized within the officials' formal, legal, institutional context.

This third IGR dimension captures the concerted, regularized actions of persons like Manager Anderson, Mayor Beame, Coordinator Brown, and former Governor Sanford as they attempted to realize their policy and administrative aims. Normally, these officials did not act randomly, capriciously, or arbitrarily; rather, their efforts were patterned, targeted, and often repeated to achieve results that required the assent of other officials spread across the wide, sometimes treacherous terrain of the IGR landscape.

The fourth distinguishing characteristic of IGR is that *all* public officials—mayors, town and city council members, governors, state legislators, members of Congress, and presidents—participate. In recent years, however, scholars have paid more attention to the IGR participation of appointed administrators. This change of focus reflects two separate phenomena: first, the increasingly important role played by public bureaucracies in government (indeed, the public employment growth depicted in figure 1-1 and table 1-3 is due to a proliferation of appointed administrators, or bureaucrats); second, the predilection of most academics interested in IGR to study state and local public administration. In other words, the concerns and interests of IGR practitioners and researchers more closely coincide in the area of administration than in the legislative, executive, or judicial areas.

A fifth and final distinctive feature of IGR is its policy component. Policy consists of intentions and actions (or inactions) of public officials and the consequences of those actions. In the context of IGR, policy is generated by interactions among all public officials. In recent decades, however, economic and political complexity have combined with rapid rates of social and technological change to reduce the capacity of courts and legislatures to deal with continuous pressures for policy change, thereby putting greater pressure on, and allowing greater latitude to, administrators in formulating and executing public policy. For example, in the Elementary and Secondary Education Act of 1965 the U.S. Congress declared its intent to improve the quality of education for socially and economically disadvantaged children. Whether there was improvement, or what constituted improvement, depended on an immense array of decisions, actions, and interactions which included:

1. the funding levels provided by the Congress;
2. the decisions of the Office of Education on whether and how to judge educational impacts;
3. past and current decisions by elected and appointed state officials responsible for educational matters—decisions that often specify the content of education and the conditions under which it takes place; and
4. actions by local school boards, administrators, and teachers who receive the funds and translate them into educational content.

Policy, then, pervades all IGR actions. And at the policy core of IGR have been fiscal policy problems, which have been chiefly allocational questions: Who shall raise what amounts by what method from which citizens? Who shall spend how much for whose benefit with what intended results? This fiscal preoccupation has sometimes skewed diagnoses of and prescriptions for reforming or improving IGR, such as adopting revenue sharing. As the Kestnbaum Commission noted in 1955, "The crucial questions now are questions of policy: What level ought to move? Or should both?" These questions, the Commission added, are ones on which the criteria for judgment "are chiefly political, economic, and administrative rather than legal."[13] Fiscal issues are ones around which both political and economic pressures rapidly converge, usually with strong force. And administrative activities are seldom insulated from the fiscal base on which they operate. Politics, economics, and administration combine to put finance at the policy center of IGR.

The five distinctive features of IGR just described (and summarized in table 1-1) reflect new directions and outcomes in the conduct of public affairs in the United States. The concept of IGR permits us to observe, classify, and accumulate knowledge about recent changes without obscuring other relevant data to which prior political concepts have attuned us.

UNDERSTANDING IGR: THE STRUCTURE OF THE BOOK

How, then, do we apply the IGR concept to increase our understanding of the system? How shall we make more visible this "hidden dimension" of government? Two approaches are employed: the conceptual-historical, and the empirical-descriptive. These approaches are sometimes used separately, sometimes combined. Chapters 2 and 3, on models and on twentieth-century IGR patterns, respectively, typify the conceptual-historical approach.

The first step to understanding IGR is to clarify the concept. In this chapter we have only scratched the surface. In chapter 2 we contrast and compare IGR and the more familiar concept *federalism*. We also

---

13. The Commission on Intergovernmental Relations, *A Report to the President for Transmittal to the Congress* (Washington, D.C., June 1955), p. 33.

construct three alternative models of interjurisdictional relationships in the United States. In chapter 3 we adopt the historical mode, describing the changes and successive phases that have occurred in IGR over the last several decades.

In chapters 4 through 7 we explore successively local, state, and national governments with respect to fiscal issues—more specifically, questions of public policy and policy choice. To do so we combine the historical and empirical approaches. That is, although in each chapter we emphasize current issues, policies, and alternatives, we also probe as far as forty years into the past, discerning a historical background for reviewing and evaluating current conditions.

In chapters 8 through 11 we again explore local, state, and national IGR, but now with respect to the attitudes and actions of officials in these jurisdictions. Since IGR focuses on "human beings clothed with office," the activities and opinions of public officials are central to an understanding of IGR. In these chapters the empirical-descriptive approach is most evident, analyzing substantial, diverse sets of contemporary data on the actions and attitudes of officials operating in IGR. This approach to IGR yields what I call "participants' perspectives": an accurate, realistic picture of "the way things work" in IGR, as seen from within.

In chapter 12, we draw together the several substantive themes separately threaded throughout the book. We assess some of the critical variables likely to shape IGR in the near future and speculate on the shape of the alternative futures.

Because many terms and other features of IGR are still novel, appendices are supplied to anticipate many of the reader's expected needs. Appendix A, for example, is a glossary of common IGR terms, abbreviations, and acronyms. A reader for whom IGR is a new concept is advised to scan it and to use it as a ready reference. Appendix B provides a short, legally oriented analysis of U.S. federalism, a concept explored in the next chapter. Remaining appendices furnish supplementary data or case examples. References to these are given wherever pertinent throughout the text.

IGR:
Concepts and Models

2

IGR AND FEDERALISM

Does the concept *intergovernmental relations* simply augment that of *federalism,* or does it in fact supersede it? *IGR* is not, I think, simply a substitute term for *federalism:* IGR include a range of activities and meanings that are neither explicit nor implicit in federalism. These differences we shall now investigate.

To the writers of *The Federalist* papers, a *federal* arrangement meant what we now mean by *confederation:* a league formed by compact or treaty among sovereign states—much like the United Nations today. The absence of an intermediate concept between those of *national* and *federal* explains why Madison, in *The Federalist* no. 39, could—correctly for his day—describe the Constitution as "neither wholly *national* nor wholly *federal.*"[1] It was by a stroke of conceptual

1. *The Federalist* papers (New York: New American Library, Mentor, 1961), p. 246. For a thorough and penetrating analysis of the framers' views of federalism see Martin

and political inventiveness that the supporters of the Constitution called themselves Federalists. They laid claim to the term that described, for the politically attentive of the time, the least-centralized system of relationships between constituent units and the central governing mechanism. We shall see below why IGR covers patterns and relationships that were not included within federalism. Each distinction yields a reason for favoring the use of IGR over federalism.

First, *federalism* is defined by the typical dictionary as "designating a form of government in which a union of states recognizes the sovereignty of a central authority while retaining certain residual powers of government."[2] Thus, although it has not precluded state-local or national-local links, federalism has historically emphasized national-state relationships. This emphasis is avoided by IGR.

A second reason for preferring IGR to federalism is that the latter has produced a legacy of legalism. That is, legal powers, formal actions, and written agreements (or disagreements) have dominated the thought and practice of federalism. Because the United States, a constitutional republic, is ostensibly governed by laws, not persons, this legal cast is understandable and justifiable. Nevertheless, IGR transcend these mainstream legal restraints and include within the IGR net a rich range of informal and otherwise submerged actions and perceptions of officials. The concept of IGR is like a small-gauge net that catches the minnows as well as the larger, more prominent fish that swim in the large river that is our political system. The net is especially useful not only in the main river channel but also in harvesting valuable catches from backwaters and sloughs.

The legal and national-state emphases of the term federalism suggest a third reason for shifting to IGR. Federalism implies a hierarchical set of power or authority relationships. The U.S. Constitution contains (Article VI, Section 2) a supremacy clause, which makes explicit, in cases of last resort, a superior-subordinate relationship. Also, note how frequently the word "down" is used in referring to states and localities: "*down* at the state and local levels." The concept IGR contains no hierarchical status distinctions. Although it does not deny the existence of such power differences, neither does it imply, as does federalism, that the national level is inherently superior.

Diamond, "What the Framers Meant by Federalism," in Robert A. Goldwin (ed.), *A Nation of States: Essays on the American Federal System* (Chicago: Rand McNally, 1961), pp. 24-41.

2. *The American Heritage Dictionary of the English Language* (Boston: Houghton Mifflin, 1969), p. 481.

A fourth reason for preferring IGR to federalism arises from the explicit policy elements developed and associated with IGR. Although writings on federalism have not excluded policy concerns, they have given them little emphasis. And writers on federalism have neglected various efforts in the past quarter-century to construct a viable body of theory that would explain how public policy is formulated and implemented. In contrast, the search for concepts and empirical results in the field of policy studies has occurred simultaneously with efforts to clarify IGR.

The intersection of interests in both IGR and policy studies has encouraged the development of a "policy choice" approach, one that "contributes to choice between better and worse policies."[3] When applied in an IGR context the policy choice approach poses questions that deal with both ends and means, substance and process. For example, in the Rural Development Act of 1972 (7 U.S.C. 2654) the Congress authorized and subsequently appropriated $3.5 million to fund 50 percent of the cost of organizing, training, and equiping rural volunteer fire departments. A student guided by the concept of federalism might ask such questions as: What is the legal basis for such congressional action? Is there a national need for rural fire protection? Have the states failed to respond to rural fire protection needs? These are necessary questions.

But a student guided by the IGR concept would pose additional questions: Who were the key national, state, and local officials instrumental in securing passage and funding for the grant program? What were their explicit and implicit aims? What, if any, alternative means to achieving these aims were considered? What formulas for distributing the funds among the states were considered and adopted? Is the grant administered through state governments? What was the process for developing the guidelines for administering the grant and for funding grant proposals? What rural communities have applied for funds? Which have received funds and which have been rejected? What have been the effects of the funding? Have rural fire insurance rates dropped? If so, by as much as or more than the grant funds? Could the same results have been achieved in a different way, for example, by contractual service agreements between city fire departments and the rural areas?

---

3. Duncan MacRae, Jr., "Sociology in Policy Analysis," *Policy Studies Journal* 2 (Autumn 1973): 4. See also, Deil S. Wright, "Intergovernmental Relations and Policy Choice," *Publius: The Journal of Federalism,* 5 (Fall 1975): 1–24.

Is this rural fire service grant program likely to remain the same, grow, or be eliminated?

It should be evident from the above questions why the concept IGR is preferred over federalism. But there is a fifth reason for such preference. Federalism has been expropriated for such varied and loose political usages that its meaning has been muddied and made imprecise. Politicians and academics have shown great ingenuity and imagination in choosing adjectives to append to the word. We have been exposed to "the New Federalism" (Nixon), "Creative Federalism" (Johnson), "national federalism" (Sundquist), "centralized and peripheralized federalism" (Riker), "cooperative federalism" (Corwin), "mature and emergent federalism" (Macmahon), and others too numerous to mention. At least *thirty-four* different "types" of federalism have been recorded. Clearly, *federalism* is a much-used and much-abused term.

Not only does such unrestrained use of the term destroy its precision and clarity, but also the invent-your-own-federalism game politicizes the term. And not only politicians do so: Academic scholars use one species of the genus federalism to argue for or against another. In short, a host of value-laden adjectives have been attached to the leading edge of a historic and significant concept and have, from whatever motives, blunted the term's meaning and thus limited its analytic utility.

Intergovernmental relations, on the other hand, has been a more protected term, if only because it is newer. Furthermore, its two multisyllabic words are resonant neither to the ear nor to the emotions. IGR, then, promises to be an improved conceptual base for exploring and aggregating past and present experiences of citizens and public officials. To fully understand the American political system of today we must use IGR.

MODELS OF NATIONAL-STATE-LOCAL RELATIONS

Having described IGR and its contrasts with federalism, we can now formulate some simplified models of IGR. Figure 2–1 represents graphically three models of authority relationships between national, state, and local jurisdictions in the United States. These models, like any other models, fall far short of displaying the complexities and realities of governance in several respects—for example, numbers and

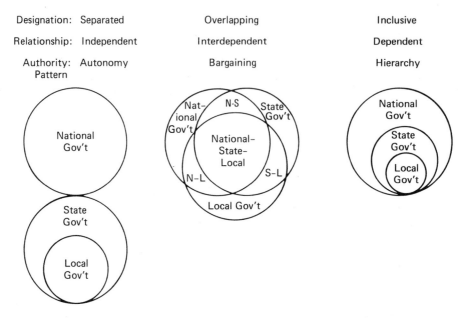

Figure 2–1. *Intergovernmental Relations Models in the United States*

types of entities, numbers and variations in personnel, fiscal resources, etc. The three models express visually the three generic types of authority relationships that can exist between political entities—the absence of authority (autonomy), dominant authority (hierarchy), equal authority (bargaining). Despite its simplicity, each model, by concentrating on the essential features of a possible IGR arrangement, guides us in formulating hypotheses. (No two models, of course, will generate identical sets of hypotheses.) By testing these hypotheses we can discover which model best fits the U.S. political system as it operates today.

The Separated-Authority Model

In the separated-authority model of IGR, sharp, distinct boundaries separate the national government and state governments. Local units, however, are included within, and dependent on, state governments. The most classic expression of state-local relations is Dillon's Rule, named after the Iowa judge who asserted it in the 1860s, which summarizes the power relationships between the states and their localities:

1. there is no common-law right of local self-government;
2. local entities are creatures of the state subject to creation and abolition at the unfettered discretion of the state (barring constitutional limitations);
3. localities may exercise only those powers expressly granted; and
4. localities are "mere tenants at the will of the legislature."[4]

For more than a century Dillon's Rule has been a nationwide guidepost in legal-constitutional relations between the states and their local governments. Hidden behind its seeming simplicity is a central issue in IGR and in the models of figure 2-1: "Who should govern?" This fundamental philosophical question clearly cannot be answered by the model, nor has Dillon's Rule succeeded in resolving it. But the model has helped frame a significant question—and that is one positive result from constructing models.

What does the separated-authority model imply concerning national-state power relationships? It implies, again, that the two types of entities are independent and autonomous; they are linked only tangentially. This model received implicit endorsement in the 1880s from Lord Bryce, an eminent Briton who visited the United States and observed its political system. He described national-state relations as follows:

> The characteristic feature and special interest of the American Union is that it shows us two governments covering the same ground, yet distinct and separate in their action. It is like a great factory wherein two sets of machinery are at work, their revolving wheels apparently intermixed, their bands crossing one another, yet each set doing its own work without touching or hampering the other.[5]

Bryce's analogy was drawn from observation and experience, but he could have cited an 1871 U.S. Supreme Court decision for a stamp of approval. In *Tarbel's Case* the Court stated:

> There are within the territorial limits of each state two governments, restricted in their sphere of action, but independent of each other, and su-

---

4. *City of Clinton* v. *the Cedar Rapids and Missouri River Railroad*, 24 *Iowa Law Review*, 455 (1868). For a recent analysis of Dillon's Rule from a policy orientation see John G. Grumm and Russell D. Murphy, "Dillon's Rule Reconsidered," *The Annals*, 416 (November 1974): 120–132.

5. James Bryce, *The American Commonwealth, Vol. I*, 2nd ed. (London: Macmillan, 1891), p. 318.

preme within their respective spheres. Each has its separate departments, each has its distinct laws, and each has its own tribunals for their enforcement. Neither government can intrude within the jurisdiction of the other or authorize any interference therein by its judicial officers with the action of the other.[6]

Both an impartial foreign observer and the institution charged with interpreting the constitution agreed, then, that *each* of the two units—the national and the state—governs within its respective sphere of authority.

What happened when the respective spheres of action put the national government and a state in conflict—when they ceased to be tangential and clashed directly? The result is well known to students of U.S. federalism. The Supreme Court became the arbiter of national-state relations. (A brief review of the Court's role in setting the boundaries of national and state powers is contained in Appendix B.) For several decades the Supreme Court, operating on the premises of the separated-authority model, attempted to set distinct, insulated spheres of national and state powers. But Court decisions in the 1930s necessitated substantial rethinking of how this model did (or did not) describe the operation of the U.S. political system.

Two scholars, Morton Grodzins and Daniel Elazar, have empirically tested the separated-authority model and found it woefully wanting, not simply for the present and recent past but for the nineteenth century as well.[7] As Grodzins put it, "Classic works are sometimes responsible for classic errors. . . . Lord Bryce was wrong, even for the period of his own observations."[8] Indeed, many students of constitutional law and history look back at Supreme Court decisions from the 1860s to the 1930s and loudly applaud the discrediting of the so-called "dual federalism" (or what we are calling the separate-authority) model. Many U.S. and state courts seemed determined to impose that model on a growing industrial society of increasingly complex and interdependent units.

IGR model builders are probably of near-unanimous agreement that the separated-authority model is obsolete and irrelevant, addressed as it is to nonexistent social and political conditions. Before dispatching

6. *Tarbel's Case,* 13 Wall, 397 (1872).
7. Morton Grodzins, *The American System: A New View of Government in the United States,* edited by Daniel J. Elazar (Chicago: Rand McNally, 1966); Daniel J. Elazar, *The American Partnership: Intergovernmental Cooperation in the Nineteenth-Century United States* (Chicago: University of Chicago Press, 1962).
8. Grodzins, *American System,* p. 7.

the model to oblivion, however, consider the Supreme Court decision of June 24, 1976. In *National League of Cities* v. *Usery* the Court, in sweeping language, ruled that the Congress did not have the authority to require that either the states or their local governments observe minimum-wage and maximum-hour laws. Declaring a 1974 federal law extending wage and hour requirements to state and city employees to be unconstitutional, the Court said the legislation violated the "attribute of state sovereignty" and held that:

> Congress has sought to wield its power in fashion that would impair the States' ability to function effectively within the federal system. . . . We hold that insofar as the challenged amendments operate to directly displace the States' freedom to structure integral operations in areas of traditional governmental functions, they are not within the authority granted Congress by [the commerce clause].[9]

The commerce clause (Article I, Section 8), which gives Congress power to regulate interstate and foreign commerce, is the legal basis for enacting the wage and hour laws. The Court's judgment that "state sovereignty" prevents the national government from enacting such laws revives elements of the separated-authority model, thus, in this one policy area at least, giving the model continued, if limited, validity.

The Inclusive-Authority Model

The inclusive-authority model is represented in figure 2-1 by concentric circles diminishing in size from national to state to local. Let us suppose that the area covered by each circle represents the proportion of power exercised by that jurisdiction with respect to the others. Suppose also that the national government wants to expand its proportion of power in relation to states and localities. Two strategies are possible: One, reduce the various powers of either the states or localities or both; or, two, enlarge the national government's circle with or without enlarging the state and/or local circles. This second strategy is often called "enlarging the pie."

Both strategies can be understood by means of game theory: a systematic way of studying behavior in decision-making situations. The theory assumes that all participants strive to optimize their behavior—

---

9. *National League of Cities* v. *Usery*, 44 *U.S. Lawyers Weekly* (June 24, 1976). See also *Wall Street Journal* (June 25, 1976), p. 1.

each trying to maximize gains and minimize losses within the limits of allowed behavior (hence the analogy with games). The outcome is seen to depend not only on the behavior of any one participant but on the responses of other participants as well.

The first strategy above, Type I, is the classic case of a three-person, zero-sum game—like poker: The sum of the players' winnings equals the sum of their losings. An illustration of this in the IGR context is the *Usery* case and the legislation requiring state and local units to meet minimum wage and maximum hour requirements. The national govern-ment attempted to exercise (expand) its power at the expense of state-local powers. The gain in national power equaled the power or discretion lost by state and local units. The latter were required—before the Su-preme Court invalidated the law—to pay increased labor costs. Thus, until the Court acted, national gains equaled state-local losses.

In game theory the second strategy above, Type II or "enlarging the pie," is called a nonconstant-sum game. All participants in this type of game can "win" or make gains. Perhaps the best IGR illustra-tion of the Type II, nonconstant sum strategy, is fiscal: the conditional grant-in-aid. The national sector can expand by raising more money to offer as grants to states and localities. The funds can be offered with conditions ("losses") imposed on the recipients. But the benefits ("winnings") are so attractive that they appear to outweigh the attached constraints. From these examples of the two strategies we would expect national IGR policies to lean far more toward Type II strate-gies (such as grants-in-aid) than toward Type I.

The inclusive-authority model serves other uses besides allowing game-theory prediction of IGR policies. The model also conveys the essential hierarchical nature of authority. The dependency relationships imply power patterns that are similar to Dillon's Rule for state-local relations. That is, states and localities would be mere minions of the national government with insignificant or incidental impact on Ameri-can politics and public policy. To the question of who governs, this model provides an unequivocal answer: the national government.

How well (and in what areas) does the inclusive-authority model describe the realities of present-day American politics, policy, and administration? Curiously enough, conservative and liberal observers alike see this model dominant in many aspects of our public life. Barry Goldwater, Ronald Reagan, and other conservatives see a powerful federal engine rolling over weakened and supine states and localities.

On the liberal side Senator Joseph Clark, as early as 1960, saw, with approval, the inception of a "national federalism": Not only was the federal government in charge (according to Clark) but it *should* be in charge.[10] A more extensive and thoughtful elaboration of the same idea appeared in practitioner-scholar James Sundquist's book, *Making Federalism Work*. Writing in 1969, in the wake of the Great Society programs, Sundquist highlighted the following:

1. "The nation for decades has been steadily coalescing into a national society" (p. 10);
2. "The Great Society was, by definition, one society; the phrase was singular, not plural" (p. 12);
3. There was "close federal supervision and control to assure that national purposes are served" (p. 3);
4. There was "centralization of objective-setting" (p. 13);
5. "Somewhere in the Executive Office must be centered a concern for the structure of federalism—a responsibility for guiding the evolution of the whole system of federal-state-local relations, viewed for the first time as a *single* system" (p. 246).[11]

Sundquist left little doubt that the national government should be in charge, but he was not convinced that it controlled a single, hierarchical system.

Other observers, especially those who have focused on the capacities or incapacities of the states, have also concluded that the states and their localities are governing entities in name only—hence their choice of the term *nominal,* or *centralized federalism.* This conclusion has been reached by four different approaches.

One approach, the power-elite perspective, sees the ship of state guided by a select and cohesive corps of national leaders at the helm. State and local governments and their political leaders are carried along like barnacles on the hull. They are insignificant and powerless to affect important political or societal choices.[12]

A second approach, the technocratic-pluralist position, identifies the dispersal of decision-making power into quasi-public or even private

---

10. Joseph Clark, "Toward National Federalism," *The Federal Government and the Cities: A Symposium* (Washington, D.C.: George Washington University, 1961), pp. 39-49.
11. James L. Sundquist with the collaboration of David W. Davis, *Making Federalism Work: A Study of Program Coordination at the Community Level* (Washington, D.C.: The Brookings Institution, 1969).
12. C. Wright Mills, *The Power Elite* (New York: Oxford University Press, 1956); G. William Domhoff, *Who Rules America?* (Englewood Cliffs, N.J.: Prentice-Hall, 1967); and G. William Domhoff, *The Higher Circles: The Governing Class in America* (New York: Random House, Vintage, 1970).

economic fiefdoms that are national in scope. The states or other entities, singularly or collectively, cannot counteract these powerful private-interest groups. This approach argues, for example, that organized medicine and the health industry control the health of the nation despite the "police power" of the states to control the health, welfare, morals, and safety of its citizens.[13]

A third approach, which might be called economic federalism, shares some views in common with the power-elite and technocratic-pluralist points of view. This perspective on the inclusive model can be summarized by excerpts from an extensive essay on the subject by Arthur S. Miller.

> I do not mean to focus upon the administrative agency, but upon the recipient of economic power—the large corporate enterprise or factory community—probably the most important of the groups in American society. These are the functional units of economic federalism and the basic units of a system of private government.

> It takes no fanciful mental gymnastics to say that the factory community operates as the recipient of delegated power to carry out important societal functions. It is the economic counterpart—and superior, be it said—of the unit of political federalism, the forty-eight state governments. It is the basic unit of functional federalism. It is a private governmental system, performing some of the jobs of government.[14]

A fourth approach to the conclusion that states and localities enjoy only a nominal existence is the administrative orientation. The states, it is argued, are little more than administrative districts of the national government, making state governors, in effect, "chief federal systems officers." In the early 1950s L. D. White, discussing "The March of Power to Washington," felt that the states were thus well on the way to becoming hollow shells.[15] By the late 1950s Miller reported the district concept as an established fact.

> So far as the traditional federal system is concerned, the implications of this change are clear. Chief among them is that, to a large extent, states today

---

13. Grant McConnell, *Private Power and American Democracy* (New York: Alfred Knopf, Vintage, 1966), especially pp. 166–195; Theodore J. Lowi, *The End of Liberalism: Ideology, Policy, and the Crisis of Public Authority* (New York: Norton, 1969).

14. Arthur S. Miller, "The Constitutional Law of the 'Security State,'" *Stanford Law Review,* 10 (July 1958): 634, 637.

15. Leonard D. White, *The States and the Nation* (Baton Rouge: Louisiana State University Press, 1953), p. 3.

operate not as practically autonomous units, but as administrative districts for centrally established policies. It is doubtless inaccurate to think of them as hollow political shells, but it does seem to be true that the once-powerful state governments have been bypassed by the movement of history. Save for "housekeeping" duties, they have little concern with the main flow of important decisions. When new problems arise, eyes swivel to Washington, not to the state capitol—where eyes also turn to the banks of the Potomac.[16]

The administrative district charge was vigorously challenged by William Anderson on the basis of his and his associates' empirical investigations in the 1940s and 1950s. Specifically addressing the grant-in-aid issue, Anderson contended that the states gained as much as the national government from the fund transfers.

In short, as administrators of federal programs under grants-in-aid the state governments have acquired something in the nature of an added check upon the national administration. Political power, like electricity, does not run all in one direction.[17]

Whatever the past state of affairs in IGR, a more recent writer, Ferdinand Lundberg, has predicted a fully fused centralized system. Lundberg has contended that all state and local governments would in future be operated from an American version of the English Home Office, such as a Department of Internal Affairs. More specifically, he foresees:

City managers and state executives will probably be appointed or declared eligible from civil service lists by the national government, although there may still be vestigial elections of purely symbolic governors, mayors, and town councilmen.

Each of the present American states, it seems evident, is destined to become pretty much of an administrative department of the central government, just as counties and cities will be subdepartments.[18]

The hallmarks of the inclusive-authority model should now be clear. One is the premise that state and local governments depend totally on decisions that are nationwide in scope and arrived at by the

---

16. Miller, "Constitutional Law," p. 629.
17. William Anderson, *The Nation and the States, Rivals or Partners?* (Minneapolis: University of Minnesota Press, 1955), p. 204.
18. Ferdinand Lundberg, *The Coming World Transformation* (Garden City, N.Y.: Doubleday, 1963), p. 18.

national government, or by powerful economic interests, or by some combination of the two. A second premise is that nonnational political institutions such as governors, state legislators, mayors, etc., have approached a condition of nearly total atrophy. A third premise is that the functions formerly performed by these now-vestigial organs have been fused into a centralized, hierarchical system.

The Overlapping-Authority Model

The inclusive-authority and separated-authority models of IGR are at opposite ends of a spectrum: In the first hierarchy prevails, while in the second the national and state governments are autonomous. The past, present, or future applicability of either model for IGR in the United States has been sharply challenged. Although there are isolated instances of such hierarchical and autonomous IGR patterns, the weight of academic research suggests that these two models describe inaccurately how the bulk of governmental operations are conducted in the United States.

The third and most representative model of IGR practice is the overlapping-authority model (see figure 2–1). The overlay among the circles conveys three characteristic features of the model:

1. Substantial areas of governmental operations involve national, state, and local units (or officials) simultaneously.
2. The areas of autonomy or single-jurisdiction independence and discretion are comparatively small.
3. The power and influence available to any one jurisdiction (or official) is substantially limited. The limits produce an authority pattern best described as bargaining.

Bargaining is used in the common, dictionary sense of "negotiating the terms of a sale, exchange, or agreement." In the IGR context, sale is far less relevant than exchange or agreement. Wide areas of IGR involve exchanges or agreements. For example, the national government offers more than 1000 assistance programs to states and localities in *exchange* for their *agreement* to implement a program, carry out a project, or pursue any one of a wide variety of activities. Of course, as part of the bargain the recipient of assistance must usually agree to such conditions as to provide matching funds and to meet accounting, reporting, auditing, and performance requirements.

A federal grant to New York City for public housing might be viewed as a bargaining-exchange relationship. The "feds" have the money—no one else gives housing and urban renewal grants. New York City is the "hands down" leader in producing maximum results with public housing dollars. In fact, there are other competitors or bargainers for the public housing dollars but few who can effectively compete with New York City. Its officials appear to be leaders at bargaining for public housing.

This example has numerous implications, four of which merit our attention. First, exchanges transfer resources and influence across governmental boundaries, making it possible to alter authority relationships among participants (officials). Second, power in the overlapping-authority model tends to be widely dispersed; consequently, although it is not uniformly distributed, it is nearly so.

Third, this model does not presuppose exclusively cooperative or competitive relationships among participants. In this respect it avoids built-in conclusions that collaboration or consensus prevail over conflict and cleavage. It leaves the matter open for case analyses and empirical investigations of IGR operations.

Fourth, as the positioning of the circles in figure 2-1 implies, national-state-local relations are the largest domain, while modest areas of autonomous action (the nonoverlapping areas of the circles) remain to each respective jurisdiction. This distribution reflects the interdependence that appears to permeate IGR.

In sum the chief characteristics of the overlapping-authority model are:

- limited, dispersed power
- interdependence
- limited areas of autonomy
- bargaining-exchange relationships
- cooperation and competition

SUMMARY

Senator Muskie called IGR the "hidden dimension" of government. But the concept of IGR now makes visible previously unnoticed aspects of our political system. Unlike federalism, IGR avoids an emphasis on national-state relations, goes far beyond legalism, does not presume hierarchical relationships, incorporates an extensive range of policy-connected interests, and is a more neutral concept than the often-politicized federalism. Professor Michael Regan has put the contrast of terms succinctly. He contends that "old style" federalism is defunct but that "new style" federalism is "alive and well and living in the United States. Its name is intergovernmental relations."[19]

Three models were developed of how IGR operates in the United States. The separated-authority model posits national-state authority relationships as autonomous. The two jurisdictions have separate spheres of power and control. This model has been much criticized, and rightly so, for failing to fit the actual operating features of national, state, and local relationships. However, we may sometimes find elements of this model accurately represented in a particular case or problem area.

At the opposite pole is the inclusive-authority model. Here hierarchy dominates, and local or state governments are viewed as mere appendages of a powerful national government in control of a centralized system. Some observers think that this model accurately describes the current state of IGR in the United States; others believe it will be years before state and local governments lose all political significance and become little more than administrative districts of Washington, D.C.

The overlapping-authority model describes IGR as patterned, interdependent, and bargained behavior among national, state, and local officials. Contacts and exchanges between officials may be cooperative or competitive; the determining factors may include: the policy issue or problem, the status (elected or appointed) of the officials, the partisan leanings of participants, and the constituency (city, state, or national) being represented. The overlapping-authority model best describes the contemporary realities of IGR and is elaborated throughout this book.

---

19. Michael D. Regan, *The New Federalism* (New York: Oxford University Press, 1972), p. 1.

IGR in the Twentieth Century

3

IDENTIFYING CHANGES

What we have learned so far about IGR now enables us to analyze recent U.S. political experience in the light of the concept. We will concentrate on the twentieth century, with occasional references to earlier political experience. Since 1900 major changes have occurred in the scope of activities and the relationships among national, state, and local governments. Selected statistics for the past sixty years convey the dramatic shifts that have occurred in IGR. Table 3–1 furnishes various financial indicators for each governmental level for the years 1913 and 1975, which are respectively the earliest and latest years of this century for which census data are available.

In 1913 the federal government was modest in size. It spent slightly less than a billion dollars; this was less than 3 percent of GNP and about 30 percent of all national-state-local outlays. Federal outlays were $10 per capita, and federal aid (in cash) was virtually nonexistent—only $12

Table 3-1. *Intergovernmental Relations Then and Now: Selected Financial Comparisons from 1913 and 1975*

	1913	1975
National Government Expenditures:		
a. Dollar amount (billions)	.970	340.7
b. Per capita dollars	10	1599
c. Percent of GNP	2.5%	23.5%
d. Percent of all public outlays	30.2%	61.1%
e. Federal aid (billions)	.012	49.6
State Government Expenditures:		
a. Dollar amount (billions)	.372	120.7
b. Per capita dollars	4	566
c. Percent of GNP	.9%	8.3%
d. Percent of all public outlays	11.6%	21.6%
e. State aid (billions)	.091	52.0
Local Government Expenditures:		
a. Dollar amount (billions)	1.9	96.2
b. Per capita dollars	19	451
c. Percent of GNP	4.7%	6.6%
d. Percent of all public outlays	58.3%	17.3%
Employment (thousands):		
National	470	2760
State	—	2742
Local	—	7369
Exhibit: Gross National Product (GNP)		
(billions)	39.6	1450.6

Sources: *Facts and Figures on Government Finance,* Tax Foundation, Inc., 1975; Bureau of the Census, *Historical Statistics on Government Finances and Employment,* Vol. 6 of 1967 Census of Governments; Bureau of the Census, *Governmental Finances in 1974-75,* GF75, No. 5 (Washington, D.C.).

million. Contrasts with 1975 are dramatic: In 1975 per capita outlays were nearly $1600 and federal aid almost $50 billion. By 1975 federal expenditures constituted 61 percent of all public outlays and over 23 percent of GNP.

The state figures reveal a similar drastic shift. Total state expenditures in 1913 were substantially below a half-billion dollars—less than 1 percent of GNP and under 12 percent of all public-sector outlays. By 1975 the expenditure figure exceeded $120 billion—over 8 percent of GNP and more than one-fifth of all public outlays. State per capita outlays leaped from $4 to $566 per person over the sixty-year span, and state aid moved from under $100 million to more than $50 billion.

At the local level there was also extensive growth—from under $2 billion in outlays to nearly $100 billion. But percent of GNP did not demonstrate dramatic growth, and indeed the proportion of all public outlays dropped from 58 percent to 17 percent. This drop might seem strange if we recall the massive growth in municipal services, local schools, etc., that have occurred in the past sixty years. Have local governments lost power in the IGR arena? That *may* be the case, but these data are neither precise nor encompassing enough for making inferences about power shifts.

As we saw in chapter 2, in discussing IGR strategies and game theory, we must be cautious about what "losing" means. From the three figures for percents of all public outlays it might be claimed that between 1913 and 1975 the national and state governments approximately doubled their power—from 30 percent to 60 percent for the national government and from 11 percent to 21 percent for the states—at the expense of local units. This claim, however, rests on the assumption of a zero-sum relationship (total gains equal total losses) between the players. What evidence would show that the states and/or the federal government have taken power away from local units? Depending on the issue or policy problem, widely varying types of evidence might be offered: for example, specific changes in legal authority, restricted discretion in determining service levels or tax rates; judgments by local officials that they have lost significant legal, fiscal, personnel, or service authority. Valid inferences about an IGR power shift require firm data, carefully gathered, reliably marshaled, and clearly interpreted.

The few fragments of information provided in table 3-1 fall far short of such high standards. In fact, we may use local expenditures as a case in point to show the care and precision required when marshaling figures. What is not clear from table 3-1 is that local expenditures ($96.2 billion in 1975) are total local outlays from *own-source revenues*. Thus, although outlays for utility operations and trust fund expenditures (for example, respectively, water and pension funds) are included in each set of outlay figures, outlays drawn from interlevel payments are necessarily excluded from the recipient jurisdiction's figures. That is, federal aid is recorded as an outlay only for the federal level; likewise, state aid enters only as a state expenditure even though it is ultimately spent by a local jurisdiction (say a school district).

A more meaningful and accurate picture will emerge if we make two definitional changes and observe the results. The first shift is from

total expenditure to *general* expenditure: A general expenditure is a
government outlay used for broad, discretionary purposes, and is defined by the Bureau of the Census as all government expenditures other
than utility expenditures, liquor-store expenditures, and insurance-
trust (Social Security) expenditure. Depending on governmental level
these exclusions from *total* expenditures to arrive at *general* expenditures can be substantial; for example, $88 billion in federal Social
Security outlays, $15 billion in local utility expenditures.

A second definitional change is to the concept of *direct outlays,*
that is, recording the outlay as spent by the actual final disburser of
the dollars. This, of course, means that substantial federal aid and all
state aid is recorded as expenditure by local units. By these definitional
changes we get the following 1975 amounts and proportions for *direct
general* expenditures by level of government:

	(Billions)	% of Total
Federal:	$203.1	47.0
State:	86.3	19.9
Local:	143.1	33.1
	$432.5	100.0

By a mere switch in fiscal terms local government is restored to a more
significant place in IGR than suggested by the $96.2 billion in table
3-1. Also, combined state-local expenditures now exceed national
outlays. Need the caution be repeated about carefully constructed evidence and precise inference?

Expenditures, of course, cover only one side of the governmental
purse or fisc: To spend money governments must raise money. There
are three broad categories of general, or discretionary, revenue: (1)
taxes, (2) fees and miscellaneous revenue, and (3) intergovernmental
revenue. What have been the long-term trends in these revenue sources
for the three levels of government? Table 3–2 provides an array of proportions from which several conclusions may be made.

The extreme right column in table 3–2 indicates, in billions of
dollars, the general revenues received by each level of government.
For all three levels the amounts show progressive increases between
1913 and 1975: for the national government, from less than $1 billion

Table 3-2. *Trends in General Revenues by Level of Government and Revenue Source, 1913-1975*

	Revenue Source				Total General Revenue
	Taxes	Charges & Misc.	Intergovt'l	Total	
	(percentages)				(billions)
National					
1913	68.8	31.2		100.0	$ .9
1922	79.9	20.1		100.0	4.2
1932	71.3	28.7		100.0	2.5
1940	78.8	21.2		100.0	6.2
1950	87.8	12.2		100.0	40.1
1960	88.4	11.6		100.0	87.1
1970	89.3	10.7		100.0	163.6
1975	85.2	14.3	0.5	100.0	223.3
State					
1913	80.0	15.7	4.3	100.0	.4
1922	75.5	14.4	10.1	100.0	1.3
1932	78.0	11.0	11.0	100.0	2.4
1940	75.6	7.9	16.5	100.0	4.4
1950	70.4	8.1	21.5	100.0	11.3
1960	65.9	9.4	24.7	100.0	27.4
1970	61.7	12.3	26.0	100.0	77.6
1975	59.6	12.3	28.1	100.0	134.6
Local					
1913	79.9	14.2	5.9	100.0	1.6
1922	79.4	12.3	8.3	100.0	3.9
1932	75.1	10.6	14.3	100.0	5.7
1940	64.8	7.4	27.8	100.0	6.9
1950	57.0	11.4	31.6	100.0	14.0
1960	54.8	14.6	30.6	100.0	33.0
1970	48.0	15.5	36.5	100.0	80.9
1975	41.9	15.7	42.4	100.0	146.3
					1975 total: $504.2

Sources: Bureau of the Census, *Historical Statistics on Governmental Finances and Employment,* Vol. 6 of the 1967 Census of Governments, Topical Studies, No. 5, Tables 3,5,6; Bureau of the Census, *Governmental Finances in 1969-70,* GF70, No. 5, Table 4; Bureau of the Census, *Governmental Finances in 1974-75,* GF75, No. 5 (Washington, D.C.), Table 4.

to more than $220 billion; for the states, from less than $0.5 billion to about $135 billion; and for local units, from $1.6 billion to nearly $150 billion. The sum of these three general revenue amounts in 1975 exceeded $500 billion. And the proportions were national, 44 percent; state, 27 percent; and local, 29 percent. Recall, however, that intergovernmental funds are included as a category of *general revenue*. They therefore heavily influence any inferences or conclusions we might draw from these proportions. How much these transfers affect the state and local situation can be appreciated by reporting the intergovernmental revenue amounts for 1975:

To state from national:	$36.1 billion
To local from national:	$10.9 billion
To local from state:	$51.1 billion

It is evident that massive amounts of money flow through the financial pipelines of the IGR system. That the levels and jurisdictions overlap and are interdependent is seldom more evident than in the financial field. (This fiscal interdependence will be further explored below.)

Let us approach the long-term change in fiscal positions as if the autonomous or separated-authority model of IGR were operative. How much revenue does each level of government raise "on its own"— that is, excluding intergovernmental transfers from the aggregations and computations? The figures below show, for 1913 and 1975, the own-source revenues of each level operating as if they were separate and autonomous entities.

	General Revenues from Own Sources			
Level	1913	1975	1913	1975
	(billions)		(percentages)	
National	.96	222.0	33.6	55.1
State	.36	96.8	12.6	24.0
Local	1.54	84.4	53.8	20.9
Totals	2.86	403.2	100.0	100.0

The picture painted by these figures differs from the one displayed by the previous expenditure and revenue data, in which state and local finances outstripped national. In 1913 they did indeed; about two-thirds of all own-source revenues in that year were raised by local and state governments. By 1975 the situation was not exactly reversed but the national level clearly "out-revenued" the states and localities by 55 to 45 percent. This shift, or near reversal, is only one modest indicator of the revenue strength or tax-raising ability of the national government.

Of more significance in table 3–2 than the absolute amounts of general revenue are the proportions among the main sources of that revenue. In 1913 the national government secured nearly one-third of its revenues from miscellaneous sources, but since 1950 it has relied on taxes for 85 percent or more of its general revenues. State governments have become progressively less reliant on taxes; in 1975 less than 60 percent of general revenues came from this source, in contrast to 80 percent in 1913. Local units also obtained 80 percent of their general revenues from taxes in 1913, but by 1975 the proportion from this source had plummeted to nearly 40 percent. These declines in reliance on taxes are explained by the progressive increases in intergovernmental revenue.

Since 1970 more than one-fourth of the states' general revenue has been obtained from the national government. Dependence on this source has consistently increased since the turn of the century. In a like manner, local governments have become, in the aggregate, heavily dependent on revenues received from the state and national governments. In 1975 these two sources produced over 40 percent of all local revenues. That is, more than 40 percent of local officials' revenues come from sources beyond their direct control. Thus, whereas the substantial fiscal links among national, state, and local governments earlier suggested *interdependence,* local governments in fact seem to be *dependent.* (How this dependence affects local officials' actions and attitudes will be explored in chapter 8.)

The different *types* of local jurisdiction—counties, municipalities, school districts, townships, and special districts—vary in their revenue-raising abilities and in their reliance on intergovernmental revenues. Some of that variation is shown as near-term trends in table 3–3, for selected years from 1932 to 1975 by type of local unit. Of the numerous points for comparison and comment, we will look most closely at the percentages for intergovernmental revenue.

County governments in 1932 relied on intergovernmental transfers for less than 20 percent of their general revenue. By 1942 the proportion had increased to nearly 40 percent, where it remained until recently, when it rose to approximately 45 percent.

Table 3-3. *General Revenue Trends by Type of Local Government and Revenue Component, 1932-1975*

Type of Local Gov't and Revenue Component	1932	1942	1952	1962	1975
Counties			(percentages)		
Taxes	69.8	53.3	48.9	48.9	38.5
Charges & misc.	10.8	8.7	11.9	12.5	16.6
Intergovt'l revenue	19.4	38.0	39.2	38.6	44.9
	100.0	100.0	100.0	100.0	100.0
(Actual $ in billions)	(1.3)	(1.7)	(3.9)	(8.5)	(32.9)
Municipalities					
Taxes	77.6	74.4	65.9	60.4	42.4
Charges & misc.	13.0	9.8	15.0	19.2	18.2
Intergovt'l revenue	9.4	15.8	19.1	20.4	39.4
	100.0	100.0	100.0	100.0	100.0
(Actual $ in billions)	(2.7)	(3.1)	(6.4)	(13.1)	(49.9)
School Districts					
Taxes	68.4	60.0	52.3	51.8	43.2
Charges & misc.	4.6	4.9	5.2	7.4	7.5
Intergovt'l revenue	27.0	35.1	42.5	40.8	49.3
	100.0	100.0	100.0	100.0	100.0
(Actual $ in billions)	(1.4)	(1.8)	(5.1)	(14.1)	(52.9)
Townships					
Taxes	83.8	73.5	61.1	70.0	61.2
Charges & misc.	6.5	5.0	6.1	7.5	9.2
Intergovt'l revenue	9.7	21.5	32.8	22.5	29.6
	100.0	100.0	100.0	100.0	100.0
(Actual $ in billions)	(0.3)	(0.3)	(0.9)	(1.6)	(5.6)
Special Districts					
Taxes	69.0	46.4	23.9	25.0	15.2
Charges & misc.	27.1	52.6	64.9	53.9	47.8
Intergovt'l revenue	3.9	1.0	11.2	21.1	37.0
	100.0	100.0	100.0	100.0	100.0
(Actual $ in billions)	(0.1)	(0.2)	(0.7)	(1.8)	(8.3)

Sources: Bureau of the Census, *Historical Statistics on Governmental Finances and Employment,* Vol. 6 of the 1967 Census of Governments, Topical Studies, No. 5, Table 7; Bureau of the Census, *Governmental Finances in 1974-75,* GF75, No. 5 (Washington, D.C.), Table 16.

The trend for municipalities showed a still more accentuated rise in dependence on intergovernmental revenue—from less than 10 percent in 1932 to nearly 40 percent in 1975. More notably, the reliance on outside revenues jumped most sharply between 1962 and 1975 (from 20 percent to 39 percent). Thus, heavy municipal dependence on federal and state fiscal assistance is relatively recent.

Such heavy reliance on outside sources is not new to local school districts. As early as 1942 more than one-third of their revenues came from external origins, almost exclusively from state governments. Since 1952 the proportion has ranged between 40 to 50 percent, in recent years closing in on the higher figure. Of the external revenues received in 1975, about $4 billion, or 8 percent, of general school revenues originated with the national government.

Although townships show an inconsistent reliance on external revenues, the overall trend is similar to that of other jurisdictions—increased reliance. About 30 percent of township general revenues come from this source—the lowest proportion for any of the five types of units. Special districts are more dependent on outside revenues and have dramatically increased that reliance between 1952 and 1975.

Three observations summarize the fiscal revolution that has occurred among local governments in recent decades. First, every type of local jurisdiction has become reliant on resources provided by national and state governments. Second, school districts remain the most dependent on external aid. Third, municipalities and special districts, in the aggregate, sharply increased their dependence on state and national assistance between 1962 and 1975. For a better understanding of the forces underlying these trends, IGR in this century must be analyzed according to discrete periods or phases.

PHASES OF IGR

It is an accepted fact that since 1900 the U.S. political system has experienced changes bordering on major upheavals. What were the frequency, mechanisms, directions, and effects of such changes? To answer such questions, and to gain a better grasp of our political system, we shall identify and analyze five phases of IGR.

The five phases and their approximate periods of prominence are:

Conflict:	19th century-1930s
Cooperative:	1930s-1950s
Concentrated:	1940s-1960s
Creative:	1950s-1960s
Competitive:	1960s-1970s

A condensed chart of the phases is provided in table 3-4.

For each of the five IGR phases three main components are considered (see the second through fourth columns of table 3-4). First, what policy issues dominated the public agenda during each phase? Second, what dominant perceptions did the chief participants seem to have and be guided or directed by in their behavior in each phase? Third, what mechanisms and techniques were used to implement intergovernmental actions and objectives during each period? The fifth column of the table lists a metaphorical characterization of each phase.

It must be emphasized that the dates for each period are approximate. Indeed, the phases actually overlap. Hence, the importance of the idea of *climax period*—not only because it conveys a time of peak prominence but because it does not preclude the continuation of a phase beyond the dates given. For example, although the conflict phase *climaxed* before and during the 1930s, conflict patterns did not end then, but have since recurred.

Thus, like successive, somewhat porous strata that have been superimposed on each other (by the interactions and perspectives of public officials), no phase ends at an exact point—nor does it in fact disappear. Each phase is continuously present in greater or lesser measure, bearing the weight, so to speak, of the overlying strata and producing carry-over effects much wider than the climax periods indicated in table 3-4. Indeed, the present state of IGR results from multiple overlays of each of the five phases. The task of an IGR analyst is like that of a geologist—to drill or probe the several strata and from the samples make inferences about the substructure of the terrain.

Conflict (1930s and Before)

The conflict phase of IGR centered on identifying the proper spheres of governmental powers and jurisdiction and defining the boundaries of officials' actions. This emphasis operated at the state-local levels as well as between national and state governments. Dillon's Rule,

Table 3-4. *Phases of Intergovernmental Relations*

Phase Descriptor	Dominant Policy Issues	Participants' Perceptions	IGR Mechanisms	Federalism Metaphor	Approximate Climax Period
Conflict	Defining boundaries Proper spheres	Antagonistic Adversary Exclusivity	Statutes Courts Regulations	Layer cake	19th century–1930s
Cooperative	Economic distress International threat	Collaboration Complimentarity Mutuality Supportive	National planning Formula grants Tax credits	Marble cake	1930s–1950s
Concentrated	Service needs Physical development	Professionalism Objectivity Neutrality Functionalism	Categorical grants Service standards	Water taps (focused or channeled)	1940s–1960s
Creative	Urban-metropolitan Disadvantaged clients	National goals Great society Grantsmanship	Program planning Project grants Participation	Flowering (proliferated and fused)	1950s–1960s
Competitive	Coordination Program effectiveness Delivery systems Citizen access	Disagreement Tension Rivalry	Grant consolidation Revenue sharing Reorganization Regionalization	Picket fence (fragmented)	1960s–1970s

an assertion of state supremacy, was also an example of the search for the exact limits of local government powers. The national, state, and local officials who searched for precise specification of their respective powers assumed that those powers would be mutually exclusive. Moreover, the officials seem to have expected opposition and antagonism to be part of the normal process of learning who is empowered to do what.

These attitudes were anchored in the deeper societal values of competition, corporate organizational forms, and efficiency. Elements of this phase remain today in metropolitan areas, in the search for the one political jurisdiction that can perform a particular function most efficiently. Much of the impetus to reform and reorganize metropolitan government arises from civic leaders' views that present functions and programs are being performed by units that are too small, inefficient, and ineffective. Most metropolitan reorganization efforts are directed toward identifying those functions best performed by large entities and reallocating them to an existing or new areawide government. This rearrangement and consolidation of functions rests on the assumption that activities can be neatly and appropriately defined by governmental boundaries.

Sorting out roles and specifying clear boundaries is a hallmark of the conflict phase. The tendency comes from long-established traditions in American politics and especially in legal-constitutional traditions. An early, classic Supreme Court decision firmly established the conflict-oriented pattern in one policy arena with special relevance for IGR—finances. The case of *McCulloch* v. *Maryland* is most often remembered for its interpretation of the "necessary and proper" clause (Article I, Section 8, clause 18 of the Constitution) and specifically for sustaining the power of the national government to establish a bank.[1] (The case is discussed in Appendix B.)

What is often overlooked in writings about this case is that a Maryland tax on bank notes was invalidated with respect to federal bank notes. Chief Justice John Marshall's statement that "the power to tax involves the power to destroy" is frequently cited in connection with the decision (and is also cited by a much wider group of complainers about high taxes). Usually also forgotten in this case is that Marshall took an unnecessary, or at least discretionary, second step in striking down the Maryland tax—which, it should be mentioned, was assessed

1. *McCulloch* v. *Maryland,* 4 Wheaton 316 (1819).

against *all* bank notes issued by financial institutions not chartered by the Maryland legislature. On its face the tax was not discriminatory against U.S. government obligations. Marshall could have stopped once he upheld national authority to create the bank. His (and the Court's) negation of the Maryland statute rested on an unstated premise that the state of Maryland was intent on obstructing and frustrating actions of the national government.

Marshall, in other words, viewed the relationship between national and state officials as one in which adversaries acted to hinder and oppose each other's aims. Chief Justice Marshall, then, serving as the referee in a boxing match between national and state officials, awarded, in the McCulloch-Maryland fight, a TKO to the national government— a decision that was highly consistent with his nationalist views.

Marshall's decision in *McCulloch* did far more, however, than assist and assert national supremacy. It was the opening round in a century and a half of battles between national and state-local taxing authorities over who could or could not tax what activities of "opposing" jurisdictions. Although this lengthy struggle is often described simply as the intergovernmental tax immunity doctrine, it was far from that simple. As late as the 1930s the courts had so extended this doctrine that the salaries and wages of federal government employees were not subject to state income taxation, and compensation paid state and local government employees was not subject to federal income taxation! (If the latter condition prevailed today there would be an even greater incentive to seek and secure employment with state or local governments.)

Fortunately (or unfortunately) the Supreme Court beat a strategic retreat from these and other extremes associated with the *constitutional* issues.[2] But statutory and discretionary features of intergovernmental tax immunity are still very much with us. We cite only a few of the remaining issues which are, as the Kestnbaum Commission said, matters of policy:

1. There is no federal taxation of the income earned as interest payments on state or local debt obligations.
2. There is no levying and collecting of local property taxes on federally owned property.
3. There is no collection of state or local sales taxes on retail sales of food, tobacco, and alcohol on military bases and installations.

---

2. *Graves* v. *New York ex rel. O'Keefe,* 306 U.S. 466 (1939).

On the last item a recent study estimated that state and local governments thereby lose nearly $400 million annually in sales and excise tax revenues. An additional estimated $100 million in state income tax revenues was lost because of tax avoidance or evasion by military personnel, from whose compensation no state or local income tax is withheld.[3] Needless to say, state and local tax officials are concerned about these lost revenues, just as federal treasury personnel have long been bothered by the exemption from the federal income tax of income from interest on state and local government bonds. These and other issues have produced many studies, numerous legislative proposals, and a few court cases.

The tax immunity issue illustrates how problems of jurisdiction and authority were resolved in the conflict phase of IGR: chiefly by court decisions and statutory provisions. Behind these formal instruments was a set of perceptions by the chief participants. Those views were cut from the same cloth of hostility and suspicion that governed John Marshall's outlook. Participants saw each other in adversary roles across boundaries, and expected differences of opinion if not outright antagonism.

But social and economic complexity outgrew the abilities of state and national legislative bodies and courts to resolve conflicts—for example, state regulation of railroad rates or grain elevator charges, and national legislation regulating interstate commerce. One response was to create regulatory agencies and commissions to referee boundary disputes. L. D. White, for example, points to the Interstate Commerce Act of 1887 as the first significant breach of the "administrative settlement" between the nation and the states.[4] Attempts by national and state officials to specify the scope of federal regulatory power under the commerce clause have since expanded to the point that all electric generating and transmission companies fall under the rate-making authority of the Federal Power Commission.

Illustrations of continued adversary, conflict-oriented patterns of national-state relations abound, even to the present day. For example, environmental and health concerns precipitated a jurisdictional dispute over the spheres of national and state power to regulate the safety levels of a nuclear generating plant in Minnesota. National standards

3. Advisory Commission on Intergovernmental Relations, *State Taxation of Military Income and Store Sales* (Washington, D.C., July 1976, A-50), p. 2.
4. Leonard D. White, *The States and the Nation* (Baton Rouge: Louisiana State University Press, 1953), pp. 9–10.

set by the Atomic Energy Commission (AEC) specified one level of allowable millirems of radiation escaping from the reactor into the atmosphere, whereas the Minnesota Pollution Control Agency set its level at only two percent of the AEC's. The Northern States Power Company brought suit in federal court challenging the state standards and requesting permission to construct the nuclear power plant without regard to them. At issue in the case was the application and intent of federal statutes dealing with atomic energy. The court ruled in favor of the exclusive jurisdiction of the national government and invalidated the more restrictive state regulations.[5]

Recent court decisions probably come as close to reflecting current economic realities, social interdependencies, and technological necessity as pre-1937 courts and legislatures thought they were reflecting economic, social, and technological separatism. That supposed separatism—however limited or restricted in practice—gave credence to the metaphor of "layer cake federalism" to describe exclusive or autonomous spheres for national, state, and local governments.

Cooperation (1930s–1950s)

Several authors have ably argued and amply demonstrated that intergovernmental collaboration has existed in the United States throughout the nineteenth and twentieth centuries. It is less clear, however, that such collaboration was of major significance or the dominant fact of our political history. Nevertheless there is one period in which complementary and supportive relationships were most prominent and had high political significance. That period is the cooperative phase prominent for approximately two decades, from the 1930s into the 1950s.

The prime issues of concern to the nation during the period were the alleviation of widespread economic distress and responses to international threats. It seems logical and natural that internal and external challenges to national survival would bring public officials into closer contact and collaboration.

The means for such increased collaboration were several and

---

5. *Northern States Power Co.* v. *State of Minnesota,* 447 F. 2nd 1143 (1971); see also Harry Foreman (ed.), *Nuclear Power and the Public* (Minneapolis: University of Minnesota Press, 1970); *Science,* 171 (January 8, 1971): 45; and Phillip M. Boffey, "Nuclear Energy: Do States Lack Power to Block Proliferation of Reactors?" *Science,* 191 (January 30, 1976): 360–361.

varied. Pertinent for our concerns are such policy innovations as national planning, tax credits, and formula-based grants-in-aid.

- In 1933 the National Resources Planning Board was created; among other things, it stimulated considerable policy planning at the state and local levels.
- The tax credit was as a major policy innovation, enacted for the first time in the joint federal-state unemployment compensation program. The tax credit (or tax offset) is simply a tax rebate or forgiveness scheme conditional on the beneficiary's meeting specified requirements—in this case the state government must pass an acceptable program covering unemployed workers.
- More than a dozen conditional grants-in-aid were enacted during the depression, programs that offered funds to state and/or local governments provided the recipients met the conditions attached. Public health and welfare were the focus of most grants, such as health services, old age assistance, aid to dependent children. Also, these federal funds were distributed among the states according to a prescribed formula, hence the term "formula grants."

During the war years special emergency funding arrangements that were instituted during the depression years were revived in selected areas. As one observer noted in 1943:

> Cooperative government by federal-state-local authorities has become a by-word in the prodigious effort to administer civilian defense, rationing, and other war-time programs. Intergovernmental administration, while it is a part of all levels of government, is turning into something quite distinct from them all.[6]

The IGR collaboration that persisted during these years was in effect on varied and unusual occasions. When President Truman took action against the steel mills during the Korean War in 1952 he polled state governors for their views prior to his attempt at seizure.

The prime IGR mechanism—as well as the major legacy—of this cooperative period was fiscal. Substantial, significant fiscal links were firmly established, and were harbingers of more to come. They also stimulated a new metaphor of intergovernmental patterns: the well-publicized "marble cake," which appears to have been created in the

---

6. Arthur W. Bromage, "Federal-State-Local Relations," *American Political Science Review,* 37 (February 1943): 35.

early 1940s by Professor Joseph McLean of Princeton University to contrast with the layer cake conception. But Professor Morton Grodzins was probably the person who best popularized and elaborated the concept behind the metaphor.[7]

Grodzins argued that American government was erroneously seen as a three-layer cake. "A far more accurate image," he said, "is the rainbow or marble cake, characterized by an inseparable mingling of differently colored ingredients, the colors appearing in vertical and diagonal strands and unexpected whirls [*sic*]."[8] Grodzins effectively illustrated his point with a rural county health official called a "sanitarian":

> The sanitarian is appointed by the state under merit standards established by the federal government. His base salary comes jointly from state and federal funds, the county provides him with an office and office amenities and pays a portion of his expenses, and the largest city in the county also contributes to his salary and office by virtue of his appointment as a city plumbing inspector. It is impossible from moment to moment to tell under which governmental hat the sanitarian operates. His work of inspecting the purity of food is carried out under federal standards; but he is enforcing state laws when inspecting commodities that have not been in interstate commerce; and somewhat perversely he also acts under state authority when inspecting milk coming into the county from producing areas across the state border. He is a federal officer when impounding impure drugs shipped from a neighboring state; a federal-state officer when distributing typhoid immunization serum; a state officer when enforcing standards of industrial hygiene; a state-local officer when inspecting the city's water supply; and (to complete the circle) a local officer when insisting that the city butchers adopt more hygienic methods of handling their garbage. But he cannot and does not think of himself as acting in these separate capacities. All business in the county that concerns public health and sanitation he considers his business. Paid largely from federal funds, he does not find it strange to attend meetings of the city council to give expert advice on matters ranging from rotten apples to rabies control. He is even deputized as a member of both the city and county police force.[9]

From this and numerous other examples Grodzins concluded that the American system of governance was one of shared functions where "It is difficult to find any governmental activity which does not involve

---

7. Morton Grodzins, "The Federal System," in *Goals for Americans: Report of the President's Commission on National Goals and Chapters Submitted for the Consideration of the Commission* (Prentice-Hall, Spectrum, 1960), pp. 265-282.

8. Ibid., p. 265.

9. Ibid.

all three of the so-called 'levels' of the federal system."[10] Undergirding these shared functions was an implicit—and sometimes explicit—mood and pattern of behavior among participants: collaboration, cooperation, and mutual assistance.

Concentrated (1940s–1960s)

Through the Truman-Eisenhower-Kennedy years IGR became increasingly specific, functional, and highly focused—in short, concentrated. From 1946 to 1961 twenty-one major new grant-in-aid programs were established, nearly doubling the total enacted in the depression era. With this expanded use of categorical grant programs came increased attention to service standards: Administrative rules and regulations rather than statutes began to govern award criteria, reporting, performance requirements, etc.

Guiding this growing programmatic and functional emphasis were corps of professionals in each of the specialized grant fields—for example, construction of airports, hospitals, and highways; slum clearance and urban renewal; urban planning; waste treatment; library construction. In the late 1950s education was added as being important to defense—a response to major Soviet advances in scientific, technical, and aerospace fields. The pervasiveness of professionalism enhanced the emphasis on service standards by covering the domain with a cloak of objectivity and neutrality. As Herbert Kaufman has argued, the emergence of objectivity and neutrality, or of "neutral competence" as he calls it, in public administration militates against continued control of policy by a strong executive leader.[11] Moreover, Professor Frederick Mosher locates the triumph of the "professional state" in the public service in the 1950s.[12]

Toward what problems and needs were these expanded IGR programs and burgeoning professional involvement directed? Two general targets appear to be most prominent. One was a capital works, public construction, physical development push. Between 1946 and 1960 state and local capital outlays increased twelvefold while current operating expenses rose by a multiple of four. Federal grants for high-

---

10. Ibid., p. 266.

11. Herbert Kaufman, "Emerging Conflicts in the Doctrines of Public Administration," *American Political Science Review,* 50 (December 1956): 1057–1073.

12. Frederick Mosher, *Democracy and the Public Service* (New York: Oxford University Press, 1968), especially chapter 4, "The Professional State."

ways, hospitals, sewage plants, and airports underwrote much of the state-local effort to meet deferred wartime needs and also responded to changing technology and population configurations—especially that of suburbanization.

A second motive force propelling intergovernmental action in this period was the political realization that government was capable of responding to particularistic, middle-class service needs. The most significant effect of the New Deal may have been to make the middle class acutely aware of the positive and program-specific capabilities of governmental action. Effective political action generated by this awareness came after World War II and was reinforced by several conditions.

One, again, was suburbanization. Suburbia, the urban frontier, seemed to preserve if not reinforce the Jeffersonian myth of self-governing "ward republics": the ideal that each small place should be governed solely by its denizens. Suburbia was greatly in need of public services—schools, sewers, roads. And how better to provide them than to secure external assistance while retaining local decision-making authority?

A second, related favoring condition was that IGR mechanisms seemed to preserve substantial local political control. In this respect the techniques of grants, service standards, construction projects, etc., matched the local traditions of initiative and voluntary participation. In addition, IGR techniques fitted middle-class values of professionalism, objectivity, and neutrality. It appeared that objective program needs rather than politics were being served. Like governmental reforms at the turn of the century (for example, the council-manager plan, at-large elections), IGR appeared to remove programs from the seamy side of pork-barrel politics.

These principled political values coincided with an important structural change at the national level: at legislative reorganization of the Congress in 1946. For IGR the most significant result of this event was the creation of standing committees with explicit program emphases. These congressional committee patterns soon became the channels for access and leverage points for influencing program-specific grants.

Because the flow of influence combined with the concentrated or focused flow of funds in the 1946–1961 period, the national government had become an established reservoir of fiscal resources to which a rapidly increasing number of water taps were being connected. Funds could be made to flow best by those (the program professionals) knowledgeable at turning on the numerous spigots. Although cooperation was prominent during this period, it occurred in concentrated and selectively channeled ways.

The "water tap" phase of IGR is sketched diagrammatically in figure 3-1. Lines connecting the national-state and state-local spending sectors show the intergovernmental flow of funds for 1950. During this phase of IGR the interconnectedness and interdependency of national-state-local relations was confirmed and solidified. Links among national, state, and local officials, especially at the administrative level, had long been present. This is merely one way of recalling that the confirmed features of one phase has antecedents in one or more prior phases.

What is somewhat surprising, however, is just how solidified the programmatic and functional connections had become by the late 1950s. The benefits conferred, the interests satisfied, and the political support realized by *administrators* as well as legislators combined to

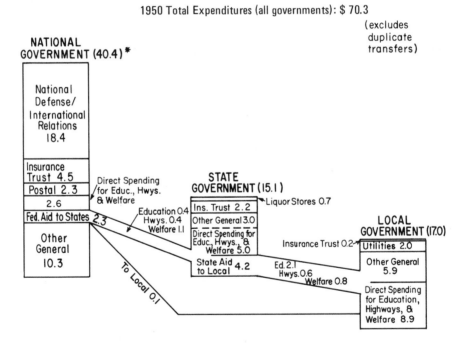

* Excludes interest on the national debt ($ 4.4 billion)

Figure 3-1. *Public Expenditures by Type and by Level of Government, and the Intergovernmental Flow of Funds, Fiscal Year 1950 (in billions of dollars)*

Source: Bureau of the Census, *Historical Statistics on Governmental Finances and Employment* (Washington, D.C.: Government Printing Office, 1969).

produce potent political alliances around specific grant programs. The solidification and strength of the interests associated with categorical grant programs did not go unnoticed elsewhere. As early as 1955 some local officials, especially mayors, lamented the growth of "vertical functional autocracies" composed of program professionals at national-state-local levels.[13] Attacks on, or even efforts to cope with, the concentration of forces favorable to categorical grant programs did not fare well. Consider one major example.

On June 24, 1957, in Williamsburg, Virginia, President Eisenhower addressed the assembled governors at their annual conference. Bemoaning the drift of pressures, programs, and financing toward Washington, the president offered to work with the governors in an effort:

1. to designate functions which the states are reading and willing to assume and finances that are now performed or financed wholly or in part by the Federal Government;
2. to recommend the Federal and state revenue adjustments required to enable the state to assume such functions; and
3. to identify functions and responsibilities likely to require state or Federal attention in the future and to recommend the level of state effort, or Federal effort, or both, that will be needed to assure effective action.[14]

From this invitation emerged the so-called Joint Federal-State Action Committee, composed of six governors and six federal executive-branch officials (such as Secretary of the Treasury). The Joint Committee labored for two and a half years to turn some grant programs (and revenues) back to the states.[15] The strategy was a notable failure. In the forefront of the numerous obstacles were the interests welded around two of the categorical grant programs proposed for "return" to the states—vocational education and construction of waste-treatment facilities.

13. *An Advisory Committee Report on Local Government,* submitted to the Commission on Intergovernmental Relations (Washington, D.C.: Government Printing Office, June 1955), p. 7.
14. "Address to the 1957 Governors' Conference, Williamsburg, Virginia," *Public Papers of the Presidents—Dwight D. Eisenhower, 1957,* pp. 494-495.
15. *Final Report of the Joint Federal-State Action Committee to the President of the United States and to the Chairman of the Governors' Conference* (Washington, D.C.: Government Printing Office, February 1960). For discussions and evaluations of the work of the Joint Federal-State Action Committee see Grodzins, "The Federal System"; James A. Maxwell, "Recent Developments in Federal-State Financial Relations," *National Tax Journal,* 13 (December 1960): 310-319; William B. Shore, "Developments in Public Administration: Intergovernmental Relations—Satisfactions and Problems," *Public Administration Review,* 19 (Winter 1959): 65-69.

The interests opposing such a fiscal return to the states were members of the program-authorizing congressional committees; federal agency personnel; state and local professionals in vocational education and sanitary engineering; agricultural interests (where much vocational-education support went); many mayors; and some governors. In addition to this arrayed opposition, there was a basic political-fiscal flaw in the "return-it-to-the-states" strategy. To compensate the states for picking up these programs the Eisenhower administration was ready to recommend enactment of a 4 percent tax credit on local telephone service—that money becoming directly available to the states as tax revenue. The credit would have yielded $148 million in new revenue to the states and an equivalent loss to the U.S. Treasury.

This appeared to be a "good deal" for the states since the two grant programs proposed for return totaled only $84.5 million in revenue. But the states, like the program-associated interests, were not buying. The reasons are complicated and require lengthy explanation, but they can be gleaned from analysis of the following examples of monies gained and lost by the tandem proposals in particular states.[16]

Selected States	Yield from 4% Telephone Tax Credit	Federal Grants (in 1956) for Voc. Ed. and Waste Treatment
	(millions of dollars)	
New York	22.5	5.1
Illinois	11.0	3.4
Massachusetts	5.5	1.2
California	16.3	3.9
Mississippi	.8	2.1
South Carolina	.9	1.7
Kentucky	1.6	2.1
North Dakota	.3	1.0

In short, the states (or the governors) could not come close to presenting a united front in dealing with national officials—the president and Congress. Furthermore, members of Congress from states that would

---

16. *Federal-State-Local Relations: Joint Federal-State Action Commitee,* hearings before the Intergovernmental Relations Subcommittee of the Committee on Government Operations, House of Representatives, 85th Congress, 2nd Session, February 18, 1958, p. 26.

lose under the exchange held influential positions on key congressional committees.

Eisenhower's somewhat oblique attack on the focused, functional, and concentrated character of categorical grants came off rather badly, although the Joint Federal-State Action Committee was useful in other respects. For one, it kept national government's attention on IGR during the years between the termination of the Kestnbaum Commission on Intergovernmental Relations in 1955 and the creation of the permanent Advisory Commission on Intergovernmental Relations (ACIR) in 1959.

How did one governor (who, incidentally, opposed the Joint Action Committee's proposal to dam established funding channels) assess the general condition of grant programs? What might be the outlook of a governor who wished to improve regulation of the rate of fund flows or to target them in slightly different directions? Speaking at the time of the Joint Federal-State Action Committee's proposals in 1958, Governor Orville Freeman of Minnesota observed:

> Some of the worst features of bureaucratic control are manifest in the Federal-aid programs. Some administrative forms are so complex that they make administration unnecessarily unwieldly. States frequently experience troublesome delays in obtaining needed decisions from regional and national offices. Sometimes authority to act in behalf of Federal agencies is not clearly spelled out; at times Federal agents will be too indecisive, at other times too arbitrary.

> The many Federal-aid programs are conceived, established, and managed independently of each other. No central or single mechanism coordinates programs which often affect each other. The Joint Action Committee might very well consider establishment of an administrative mechanism at the national level that would be responsible for bringing the numerous aid programs into balance with each other and for helping States maximize their participation in the aid program.[17]

Creative (1950s–1960s)

The pilings if not the full foundations for the creative phase of IGR were implanted in the cooperative and concentrated periods.

---

17. *To Establish an Advisory Commission on Intergovernmental Relations,* joint hearings before the Intergovernmental Relations Subcommittee of the House Committee on Government Operations and the Senate Committee on Government Operations, 86th Congress, 1st Session, June, 1959, pp. 187–189.

The period of ascendancy of the creative phase marks a time of movement toward decisiveness rather than drift in American politics and public policy. The election of a heavily Democratic Congress in 1958 and the 1964 landslide victory for President Lyndon Johnson are the seminal political events of this phase of IGR. An added input that contributed to direction and cohesiveness, if not decisiveness, was the report of the Eisenhower-appointed President's Commission on National Goals. The Commission, appointed partially in response to the Russian challenge of Sputnik, was created in 1959 and reported in 1961.[18]

The term *creative* is applied to this period partly because of President Johnson's usage of the slogan "Creative Federalism," and partly because of the many novel initiatives in IGR. Three IGR mechanisms were prominent: (1) program planning, (2) project grants, and (3) popular participation. The first refers to federal legislative and administrative requirements that comprehensive local, areawide, or statewide plans be submitted and approved prior to the receipt of grant funds. Project grants, which now number over 400, are authorizations for which individual, project-type proposals must be submitted. Project grants involve not only extensive (often elaborate) proposals or requests but also far greater discretion in the hands of grant administrators than formula grants, in which statutory or administrative formulas determine recipient entitlements. How much popular or client participation there should be is conveyed concisely by the Economic Opportunity Act: There should be "maximum feasible participation" in program operations by clients/recipients.

The sheer number of grant programs alone is sufficient to set this period apart from all others. In 1961 the ACIR identified approximately forty major grant programs that had been enacted prior to 1958 and were still in existence.[19] By 1969 there were an estimated 150 major programs, 400 specific legislative authorizations, and 1300 different federal assistance activities for which monetary amounts, application deadlines, agency contacts, and use restrictions could be identified.[20] Of the 400 specific authorizations 70 involved direct national-to-local

---

18. Grodzins, "The Federal System."

19. Advisory Commission on Intergovernmental Relations, *Periodic Congressional Reassessment of Federal Grants-in-Aid to State and Local Governments* (Washington, D.C.: June 1961, A-8).

20. *1969 Listing of Operating Federal Assistance Programs Compiled during the Roth Study,* House of Representatives, 91st Congress, 1st Session, Doc. No. 91–177. It is very easy to play a "numbers game" in counting federal grant or assistance programs. The figures cited are not precise or definitive results but merely highlight the extent, growth, and diversity of federal aid during the creative phase.

disbursements, thus bypassing the states. In one two-year span (1964–1966) over 100 project grant programs were enacted. In dollar magnitude federal grants jumped from $4.9 billion in 1958 to $23.9 billion in 1970. There was also a major expansion in state government IGR fiscal activities. State aid to local governments rose from $8.0 billion to $28.9 billion between 1958 and 1970.

Numbers and dollars alone do not distinguish the creative phase. Planning requirements, for example, were attached to sixty-one new grant programs enacted between 1961 and 1966.[21] In 1965 President Johnson sought to apply cost-effectiveness techniques, developed in the Defense Department, to the entire federal administrative establishment. The approach was called Planning-Programming-Budgeting-Systems (PPBS), and among other aims it attempted to tie national, state, and local objectives more closely together.[22] The tremendous increase in project grants over formula grants further diversified the activities supported by federal funds and further increased the autonomy and discretion of program professionals. Finally, the public-participation requirements tied to some grants increased the complexity of managerial activities and of calculations and occasionally added to the chagrin of officials charged with grant allocation choices. The task of securing and spending federal funds involved extensive administrative skills, substantial resources, and expert timing. Success often was defined simply as getting everyone in on the act but still getting action. In several instances federal funds, especially Office of Economic Opportunity (OEO) antipoverty program funds, were seen as sources of support with which to "fight city hall."

This phase of IGR has sometimes been called a period of the "project-categorical grant explosion." An analysis of grant-in-aid developments by the ACIR in 1967 highlighted the following features:

- proliferation of grants;
- expanding use of project grants;
- increasing variety of matching ratios;
- introduction of special incentive grants;

---

21. Advisory Commission on Intergovernmental Relations, *Fiscal Balance in the American Federal System*, Vol. I (Washington, D.C.: October 1967, A-31), pp. 175–181. This volume, and especially chapter 5, "Federal Grant-in-Aid Programs—Trends and Problems," is an excellent review and appraisal of IGR at the peak of the creative phase.
22. A perceptive analysis of Creative Federalism, PPBS, and IGR policy issues of the 1960s set in a long-term historical context is Harry N. Scheiber, "The Condition of American Federalism: An Historian's View," a study submitted by the Subcommittee on Intergovernmental Relations to the Committee on Government Operations, U.S. Senate, 89th Congress, 2nd Session, Committee Print, October 15, 1966.

- use of multifunctional or multiple-program grants (for example, economic development);
- diversification of eligible recipients;
- increasing grants to urban areas;
- inflexible administrative and fiscal requirements;
- extensive mandating of planning requirements;
- variability in federal regional administration.[23]

To what ends were these massive federal initiatives directed? What were the chief policy issues addressed by this creative activism? At the risk of great oversimplification we can identify two major policy themes: one, an urban-metropolitan focus; two, attention to the disadvantaged through antipoverty programs and aid-to-education funds. The second policy theme needs little documentation. With respect to the first, between 1961 and 1969 the percentage of all federal aid that went to urban areas or SMSAs increased from 55 percent to 70 percent (from $3.9 billion to $14.0 billion).[24]

Policies focusing on urban problems and disadvantaged persons reflected significant views held by important actors. The presidential speech in which Creative Federalism was first mentioned also contained a phrase of broader popularity: the Great Society. We have already noted the centralizing and unitary character of the term. How much Johnson's consensus politics owed to the popularity of "national goals" efforts in the late 1950s and early 1960s is unknown.[25] A unitary emphasis was, however, quite clear, and the perspective of the president on the need to centralize objective-setting made PPBS a natural offshoot of the view that our governmental system was single and unitary.

Accompanying these national, unitary perspectives was the outlook and behavior of IGR participants standing under the shower of federal dollars. With the expansion in dollar size and numbers of grants a grantsmanship perspective grew rapidly and widely, but it took especially deep root around the poverty and project grant programs. Playing the federal grant "game" became a well-known but time-consuming activity for mayors, city managers, county administrators, school officials, governors, and, of course, program professionals.

Several illustrations underscore the grantsmanship games played

23. ACIR, *Fiscal Balance*, p. 260.
24. *Special Analysis, Budget of the United States, Fiscal Year 1971* (Washington, D.C.: Office of Management and Budget, 1970), pp. 228-229.
25. For a review of five major works during 1960-1961 that focused on national purposes, goals, and policies, see William L. C. Wheaton, "Made in U.S.A.: Goals for America," *Journal of the American Institute of Planners,* 27 (August 1961): 221-224.

by local officials. Catawba County, in central North Carolina, with a population of about 80,000, hired a private consulting firm as "grant lobbyists to help them secure federal monies and to manage the accompanying red tape." The county agreed to pay the firm $8000 annually to help find, secure, and manage federal grants.[26]

Edward Zorinsky became mayor of Omaha, Nebraska, in 1973. He soon found that the city's major grant-acquisition efforts in the late 1960s made commitments to match many of the federal monies with "in-kind services," that is, parts or all of the salaries, space, supplies, etc., that the city was already providing. At his first cabinet meeting with department heads Zorinsky asked each administrator to determine what percentage of the hours per person in their own offices and in their departments as a whole were being used as in-kind matching for federal grants. The Mayor explained his action with a question: "Are we going to wake up some morning and find that only 25 per cent of city employees are working on city business?"[27]

A final example comes from a large California city, San Jose (population 450,000). By 1970 most responsible elected and administrative officials had been turned into grantsmen—applying for federal dollars simply because they were available and making commitments of local matching funds without sufficient regard for their own priorities. Mayor Norman Mineta secured a $200,000 grant from HUD for the purpose of providing him with the staff to review and assess all federal grant program applications originating within and affecting San Jose. (In bureaucratic lingo this was called the CERC process option under the PV program in anticipation of CDRS: Chief Executive Review and Comment process, part of the Planned Variations experiment as a precedent for Community Development Revenue Sharing.) It should be noted that Mayor Mineta's review covered grants to agencies and groups that were not a formal part of city government: schools, community action agencies, neighborhood health centers.

But the mayor and his staff chief on the project, James King, soon found that the CERC power could not be exercised. The simple but somewhat astounding reason was that there was no one source of information on all the federal grants entering San Jose; nor were there only a few—there were many. Moreover, there was not even a single

---

26. *Chapel Hill Newspaper,* February 23, 1970, editorial: "Hiring a Consultant Is the Latest Fad."

27. *Omaha World Herald,* July 18, 1973, "Mayor Seeks Time Spent on Federal In-Kind Services."

total for just their own city agencies. As a result, King spent the entire $200,000 grant and a full year of time just to assemble a booklet summarizing the nature and extent of the projects involving federal aid to San Jose. King's compilation disclosed that the federal government had agreed to provide $56.4 million to the city and, to the surprise of the mayor and other municipal officials, San Jose was committed to matching those monies with about $20 million in local contributions.[28]

There is a paradox in the creative phase of IGR: Federal grants proliferated in number and expanded massively in scope and dollar magnitudes; yet the diversity that encouraged grantsmanship originated in political and policy assumptions that derived from common (if not exactly unitary) conceptions about the aims of society. Thus, both fusion as well as proliferation equally characterize this IGR phase. Figure 3–2 shows visually the interconnectedness of IGR at the end of the creative period. The connections between national-state and state-local sectors are broad, and the segments form a closely linked system. At the same time the identical federal-state and federal-local "pipes" are penetrated by scores, if not hundreds, of small, grant-specific "tubes."

The visual contrast between figures 3–1 and 3–2 helps confirm the shift from a focused to a fused-proliferated phase of IGR. Although figure 3–2 conveys the interconnectedness and interdependence of national, state, and local levels, it does not convey the diversity and proliferation of national-state and national-local links. There is at first glance an appearance of fusion, but the scores of diverse, discrete categorical grants produce great variety and profusion—a flowering federalism.

Competitive (1960s–1970s)

The proliferation of grants, the clash between professionals and participation-minded clients, the gap between promise and performance, and the intractability of domestic urban and international problems all contributed to a malaise, and IGR entered a new phase. Central policy issues were restored when the administrative consequences of executive-legislative policy whirlwinds in the mid-1960s became the center of attention during the late '60s and '70s. Issues associated with bureaucratic behavior, administrative competence (or

---

28. *National Journal,* "The New Federalism: Theory, Practice, Problems" (Washington, D.C.: Government Research Corporation, March 1973), p. 7.

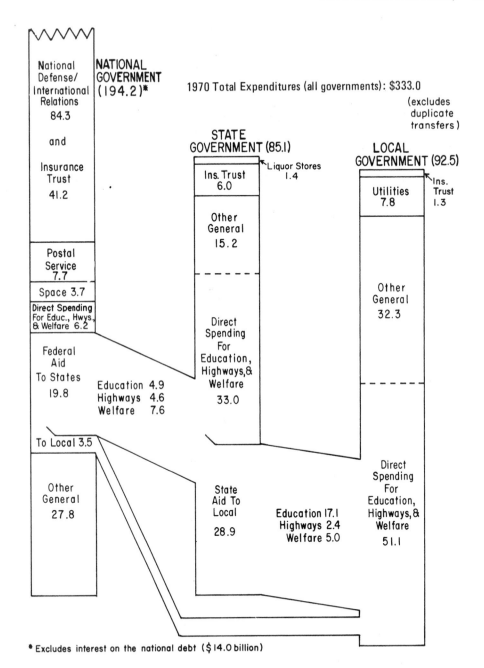

National Defense/ International Relations 84.3

and

Insurance Trust 41.2

NATIONAL GOVERNMENT (194.2)*

1970 Total Expenditures (all governments): $333.0

(excludes duplicate transfers)

Postal Service 7.7

Space 3.7

Direct Spending For Educ., Hwys., & Welfare 6.2

Federal Aid To States 19.8

Education 4.9
Highways 4.6
Welfare 7.6

To Local 3.5

Other General 27.8

STATE GOVERNMENT (85.1)

Ins. Trust 6.0

Liquor Stores 1.4

Other General 15.2

Direct Spending For Education, Highways,& Welfare 33.0

State Aid To Local 28.9

Education 17.1
Highways 2.4
Welfare 5.0

LOCAL GOVERNMENT (92.5)

Utilities 7.8

Ins. Trust 1.3

Other General 32.3

Direct Spending For Education, Highways,& Welfare 51.1

* Excludes interest on the national debt ($14.0 billion)

Figure 3-2. *Public Expenditures by Type and by Level of Government, and the Intergovernmental Flow of Funds, Fiscal Year 1970 (in billions of dollars)*

Source: Bureau of Census, *Governmental Finances in 1969-70* (Washington, D.C.: Government Printing Office).

incompetence), and implementation came to the forefront. One talisman earnestly sought was coordination within and among programs, and within and among levels. Others in close association were program accomplishment, effective service delivery, and citizen access. In such a political climate candidates for office from the presidency on down focused attention on administrative performance, or lack thereof, and on organizational structures and relationships that either hindered or helped the delivery of public goods and services.

A sharply different tack was taken regarding appropriate IGR mechanisms. Pressure grew to alter and even reverse previous grant trends. It was proposed that numerous grant programs be consolidated under the rubric of "special" revenue sharing. General Revenue Sharing was proposed and popularized and ultimately enacted under a Republican president, Nixon, who urged it as a means of improving program effectiveness and strengthening state-local governments, especially elected officials in their contests with federal bureaucrats. With the strong support of mayors and governors, General Revenue Sharing slipped through a divided Congress. That same president, in 1973, also sought mightily to stem or reverse the flow of grant funds by massive use of impoundment. On the federal administrative scene moves were made toward regionalization and reorganization.

A flood of other developments in the late 1960s and early 1970s underscored the competition present in the system and also signaled efforts to reduce it. Perhaps the more visible actions and initiatives came at the national level, but numerous potentially significant policy shifts occurred at the state and local levels. The trends that induced competition and those that eased competitive tendencies are both too numerous to mention. Three policy patterns illustrate tension-promoting developments: (1) economic opportunity programs and their chief implementation mechanisms—community action agencies; (2) "white flight" and the polarization of central cities and suburbs, especially along racial lines; and (3) elimination of some grant programs and funding reductions of others—some by the impounding of funds—by the Nixon administration in 1973.

Of the countervailing tendencies toward reduced tensions several can be mentioned. At the local level, prompted and supported by national action, councils of governments sprang into existence in large numbers. One major aim was to foster metropolitan and regional coordination, especially through the grant review and comment process (under OMB circular A-95). At the state level, herculean tax efforts were made to: (1) expand state services, (2) greatly increase state aid to local governments (see figure 3-2), and (3) meet the enlarged state-level obligations to match the vastly expanded federal grant monies. At the national level tension-reducing aims were reflected in such actions as new departures with interstate compacts, the Partnership for Health Act (P.L. 89-749), the Intergovernmental Cooperation Act of 1968 (P.L. 90-577), and the Intergovernmental Personnel Act of 1970 (P.L. 91-648).

The developments noted above reflected contrasting perspectives that old as well as new participants brought to IGR. For example, in 1966 Senator Edmund Muskie stated: "The picture, then, is one of too much tension and conflict rather than coordination and cooperation all along the line of administration—from top Federal policymakers and administrators to the state and local professional administrators and elected officials."[29] Similar views about unwarranted disagreement, tension, and rivalry among officials prompt calling this phase of IGR "competitive."

Yet the competition differs in degree, emphasis, and configuration from the interlevel conflict of the older, "layer cake" phase. It is more modulated and reflects the lessons learned from the intervening periods of cooperation, concentration, and creativity. For example, during the current competitive phase most officials appear reasonably realistic about the interdependencies within the system and about the inability to turn the clock back in IGR. The three federal statutes cited above reflect reasoned, realistic approaches to IGR.

The nature of the competition in the present IGR phase is indicated in part by Senator Muskie's remarks about professional program administrators and state-local elected officials. This tension between the policy generalists, whether elected or appointed, and the program-professional specialists currently produces great friction in IGR. This cleavage is another reason for describing this phase of IGR as competitive. Figure 3-3 depicts the fractures and rivalry characterizing this phase, and thereby suggests the appropriateness of the picket fence metaphor referred to in Terry Sanford's *Storm over the States* (mentioned in chapter 1).[30] The seven public-interest groups, often called the PIGs or the Big Seven, have parted ways from the program or functional specialists. Because of the common interests that the Big Seven hold in revenue sharing, grant consolidation, and similar proposals, they

29. *Congressional Record,* U.S. Senate, 89th Congress, 2nd Session (1966), p. 6834.
30. Terry Sanford, *Storm over the States* (New York: McGraw-Hill, 1967), p. 80.

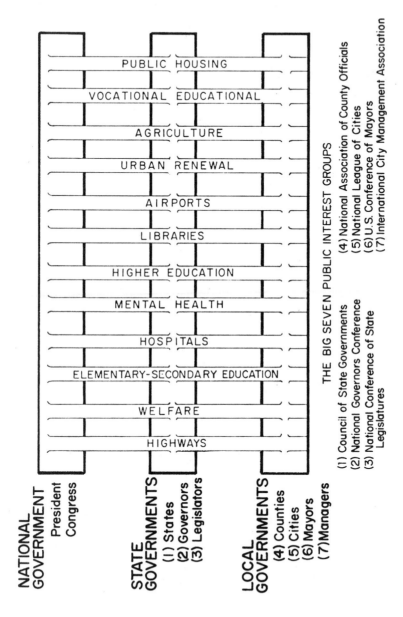

NATIONAL
GOVERNMENT

President
Congress

STATE
GOVERNMENTS

(1) States
(2) Governors
(3) Legislators

LOCAL
GOVERNMENTS

(4) Counties
(5) Cities
(6) Mayors
(7) Managers

PUBLIC HOUSING

VOCATIONAL EDUCATIONAL

AGRICULTURE

URBAN RENEWAL

AIRPORTS

LIBRARIES

HIGHER EDUCATION

MENTAL HEALTH

HOSPITALS

ELEMENTARY-SECONDARY EDUCATION

WELFARE

HIGHWAYS

THE BIG SEVEN PUBLIC INTEREST GROUPS

(1) Council of State Governments
(2) National Governors Conference
(3) National Conference of State
     Legislatures

(4) National Association of County Officials
(5) National League of Cities
(6) U.S. Conference of Mayors
(7) International City Management Association

Figure 3–3. *Picket Fence Federalism: A Schematic Representation*

have reasserted the executive leadership doctrine and have challenged the program professionals' doctrine of neutral competence.[31]

A second type of competition can also be discerned from figure 3-3: the competition among the several functional program areas. Each picket represents an alliance among like-minded program specialists or professionals, regardless of the level of government in which they serve.

These interlevel loyalties were identified earlier and criticized by elected officials as "vertical functional autocracies." Other epithets used to label these patterns are: balkanized bureaucracies, feudal federalisms, and bureaucratic baronies. These terms emphasize both the program specialists' degree of autonomy from policy control by political generalists and also the separateness and independence that one program area has from another. Hence, interprogram, interprofessional, and interagency competition is encouraged. This competition and the generalist-specialist split combine to validate the "picket fence" model as best describing the most recent phase of IGR.

Both competitive patterns were expressed by local officials, who were quoted by James Sundquist. One such official, the director of a local model cities program, speaking in the late 1960s, contended that "Our city is a battleground among federal Cabinet agencies."[32] Similar sentiments came from mayors and city managers whose limited control and coordination powers over federal programs caused them to feel like spectators of the governmental process in their own cities. If, in fact, this competitive model is applicable to IGR today, then to recognize these tensions and cleavages would seem to be the first-order task of those seeking changes and improvements in IGR.

---

31. The most thorough analysis of political action by the public interest groups is Donald H. Haider, *When Governments Come to Washington: Governors, Mayors, and Intergovernmental Lobbying* (New York: The Free Press, 1974). See also Samuel H. Beer, "The Adoption of General Revenue Sharing: A Case Study in Public Sector Politics," *Public Policy*, 24 (Spring 1976): 127–195. Other illustrative and descriptive material may be found in: Arlen J. Large, "Taming the Octopus: States Weary of Being Bypassed, Open a Lobbying Office," *Wall Street Journal*, September 1, 1967; "Public Interest Groups," *Public Management*, 53 (December 1971): entire issue; Jonathan Cottin, "Washington Pressures: National Governors' Conference," *National Journal*, February 28, 1970, pp. 454–459; William Lilley, III, "Washington Pressures: National League of Cities—U.S. Conference of Mayors," *National Journal*, May 23, 1970, pp. 1098–1105; William Lilley, III, "Washington Pressures—Friendly Administration, Growth of Suburbs Boost Counties' Influence," *National Journal*, May 29, 1971, pp. 1127–1143; *Man In Washington Service*, (Washington, D.C.: National League of Cities—U.S. Conference of Mayors, September 1973); David Grizzle, "The Intergovernmental Lobby: A Response to Changing Federalism," unpublished senior honors essay, Harvard College, 1975.
32. Sundquist, *Making Federalism Work*, p. 7.

The contrasting and competitive features of the present phase of IGR can be portrayed according to what might be called the participants' perspectives approach. It stems from the simple question: How do national, state, and local officials each perceive the position and perspectives of the other participants in the IGR bargaining-exchange process? These perspectives are expressed visually by the inverted pyramid, diamond, and hourglass shapes of figure 3-4. Each geometric pattern is a simplified representation of how national, state, or local officials see their own and other participants' perspectives in the IGR system.[33]

For example, national officials judge their own views of problems and policies as broad, extensive, circumspect, and wide-ranging; they judge state-level officials as having more limited, narrower perspectives than their own; and they judge local officials as holding a highly restricted, particularistic, even parochial set of perspectives. Federal officials have been known to describe some local officials as "pip-squeak mayors" "fly-by-night city managers." A less extreme expression of such perceptions came from the mid-level federal career official who, shortly after the 1967 Detroit riot, told Governor Romney of Michigan and Mayor Cavanaugh of Detroit that federal officials knew better than they the riot's likely causes and cures.

State officials see participants' perspectives in diamond form, judging their own as wide-ranging, potent, and broadly appropriate to the problems they face—that is, they see themselves in the middle and sitting astride the IGR system. State officials see the views of national officials as constricted, narrow, and inappropriately attuned to the special circumstances and conditions of the states; and they see the perspectives of local officials as limited, particularistic, and too narrow in scope.

Seen from the local level, IGR perspectives conform to an hourglass shape. Local officials see common and compatibly broad outlooks shared by themselves and national participants; but they see narrow and limiting perspectives as dominant at the state level. This fits the frequently mentioned charge by local officials that the states are the "bottlenecks" of the entire IGR system. The constricted character of the states as conduits, according to local officials, helps explain why the states are increasingly bypassed in direct national-local

---

33. This discussion follows closely Deil S. Wright, "Revenue Sharing and Structural Features of American Federalism," *The Annals*, 419 (May 1975): 115-118.

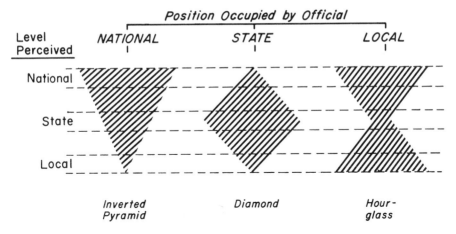

Figure 3-4. *Intergovernmental Perspectives: Officials' Outlook on the Federal System*

flows of funds (see figures 3-1 and 3-2). Direct national-local dollars in 1975 were $10.9 billion (including General Revenue Sharing of about $4 billion), whereas in 1950 they were $0.1 billion, in 1970 $3.5 billion.

These graphic characterizations of officials' perspectives are unquestionably crude and do not express variations by types of officials and the diversity among the units. Nevertheless they emphasize that among differently situated officials contrasting outlooks predominate. Equally important is how much participants at each level see others as having outlooks different from their own. The aggregate effect of these multiple contrasting perspectives is a pattern of cleavages and competition. If all three geometric shapes are overlaid on each other, the result is a jagged pattern, exemplifying the tension, rivalry, and disagreement indicated in table 3-4 as characteristic of the current, competitive phase of IGR.

SUMMARY

From the perspective of IGR, the U.S. political system of this century discloses several significant shifts in national-state-local relationships. Financially the entire system has become increasingly interdependent, and the states and local units depend more than ever before on external, intergovernmental sources of revenue. Over one-fourth of all state general revenues come from the federal government, and more than 40 percent of local government revenues are secured from state and federal sources.

Among types of local governments, school districts and counties are the most dependent on external aid; both obtain slightly less than half of all revenues from intergovernmental aid. The most striking of recent local government fiscal trends, however, is the rapidly increasing reliance of cities on external support: About 40 percent of municipal revenues come from that source. Special districts, while far smaller in fiscal aggregates, have increased their fiscal dependency at rates similar to those of the cities.

The past several decades of U.S. political developments can be understood as having five IGR policy phases: conflict, cooperation, concentration, creativeness, and competition. Each of these policy thrusts, while climaxing during successive periods, has exercised a lasting impact on IGR through the 1970s. Recent tensions among officials involved in IGR, specifically the rivalry between policy generalists and program professionals, are best depicted as "picket fence federalism." Regardless of the phase or its policy problems, the most significant indicators of the state of IGR are the officials' perspectives and their views of other IGR participants.

Intergovernmental Finances:

Local Profiles and Policies

4

LOCAL GOVERNMENT FINANCES

Despite a presumed legal subjugation to state government, local governments are important participants in the total system of intergovernmental overlapping and interdependency. Local governments not only invent and initiate important public programs, they also implement major programs and policies emanating from state and/or national governments.

The policy blend that occurs at the local government level can be described by means of aggregate data—the approach adopted here. (Later, in chapter 8, we describe the blending process by using data on the attitudes and actions of local officials.) With this focus we analyze employment data, revenue figures, and expenditure amounts. We then examine the complex merging of IGR policy at the local level by looking at the estimated impacts of General Revenue Sharing funds on city and county programs and policies.

All types of local units have become more dependent on external sources for revenues. And although most local jurisdictions, especially cities and counties, have greatly increased their own tax efforts, they have done so at a slower rate than the one at which their reliance on outside resources has expanded. Table 4-1 and figure 4-1 provide both tabular and graphic data demonstrating dramatic revenue rises between 1942 and 1975 as well as the movement toward a more balanced, diversified, and interdependent revenue base for all local units.

Given the steep rise in revenues from all sources, a citizen, tax-payer, or student of local government might well ask: Why is there constant reference to an urban fiscal crisis? Why are many large central cities teetering on the brink of bankruptcy? There are many possible explanations for the "crisis" of local finances. The most commonly cited reasons can be briefly listed:

1. Inflation, energy, and environmental problems, including the weather, have conspired to deal harsh blows to cities and other local entities; fate has dealt local governments a poor hand.
2. Public policies of an IGR nature, some deliberate and some un-witting, have produced results that are discriminatory and unwise; e.g., welfare responsibilities lodged at the local level; real estate development and mortgage policies that promote urban sprawl and service chaos; transportation policies that promote dispersal of persons and of wealth and that also con-sume much natural energy.
3. Governmental rigidities, balkanization, and chaos have resulted from the small, inefficient size of government units in both urban and rural areas.
4. Localities have failed to produce or acquire persons with the political leadership, the policy management skills, and the administrative abilities to cope with the societal needs and public service demands placed on cities, counties, and other local jurisdictions.

The following reason is actually not a reason at all but a dismissal of the claim that a critical problem exists:

- There is no "crisis"; it is merely a matter of perceptions, of problem definition, and relative comparisons in which U.S. cities, counties, and other entities are actually viable but have been deluded into "crying wolf" at every turn of the budget cycle.

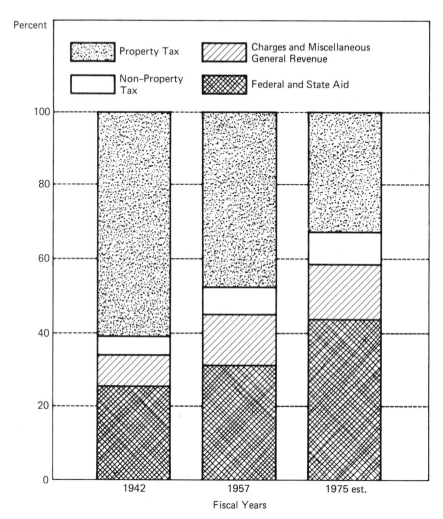

Figure 4-1. *Distribution of Local General Revenue by Major Source, 1942–1975*

Source: Advisory Commission on Intergovernmental Relations, *Significant Features of Fiscal Federalism: 1976 Edition* (Washington, D.C.: Government Printing Office, 1976), pp. 36, 37.

Table 4-1. *Trends in Revenue Systems of Local Governments in the U.S., 1942–1975*

	All Local Governments		Percent Distribution by Type of Government			
Fiscal Year	Amount (millions)	Percent Distribution by Source	Cities	School Districts	Counties	Townships and Special Districts
	Total General Revenue (Local Revenue and Federal-State Aid)					
1942	$7,071	100.0%	37.0%	33.7%	22.0%	7.3%
1952	16,952	100.0	32.0	38.4	20.7	8.9
1957	25,916	100.0	30.3	41.9	19.5	8.3
1967	59,383	100.0	26.8	47.0	17.8	8.5
1971	93,868	100.0	27.1	46.4	18.4	8.2
1974	133,994	100.0	28.2	43.5	19.3	9.0
1975 est.	147,700	100.0	28.4	42.9	19.5	9.1
	Intergovernmental Revenue (Federal and State Aid)					
1942	1,785	25.2	24.0	43.8	27.8	4.5
1952	5,281	31.2	18.7	49.9	26.2	5.2
1957	8,049	31.1	17.6	53.6	23.5	5.3
1967	21,338	35.9	17.7	58.2	18.5	5.5
1971	36,375	38.8	21.1	55.1	18.6	5.2
1974	57,253	42.7	24.0	49.6	19.6	6.7
1975 est.	64,000	43.3	24.2	49.0	18.9	7.0

General Revenue From Local Sources (Taxes and Charges)

1942	5,286	74.8	41.4	30.3	20.0	8.3
1952	11,671	68.8	38.0	33.3	18.3	10.5
1957	17,866	68.9	36.1	36.6	17.7	9.6
1967	38,045	64.1	32.0	40.5	17.4	10.1
1971	57,491	61.2	30.9	40.8	18.2	10.1
1974	76,742	57.3	31.3	38.9	19.1	10.8
1975 est.	83,700	56.7	31.6	38.3	19.3	10.8

Local Property Taxes

1942	4,344	61.4	39.0	32.9	20.1	8.0
1952	8,282	48.9	32.7	39.2	19.8	8.3
1957	12,385	47.8	29.7	42.8	19.2	8.3
1967	25,186	42.4	24.8	48.9	18.5	7.8
1971	36,726	39.1	23.3	50.3	18.3	8.0
1974	46,452	34.7	23.0	50.0	18.4	8.6
1975 est.	49,220	33.3	22.7	50.1	18.5	8.7

Source: Advisory Commission on Intergovernmental Relations, *Significant Features of Fiscal Federalism: 1976 Edition* (Washington, D.C.: Government Printing Office, 1976), pp. 36, 37.

The four explanations run the gamut of assigning blame to environmental, national, state, and local conditions. (The last item listed, the dismissal, is of course not amenable to remedy by public policy; it is more a psychological problem—whether of local politicians or of the observers who hold the stated view cannot be said here.) Which one or combination of the several contentions accounts for the current condition of local fiscal affairs? The search for an answer must begin with data that reveal recent circumstances and contemporary features of the local financial scene. The data used are selective in several senses—the most prominent one is their restriction to cities and counties, with a heavy emphasis on the former. These are, however, the primary jurisdictions of local government throughout the nation: They raise and spend more than two-thirds of all local dollars. Five principal features examined are: (1) public employment, (2) taxes and intergovernmental revenue, (3) revenue variations, (4) expenditures, and (5) General Revenue Sharing impacts.

PUBLIC EMPLOYMENT

In 1975 municipal governments employed over 2.5 million workers, full-time and part-time. On a full-time equivalent (FTE) basis city employment was 2.15 million, and the annual payroll nearly $26 billion. Ten years previously municipal payrolls totaled less than $10 billion annually for FTE employment of 1.6 million.[1] FTE employment in cities per 10,000 population has increased consistently in recent years. The figures (ratios of public employees per 10,000 population) are:

1962:127	1972:153
1967:146	1975:162

City employment trends for various functions show a mixed picture not unrelated to larger economic trends and to state and national IGR policies. Listed in table 4-2 are average annual rates of change in city employment for various functions by four time periods from

---

1. U.S. Bureau of the Census, *City Employment in 1975*, GE 75–No. 2 (Washington, D.C.: Government Printing Office, 1976), Table 1, p. 5; and *City Employment in 1966*, GE–No. 3, Table 1, p. 4.

Table 4-2. *Average Annual Change in Municipal Employment by Type of Function for U.S. Cities, 1962-1975*

Function	Average Annual Change			
	1962-67	1967-72	1972-75	1974-75
	(percentages)			
Police	2.8	4.3	3.1	1.6
Fire	2.2	2.9	0.6	0.3
Sanitation	1.8	0.1	-0.3	-3.8
Utilities	0.3	0.6	1.9	-0.6
Welfare	11.2	2.9	-0.6	-5.9
Health	1.5	6.6	0.3	-1.6
Hospitals	1.3	1.8	-0.5	-2.5
Highways	0.5	1.3	2.7	5.5
Parks/Recreation	2.5	2.6	5.5	9.9
Housing/Urban Renewal	6.5	9.8	3.4	5.5
Total (All functions)	2.9	3.4	1.8	0.7

Source: U.S. Bureau of Census, *City Employment in 1975,* Series GE75-No. 2 (Washington, D.C.), Table 1.

1962 to 1975. With some exceptions they generally show either lower rates of increase or actual declines in the 1972-1975 period, a span during which General Revenue Sharing (GRS) appeared on the local and municipal scene.

The varying rates, both overall and by specific function, are the result of an array of influences several of which could be traced to IGR factors. For example, the substantial federal aid to highway, recreation, and housing functions may explain in part the higher growth rates for these three functions. But if so, then why did welfare, health, and hospitals—functions also receiving extensive federal aid—show slowed growth or actual declines? An alternate IGR factor may have contributed to this pattern—the transfer of functions by municipalities to other units.

Results of a survey published by the ACIR indicate that between 1965 and 1975 in more than 1000 cities there was a total of 1708 transfers of a function from one unit of government to another.[2] The four functions most transferred were sanitation (including sewage treatment), police or law enforcement, health, and welfare. These

2. Advisory Commission on Intergovernmental Relations, *Pragmatic Federalism: The Reassignment of Functional Responsibility* (Washington, D.C.: Government Printing Office, July 1976, M-105).

functions, accounting for almost 1000 transfers, show slow or declining public employment growth rates for cities. More precise, detailed evidence is required to confirm that federal aid and functional transfers contribute significantly to the variations in municipal employment appearing in table 4-2. These suppositions, then, should be regarded as merely hypotheses; it is imperative that IGR variables be taken into account in looking for explanations of policy changes.

County government is a jurisdiction no longer consigned, like Uranus, to the outer reaches of the governmental solar system. The IGR orbits of the nearly 700 counties with populations above 50,000 are now nearer the center of the system of governance. Counties, with FTE employment of 1.4 million persons in 1975, hire people and spend money at approximately two-thirds the hiring and spending levels of municipalities. In addition, the growth rates for county spending and employment are both well above those for cities.[3] The average annual increase in FTE employment for counties in recent periods is:

Period	Average Annual Increase (%)
1962–67	4.4
1967–72	5.0
1972–75	4.3
1974–75	4.8

An analysis of rate changes, over the four periods, for specific functions reveals only two areas of employment decline among twelve functions. Representative change rates for functions in the 1972-1975 period are:

Welfare	1.7%	Parks/Recreation	9.5%
Hospitals	2.3	Airports	6.1
Health	9.4	Correction	9.6
Police	6.4	Libraries	6.4
Fire	10.1		

High rates of change are the hallmarks of policy making and administration in county government. The substantial increases are sustained (after

---

3. U.S. Bureau of the Census, *County Government Employment in 1975*, GE 75–No. 4 (Washington, D.C.: Government Printing Office, 1976), Table 1, p. 5.

holding population constant by using the FTE employment ratio per 10,000 population). In recent years the ratios have climbed as follows:

1962:49	1972:69
1967:62	1975:76

It was perhaps prophetic that Professor Snider's early (1936) use of "intergovernmental relations" in print was in a discussion of county government. The importance of county government to IGR and to American politics and policy deserves special emphasis if only because the recognition has been so slow in coming.

TAXES AND INTERGOVERNMENTAL REVENUE

In 1975 the 18,517 U.S. municipalities received a total of $49.9 billion in general revenues: $30.2 billion in own-source revenue and $21.1 billion in taxes. Intergovernmental revenue totaled $19.6 billion, with $13.1 billion from state government, $0.7 from other local governments, and $5.8 from the national government, including $2.2 billion in GRS funds.[4]

These amounts have little meaning without other data as a basis for comparison. A picture of the changing complexion of municipal finances can be obtained quickly from a ten-year perspective on city taxes, charges, and intergovernmental revenues. Table 4-3 provides both absolute amounts and proportions for 1965 and 1975.

Among own-source revenues cities currently rely less on taxes generally and significantly less on property taxes specifically. Although percentages have declined, the actual yield of property taxes has doubled, from $6.5 to $13.0 billion during the decade. Sales and other taxes, chiefly city income taxes, have produced sharply increased monies. Charges and miscellaneous revenues have also risen steeply, tripling in dollar amount over the decade.

Intergovernmental revenues demonstrate clearly the ten-year "hidden" revolution in municipal finances. Actual revenues increased nearly sixfold as federal dollars rose by a multiple of ten and state

---

4. U.S. Bureau of the Census, *City Government Finances in 1974–75,* GF 75-No. 4 (Washington, D.C.: Government Printing Office, 1976), Table 1, p. 5.

Table 4-3. *General Revenue Sources of U.S. Municipalities by Type of Revenue Source, 1965 and 1975*

Revenue Source	1965	1975	1965	1975
			(percentages of	
	(billions of dollars)		respective totals)	
Own Sources				
Taxes	9.289	21.135	75.2	70.0
Property	6.537	13.046	52.9	43.2
Sales	1.795	4.555	14.5	15.1
Other	.957	3.534	7.8	11.7
Charges & misc.	3.060	9.071	24.8	30.0
Total	12.349	30.206	100.0	100.0
Intergovernmental				
National	.557	5.844	15.8	29.8
State	2.745	13.053	77.7	66.4
Local	.232	.751	6.5	3.8
Total	3.534	19.648	100.0	100.0
Total General Revenue	15.884	49.853		
Intergovt'l as Percent of Total General Revenue			22.2	39.4
Intergovt'l as Percent of Own-Source Revenue			28.6	65.0

Sources: U.S. Bureau of the Census, *City Government Finances in 1964-65,* Series GF-No. 5, Table 3; and *City Government Finances in 1974-75,* Series GF-No. 4 (Washington, D.C.), Table 3.

monies by a multiple of five. The two sets of proportions in the two bottom entries in table 4-3 indicate the greatly increased reliance of cities on external support. Intergovernmental revenue approached 40 percent of total general revenue in 1975, contrasted with 22 percent in 1965. During both the creative *and* the competitive phases of IGR a major urban-oriented fiscal shift was in process. That policy shift is dramatized more starkly by the ratio of intergovernmental revenue to municipal own-source revenues; the ratios changed from less than $1 of IGR per $3 of own-source, to almost 2:3.

What was the composition of this IGR fiscal turnabout? What were the respective roles of the national and state governments? The questions have been partially answered by noting that between 1965 and 1975, federal aid increased tenfold, from nearly $600 million to nearly $6.0 billion. But the relative dependence on federal aid is equally significant: By 1975 nearly 30 percent of the cities' intergovernmental revenue came directly from Washington, D.C. In actuality, both the dollar amount and the proportion understate the dependence on federal funds, for *state* monies include substantial but indeterminant amounts of *federal* dollars that are received by cities—grants for waste treatment, law enforcement, etc. Despite the flow of those monies through state coffers, it seems certain that city (and other local) officials are well aware of the ultimate source—and are made more conscious of it by the accompanying federal guidelines and restrictions.

There is another body of data on federal aid to the cities: Federal budget analyses have occasionally provided data on federal aid to local units in SMSAs. The federal aid goes to all types of local units, not just cities, but the figures still provide a crude measure of by how much federal aid policies favor the cities. Program breakdowns of these SMSA-directed funds in Appendix C show an increase from $3.9 billion in 1961 to $35.9 billion in 1975. The proportions of total federal aid allocated to local units in SMSAs are, for selected years:

1961:54.7%	1969:69.3%
1964:55.1%	1976:70.1%

Two themes draw together this analysis of city/urban finances and IGR. First, city governments and their decision-making officials have become increasingly, and heavily, reliant on federal funds as a source of revenue. Second, federal policy has responded by emphasizing metropolitan areas in aid programs. Revenue patterns, however, are not uniform but vary by city size.

REVENUE VARIATIONS

To what extent do cities in different size groupings vary in their revenue sources, specifically in their reliance on state and federal aid, and is there much variation over time? The percentages in table 4-4 provide a basis for an answer. For the years 1965 and 1975 and arrayed by city-size groups, the figures indicate three major revenue sources: own-source, federal aid, and state aid. Comparisons are possible both vertically by city size and horizontally over time.

In 1965 cities of over 500,000 persons were less dependent on

Table 4–4. *General Revenue Sources of U.S. Cities by Type of Revenue and City Size, 1965 and 1975*

City Size	1965					1975				
	No. of Cities	Own-Source Revenue	Federal Aid	State Aid	Total*	No. of Cities	Own-Source Revenue	Federal Aid	State Aid	Total*
		(percentages)					(percentages)			
1,000,000 and over	5	77.1	1.8	21.1	100.0 (4.9)	6	52.8	7.7	39.5	100.0 (16.6)
500,000– 999,999	17	73.7	7.8	18.5	100.0 (2.2)	20	59.5	19.8	20.7	100.0 (6.6)
300,000– 499,999	21	82.0	4.0	14.0	100.0 (1.1)	20	63.8	16.0	20.2	100.0 (3.1)
200,000– 299,999	19	84.5	3.0	12.5	100.0 (0.6)	17	62.7	15.9	21.4	100.0 (1.7)
100,000– 199,999	68	80.7	3.2	16.1	100.0 (1.3)	95	66.1	13.0	20.9	100.0 (4.3)
50,000– 99,999	180	81.6	2.9	15.5	100.0 (1.6)	229	69.0	11.9	19.1	100.0 (4.6)
Under 50,000	17,690	82.7	1.3	16.0	100.0 (3.9)	18,130	69.4	11.3	19.3	100.0 (12.1)
All Cities (weighted)	18,000	78.9	3.6	17.5	100.0 (15.7)	18,517	61.5	11.9	26.6	100.0 (49.1)

*Billions of dollars in parentheses.
Sources: Bureau of the Census, *City Government Finances in 1964–65*, Series GF – No. 5, Table 3; and *City Government Finances in 1974–75*, Series GF75 – No. 4 (Washington, D.C.), Table 3.

own-source revenues than those below this size. The smaller cities tended to be the most self-reliant. Cities of vastly different sizes showed only a small difference in such reliance—less than 10 percentage points. By 1975 not only was the point spread larger but a clearer, more consistent relationship was evident between size and reliance on external aid. Slightly more than half the general revenues of cities over 1,000,000 were self-generated compared to more than two-thirds of general revenues for cities below 100,000. The smaller the city, the greater the reliance on own-source revenue.

In 1965 the proportion coming from federal aid for all cities was 3.6 percent. Only cities in the two categories between 300,000 and 1,000,000 were above this weighted average figure, and the five largest cities over 1,000,000 were near the bottom in percentage of reliance on federal monies. Somewhat surprisingly, the same group, enlarged to six cities, was again lowest in 1975. This finding runs counter to conventional wisdom that the largest cities with the most skilled professionals draw down more than their share of federal funds.

These large cities, however, appear to have adopted the compensatory strategy of emphasizing the acquisition of state funds: Nearly 40 percent of their general revenue came from their respective states. This figure, combined with 7.7 percent from federal aid, made them most dependent on external sources of support. It is not surprising, then, that Mayor Beame had ample precedent for carrying the battle for New York City's solvency to Albany as well as to Washington, D.C.

A vertical scan of the federal aid figures for 1975, excluding the percentage for the six largest cities, does lend some credence to the skilled-grantsmanship hypothesis. The proportions drop as one proceeds down the scale of city size, suggesting that the larger cities are more skilled, and successful, in obtaining federal dollars. Nevertheless, a couple of qualifying circumstances cause lingering doubts: The proportionate dependence on federal aid appears to be a function of how aggressive cities in each size bracket are in (a) raising revenue locally and (b) acquiring state aid.

These contaminating effects can be circumvented by calculating how aggressively each city-size group solicits federal aid, as indicated by the per capita federal dollars they acquired:[5]

---

5. U.S. Bureau of the Census, *City Government Finances in 1964-65* and *1974-75* (Washington, D.C.: Government Printing Office, 1966 and 1976), Table 4, p. 8 in both publications.

City Size	Federal Aid Per Capita	
	1965	1975
Over 1,000,000	$ 5.09	$ 70.34
500,000–999,999	14.64	100.82
300,000–499,999	5.31	64.68
200,000–299,999	3.78	60.96
100,000–199,999	4.37	42.73
50,000– 99,999	3.76	33.49
Under 50,000	2.84	21.84
All Cities	4.79	43.06

No clear or consistent pattern prevailed in 1965, but that was prior to the full impact of the creative phase of IGR and the project-categorical grant explosion. For 1975, again with the exception of the very largest cities, there is a clear, consistent pattern that appears to confirm our hypothesis: Though we cannot say without fear of contradiction that grantsmanship skill is linked to city size, the presumption is in favor of a positive relationship.

Does the skilled-grantsmanship hypothesis also apply to counties? Is there a positive relationship between per capita federal aid and county population size? The per capita figures in table 4–5 put considerable doubt on the hypothesis for counties in the three recent years for which data are available.

Table 4–5. *Per Capita Intergovernmental Revenue of U.S. Counties by Population Size, 1973, 1974, 1975*

County Population	Number of Counties	Per Capita Intergovernmental Revenue		
		1973	1974	1975
		(per capita dollars)		
300,000 and over	109	80.32	85.22	86.34
200,000–299,999	68	62.85	65.67	74.34
150,000–199,999	50	48.82	54.76	60.76
100,000–149,999	106	51.82	60.48	67.00
Under 100,000	2,711	47.97	66.81	75.84
All Counties	3,044	64.35	74.00	79.13

Sources: U.S. Bureau of the Census, *County Government Finances in 1972–73*, GF73 - No. 8, (Washington, D.C.), Table 3; and similar sources for 1974 and 1975.

Rather than consistently declining with decreasing county size, per capita IGR revenue appears to show a U-shaped pattern. Especially in 1974 and 1975 the largest and the smallest counties secure the highest funding levels from intergovernmental sources. The raw data, however, are not precise enough for directly testing the federal aid hypothesis, since *all* intergovernmental revenue, both state and federal, is included in the per capita figures. Separate data on neither federal nor state funds received by counties are available. Thus, there are too little published data on county revenue sources to permit a replication of the revenue analysis performed for cities. The only separation within the intergovernmental total is the amount of GRS received. It is still possible, then, to examine IGR impacts on counties with existing data; table 4-6 provides results of the revenue source analysis and furnishes 1975 breakdowns by county size.

Between 1965 and 1975 counties modestly increased their relative reliance on external funding, from 40 to 45 percent. However, the 1975 proportion reflects the presence of GRS, which alone added about 5 percentage points to the intergovernmental revenue proportion. Thus it appears that without GRS counties would not have increased their dependence on outside revenues, despite policies and programs launched during the creative phase of IGR. A counterpoint should be noted: In 1965 counties were already 40 percent dependent on intergovernmental revenue, a level reached by cities only in the 1970s.

Does the ratio of dependence on outside revenues vary among counties by population size? The lower section of table 4-6 permits a straightforward response: No. In fact, there is strikingly little variation among the figures in any one of the several revenue-source columns. The modest difference between the largest and smallest counties in their reliance on taxes shows no pattern by size. These results, applying to groups and not refined to any precision, of course neither confirm nor deny the possibility of an underlying consistent relationship. Grouping counties by size discards an immense amount of discrete data about the individual counties. Lacking a thorough (and costly) analysis of each of the 3044 counties, we tentatively conclude that county size is not systematically related to revenue source patterns.

The picture does not change if percentages are replaced by per capita figures, as table 4-6 also shows. GRS appears to be spread among counties with a remarkable uniformity—except for counties under 100,000. Those counties enjoy a special advantage, one that

Table 4-6. *General Revenue Sources of U.S. Counties by Type of Revenue Source in 1965, 1970, and 1975; and by County Size for 1975*

Revenue Source	Year		
	1965	1970	1975
	(percentages)		
Own-source	59.5	58.7	55.1
Taxes	78.4	73.4	69.8
Charges & miscellaneous	21.6	26.6	30.2
Intergovt'l revenue	40.5	41.3	44.9*
Total (amount in billions)	100.0 ($10.4)	100.0 ($17.7)	100.0 ($32.9)

		Revenue Source						Per Capita from:	
County Size	Number of Counties	Taxes	Charges & Misc.	General Revenue Sharing	Other Intergovt'l	Total	Billions of Dollars	Intergovt'l Revenue	General Revenue Sharing
		(percentages)							
300,000 and over	109	42.2	14.7	3.8	39.2	100.0	$16.8	$86.34	$7.64
200,000–299,999	68	36.3	17.4	4.6	41.7	100.0	2.7	74.34	7.34
150,000–199,999	50	39.2	16.5	5.3	39.0	100.0	1.2	60.76	7.30
100,000–149,999	106	36.8	17.4	4.9	40.9	100.0	1.9	67.00	7.14
Under 100,000	2,711	33.2	19.5	6.4	40.9	100.0	10.4	75.84	10.34
All counties	3,044	38.5	16.7	4.8	40.0	100.0	32.9	79.13	8.50

*Includes 4.8 percent ($1.6 billion) from general revenue sharing.
Source: U.S. Bureau of the Census, *County Government Finances in 1974–75*, GF75 – No. 8 (Washington, D.C.), Table 3, p. 9.

could be undoubtedly traced to one or two provisions in the exceedingly complex formula under which GRS monies are distributed.

In the foregoing discussion the reader may have detected a note of apprehension or criticism implicit in the description of the increased reliance of cities on external revenue sources. Such terms as "heavily reliant" and "dependent" were used. A more favorable way to describe these revenue changes is to say that cities have moved toward more-balanced and diversified revenue systems. That is, the revenue shifts are matters of fact on which one may impose different values and judgments. My view is one of more than mild concern that cities may have incurred greater costs, complications, and commitments than anticipated by assiduously or unthinkingly pursuing federal and state funds. Not all—and perhaps not most—cities chase federal or state dollars "assiduously or unthinkingly." Some city officials may perceive no other alternative or find that an "appeal upstairs" is the line of least resistance. This charge was often leveled against New York City Mayor Beame. However, local officials have been feeling a growing (though poorly documented) concern and skepticism about the acquisition and use of federal (or state) monies. Yet at the same time they feel needy and are eager to acquire these external revenue resources. This mixture of feelings is described and analyzed in chapters 8 through 11.

EXPENDITURES

For what purposes do cities spend their variously generated revenues? How does the acquisition or acceptance of federal and state aid affect the complexion of municipal outlays? The first question, while the easier to answer, is the less interesting. The second is very interesting and highly significant, yet it is among the most difficult of IGR questions to answer.

Table 4-7 breaks down per capita municipal outlays for direct general expenditures in 1965 and 1975. As direct outlays these amounts contain the federal and state funds received by the cities. There are few surprises in the columns. However, the education figures may warrant comment since they reflect the outlays of nearly 500 cities in which the school system is a "dependent" entity, that is, a department of the city government. That many of these dependent systems are in

Table 4-7. *Per Capita Direct General Expenditures of U.S. Municipalities in 1965 and 1975*

Function	1965	1975	Increase Ratio (1975 ÷ 1965)
	(per capita dollars)		
Health	$ 1.80	$ 6.68	3.7
Welfare	7.97	28.34	3.6
*Housing/Urban Renewal	1.79	6.23	3.5
Interest on Debt	5.18	16.90	3.3
*Hospitals	6.26	18.82	3.0
*Sewerage	3.10	8.55	2.8
*Education	18.05	46.48	2.6
Police	14.94	38.91	2.6
General Control	4.02	10.61	2.6
Parks/Recreation	6.66	16.75	2.5
Libraries	2.29	4.65	2.4
Financial Admin.	2.50	6.03	2.4
*Public Buildings	1.51	3.59	2.4
Fire	9.85	21.37	2.2
Sanitation	6.09	12.99	2.1
*Streets	8.40	16.14	1.9
Other	13.71	49.73	3.6
Capital Outlay	30.02	70.56	2.4

*Excludes capital outlay amounts which are aggregated in the "Capital Outlay" category.
Sources: Bureau of the Census, *City Government Finances in 1964-65,* Series GF-No. 5, Table 4; and *City Government Finances in 1974-75,* Series GF75 - No. 4 (Washington, D.C.), Table 4.

large northeastern cities accounts in part for the substantial per capita amounts.

Except for education, the "stuff" of city government consists of functions conventionally associated with municipalities—streets, sewers, police, fire, sanitation, health, libraries, parks, etc. The 1965–1975 change ratios, however, disclose features with IGR policy implications. *Excluding* capital outlays, four functions—welfare, hospitals, health, and housing/urban renewal—increased in per capita costs by multiples of three or greater. These four functions have at least two distinctive characteristics in common: (1) They are heavily supported with federal funds, either directly or indirectly, through the state, (2) They involve intensive provision of personal services. These two features may have combined to push municipal costs for these functions to exceptional heights. Depending on matching requirements and competing claims, substantial own-source revenues may have been allocated by cities to support these four functions over other activities. In short, federal aid may have pushed, or pulled, or otherwise stimulated the spending of city funds for these functions rather than for other purposes. The influence of other factors, such as rapidly rising hospital costs and burgeoning welfare rolls, cannot be discounted.

We cannot be certain about federal aid effects since we lack the data with which to reconstruct in detail the decision-making processes of municipal officials in thousands of cities over a ten-year period. What specific program alternatives did municipal policy makers consider when confronted by competing options in the form of (a) attractive, externally supported programs versus (b) desirable but unsupported conventional municipal activities? We know the results but we do not know the dynamics of the choice processes.

The problem of identifying the effects of external aid would be no less severe even if *all* municipal activities received some type of outside aid. The priorities and preferences of city officials would still have to be located and compared against the implicit policy preferences built into the aid programs in the form of matching ratios and total funds available. In short, it is exceedingly difficult to trace with great precision the fiscal, programmatic, or functional effects of federal or state aid on cities (or other units).

Before examining one such trace effort, a final comment on Table 4–7 is warranted. Note that between 1965 and 1975 interest on debt was another category that was multiplied by more than three. Between 1965 and 1975 the amount of long-term city debt outstanding nearly doubled from $29.3 billion to $55.8 billion. If the outstanding debt doubled, why did the per capita carrying charge more than triple? It did so because (a) borrowing rates increased, (b) municipal tax bases did not keep pace with rising debt charges, and (c) a higher percentage of capital outlays was financed by borrowed funds in 1975 than in 1965. New York City is a classic case fitting all three points.

GENERAL REVENUE SHARING IMPACTS

The State and Local Fiscal Assistance Act of 1972 is informally known as General Revenue Sharing (GRS), although nowhere in the statute and committee reports does the term appear. The legislation (P.L. 92–512) was passed and signed with much fanfare; President Nixon even chose Independence Hall in Philadelphia to commemorate the start of a "New American Revolution": the transfer of power back to state and local governments. The act, of course, provided approximately $30 billion for general, relatively unrestricted use over the 1972–1976 period. Funds were distributed by a formula to the fifty states and nearly 39,000 local units—cities, counties, townships, American-Indian tribes, and Alaskan native villages.

Did GRS indeed have a "revolutionary" impact on cities, counties, and other recipients? How, if at all, did the funds change local expenditure patterns, and by how much? What were the "actual uses" to which GRS monies were put? How, and by whom, were the decisions made on the use of GRS funds? These questions pose a formidable task— all the more herculean because, again, tracing the effects of an external source of funds, even if formally specified for a particular activity, is a tricky assignment.

Fortunately, GRS captured not only the attention of public officials but also the interest of numerous researchers across the country— lawyers, economists, political scientists, sociologists, and organization theorists. Hundreds of studies, scores of articles, and several books make GRS the most extensively analyzed IGR policy question of this decade and perhaps of this generation. Instead of trying to best the flood of research and writing, we will examine findings in only four GRS issue areas: (1) fiscal, (2) program, (3) decision-making, and (4) citizen involvement. The focus of attention will be GRS impacts on cities.[6]

---

6. The following discussion relies heavily on two major sources and research-based national studies, which thus permitted estimates or inferences about GRS impacts across all U.S. cities or local governments. The sources are: National Science Foundation/ Research Applied to National Needs, *General Revenue Sharing Research Utilization Project,* Volume 4, *Synthesis of Impact and Process Research* (Washington, D.C.: Government Printing Office, December 1975), 139 pp.; and F. Thomas Juster (ed.), *The Economic and Political Impact of General Revenue Sharing* (Washington, D.C.: National Science Foundation/Research Applied to National Needs, April 1976). The former will be cited as NSF/RANN, *GRS Research;* the latter is noted as Juster, *Economic and Political Impact.* An example of GRS impact research that focuses in depth on a few jurisdictions is Richard P. Nathan et al., *Monitoring Revenue Sharing* (Washington, D.C.: The Brookings Institution, 1975). A follow-on volume is Richard P. Nathan et al., *Revenue Sharing: The Second Round* (Washington, D.C.: The Brookings Institution, 1977).

GRS Fiscal Impacts

GRS monies may have had five different fiscal impacts. They may have:

1. maintained or increased operating expenditures,
2. maintained or increased capital outlays,
3. stabilized or reduced taxes,
4. stabilized or reduced borrowing, and
5. added to any surplus in the city's accounts.

The first two are expenditure effects, the third a tax effect, and the fourth a borrowing-related impact. The fifth is simply an increase in cash balance(s). Because GRS funds carried virtually no use restrictions, it was theoretically possible for all five effects to have occurred at the same time in one local jurisdiction. For example, a city receiving $100,000 might have used $30,000 for salary increases (operating expenditures), $40,000 for street construction (capital), reduced taxes by $15,000, used $10,000 to pay off indebtedness (borrowing), and kept $5000 in the bank.

Indeed, the amounts cited are proportionately very close to the estimated nationwide fiscal impacts of GRS on localities. GRS uses were estimated as: operating, 27 percent; capital, 40 percent; tax effects, 16 percent; borrowing effects, 8 percent; additions to surplus, 3 percent; and undetermined, 6 percent.[7] These estimates, based on a national sample of cities, counties, and townships, covered $4.1 billion in GRS monies allocated in the fiscal year 1974.

However, some notable differences in fiscal impacts depended on city size. Large cities, those over 300,000, were far more likely to have used GRS funds for operating outlays—63 percent of monies were traced to this use. This use appeared to reflect the severe or dire financial condition(s) of these cities. Capital outlays, estimated above 50 percent, were highest in smaller cities, those under 25,000. It was frequently remarked, partly in jest, that these units had no pressing uses for the money and therefore "sank" it by constructing streets, sewers, buildings, and other capital works. Cities in the range of 100,000–300,000 were highest in tax and borrowing effects, with nearly 60 percent of the GRS funds estimated as reducing taxes (42 percent) and reducing borrowing (16 percent).[8] Evidently some cities were fis-

---

7. Juster, *Economic and Political Impact,* p. 25.
8. Ibid.

cally solid enough that GRS spared them the need to raise taxes or increase borrowing, or indeed even allowed some to reduce property taxes.

Estimates on the use of GRS funds in the 1975 fiscal year were not dramatically different from 1974 uses, although the tax effects rose from the 16 percent of 1974 to almost 25 percent of the $4.2 billion allocated in 1975. Variations in use according to city size in 1975 resembled the 1974 pattern.[9]

Did cities, in 1975, use their GRS funds in markedly different ways from how they spent their non-GRS funds? This question can be addressed by comparing aggregate expenditures for all cities in 1975 with estimated GRS used by cities for operating, capital outlays, and borrowing:

Type of Use	Estimated GRS Uses by Cities	Aggregate Expenditures All Cities
Operating	41%	69%
Capital Outlay	45	20
Debt (Borrowing)	7	5
Other	7	6

A dramatic departure from "normal" city uses occurred in the allocation of GRS funds for capital outlays. Whereas only 20 percent of all municipal expenditures were capital outlays, an estimated 45 percent of GRS monies were. One frequently offered explanation for this "bricks-and-mortar" emphasis in GRS usage was the temporary status and short (five-year) duration of GRS: Many local units or decision makers were hesitant to hire personnel, fearing that possible termination of GRS in 1976 would leave them with overcommitted expenditures and under-realized revenues.

GRS Program Impacts

How much of GRS funds were employed to support existing programs and activities rather than to fund new and innovative ones? Did GRS monies have greater impacts on the financing of police and fire protection or health and hospitals? Did GRS help the elderly, the poor,

---

9. Ibid., p. 27.

and the young? The initial (1972) legislation authorizing GRS contained a list of eight "priority expenditure" categories for which GRS monies were to be used and reported to the U.S. Treasury in official "Actual Use Reports." The priority outlays for local governments were:

1. public safety
2. environmental protection
3. public transportation
4. health
5. recreation
6. libraries
7. social services
8. financial administration

These categories were included in the 1972 Act as a concession (or sop) to sentiment favoring some control or direction by Congress over the use of the funds. In fact, the priority categories and the actual use reports were a charade and were eliminated in the 1976 renewal of GRS. To all intents and purposes they were meaningless because once GRS money entered the financial accounts of a local unit the dollars became fungible, that is, interchangeable with or replaceable by other funds.[10]

The fungibility of GRS monies explains why, despite the legislative requirement that GRS funds actually be "expended" for the specified purposes, it was a simple matter for cities, if they so desired, to use GRS to reduce property taxes. That end was achieved with 15–25 percent of GRS dollars by officially reporting, for example, that the monies paid police and fire salaries. But the property tax levels that had previously supported public safety salaries were simply reduced by the amount of added GRS funds.

This digression on the apparent mechanics of GRS and local fiscal ingenuity contains several policy implications. First, GRS recipients were free to use the funds—which, remember, were fungible—for virtually any purpose they chose. They merely had to mask the actual program impact by reporting GRS usage in one of the formally specified categories.[11] Fungibility did not, however, prevent researchers from arriving at best estimates of the program impacts of GRS. The chief research and estimation strategy was extensive, multiple interviews with local executives, chief administrators, and finance officers. For all local units the 1975 program use estimates for GRS are shown below as percentages of the $4.2 billion allocated in 1975.[12]

---

10. A precise, detailed analysis of issues associated with the inclusion of these "priority" categories in the GRS act is Otto G. Stolz, *Revenue Sharing: Legal and Policy Analysis* (New York: Praeger, 1974), pp. 75–83.
11. NSF/RANN, *GRS Research;* see especially discussions of "fungibility" and "displacement effects."
12. Juster, *Economic and Political Impact,* p. 58. It cannot be claimed that interviews

public safety	24%	health	7%
transportation	17	administration	6
other unspecified	13	education	4
environment	12	social service	3
amenities (recreation, libraries)	11	land use	2

Public safety—police and fire protection—was the chief program beneficiary of GRS. It is perhaps more than a coincidence that public safety
activities, historic and basic functions of local government, have not
enjoyed direct or major financial aid from state or national governments. Nor has transportation (apart from highways), the second leading program beneficiary of GRS. Education, health, and social service,
all programs heavily supported by national and/or state funding, received only modest or tiny benefits from GRS. In short, it appears that
local units used GRS to offset the dominant spending patterns fostered
by federal and state aid. One justification for enacting GRS was that it
represented a "new type" of federal aid. How it was used evidently
differed sharply from how other kinds of federal aid were used.

Did GRS funds have program impacts that, in the aggregate,
sustained the typical pattern of local expenditures, or did their allocation depart from normal program priorities? There were some distinct
but not radical departures from typical patterns, as the selected program
comparisons for 1974 show:[13]

Program	Estimated GRS Impact	Typical Local Outlays
Public Safety	21%	17%
Environment	10	11
Transportation	17	11
Amenities	14	6
Education	4	15
Health	7	8
Social Services	4	8

In four program or functional areas there are noteworthy GRS-based

---

with key local officials necessarily produced valid or precise figures on the "true" or
ultimate impact of GRS. Interviewing was essentially a strategy for securing the best-
informed judgments about fiscal and other impacts of GRS. To ascertain with greatest
accuracy the fiscal impact of GRS we would need to know what a unit's expenditure
pattern and tax level would be in the absence of GRS.
13. Ibid., p. 57; and *City Government Finances in 1974-75*, p. 2.

departures from typical expenditure patterns. The two largest discrepancies involve amenities (libraries, recreation) and education.

What population groups benefited from GRS outlays? If recreation programs, library construction, etc., received special emphasis from GRS support, were the facilities and services in low-income areas, where the poor would be the primary beneficiaries? The question of who benefits posed insuperable barriers to researchers attempting to trace the ultimate impacts of GRS. For every Amanda Jones in a southern town who benefited from a GRS-supported housing repair loan another researcher might identify a tennis court constructed by GRS funds in Beverly Hills. It proved impossible to develop workable instruments and precise data that would allow consistent and systematic accumulation of evidence on what racial, economic, age, or other groupings benefited more (or less) from GRS.[14]

One general observation did appear warranted by the extensive probing into GRS uses by local officials. GRS appeared to stimulate only an insignificant or infinitesimal amount of FTC: *F*rivolity, *T*hievery, and *C*hicanery. Before, during, and shortly after the enactment of GRS many opponents expressed fears that such uses would be prominent, if not extensive. As one opponent put it: "If revenue sharing is passed, half the mayors of this country won't know what to do with the money and the other half will steal it!" This dire view turned out to be light-years removed from reality.

GRS Impacts on Local Decision Making

Proponents of GRS argued that it would strengthen local governments and make them more effective. Most of the debate around this issue was cliché-ridden, unenlightening, and studiously vague on what "strength" and "effectiveness" meant. Evaluative research, of course, requires precision, so the problem was redefined: Did GRS enhance a local unit's capacity to make decisions?[15] The key phrase, "capacity to make decisions," has three components:

1. the ability to plan, control, and modify expenditure and tax policies as well as assimilate citizen views into the budget process;

---

14. Juster, *Economic and Political Impact*, pp. 64–66; and NSF/RANN, *GRS Research*, discussions of "minorities," "poor," and "redistributive effects."
15. Juster, *Economic and Political Impact*, pp. 143–163.

2. the ability to define, address, and act on community problems; and

3. the promotion and adoption of new and innovative programs.

Nationwide representative samples of local chief executives and
finance officers were asked whether GRS made expenditure planning
more or less difficult. More than 60 percent of them responded that
GRS had made fiscal planning less difficult; over one-fourth detected
no change because of GRS; and about 10 percent indicated that GRS
had made their fiscal planning efforts more difficult.[16] As to how GRS
improved planning ability, three reasons dominated:

1. the five-year certainty of the program,
2. the simple availability of more money, and
3. the opportunity to make "needed expenditures."

GRS had been touted with the slogan, "More money with greater certainty"; the responses and views of local officials powerfully echo that
contention. In addition, slightly over one-third of the local executives
and finance officers reported that GRS helped them improve their
processes of priority setting.

To what extent did GRS help local officials define, address, and
act on community problems? Here the reaction to the impact of GRS
was more mixed and dubious. A majority of local officials reported that
GRS had a positive impact on what they perceived to be their most
pressing problems. But these officials felt better off only because GRS
provided an increment of funds that did not have to be raised locally
and that could therefore be spent more freely. One researcher concluded: "There is little evidence to suggest that GRS has stimulated
any mechanisms for improving the way in which local governments
identify new problems or modify programs to more efficiently address
old ones."[17]

Some proponents of GRS argued that it would revive innovation
and experimentation within local and state governments. With flexible and supplementary funds, it was claimed, local officials would be
less hesitant to design novel programs and approaches than if they were
using hard-earned own-source local tax monies. How well did this aim
of providing GRS as venture or "risk" capital work out in practice?

Again the responses of officials are not conclusive. There is diffi-

_____

16. Ibid., p. 144.
17. Ibid., p. 158.

culty in determining what represented a truly new program or an activity supported by GRS that was significantly different from existing operations. Despite these hazards of definition and judgment some findings do warrant recognition. The percentages of local finance officers indicating that 0–3 new programs were stimulated by GRS in 1974 were:[18]

Number of New Programs	
0	40%
1	30
2	9
3	21

In two-fifths of the communities, then, no new programs were associated with the advent of GRS, but in one-fifth of the units there were at least three such new programs. Although the number of new programs varied little by city size, the bulk of the new programs in larger cities was in public safety, health, and environment, and in smaller cities in transportation, recreation, and libraries. In the smaller cities most new programs stimulated by GRS took the form of capital projects; in the larger cities GRS prompted new programs that required current operating expenses, such as employing youth in recreation programs.

GRS was a stimulus to initiate some new programs in some cities. Exactly how innovative and significant these programs were remains an open question despite extensive research on the issue. Judgments on "progress" traceable to GRS undoubtedly vary widely within any community and between any two communities — which leads to the final issue with respect to the impact of GRS.

GRS Impacts on Citizen Participation

The citizen participation "revolution" of the 1960s had not spent itself by the time GRS was enacted in 1972. It was an issue closely and controversially associated with the GRS debate. Advocates of GRS contended that the transfer of money and power to local and state govern-

---

18. Ibid., p. 159.

ments would generate public interest and more meaningful participation. Critics of GRS argued that the levels of citizen action attained under Great Society programs of the OEO type would evaporate without some type of mandate for citizen input.

The GRS legislation, of course, contained no participation require-ments—only the stipulation that the funds be spent in accordance with applicable state statutes and local ordinances. Many statutes and ordi-nances, however, require public hearings on the city budget, bond authorizations, and capital projects. GRS proponents claimed there would be strong incentives for citizens to participate because of the *discretionary* funds available from GRS allocations. Opponents stressed that GRS decisions made in the absence of citizen participation would be elitist. Both GRS proponents and opponents assumed that citizen input was both desirable and effective in influencing decisions.

Three questions help to focus discussion on the issues of citizen input and GRS:

1. Did local officials, in the absence of participation requirements, seek citizen input on GRS uses?
2. How did local officials judge the nature and character of any citizen involvement in GRS decisions?
3. Did citizen participation as perceived by local officials make any apparent difference in GRS-related fiscal processes and policy outcomes?[19]

Public budget hearings are a nearly universal phenomenon in U.S. cities; only about 5 percent of all cities over 10,000 do *not* hold them. (For cities under 10,000 the proportion not holding hearings is considerably higher, around 30 percent.) But were GRS monies in-cluded, or "merged," in the city budget, or were they held separate and distinct from both the formal budget and the fiscal decision pro-cess? In over 80 percent of the cities GRS monies were handled as funds apart from all other revenues. And in 1973, the first year of GRS, in only about 40 percent of the cities were special hearings held on these distinct funds—a considerably smaller percentage than for the usual budget process. Also, there was a strong association between city size and the convening of special public hearings on GRS. In 1973 nearly two-thirds of the largest cities held hearings; less than one-third of the smallest did. These proportions dropped substantially in 1974.

19. The following discussion relies on data in Juster, *Economic and Political Impact,* pp. 165–182. See also NSF/RANN, *GRS Research,* "Citizen Participation."

Formal public hearings were only one way of learning citizen sentiment on GRS. About 15 percent of cities set up special citizens' advisory groups to advise officials on the budget generally and on GRS funds specifically; in more than two-thirds of these cities the advisory bodies were prompted by GRS. Such groups were employed in so small a percentage of cities because officials in most cities opposed their creation. When asked whether they favored changing GRS provisions to require the creation of citizen advisory groups on GRS usage the distribution of opinions among city officials was: strongly opposed, 60 percent; somewhat opposed, 22 percent; somewhat favor, 12 percent; strongly favor, 6 percent.

Apart from officials' preferences on citizen involvement, did the officials think that GRS had any impact on public awareness and interest in how the city allocated its resources? Did GRS elevate citizen interest, as measured by attendance at hearings, expressions of opinions, and criticisms of the way GRS funds were used? Most city executives judged citizen activity attributable to GRS to be very limited; in only about 5–15 percent of the cities (the percentage varied according to the specific question asked) did city executives affirm increased citizen activity.

There was, however, much more perceived GRS-stimulated *group* activity: in over 40 percent of the cities as a whole and in 80 percent of the larger cities. In fact, on nearly all measures city size was positively associated with higher perceived levels of GRS-related individual and group actions. As one researcher put it: "group involvement in large cities was perceived as more active, conflictual, and concentrated in social service groups than it was in smaller cities."[20]

Did GRS-stimulated citizen participation, however modest or low (depending on one's point of view), make any difference in the fiscal processes and outcomes? In operational terms an affirmative answer would require that such involvement: (a) made it easier for officials to learn community preferences and (b) alerted city leaders to new community issues and problems. Both of these conditions prevailed, in general, to a very high degree. Citizen action stimulated by GRS definitely affected city officials' perceptions of community concerns.

The proof of the pudding is in the eating: Did citizen involvement make a difference in how the GRS dollars were allocated among programs? Or, to take a specific, highly visible policy issue, in cities where individuals and groups were more visible and vocal, did more money

---

20. Juster, *Economic and Political Impact,* p. 174-5.

go to health and social services? Although the absolute proportions of GRS going for health and social services in cities were small, there was a consistent positive relationship between higher participation and greater funds for these services. The outcomes of participation in general can be summarized by the conclusion of one research study:

> In sum, the data are consistent with the idea that formal participatory mechanisms allow citizen involvement which pushes local governments (particularly cities) into new problem areas. They are also consistent with another interpretation: that officials interested in moving into new problem areas consult citizens before doing so.[21]

General Revenue Sharing ranks among the most prominent IGR fiscal programs since World War II. National in scope but primarily local in focus, it produced, not surprisingly, widely varying results that are also subject to widely varying interpretations. In reaching over 38,000 local units it is also understandable that no one conclusion adequately or accurately summarizes its contrasting impacts. In that respect it suitably reflects the character, content, and diversity of IGR in the 1970s.

SUMMARY

Programs and policies pursued by local governments in the United States are a blend of local initiative and state-national influences felt chiefly through the flow of funds. Because local units are increasingly dependent on external fiscal sources, few local policies and activities are insulated from external influence. City and county employment trends are affected by federal aid policies and by the transfer of functions between governments—IGR reallocations, among local units and officials, of responsibility for funding and implementing programs. Federal aid policies have undergone a distinct shift toward urban areas; larger cities secure a higher proportion of their revenue and more dollars per capita from federal aid than do smaller municipalities. Counties, however, do not follow the pattern of revenue dependence related to population size. Dependence on external revenue appears to have direct effects on the rates of change in city expenditures. Those

---

21. Juster, *Economic and Political Impact,* p. 182.

functions receiving substantial federal or state aid are among those with the highest increase in city outlays.

Tracing the exact effects of federal (or state) aid on local expenditure levels is not a simple task because of the fungibility of dollars and the difficulty of ruling out the influence of other variables. Nevertheless, researchers have arrived at best estimates of the fiscal impacts of General Revenue Sharing. Researchers also identified other changes induced by GRS in municipal operations. An estimated 40 percent of GRS monies in 1974 and 1975 financed capital works projects, about one-fourth was spent as operating outlays, and roughly one-fifth was used to reduce local taxes. Larger cities, ones usually in more dire fiscal straits, tended to use GRS monies more for operating than for capital outlays. There were distinct departures in the use of GRS funds from the usual expenditure patterns of cities: more for capital works, transportation, recreation, libraries, and public safety; less for education.

Local officials reported that GRS helped their fiscal planning, but it was not given very high marks on improving local decision-making capacities or for stimulating substantial numbers of new programs. Neither did GRS stimulate an outburst of citizen participation that influenced local decision makers in the use of those funds. Indeed, local officials were overwhelmingly *opposed* to such participation. Citizen activity attributable to GRS tended to occur more often in the larger cities and to be associated with decisions allocating GRS to health and social services uses.

GRS was touted by some as a "great experiment." The experiment lacked clear or precise hypotheses. It is therefore not surprising that the findings were mixed. The diversity of nearly 39,000 recipient jurisdictions and the policy blending process at the local level virtually assured varied and mixed results—results that are representative of the overlapping, interdependent, nonhierarchical model of IGR.

Intergovernmental Finances:

State Profiles and Policies

5

INTRODUCTION

The overlapping-authority model has special applicability to state governments. The thesis of this chapter is that the states are confronted with the most extensive and intensive IGR involvements of any jurisdiction in the U.S. political system. This argument will be developed and documented with fiscal data, data similar to those used in figure 3-2, which shows the flows of funds (for 1970) between national, state, and local governments. Indeed, that figure supports the thesis that the states occupy a crucial intermediary role in IGR. The states are linchpins holding the overlapping model together.

A modest fraction of federal funds flows to the states as part of the federal efforts to influence the scope, direction, and content of state policies. (A much smaller fraction bypasses the states and flows directly to local units.) Simultaneous with the "push" from the federal government, the states are subjected to powerful "pulls" from local units to support local budgets or otherwise assist in dealing with seemingly endless arrays of local issues that come to rest at the states' doorsteps. In short, state governments, in the overlapping-authority model, occupy a position in which they are subjected to intense forces from two major sources. The states' middle role and fiscal coping capacity are the two themes of this chapter.

In the fields of social psychology and small-group behavior there is frequent reference to the "two against one" pattern in three-person settings: There is a strong tendency, accentuated in ambiguous or conflict-oriented situations, for two persons to form a coalition against the third. The coalition usually forms between the two persons occupying polar positions against the third individual who holds a middle position.

Although this behavioral regularity (often termed the "dilemma of the middleman") does not entirely translate from the realm of social psychology to the arena of intergovernmental relations, this idea nevertheless can enlighten and sharpen perspectives on the fiscal role of the states in IGR. Indeed, the middleman role of the states is far from a new idea; for example, John M. Gaus published in 1950 an article, "The States Are in the Middle."[1]

REVENUE POLICIES AND FISCAL FLOWS

Figure 5-1 graphically shows the states' middleman role in 1975. The states received over $35 billion in federal aid, more than $28 billion of it for welfare, education, and highways—the three broad functional classifications covering scores of specific categorical grant programs. To see the significance of the federal "push" on the states, compare the size of the federal aid conduit to the height of the bar indicating state general spending (excluding trust and enterprise funds).

Or compare the $28 billion in federal aid to the states for welfare, education, and highways with the $54.7 billion spent directly by the states on these three major functions. Federal aid was more than half of direct state spending for these three functions. The comparison, however, is not completely valid, because an undetermined amount of

---

1. John M. Gaus, "The States Are in the Middle, *State Government*, 23 (June 1950): 138-142.

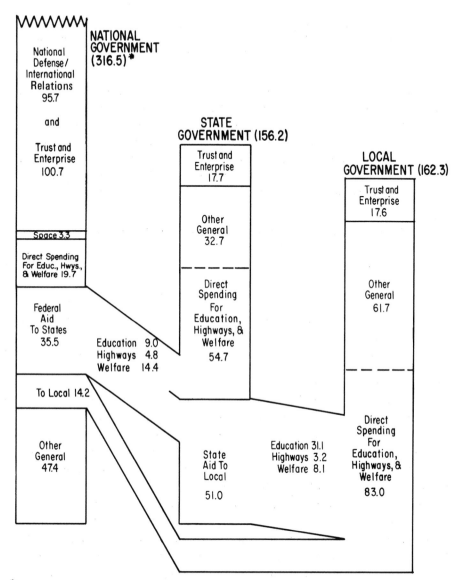

Figure 5-1. *Public Expenditures by Type and by Level of Government, and the Intergovernmental Flow of Funds, Fiscal Year 1975 (in billions of dollars)*

Source: Bureau of the Census, *Government Finances in 1974-75* (Washington, D.C.: Government Printing Office, 1976).

the federal monies are not spent *directly* by the states, but are channeled further through the IGR fiscal pipelines to local governments.[2]

Figure 5-1 also displays the direct national-local flow of funds. That flow, $14.2 billion in 1975, includes the $4.2 billion in GRS funds analyzed in chapter 4. The remaining $10 billion bypassed the states through approximately seventy-five grant programs that make local units the eligible recipients of direct national-local payments.

National-local payments, however, are overshadowed by the size of state aid to local units—$51 billion in 1975. Education aid was more than three-fifths of the total with welfare aid a distant second at $8 billion. Aid to local units constituted about one-third of *total* state expenditures and was an even larger proportion (approaching 40 percent) of state *general* expenditures. The "pull" of local programs and problems, of local politics and pressures, on the states is large, if not massive.

Two summary observations follow from this discussion and from figure 5-1. First, governments in the United States spend large amounts of money that they do not raise, and raise large amounts of money that they do not spend. (The states are, *par excellance,* the fiscal mediators of the IGR system.) Second, the extent to which national, state, and local jurisdictions are interconnected by dollar flows means that policy changes or actions at one level are likely to have important consequences at other levels. When one level sneezes, the others are apt to catch colds.

The largest connector in the IGR system of conduits is state aid to local governments. The level of state aid from 1946 to 1976 is provided in the lower part of table 5-1. From barely $2 billion in 1946 this IGR flow has accelerated to more than $56 billion in 1976. During each ten-year period state aid approximately tripled—an average annual increase of about 12 percent. Yet in the aggregate, state aid has remained remarkably stable within the range of 35-40 percent of state general expenditures.

Individual states, of course, vary greatly in their relative fiscal

---

2. Excellent analyses of policy questions associated with state aid, state-local fiscal relations, and interstate variations in state-local fiscal policies may be found in: Advisory Commission on Intergovernmental Relations, *State Aid to Local Government* (Washington, D.C.: Government Printing Office, April 1969, A-34); Advisory Commission on Intergovernmental Relations, *The States and Intergovernmental Aids* (Washington, D.C.: Government Printing Office, February 1977, A-59); G. Ross Stephens, "State Centralization and the Erosion of Local Autonomy," *Journal of Politics,* 36 (February 1974): 44-76. See also J. Fred Giertz, "Decentralization at the State and Local Level: An Empirical Analysis," *National Tax Journal,* 29 (June 1976): 201-210.

Table 5-1. *General Revenue Trends in State Finances by Major Revenue Source, 1946–1976*

Revenue Source	1946	1956	1966	1976	1946	1956	1966	1976
	(millions of dollars)				(percentages of total general revenue)			
Total general revenue	6,284	18,389	46,757	152,118	100.0	100.0	100.0	100.0
Total own-source revenue	5,419	15,093	34,511	107,401	86.2	82.1	73.8	70.6
Taxes	4,937	13,375	29,380	89,256	78.5	72.7	62.8	58.7
Sales	2,803	7,801	17,044	47,391	44.6	42.4	36.4	31.1
Income	831	2,264	6,326	28,721	13.2	12.3	13.5	18.9
Charges and misc.	482	1,718	5,131	18,145	7.7	9.4	11.0	11.9
Intergovernmental revenue	865	3,296	12,246	44,717	13.8	17.9	26.2	29.4
Exhibit: state aid to local units	2,092	6,538	16,928	56,678				

Sources: U.S. Bureau of the Census, *Historical Statistics on Governmental Finances and Employment*, Table 5; *State Government Finances in 1976*, GF 76, No. 3 (Washington, D.C.), Table 1.

support of local governments: Minnesota, New York, and Wisconsin allocate 45–50 percent of their state budgets for aid to local units; Connecticut, New Hampshire, South Dakota, and Vermont spend only 15–20 percent.

The proportions of intergovernmental revenue make it clear that the states face in two directions. As noted earlier, the percentage of state general revenue from this source has risen consistently over the three decades shown in table 5–1 as well as over the six decades displayed in table 3–2. More than one-fourth of state revenue dollars are externally derived, and more than one-third of state outlays are delivered to the treasuries of local units for ultimate disbursal.

State own-source revenues rose from just $5.4 billion in 1946 to over $107 billion in 1976 but declined as a proportion of general revenue from 86 to 71 percent. Likewise, state taxes, under $5 billion in 1946, approached $90 billion in 1976, yet as a percent of general revenue fell from almost 80 percent to below 60 percent. Income taxes and revenue from charges and miscellaneous sources became increasing shares of state general revenue; indeed, in absolute amounts income taxes have skyrocketed, especially since 1966. The sales tax, at $47 billion in 1976, remained the largest single revenue source for the states. It, too, however, has declined as a percentage of state revenues.

The states' position in the middle has put them in a fiscal squeeze, especially in the past two decades, from five viselike fiscal forces: tax sources, revenue responsiveness, tax resourcefulness, tax productivity, and intergovernmental outlays. These forces amply document the fiscal dilemma of the states as middlemen. The focal period examined, from the late 1950s to the early 1970s, covers developments during the creative and competitive phases of IGR.

TAX SOURCES AND REVENUE RESPONSIVENESS

The system of tapping the various sources of tax revenue presents the states with several difficulties in the intergovernmental tax derby. Common belief associates income taxes with the national government, sales and consumption taxes with state government, and property taxes with local governments. These assumptions are substantially correct. In 1975 more than 80 percent of national government tax revenues were derived from personal and corporate income taxes (see figure 5-2). Local governments placed similarly heavy reliance on a single tax source, the property tax, which produced $50 billion in 1975. State governments, on the other hand, depended much less heavily on a single revenue source. The $43.3 billion in state sales and gross receipts taxes provided a little over half of the states' total tax revenue in 1975; income taxes of about $25 billion furnished another third; and the remainder came from property taxes and other sources, such as license taxes and death and gift taxes.

Figure 5-2 yields several observations about the overall effects of

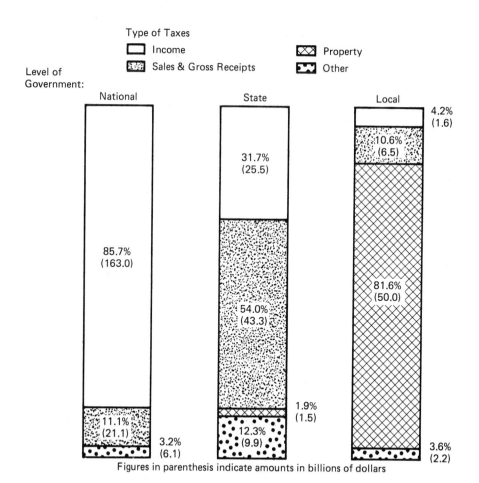

Figure 5-2. *Governmental Tax Revenue by Level of Government by Type of Tax, Fiscal Year 1975 (in percents and billions of dollars)*

revenue policies pursued by the three levels. First, there is a moderate amount of tax overlapping in our intergovernmental system; for example, all three levels derive revenues from income taxes. Second, despite this overlapping, each plane of government practices a degree of tax specialization. Third, the states' two chief revenue sources, income and sales (excise) taxes, have major competition from the national government. Fourth, the states have the most diverse of the tax structures. Finally, probably because the property tax, though significant for local governments, is relatively insignificant for state governments, the states have shown limited concern for the character, administration, and impact of this tax in the past.

These aggregate effects of diverse governmental revenue policies are essential to understanding the IGR context of state taxation policies and, indirectly, state spending policies. The fiscal issues that confront state decision makers are in large part defined by these general considerations—for example, the mixture of moderate tax overlapping with some degree of tax specialization. The states do not have, in the aggregate, one preponderant revenue source as the national and local governments do. Income and property taxes "belong" to the federal government and to local governments, respectively, but the nearest approach to state dominance in taxation is the sales tax. Yet sales taxes provide only about half of all state revenues and involve substantial overlapping, especially with local units. The states, then, compete with their own localities and, to some extent, with the federal government for a share of what is in fact the states' largest source of revenue.

Of course, state competition with localities over sales taxes is a matter of choice, since states can regulate the taxing power of local units. In recent years, however, the states have come under increasing pressure from local officials to allow local units greater discretion in matters of taxation. This trend undoubtedly will continue.

Three conclusions follow from this discussion of tax sources and the context of IGR revenue policies. First, state governments have been unable to establish unassailable hegemony over a single tax source. Some citizens and commentators consider this a virtue; others decry it. Second, when considering major tax actions, state government officials must, more than their federal and local counterparts, also take into account the policies of other government jurisdictions. The need to "look both ways before walking" makes state tax actions on tax matters more difficult and complicated. Third, the tax choices of state decision makers are also conditioned by the feature of revenue responsiveness.

Different types of taxes respond differently to economic growth; that is, they differ by how much and at what rate of change they respond to a specified change in an important economic indicator, such as personal income, gross national product (GNP), or rising property values. Calculations of the approximate responsiveness rates for major taxes in relation to changes in personal income can be made (see figure 5-3). They give further insight into how the states are caught in the middle.

Several policy implications can be drawn from the responsiveness rates displayed in figure 5-3. Because there is a lag in the elasticity of the property tax, local governments that want to maintain an existing level of services must, if other factors remain unchanged, increase property tax rates. Those "other factors" include efficiency, non-property taxing powers, state aid, and federal aid. The local fiscal bind has been a powerful incentive to secure increased state and federal assistance.

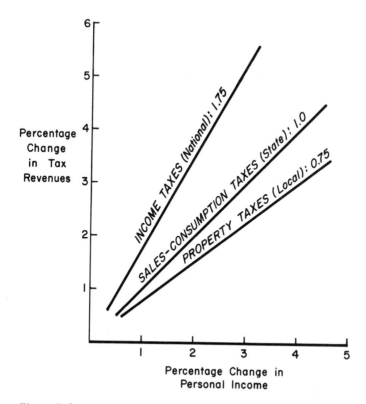

Figure 5-3. *Revenue Responsiveness (Elasticity Coefficients) to Economic Growth by Type of Tax and Governmental Level*

The steep slope of the revenue line for income taxes in figure 5-3 dramatizes the frequently mentioned productiveness of the federal income tax. It is often said—or lamented—that "There is one thing the national government is best at—collecting taxes!" For every 1 percent change in personal income, federal income tax revenues increase by 1.75 percent. (A few state income taxes have similarly high elasticities.) The larger meaning of these figures can be expressed through a historical example. During the 1960s the national government fought two "wars," one against poverty and another in Vietnam. Despite expanded financial commitments to both these efforts the national government reduced income taxes three times in the 1960s (1961, 1964, 1969). As a general observation it seems fair to say that the benefits of economic growth accrue to the national government; the burdens of public services accompanying expansion fall locally.

Where, then, does that leave the states? It leaves them in the middle. The revenue productivity of most state tax structures is roughly equal to the rate of personal income change, that is, elasticities from .90 to 1.10. This modest, intermediate responsiveness of state tax revenues leads to hard policy choices. The states are regularly called on to raise additional revenues to:

1. meet the matching requirements of increasing federal grants,
2. respond to local governments for increased state aid, and
3. expand the scope and improve the quality of state programs and services.

TAX RESOURCEFULNESS AND TAX PRODUCTIVITY

The states' policy choices are reflected in state tax efforts. The Advisory Commission on Intergovernmental Relations compiled data on tax actions taken by the 50 state legislatures from 1959 through 1971. Those legislative sessions passed 40 new taxes and enacted 468 increases in existing tax rates over the 13 years.[3] Six major types of tax were the focus of the 508 total tax actions: sales (73 actions), personal income (67), corporate income (75), motor fuel (60), cigarette (140),

---

3. Advisory Commission on Intergovernmental Relations, *State-Local Finances: Significant Features and Suggested Legislation* (Washington, D.C.: Government Printing Office, 1972, M-74), p. 177.

and alcoholic beverages (84). The tax actions relating to cigarettes and liquor tend to confirm the comment that "the easiest taxes to levy are those on vices." Apart from cigarette and liquor levies, however, there is consistency in the frequency of tax actions for the other four taxes. Hence some balancing or equilibrating factors must be at work. Tax actions are "spread around" among the major types of tax sources.

The total of 508 tax actions reflects an average of one tax increase in each of the 50 legislatures every time a legislative body convened: (Several legislatures have biennial sessions.) There was considerable variation among the states in the number of tax actions during those thirteen years. Minnesota led all states with twenty tax increases; Oregon was the lowest with three. (A major reason why Oregon had few tax increases was its heavy reliance on a state income tax, which gave Oregon's tax structure an elasticity coefficient of 1.29.) Twenty-six states had ten or fewer tax actions. On the high side of the distribution only four states had seventeen or more tax increases in those thirteen years. Note, however, that the *numbers* of actions say nothing about their financial *magnitudes*.

The financial bulk of these several hundred state tax actions was significant, as were the results. State tax revenues jumped from $14.9 billion in 1958 to $59.9 billion in 1972, an absolute increase of $45 billion and a proportionate increase of 300 percent in 14 years. But not all this state tax revenue increase reflects increases in *rates* of taxation. A substantial portion of the increased revenues was generated automatically by economic growth—a result of the elasticity of state tax structure. This built-in growth was attributable to an expanding economy, not to state policy choices.

Research by the ACIR estimated that of the $45 billion increase between 1958 and 1972, economic growth accounted for 47 percent ($21 billion) of the increase in state tax revenues; policy choice accounted for the remaining 53 percent ($24 billion).[4] The left-hand panel of figure 5-4 shows this graphically. The area enclosed by the lower and upper lines indicates the increments in state tax collections added by policy choice.

Governors and legislators are painfully aware of the political liabilities engendered by forces pressing for continuous tax hikes. A survey of 800 legislators during 1963 reported 3000 issues mentioned

---

4. Advisory Commission on Intergovernmental Relations, *Sources of Increased State Tax Collections: Economic Growth vs. Political Choice* (Washington, D.C.: Government Printing Office, October 1968, M-41), p. 1.

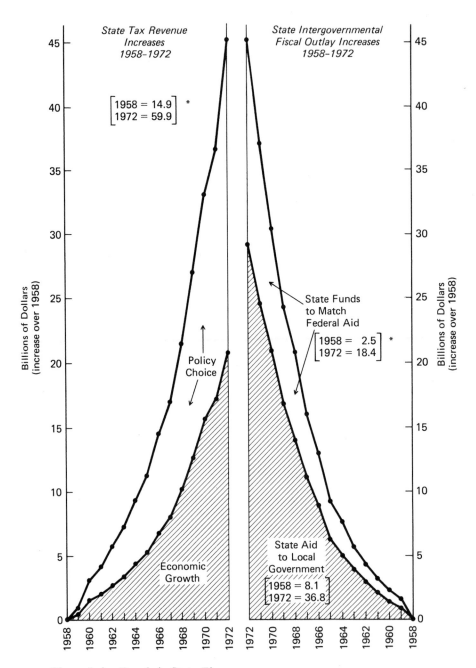

Figure 5–4. *Trends in State Finances*

*Bracketed amounts in billions of dollars.

in 20 policy areas. The leading issue was taxation, and it was mentioned by more than 20 percent of the lawmakers.[5]

The states, then, are, so to speak, where the tax action was from 1958 to 1972. State aggressiveness in taxation between 1958 and 1972 can be demonstrated by respective percentage increases in tax revenues: national government, an increase of 103 percent; state government, 302 percent; and local government, 245 percent. For once, the states held the dubious distinction of not being in the middle.

The vigorous state tax efforts in recent years have placed governors and legislators in vulnerable positions. Those who have committed themselves to continuous tax hikes have run the risk of reprisals at the polls. More than one governor has commented to the effect, "When I sign a major tax increase bill it is nearly the same as signing my political death warrant."

INTERGOVERNMENTAL OUTLAYS

Since state taxes quadrupled from 1958 to 1972, where did the $45-billion increase go? Unfortunately for the states, much of it went to meet the pressures of inflation. Between 1958 and 1972 inflation, a force ostensibly under the control of the federal government, eroded more than one-half of the current dollar increases in state tax revenues.[6] Inflation, of course, is a two-edged sword; increases costs, but it also swells state revenues. More important, however, is an assessment of the disposition of state tax revenues to the two major intergovernmental fiscal outlays of the states: aid to local governments, and spending to meet matching requirements for federal grants-in-aid.[7]

State outlays to local units rose from $8.1 billion in 1958 to $36.8 billion in 1972—a substantial increase of more than $28 billion. In the right-hand panel of figure 5–4 the area included under the lower

5. Wayne L. Francis, *Legislative Issues in the Fifty States: A Comparative Analysis* (Chicago: Rand McNally, 1967), p. 11.
6. The implicit price deflator for state-local purchase of goods and services (as a component of gross national product) rose from a base of 100 in 1958 to 184 in 1972. In other words the 1972 tax collections of nearly $60 billion are reduced, when deflated to 1958 dollars, to under $33 billion (60 ÷ 1.84). For the implicit price deflator series see *Economic Report of the President* (Washington, D.C.: Government Printing Office, 1975), p. 253.
7. This analysis draws heavily on Deil S. Wright and David E. Stephenson, "The States as Middlemen: Five Fiscal Dilemmas," *State Government,* 47 (spring 1974): 101-107.

line depicts increases in state aid to local government. The area between the lower and upper lines indicates the 1958–1972 increments in state amounts to match federal aid. This aggregate increment of about $16 billion, added to the $29 billion of local aid, totals $45 billion.

Perhaps the most striking feature of figure 5-4 is the close match between state tax increases and enlarged intergovernmental fiscal obligations: The 1958–1972 intergovernmental fiscal claims appear to have consumed all the increases in state tax revenues. This is not in fact true; the state matching amounts are slightly misleading because some federal aid funds are double counted. For instance, some federal aid coming to the states is subsequently passed on to local governments and recorded as state aid to local governments. How much federal aid is thus double counted cannot be estimated precisely, but the duplication is not likely to have exceeded $8 billion. This figure is only a best guess, but even if it were as high as $10 billion, the local and national intergovernmental impacts on the states were tremendous. Of the $45 billion in tax revenues raised from 1958 to 1972, less than 25 percent would have been available for state-determined discretionary purposes. The other 75–80 percent went to satisfy intergovernmental fiscal obligations.

A FISCAL STRAITJACKET

It is not surprising, then, that by the early 1970s governors and state legislators felt they were confined in a fiscal straitjacket. The effect that state officials had on intergovernmental expenditures apparently was highly restricted. Formulas attached to categorical grants extended from Washington, D.C., specified the amount of matching funds each state was required to provide. States were given the choice of either accepting or rejecting federal aid.

Understandably, state officials have always been reluctant to refuse grants. In fact, federal aid constitutes such a large portion of state expenditures that it could be both politically and economically unwise for governors and legislators to turn down federal money. Still, governors, at least, are not unaware of the restraints placed upon them by categorical grants.

Although state governments have considerably more discretion in allocating money as state aid to local units, such aid does not represent fully "flexible funds" at the disposal of state officials: First, state grants are often earmarked for specified functions, albeit by actions of previous legislative initiative. (Many of the functions most heavily supported by state aid are also receiving the most funding from federal grants.) Second, the states continue to increase financial assistance to their localities, which have experienced both increasing demands on their services and an unresponsive local property tax. Aside from the most basic governmental services (for example, police and fire protection), these local units have virtually always needed state and federal assistance to provide the kind and degree of public services desired by urban inhabitants. Cities have been increasingly dependent on outside aid, and the states have responded.

By 1972 the demands on their expenditures had put the states in a fiscal bind—or had tightened their straitjacket—because state aid levels were exacerbated by federal aid matching requirements. On the revenue side of the ledger, the states were suffering from what might be called financial "hypertension," or high "fiscal blood pressures."[8] That policy makers were sensitive to state tax actions and tax levels was only one crude indicator of the hypertension; two more objective indicators are contained in figures 5-5 and 5-6. Figure 5-5 displays local and state taxation as rising proportions of the gross national product. Although GNP grew substantially from 1955 to 1975, local taxes grew more, rising from 3 to 4 percent of the expanded GNP. But state tax rates increased even more dramatically as a proportion of GNP, from 3 percent in 1955 to nearly 6 percent of the enlarged GNP in the early 1970s.

Figure 5-6 displays the intensity of state tax activity during a quarter-century; the bars indicate the number of states having specified combinations of tax policies. In 1950 seventeen states levied both income and sales taxes; seven states had neither. By 1975 thirty-six states used both sales and income as sources of tax revenue, and only one state—New Hampshire—had neither tax.

The policy consequences of the herculean tax effort of the states were numerous; the two that deserve mention here are citizen opinions and state officials' search for new revenue sources. There are no sources of systematic trend data on citizen views about levels of state taxation.

---

8. For an analysis that measures variations in fiscal "hypertension" among the fifty states see: Advisory Commission on Intergovernmental Relations, *Measuring the Fiscal "Blood Pressure" of the States—1964–1975* (Washington, D.C.: Government Printing Office, February 1977, M-111).

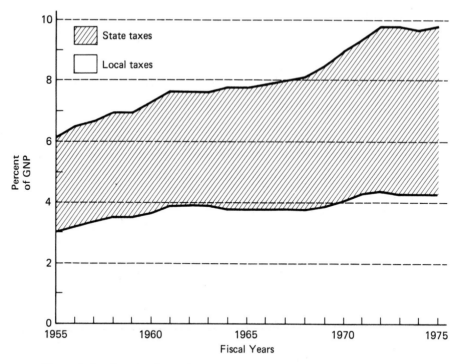

Figure 5-5.   *State and Local Taxes as a Percentage of Gross National Product, 1955 through 1975 (est.)*

Source: Advisory Commission on Intergovernmental Relations, *1974–75 Edition Federal-State-Local Finances: Significant Features of Fiscal Federalism* (Washington, D.C.: ACIR, November 1975), p. 4.

We must be content, then, to make reasonable, though tentative inferences from Gallup polling data on whether *federal* income taxes were "too high." In the early 1960s 46–48 percent of the respondents said yes, but by 1973, 65 percent said yes. The Harris surveys disclosed data possibly still more pertinent to taxpayer unrest. Asked about their sympathy for "a taxpayers' revolt where people would refuse to pay any more taxes unless spending were reduced," 43 percent of the respondents concurred with this sentiment in 1969; four years later, in 1973, 69 percent concurred.[9]

---

9. Parris N. Glendening and Mavis Mann Reeves, *Pragmatic Federalism: An Intergovernmental View of American Government* (Pacific Palisades, Calif.: Palisades Publishers, 1977), p. 141. See also Mavis Mann Reeves and Parris N. Glendening, "Areal Federalism and Public Opinion," *Publius: The Journal of Federalism* (Spring 1976): 135–167.

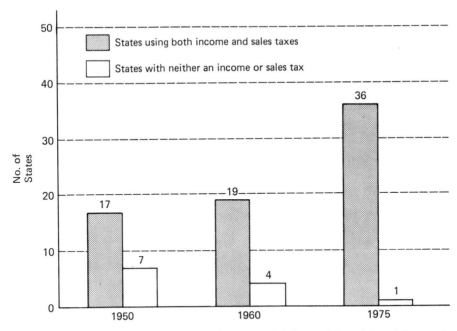

Figure 5-6. *Number of States with General Sales and Broad-Based Personal Income Taxes, as of January 1, 1950, 1960, and 1975*

Source: Advisory Commission on Intergovernmental Relations, *1974-75 Edition Federal-State-Local Finances,* p. 4.

While citizen concerns about taxation in general were escalating in the 1960s and 1970s the apprehensions of state (and local) officials were also on the rise. Faced with inflationary costs, less elastic tax revenues, years of successive tax increases, and actual or perceived citizen demands for public services, state policy makers searched anxiously for new revenue sources. The 1964 revenue sharing proposal by Council of Economic Advisors chairman Walter Heller had gained considerable attention. Starting in 1965 the National Governors Conference began beating the drums for GRS. Their wishes, along with those of thousands of other state and local officials, were not realized until 1972, but seven to eight years is perhaps the average time that a major IGR issue needs to proceed from proposal to adoption. GRS funds began to flow to the states during fiscal year 1973. What were the impacts of GRS on the states? Did GRS relieve fiscal hypertension among state officials?

GENERAL REVENUE SHARING (GRS) IMPACTS

The degree of centralization versus decentralization between each state and its local jurisdictions varies widely among the states. This centralization/decentralization measure is usually constructed from financial data, although there are other, more complex composite indices. Variations in state-raised tax revenues are one example of a financial index.[10] In 1975 state governments raised 57 percent of combined state-local tax revenues. But eight states raised more than 75 percent: Arkansas (76), Delaware (90), Hawaii (78), Kentucky (76), Mississippi (76), New Mexico (83), South Carolina (76), and West Virginia (77); and seven states raised less than 50 percent: Connecticut (49), Massachusetts (47), Nebraska (48), New Hampshire (40), New Jersey (39), New York (48), and South Dakota (46).

Despite these divergent patterns of revenue raising (and spending) among the states, the State and Local Fiscal Assistance Act of 1972 specified that of the GRS funds allocated to "state areas" a uniform fraction of one-third went to state governments. The remaining two-thirds in each state was apportioned by a distribution formula among cities, counties, and townships. Before, during, and after the enactment of GRS state officials roundly criticized this procrustean division, which failed to recognize diverse state-local differences. Their protests were to no avail then or even at the time GRS was renewed in 1976. Basically, city and county interests were simply too strong for state officials to outlobby, outmaneuver, or outmuscle.

Not all state officials, of course, were of one mind at the time GRS was first passed or was extended. Indeed, fiscal and economic matters have sparked a growing diversity among the states and have sharply split them along self-interest lines. One large-circulation magazine even called it "The Second War Between the States."[11] Another description of the cleavage is the "Snowbelt" (the northern and northeastern states) versus the "Sunbelt" (the southern and southwestern states).

These differences, as will be noted in later chapters, influence state officials' attitudes and actions with respect to federal aid formulas and other issues. But the differences spring from significant variations

---

10. U.S. Bureau of the Census, *Government Finances in 1974-75*, GF 75-No. 5 (Washington, D.C.: Government Printing Office, 1976), Table 25, p. 68.
11. *Business Week*, "The Second War Between the States," May 17, 1976, pp. 92-114.

among the states in the policies they follow. Among them are revenue raising and spending policies. The diversity of these fiscal and public-service policies among the states would lead us to expect GRS impacts to vary from state to state. They generally do.

Two independent studies, using top-level state officials as respondents—in one instance (Brazer) top legislative and executive finance officers, in the other (Wright et al.) top-level administrators heading various state departments, agencies, and boards—corroborated the diversity of GRS fiscal impacts.[12] Both analyses found that the tax effects of GRS were present chiefly among the wealthier states (as measured by per capita personal income). These states tended to be concentrated in New England or the midwest and have high tax efforts, that is, a high ratio of aggregate state-local taxes to the aggregate personal income of the state's inhabitants. A "tax effect" impact meant that GRS either produced actual tax reductions or delayed a tax increase. In contrast, capital outlay effects appeared concentrated chiefly in north-south border and southern states, most of which have low per capita incomes.

Research on the diversity of fiscal impacts among the states permitted overall estimates of GRS uses to be calculated. Two classifications of fiscal uses were developed. One was functional, for example, health, education. The other was by character, that is, operating, capital outlay, state aid to local units, tax effects, and borrowing. Approximately 20 percent of GRS monies were estimated to have affected each of the first four character categories; less than 5 percent affected state borrowing, with the remaining 15 percent undetermined.[13] The nearly even division among operating, capital, and state aid outlays (to local units) is at wide variance from the usual configuration of these components of state budgets. Like GRS at the local level, GRS uses at the state level departed significantly from regular state spending.

GRS functional uses were traced by surveying a total of several hundred heads of state administrative agencies in the fifty states. For

12. Harvey E. Brazer, "The States and General Revenue Sharing," in F. Thomas Juster (ed.), *The Economic and Political Impact of General Revenue Sharing* (Washington, D.C.: National Science Foundation/Research Applied to National Needs, April 1976), pp. 105–129; Deil S. Wright et al., *Assessing the Impacts of General Revenue Sharing in the Fifty States: A Survey of State Administrators* (Chapel Hill: Institute for Research in Social Science, The University of North Carolina, 1975).
13. Brazer, "The States and General Revenue Sharing," p. 125.

the fiscal year 1974 nearly $2 billion in state-alloted GRS funds went, in the aggregate, for the following:[14]

Education	51%	Natural resources	3%
Economic development	14	Environment	3
Criminal justice	12	General administration	3
Transportation	7	Social services	2
Health	4		

This expenditure distribution departs radically from the typical aggregate expenditure pattern of the states. In 1974, for example, the states' major direct expenditures were: education, 27 percent; welfare, 21 percent; highways, 17 percent; and health/hospitals, 10 percent.

Not only did the use of GRS funds vary considerably among the states, but the aggregate uses for functions differed greatly from normal state budget priorities. Note also that these findings confirm that GRS funds were a novel revenue source for the states, and the uses to which the funds were put strongly reflected state priorities or needs as determined by state, not federal or local, officials. In this respect GRS evidently relieved some of the states' fiscal hypertension.

The attitudes of the surveyed state officials bear out this last supposition: About two-thirds of the key legislative and executive officials felt that GRS had enabled them to develop new state-level programs, and over 80 percent believed that GRS made a difference "in [our] ability to deal with the three most important problems facing [our] state."[15] Of more than 1500 state agency heads responding, 61 percent favored the idea of GRS, and 53 percent thought that the amount of GRS funds available to the states was "too little."[16] Nevertheless, among the respondents there were decidedly different views on the desirability of GRS. Over 75 percent of the heads of staff agencies or "generalist" officials, such as budget and finance officers, were strongly partial to GRS. But the heads of line agencies, the program professionals or functional specialists, were much less favorably inclined. A bare majority of the heads of state health agencies favored GRS and only 43 percent of the welfare/income-security agency heads agreed with the idea of GRS.[17] In short, GRS exposed cleavages

---

14. Wright et al., *Assessing the Impacts,* chap. 6, pp. 1–22.
15. Brazer, "The States and General Revenue Sharing," p. 119.
16. Wright et al., *Assessing the Impacts,* chap. 2, pp. 7–11.
17. Ibid., pp. 19–22.

within the states between the programmatic specialists and political-administrative generalists: The "picket fence" does have a grounding on systematic empirical data. GRS remains both the godfather and the offspring of generalist officials at the state and local levels. For a time, at least, it appears to have eased the pressure and tension under which these officials were forced to operate.

It may seem an exaggeration to say that GRS eased the fiscal agony of the states' middleman role, for how could an additional $2 billion per year to the states make much difference amid state tax revenues of $74 billion in 1974? Furthermore, if miscellaneous revenues and non-GRS intergovernmental revenues are included, then total state general revenues in 1974 exceeded $120 billion, further reducing GRS contributions to 1–2 percent of total revenues. It would appear that the impact of GRS could only be negligible at best. The prospect that GRS could significantly alter state officials' attitudes and actions, much less start a presidentially inspired "New American Revolution," seems, then, all the more doubtful.

But appearances can be deceiving—and in this case are. It is unrealistic to compare the states' $2 billion share of GRS with the total tax or general revenues of state governments. There is evidence on how state policy officials make program and fiscal choices: They do not decide each year how to allocate or reallocate all of the $74 or $120 billion that underwrites state and local activities. Instead, they pursue decisions on budgets and programs incrementally, through marginal analysis with such questions as: What change is proposed this year? How much more resources do we have this year than last? In short, the bulk of the prior years' resources are viewed as committed and the discussion, debate, logrolling, and conflict center mostly on how to use the "new money"—the additional revenues available for discretionary use by governors and state legislators. GRS was, and perhaps still is, "new money."

In this incremental, new-money approach to state policy decisions, GRS assumes a radically altered role in state finances. From 1973 to 1974 the additional tax revenues collected by the fifty states totaled slightly over $6.1 billion (an increase from $68.1 billion to $74.2 billion).[18] State policy makers had not only this $6 billion in new money to allocate at the legislative sessions covering the 1974 fiscal year,

---

18. U.S. Bureau of the Census, *State Government Finances in 1973*, GF 73-No. 3 (Washington, D.C.: Government Printing Office, 1973), Table 7, p. 19 (for 1974, Table 7, p. 22).

they also had (guaranteed by the State and Local Fiscal Assistance Act) slightly over \$2 billion in GRS funds. In other words, GRS presented state officials with a 33 percent increase in discretionary dollars. Viewed in this context, GRS *was* an important factor in the policy decision equations of the fifty states. (Variations in the incremental impact of GRS for each state are shown by the table in Appendix D.)

GRS was a major source of "new" revenue for the states. The funds became available without the usual painful political wounds that often accompany a tax increase in the states. Because the tax clashes from the 1950s into the 1970s had unquestionably left much scar tissue, some recent and exposed, on state officials, GRS had to be attractive: It promised the pleasure of spending funds without the pain of having to raise them. Unlike any other type of federal aid, GRS required no matching, was for all intents and purposes unconditional and unrestricted, and promised to be available through 1976 and probably beyond. GRS looked like a "good deal" to the beleaguered middlemen of IGR. It was.

SUMMARY

State governments are pivotal intermediaries in the U.S. political system; they are middlemen in the overlapping-authority model of IGR. They experience financial inducements or "pushes" from the federal government and powerful "pulls" or pressures from local governments. The states hold the system together; but in so doing state decision makers face difficult policy choices, such as how to raise more revenues and how to allocate existing or expanding resources. State governments have responded to diverse IGR pressures in substantial, perhaps spectacular ways. The states have secured large amounts of additional revenue by deliberate policy choices—enacting new taxes or increasing tax rates. Over the past two decades state taxes increased *as a percent of GNP* far more than the taxes for any other governmental level. The proportions are:[19]

---

19. Advisory Commission on Intergovernmental Relations, *Significant Features of Fiscal Federalism: 1976 Edition,* vol. 1 (Washington, D.C.: Government Printing Office, June 1976, M–106), p. 31.

	Taxes as a Percent of GNP	
	1956	1975
Federal	15.9	13.2
State	3.3	5.6
Local	3.2	4.3
Total	22.4	23.1

One interpretation of these figures is that the states have been caught in a fiscal squeeze and have responded with herculean tax (and expenditure) efforts. This "fiscal hypertension" thesis helps explain, and place in context, the several themes developed in this chapter:

1. the increasing state dependence on federal aid;
2. the absence of state dominance or near-complete command of a single tax source;
3. the intermediate responsiveness (near 1.0 elasticities) of most of the revenue structures of the states;
4. the large number of state tax actions from the late 1950s to the early 1970s;
5. the political agonies of governors and state legislators in confronting difficult tax and expenditure policy choices;
6. the limited amounts of flexible or discretionary funds available to state decision makers beyond those allocated to meet IGR obligations;
7. citizens' apprehensions over increasing tax levels;
8. state officials' leadership in supporting the adoption of General Revenue Sharing; and
9. the use of GRS funds by the states for purposes that departed significantly from existing expenditure patterns.

Another interpretation of those findings is to shun the "hypertension" approach and adopt a *structural* interpretation: Although the states were indeed under some fiscal pressure, it was not from *hypertension* but was merely a structural shift in the absorption of demands for financing public services—demands that otherwise would have been absorbed by local governments or the federal government. In other words, a role change has occurred in IGR finances over the past two decades; the states have become important financiers of major domestic programs (for example, education, health, pollution control, transportation, and welfare). The states' absorption of tax and expenditure pressures eased fiscal pressures at the local level and allowed a *decline* in fiscal pressure at the national level. The data displayed earlier in this summary on taxes as a percentage of GNP support this contention.

Whichever interpretation is accepted—fiscal "hypertension" or structural change—the thesis of this chapter remains intact: The states are indispensable components in the operation of IGR in the United States.

National Finances:

Federal Assistance and Federal Aid

6

Yet to be examined in depth are the two major conduits of federal aid to the states and local units (see figure 5-1). To adequately understand IGR we must know more than just the general characteristics of federal assistance programs and how many there are and what are their aggregate dollar amounts. This chapter provides additional data on federal aid and probes in greater depth the main IGR fiscal policies of the national government. But we first need a better grasp of what is meant by federal assistance and its three monetary forms: loans, grants-in-aid, and revenue sharing. These three forms of aid are the focal points for fiscal explorations.

Two analytic themes are woven into the discussion: First, federal aid is discussed in relation to national issues and the national government's policy-making processes; second, federal aid policies are described and assessed as to their impacts on state and local governments. Throughout the discussion the reader should remember that attention is centered on the fiscal conduits in figure 5-1, which carry funds from the federal government to the thousands of state and local jurisdictions.

FEDERAL ASSISTANCE

Federal assistance as defined by the Intergovernmental Coopera-tion Act of 1968 includes "programs that provide assistance through grant or contractual arrangements and includes technical assistance programs or programs providing assistance in the form of loans, loan guarantees, or insurance" (P.L. 90–577, Sec. 107). This broad defini-tion covers an immense diversity of programs ranging from large cash grant programs, such as highway aid, to the smallest cooperative ar-rangement, such as technical assistance. For example, by an agreement with the state of Virginia, the U.S. Civil Service Commission trains selected Virginia administrative personnel on a cost-reimbursable basis. Another example of technical assistance is that of NASA's God-dard Space Flight Center to the city of Baltimore: For three years Tom Golden, a scientist-engineer at Goddard, occupied an office in Baltimore's City Hall with the explicit, full-time aim of getting various space-related technologies adopted and applied to some of Baltimore's pressing urban problems.[1]

The central intent of federal assistance is to alter the behavior, output, programs, or decisions of state and local governments. Indeed, federal assistance often attempts to prescribe within fairly narrow limits the choices exercised by state or local officials; for example, Congress has tried to mandate the use of Title I education monies (over $2 billion annually) for the benefit of disadvantaged children in local school districts. This effort, incidentally, appears notably doubtful of success.

The 1026 programs in the *1976 Catalog of Federal Domestic Assistance* are divisible into two broad types of assistance programs: those with specifically designated cash support available, and those without such support. The former programs, numbering 525 in all, are usually called *federal aid programs*. These federal aid programs can in turn be usefully divided into three classes: loans, grants-in-aid, and

---

1. National Academy of Public Administration, *The Baltimore Applications Project: A New Look at Technology Transfer* (Washington, D.C.: Goddard Space Flight Center, Na-tional Aeronautics and Space Administration, March 1977).

Table 6-1. *Federal Aid by Major Type, 1970 and 1975*

	Year	
Type of Aid	1970	1975
	(in billions of dollars)	
Loans—net	.3	.2
(gross disbursements)	(1.5)	(1.6)
Grants-in-Aid	23.3	42.5
Categorical	23.0	37.1
Block	.3	5.4
Revenue Sharing	.4	7.0
Total	24.0	49.7

Sources: *Special Analyses: Budget of the United States Government,* (Washington, D.C.: Government Printing Office); fiscal years 1972 and 1977, "Federal Aid to State and Local Governments."

revenue sharing (or unrestricted aid). Table 6-1 provides financial amounts for each of the three types of aid for 1970 and 1975. (In addition, figures on two subdivisions of grants-in-aid are provided for subsequent reference and discussion.) The rise in total federal aid from 1970 to 1975 is immediately apparent—a doubling from $24 billion to nearly $50 billion in the short span of five years. This rise constitutes an average annual increase of about 16 percent.

Another noteworthy difference is the dramatic change in the revenue sharing amount—a shift produced by the State and Local Fiscal Assistance Act of 1972. The $7 billion in this category for 1975 includes $6.2 billion disbursed in 1975 under that legislation. The major dollar increase in federal aid, however, was for grants-in-aid. Much more will be said about this type of aid and its two subdivisions, categorical and block grants. In the five-year period under review there were only slight changes in net outlays or gross disbursements for federal loans to state-local governments. The slight change in loan amounts in no way presaged the attention received by this form of federal aid in 1975.

LOANS

The role of loans in IGR finances was a featured issue late in 1975, when New York City's fiscal crisis was front-page news. The New York Seasonal Financing Act of 1975 was an unusual federal loan, for several reasons. Not only was it large ($2 billion) and directed to one city, but it required regular, systematic monitoring by the Secretary of the Treasury and his staff. Some appreciation of that process can be gained from reading a statement by then-Secretary William Simon in approving a second installment loan of $500 million. He addressed New York City officials much in the manner of a person who might be a blend of Dutch uncle and the leader in a game of "Simon says." (See Appendix E for Simon's statement.)

Although the New York City loan may be exceptional in several respects, federal aid in the form of loans has numerous, long-established precedents. In 1975, for example, federal loans to states and local governments for only six major functions totaled over $1.5 billion.[2] These functions and the amounts loaned (in millions) were:

National Resources	$ 10	Education	8
Commerce-Transportation	37	Health	61
Community Development	760	Public Housing	645

However, because loan repayments offset total loans, net expenditures were only $200 million in 1975 (down from $300 million in 1970).

The latitude that the federal government enjoys as a lender is in sharp contrast to the discretion that most states must exercise as borrowers. In the early and middle nineteenth century, state governments made extensive use of loans for the tools of economic development: railroads, canals, bridges, etc. Mismanagement and default on these obligations produced adverse political reactions and debt restrictions that are still enshrined in many state constitutions. In twenty-eight states borrowing is so restricted that general-obligation debt may be incurred only if the bonds are approved by a statewide popular referendum. And in eleven states special restrictions apply, such as limiting obligation to a percentage of property values. In the remaining eleven states, however, there are few limits on state borrowing power.[3]

The restrictiveness of state debt limits has contributed to the heavy use of two alternate debt-related policies of IGR; (1) expansion of federal loan programs available to the states and localities, and (2)

---

2. *Special Analyses, Budget of the United States Government, Fiscal Year 1977* (Washington, D.C.: Office of Management and Budget, 1976), Table O-10, p. 274–275.

3. Richard E. Wagner, "Optimality in Local Debt Limitation," *National Tax Journal,* 23 (September 1970): 297–305. Wagner notes that in the 1840s over 50 percent of all state debt was in default, and in the 1870s up to 20 percent of all local debt was in default.

massive state and local borrowing by use of revenue bonds (nonguaranteed obligations) that escape constitutional (and other) constraints. Between 1960 and 1975, long-term, nonguaranteed debt outstanding for both states and local governments increased by a multiple of about 3.5:[4]

	State Gov'ts	Local Gov'ts
	(in billions)	
1960	$ 9.2	$15.9
1965	14.4	23.4
1970	21.2	34.9
1975	33.8	52.1

State limitations on state and/or local borrowing have several consequences for IGR. First, there is evidence that such limits, rather than encouraging taxation in place of debt financing, simply depress state and local own-source spending. In other words, debt limits systematically restrict the extent to which state and local governments will finance programs on a pay-as-you-go basis.[5] Second, if demands for state and local services remain strong, this dampening effect is a direct stimulus to secure loans or grants (or revenue sharing) from the federal government. Third, the federal government's borrowing capacity is immense, especially in comparison to state-local borrowing capacities.

Because programs for which states either lend or borrow generally must be self-supporting, they are invariably revenue-producing projects or public facilities. In contrast, federal loans enjoy greater flexibility of program objectives, including loans that, like college student loans, are capital investments in human resources. This flexibility stems not only from the national government's powerful credit position but also from the legal latitude it enjoys. The constitutional provision of Article I, Section 8 concerning taxing and spending for the "general welfare" has been broadly interpreted by the courts. Thus, the national government, as a matter of policy, can make soft or risky loans, or loans with

4. U.S. Bureau of the Census, *Governmental Finances in 1974–75*, GF 75-No. 5 (Washington, D.C.: Government Printing Office) Table 14, p. 26. Data for prior years drawn from the same publication for each respective year.
5. Thomas S. Pogue, "The Effect of Debt Limits: Some New Evidence," *National Tax Journal*, 23 (March 1970): 36–49; John Shannon, Michael Bell, and Ronald Fisher, "Recent State Experience with Local Tax and Expenditure Controls," *National Tax Journal*, 29 (September 1976): 276–285.

forgiveness and contingent repayment provisions, whereas most states find it difficult to do so because of constitutional and other legal obstacles.

Another IGR impact of federal loans is the reputed advantage enjoyed by the more advanced and professionalized states (and localities). Information about available loans is not universally or uniformly distributed to all potential applicants, whether states, local units, or individuals. In addition, the procedural requirements are sufficiently complex and the loan purposes so specialized that major advantages *might* accrue to the state or local government with greater resources of time and talent. Two points should be emphasized: First, the suggested association between federal loans and "resourceful" state and local governments is only a hypothesis, not a confirmed finding; second, even if confirmed to exist, this pattern may or may not be an intended policy goal of federal loans.

The policy goals of federal-state or federal-local loans have a programmatic bias similar to the income tax exemption feature on state-local government bonds; that is, such loans favor public works or capital asset types of outlays. Exceptions are the person-oriented education loans made by the national government (and a few states). In short, loans favor durable (physical) goods rather than other types of aid that might promote or amplify human resources. This programmatic bias is not necessarily undesirable, but it is important to consider whether it yields greater benefits than another would.

Loans from the national government to states and localities should not be overlooked in their policy significance merely because they make a miniscule net drain on the U.S. treasury: The example of New York City is a recent reminder that loans have important IGR policy effects. Far greater in magnitude, however, is the second category of federal aid: grants-in-aid.

GRANTS-IN-AID

Perhaps the best-known federal IGR fiscal tool is the federal grant-in-aid, defined as "the payment of funds by one level of government to be expended by another level for a specified purpose, usually on a matching basis and in accordance with prescribed standards or requirements."[6] Federal grants have several chief distinguishing features:

1. Congressional authorizing legislation establishes a grant program for a specified number of years or on a continuing basis.
2. Annual appropriations, which may be less than authorized amounts, provide funds for distribution among states or their subdivisions:
   a. usually in accordance with a legislatively prescribed formula,
   b. generally contingent on state or local matching funds, and
   c. based on conditions that the Congress, president, or executive agencies specify and that are agreed to by the recipient unit.
3. Allocation, supervision, review, approval, and audit responsibilities over the receiving units are performed by a federal administrative agency.
4. Funds are generally allocated to units of government rather than to individuals, nonprofit and semipublic groups, or private firms.

It should be clear, then, that a central feature of the grant device is its *conditional* character. There are limits or restrictions on how grant funds may be used. The restrictions invariably apply to the substantive or program use of monies, but normally also entail other conditions such as matching, advance planning, accounting, reporting, and personnel qualifications.

Grants may be divided into two major types according to their degree of program constraint: They may be block or categorical. The block grant (sometimes called consolidated grant) is broad in scope, and its funding is targeted toward a major purpose such as education, health, law enforcement, community development, or manpower. The categorical grant, in contrast, is specific in problem focus and intended results; for example, funds for the project grant program called "Solid Waste Disposal Training Grants," administered by EPA, can be obtained only by state agencies and specially solicited applicants for the purpose of "training persons in occupations involving the design, operation, and maintenance of solid waste disposal systems."[7]

---

6. *Federal-State-Local Relations: Federal Grants-In-Aid,* Thirtieth Report by the Committee on Government Operations, Subcommittee on Intergovernmental Relations, House Report 2533, 85th Congress, 2nd Session, August 8, 1958, p. 7.
7. *1976 Catalog of Federal Domestic Assistance* (Washington, D.C.: Office of Management and Budget, 1976), p. 766.

Until recently the block grant had been an aid strategy of interest largely to scholars and state or local officials seeking federal aid reforms; categorical grants had been the main federal aid mechanisms, as data for fiscal year 1970 confirm: Of $23.3 billion in grant funds, $23.0 billion (about 95 percent) went for categorical grants and only $300 million for block grants. An early, significant example of a block (or consolidated) grant was the comprehensive health planning and services program. Created in 1966 by P.L. 89-749, it replaced more than a dozen categorical disease grants (such as heart, cancer, tuberculosis) with a single grant for a broad range of health services. Since 1966 four additional block grant programs have been enacted covering law enforcement (1968), manpower and employment training (1973), social services (1974), and community development (1974). This shift in federal aid policies is reflected in categorical and block grant amounts for 1975 (see table 6-1): an estimated $37.1 billion and $5.4 billion respectively.[8] Categorical grant funds have dropped to 87 percent of federal grants. When general revenue sharing and general-purpose aid at $7.0 billion are included, federal aid totaled $49.7 billion in 1975: categorical grants, 75 percent; block grants, 11 percent; general-purpose aid, 14 percent.

What is the significance of this federal aid policy shift toward block grants from $0.3 billion in 1970 to $5.4 billion in 1975 and to an estimated $9.8 billion in 1977? Listing the five distinctive traits of a block grant should help to answer this question:

1. Recipient jurisdictions have fairly wide discretion within the designated program or functional area.
2. Administration, reporting, planning, and other program features are intended to keep grantor supervision and control at a minimum.
3. Formula-based allocation provisions are intended to limit grantor discretion and decrease fiscal uncertainty for the grantees.
4. Eligibility provisions are fairly precise, tending to favor general as opposed to special district governments, retraining grantor administrative discretion, and favoring state and local generalist officials over program specialists.

---

8. *Special Analyses, Budget of the United States Government, Fiscal Year 1978* (Washington, D.C.: Office of Management and Budget, 1977), p. 276.

5. Funding provisions tend toward specifying low matching requirements for recipient jurisdictions.[9]

The cumulative effect of these features, plus the substantial increase in block grant funds from 1970 to 1977, significantly reverse the trend toward proliferation and fragmentation in the grant field. Increased use of the block grant is a partial withdrawal from the position that federal officials (elected or appointed) know best what choices should be made; it is an acknowledgment that state and local officials should have a larger role in formulating the policies and programs supported with federal grants. Enactment and extension of General Revenue Sharing in 1972 and 1976 further acknowledged the enlarged state-local discretion over the use of federal aid.

Before turning to the revenue sharing component of federal aid, we must examine several additional policy considerations with respect to grants: their origins, growth, forms, and effects.[10]

Grant Origins

Prior to 1900 the chief form of federal assistance to the states was the land grant. The first prototype cash grant, enacted in 1887, financed state-operated agricultural experiment stations. That was the year singled out by Professor Leonard D. White as the breach point of the original "administrative settlement" that had kept the federal bureaucracy small and had minimized federal-state overlapping. Before this "breach point," according to White, state and local governments

---

9. Carl W. Stenbert and David B. Walker, "The Block Grant: Principles, Practice, Prognosis," Washington, D.C.: Advisory Commission on Intergovernmental Relations, April 1976. See also, "The Pattern of Federal Assistance to State and Local Governments," testimony of David B. Walker, Assistant Director, Advisory Commission on Intergovernmental Relations, before the Intergovernmental Relations and Human Relations Subcommittee of the House Committee on Government Operations, July 10, 1975. As part of a massive study assessing and proposing policies that affect the intergovernmental grant system the ACIR has produced the following reports on block grants: *Block Grants: A Roundtable Discussion* (A-51, October 1976); *Safe Streets Reconsidered: The Block Grant Experience, 1968–1975* (A-55, January 1977); *The Partnership for Health Act: Lessons from a Pioneering Block Grant* (A-56, January 1977); *Community Development: The Workings of a Federal-Local Block Grant* (A-57, March 1977).

10. Portions of the following discussion on grants draws on material from Deil S. Wright, *Federal Grants-In-Aid: Perspectives and Alternatives* (Washington, D.C.: American Enterprise Institute for Public Policy Research, 1968). For a useful (but dated) collation of historical highlights involving grants-in-aid and other IGR events see W. Brooke Graves, *Intergovernmental Relations in the United States: An Annotated Chronology* (Chicago: Council of State Governments, 1958).

met, unaided, the nation's multiplying domestic needs, and during the nineteenth century "the states and the cities became the busy workshops of the administrative world."[11]

The next landmark period of grant creation was 1914-1921, when grants were enacted to support agricultural extension, highway construction, vocational education and rehabilitation, and maternal and child health. These programs marked the beginning of the "modern" grant period and contained such features as an apportionment formula for fund distribution among the states; matching requirements; advance approval of state plans; and detailed planning, administrative, and reporting requirements.

The maternal and child health legislation resulted in celebrated Supreme Court challenges to the legality of grants-in-aid and to the spending power of the federal government. In the cases of *Frothingham* v. *Mellon* and *Massachusetts* v. *Mellon,* in 1923, the Court denied challenges to the act on the grounds that neither a state nor a taxpayer had legal standing to bring suit against a national expenditure.[12] A few years later (1936), in *U.S.* v. *Butler,* the Court concurred in a broad interpretation of the power of the national government to spend money.[13] The Court's broad interpretation of the "general welfare" clause holds today. The power to tax (and spend) for the general welfare is not limited to the other enumerated and implied powers specified in the Constitution. In short, the spending power of the national government was declared, and remains, virtually unlimited as to purpose—provided, of course, that the president and the Congress can agree on the purpose(s).

What forces, then, contributed to the invention, expansion, and justification of this particular device? The forces have been legal, economic, political, and programmatic.

We have just noted the legal basis for sustaining the expenditure of funds for grants-in-aid: the Supreme Court's interpretation of the national government's constitutional powers. An associated legal consideration on the revenue side was the enactment of the Sixteenth

---

11. Leonard D. White, *The States and the Nation* (Baton Rouge: Louisiana State University Press, 1953), p. 10. For a bibliography on IGR see Deil S. Wright and Thomas E. Peddicord, *Intergovernmental Relations in the United States: Selected Books and Documents on Federalism and National-State-Local Relations* (Philadelphia, Pa.: Center for the Study of Federalism, Temple University, 1973).

12. Frothingham v. Mellon and Massachusetts v. Mellon, 262 U.S. 447 (1923).

13. United States v. Butler, 297 U.S. 1 (1936). See also *The Constitution of the United States of America: Analysis and Interpretation* (Washington, D.C.: Government Printing Office, 1964), pp. 144-149 for a discussion of "Spending for the General Welfare."

Amendment empowering the national government to tax income from whatever source derived. The amazing productivity of the income tax has facilitated fund-raising to finance grant outlays.

The productivity of the income tax could also be construed as an economic as well as a legal underpinning for grants. While national tax revenues expand at a greater rate than the GNP does, state and local revenues have lagged behind citizens' desires and demands for public services. Grants are a means of bridging this gap between revenues and expenditures. Another, more sophisticated economic factor helps explain the use of grants: the concept of externalities, or spillovers. Economists use these terms to denote the consequences, both positive and negative, that spread beyond the boundaries of one or more jurisdictions in which given behavior or an event occurs. For example, a negative externality occurs when a city pollutes a river for downstream users; a positive externality would occur when a state provided excellent higher education but a high percentage of its graduates migrated to other states. The burdens or benefits that cross jurisdictional boundaries form an economic rationale for instituting a system of grants. The grants either compensate a unit or provide it incentives by underwriting the costs of the externalities.

Political factors have played a strong role in the creation of grant-in-aid programs. (This may seem a simple truism or a tautology, since it is hard to imagine a statute that does not involve some degree of political consideration, yet it must be kept in mind.) One factor is a strong and continued preference for local or state activity as opposed to federal action. The apparently unabated citizen preference for localism favors continued active use of grants. A second political factor is the noncentralized character of the U.S. political party system. Morton Grodzins has argued most persuasively that the undisciplined nature of political parties produced the noncentralized character of IGR.[14] The grant device is merely a means to cope with political realities.

A third political factor linked to grants is presidential initiative. For centralizing presidents such as Franklin D. Roosevelt and Lyndon B. Johnson, grants were important instruments for achieving their policy and political aims. Even Eisenhower and Nixon, two presidents philosophically inclined to decentralization, found issues associated with grants a fertile field for policy initiatives; that is, highways and education for Eisenhower, block grants and revenue sharing for Nixon.

---

14. Morton Grodzins, "American Political Parties and the American System," *Western Political Quarterly*, 13 (December 1960): 974–998.

The IGR policy positions of the Democratic and Republican parties and presidents from both parties have varied. For example, the 1924 Democratic platform contained a plank on "the rights of states" which condemned the "centralizing and destructive tendencies of the Republican Party [which attempts] to nationalize the functions and duties of the states."[15]

A fourth political force generating, extending, and expanding grant programs is the "triple alliance" made up of an interest group, a congressional subcommittee, and an administrative agency responsible for the grant program. The interest group, in many instances, is virtually identical to the vertical functional "pickets" described, in chapter 3, in the competitive, or "picket fence," phase of IGR.

The triple alliance is focused toward substantive policy questions. This focus leads directly to a final factor contributing to the creation of grants, that is, programmatic considerations. Grants are ostensibly designed to meet a need or to cope with or alleviate a problem. Grant programs address substantive policy concerns or purposes. These purposes may or may not be specified in the grant legislation, and even when specified, may be broad and ambiguous. The absence of explicit, clearly specified purposes, of course, makes the task of evaluating grant programs very difficult. Yet from the array of existing grants several implicit and explicit aims may be gleaned, among them: stimulate new programs; maintain minimum service levels; raise service levels; equalize services; improve administrative and program performance; promote community or regional economic development; counter the business cycle and stabilize the national economy; ease special hardship conditions; encourage experimentation or pilot demonstrations; and encourage planning. These and other purposes have served as energizers for major expansions in grant programs.

Grant Growth

So far our discussion of grants has emphasized their numbers and proliferation and their complexity and problems. A quarter-century perspective on the fiscal magnitude of grants and their fiscal significance will demonstrate why they became a focal point for reform efforts and policy changes in the 1970s. Table 6–2 provides pertinent

---

15. Kirk H. Porter and Donald Bruce Johnson, *National Party Platforms: 1840–1964* (Urbana: University of Illinois Press, 1966), p. 249.

Table 6-2. *Impact of Federal Grant Outlays Relative to Governmental Expenditures, 1950-1978*

| | Grants (millions) | Federal Grants as a Percent of: | | State and Local Outlays[b] |
| | | Federal Outlays | | |
		Total	Domestic[a]	
1950	$ 2,253	5.3	8.8	10.4
1955	3,207	4.7	12.1	10.1
1960	7,020	7.6	15.9	14.7
1965	10,904	9.2	16.6	15.3
1970	24,018	12.2	21.1	19.4
1971	28,109	13.3	21.4	19.9
1972	34,372	14.8	22.8	22.0
1973	41,832	17.0	24.8	24.3
1974	43,308	16.1	23.3	22.7
1975	49,723	15.3	21.3	23.2
1976	59,037	16.1	21.7	24.7
1977 estimate	70,424	17.1	23.1	26.7
1978 estimate	71,581	16.3	22.3	25.0

[a]Excluding national defense and international programs.
[b]As defined in the National Income Accounts.
Source: Special Analysis O, *Budget of the United States Government, 1978, Special Analyses* (Washington, D.C.: Government Printing Office, 1977), p. 273.

data from 1950 through 1978 (estimated). In absolute dollars, grants rose from about $2.3 billion in 1950 to more than $70 billion in 1977 and 1978. These federal aid outlays more than doubled in each of three five-year spans: 1955-1960, 1965-1970, and 1970-1975. Despite the decentralizing doctrines of the New Federalism, federal aid outlays still doubled between 1972 and 1977. The average annual rate of growth in grants has been about 15 percent.

There are several explanations for the increases. One is that the amount of the increases is inflated, because the budget table fails to separate General Revenue Sharing (GRS) from the "grant" totals. Making that separation would subtract approximately $6 billion from each of the 1973-1977 amounts, to conform to the more restricted use of the term *grant* within the total scheme of federal aid. Another explanation for recent increases is that Nixon's New Federalism was not uniformly or universally decentralist in its doctrines. On the contrary, one component of the New Federalism, national responsibility for income security, had centralizing administrative and fiscal effects. The recent large increases are all the more noteworthy because of the strong opposition to new categorical grant programs by the Nixon and Ford administrations. Yet nearly 100 more grant programs were created in the Nixon-Ford years. Like Eisenhower, Nixon was unable to stop growth in the number of grant programs; and the dollar growth in grants continued at an equal or greater pace. The 1970 to 1977 large dollar increases have been chiefly in existing grant programs. The concentration of funds in a few large programs is evident from a single statistic. Of the 525 existing grants, the 25 largest constitute 82 percent of the total monetary outlays.

The changing significance of grants in the larger federal and state-local fiscal contexts is apparent from the proportions in the other three columns of table 6–2. In the 1950s grants were about 5 percent of all federal expenditures and 9–12 percent of federal domestic outlays; by 1965 they approximated 10 and 15 percent respectively; and by the early 1970s almost 15 and more than 20 percent respectively. These proportions attest to the increased attention that intergovernmental policy matters have received from the president, the Congress, and federal administrators. In relative as well as absolute terms grants have become so large that they draw, if not demand, the attention of national policy makers. Grants currently constitute more than one-fifth of the domestic budget.

The increasing significance of grants at the state-local level is indicated by the rightmost column of table 6–2. Federal funds have become a regularly rising proportion of the aggregate state-local sector. Between 1950 and 1978 the leaps have been progressive, from 10 to 15 to 20 to 25 percent. The estimate for 1978 shows a slight drop but the share remains above 25 percent. To say that state and local officials must pay attention to actions in Washington is an understatement; what happens in D.C. is part of the daily operating realities for numerous state and local officials.

If the approximate 1-to-2 ($1 of state-local money to $2 of federal) matching requirements that accompany the federal funds are taken into account, it is not unlikely that from one-third to two-fifths of aggregate state-local budgets are directly influenced by federal grant dollars. But because dollars in state and local budgets are not neatly compartmentalized, the indirect effects of these grant funds could be substantially greater. Moreover, because state or local jurisdictions show large variations around these mean proportionate impacts, the direct and indirect effects of federal funds probably exceeds 50 percent of the budgets of some states and many local units.

Table 6–3. *Functional Distribution of Federal Grants-in-Aid (in percents)*

	1952	1957	1962	1967	1972	1975	1977[a]	1978[a]
Natural resources & environment	1	1	2	2	2	5	7	8
Agriculture	4	9	6	3	1	1	b	b
Commerce & transportation	18	24	36	27	15	12	12	14
Community development	1	1	3	6	9	7	8	8
Education, employment, & social services	9	8	8	25	26	23	22	20
Health	8	4	5	10	17	18	18	19
Income security	57	49	38	25	26	19	18	18
Revenue sharing	2	3	2	2	1	14	13	11
Other	–	1	–	–	1	2	2	2
Total	100	100	100	100	100	100	100	100

[a]Estimated.
[b]Less than 0.5%.
Source: Special Analysis O, *Budget of the United States Government, 1977, Special Analyses,*
p. 261; 1977 and 1978 estimates from the Special Analysis for 1978 (Washington, D.C.), p. 271.

Not only have grants increased in number and fiscal significance through the years, they have also shifted in functional focus. Table 6–3 shows grant priorities by broad functional categories over the past quarter-century. The proportions are based, of course, on constantly increasing and widely varying dollar amounts (indicated earlier in table 6–2).

Prior to 1967 the commerce and transportation and the income security categories, although declining from percentages of earlier years, nevertheless commanded the bulk of grant funds; highways and public assistance were, respectively, the major grant programs in these two functional fields. By 1967, however, education and associated services had come to receive one-fourth of all grant funds, and the two aforementioned categories continued to decline. The relative decline in the commerce and income-security functions continued into the 1970s as education and revenue sharing gained still more prominence. Since 1967 community development has occupied a noteworthy niche, and since 1975 natural resources (environment and energy) have experienced a sharp rise.

Examination of the estimated 1977 and 1978 distributions leads to one evident conclusion about grant priorities among functional fields: Grant funds are more nearly uniformly dispersed among the major functions than at any other time in the past twenty-five years.

This dispersal, along with the programmatic reasons given earlier, also explains the absolute growth of grants. Congressional committees, executive branch agencies, interest groups, and professional associations from all segments of society and the economy—and representing virtually every interest—have pressed to get "a piece of the action" in the federal grant policy arena.

Classifications of Grants

Grant programs can be classified in many ways. We have already described one classification scheme, based mainly on the degree of program specificity and grantor control: the division between categorical and block grants. Another scheme already mentioned is the distinction between project and formula grants; of 525 cash-supported grant programs, over 400 were project grants, about 100 were formula grants, and the remainder were a mix of both. Project grants require positive action by a prospective recipient to secure funds, whereas formula grants are divided among all qualifying units as a matter of entitlement. Thus, project grants require voluntary involvement and gamesmanship among recipients, but formula grants allocate pre-fixed amounts according to one or more distributional factors.

Another major way of classifying grants is according to their matching requirements. Some grants do not require matching funds from recipients, while others have low matching ratios, for example, 1:2, 1:3, 1:9. A lesser number of grants have high matching ratios, such as 1:1 or 2:1.

Grants can also be classified by intended or eligible recipient, for example, state governments as opposed to local units; or, more specifically, general governments as opposed to special districts; or among types of local unit (say city as opposed to county). There are several additional ways in which grants could be classified. Among these are: open-ended versus closed-ended, regular versus variable matching, cash versus in-kind matching.

To describe the configuration of grant programs and to examine their effects, we will use three of the classification schemes: those of eligible recipient, matching requirement, and formula/project. Table 6-4 provides information on numbers of grants with various combinations of these three grant features and their dollar amounts. The ACIR study from which the data are drawn analyzed 100 major grant programs for the year 1972, when grants totaled nearly $36 billion.

Revenue sharing had not yet been included in grant totals. For seventy-five grants, totaling more than $32 billion, it was possible to identify where each fit in one of the sixteen cells in table 6-4—that is, its unique combination of these three criteria.

The table reveals prominent grant policy patterns. Not surprisingly, the states were the primary recipients of federal grants, receiving nearly $27 billion in formula and project grants—almost 85 percent of the total grant funds identified in this analysis. Although the states were primary recipients of almost $3 billion in project grants, the greater bulk of the grants were formula. And whereas it required thirty-six grant programs to disburse the $3 billion in project monies, only eighteen formula grants spread eight times that much money among the states. Local units were primary clients for more than $5 billion in grant funds, more than 85 percent of them project grants. Thus, local units must rely heavily on grantsmanship and gamesmanship.

Totals in the rightmost column of table 6-4 reveal a heavy bias toward low matching ratios for federal grants. In 1972 about $4.7 billion (about 15 percent of the total) was available without any state-local match, and $25.6 billion (about 80 percent) was in the low matching classification. The states were the primary recipients of nonmatching grants: Of twenty-eight grants totaling some $4.7 billion only five programs totaling slightly over $1.1 billion were available in 1972 to local units as nonmatching grants:

Disaster relief preparedness	$ 90 million
Work experience and training	228
Emergency school assistance	70
Manpower development and training	143
School assistance in federally affected areas (formula)	599

No doubt these funds occasioned a high degree of competition and grantsmanship.

Of the twenty-three nonmatching grants to the states, three were formula grants:

Elementary and secondary education	$1,883 million
Jobs	37
Landscaping and scenic enhancement	2

Table 6–4. *Number of Federal Grants and Dollar Amounts by Matching, Recipient, and Classification Schemes, 1972*

Primary Recipient State or Local Matching Requirement	States		Local Units		Totals
	Formula	Project	Formula	Project	
	(millions of dollars; numbers of grants in parentheses)				
None	$ 1,922(3)	1,680(20)	599(1)	529(4)	4,730(28)
Low (less than 1:1)	20,842(10)	1,155(12)	156(1)	3,452(8)	25,605(31)
High (1:1 or higher)	1,129(4)	125(4)		517(6)	1,771(14)
Undetermined	16(1)			87(1)	103(2)
Totals	$23,909(18)	2,960(36)	755(2)	4,585(19)	$32,209(75)

Source: Advisory Commission on Intergovernmental Relations, *Federal Grants: Their Effects on State-Local Expenditures Employment Levels, Wage Rates* (Washington, D.C.: Government Printing Office, February 1977, A-61), p. 27.

The first of these is the large federal aid-to-education program that channels funds through the states. The last, a "dribble" grant, is a remnant of the billboard-removal program along interstate highways. Because it could not directly and legally prohibit advertising signs along major federally supported highways, the federal government provided a small supplementary grant designed to induce the states to regulate roadside advertising. Most states complied to get the "free" money.

Grant Effects

The effects that grants have on a particular receiving jurisdiction can be described with greater specificity and precision than we have yet done. Two broad types of jurisdiction-specific effects can be identified: those that are fiscal and those that affect policy choice. Although the two types of effects are not separable in practice, they can be separated for analysis.

Fiscal Effects.   Do grants that a state or a local unit receives alter or "distort" its expenditure patterns? For example, do grant monies with matching requirements pull funds away from programs that might otherwise be funded to raise the matching amount and obtain the grant? As we see later, many state officials believe that federal grants skew or unbalance state programs. But is there hard evidence to support this frequently mentioned, controversial fiscal effect of grants? Despite a substantial amount of research on the issue, there is no simple, unqualified answer.

To more clearly understand the question, let us identify three possible fiscal effects that a grant could have: stimulative, additive, and substitutive. First, the grant could *stimulate* the recipient unit to put up any matching funds necessary to secure the grant and provide the service or program. This condition, however, although commonly supposed to occur, rests on an unsatisfactorily loose definition of fiscal stimulation. It equates stimulation with the receipt of any type of matching grant solely because outside (federal) funds were secured. The extensiveness of grantsmanship—chasing federal dollars because they are there—suggests a rethinking of the concept. I contend that a *stimulative* fiscal effect occurs only when the recipient unit raises its financial support for the grant program or project by *more* than the required matching amount. By this standard a federal grant would be stimulative not simply because a unit "chased" and obtained it but rather because the unit did *more* than the bare minimum needed to secure the funds. Since doing the minimum is so widespread a practice—is perhaps nearly universal—it is useful to have a more rigorous standard of recipient response.

The second type of fiscal effect from a grant is *additive,* meaning that the expenditure increase from the grant is equal to the amount of the grant plus any matching funds supplied by the recipient. (Thus our definition of *additive* is identical to the definition of *stimulative* that was dismissed above.) Of course, if no match is required, then the *additive* effect would be identical to the amount of the grant. It might appear on the surface that every grant must be additive: Whether matched or not, when a unit or agency receives a grant it is virtually certain to spend all the money. To do otherwise would be to commit a cardinal sin of grantsmanship—namely, to leave the impression that not all the requested monies were needed.

But a clear distinction must be drawn between *spending* the grant monies, that is, paying salaries, and the net fiscal effect of *receiving* the grant in the first place. Just as money to match a grant may "pull away" funds from another program, so may the receipt of other grants release funds to be allocated to an activity that is not grant-assisted; or the recipient might be able to reduce or hold down taxes. In its actual fiscal effect, then, a grant could either "pull toward" or "push away" funds from the grant-assisted program. For our purposes we will use the term *substitutive* to apply to the latter case, that is, where a grant permits a shifting of a recipient's own-source funds away from the aided program.

An illustrative substitutive effect occurred in North Carolina in 1975. Block grant manpower (CETA) funds were available for hiring temporary summer employees in the State Division of Highways. The news article and chart in Appendix F, "Federal Job Money Is Going Awry," reveal the pattern and process by which the State Highway Division was able to conserve its own "hard" money. The Highway Division used CETA funds to hire temporary employees who, without those funds, would probably have been financed from state resources. However, more employees were hired in 1975 than in 1974.

If CETA funds were, in part, *substitutive,* where did the state funds go that were thus released? Here we enter a fiscal thicket that is well nigh impenetrable. We cannot trace a path through the dense, tangled brambles and bushes of (in this instance) the North Carolina state budget. We can say, however, that the substitutive effect of a grant is evident from this case, and thus that these monies are *fungible,* or interchangeable.

Let us now rephrase our original question on the fiscal effects of federal grants: Are federal grants stimulative, additive, or substitutive? Depending on the recipient unit, the function or program supported, and the grant, any one of the three fiscal effects might occur. One of the more sophisticated of many recent studies of aggregate grant effects, relying on simultaneous equation analysis, produced rather interesting results.

Professor Thomas O'Brien studied combined state-local expenditures for the forty-eight continental states from 1958 through 1966.[16] To draw inferences about state-local own-source outlays, he subdivided grants and state-local expenditures by major functional categories and subtracted the federal grant amounts. His results, indicated below, are measures or coefficients that show the dollar and cents increase in state-local own-source expenditures for each $1.00 of federal aid received.

Education	$1.64	Highways	.04
Health	.67	Other expenditures	.44
Welfare	.53	Total general exp.	.52

That is, for each dollar of federal aid received there was an increase in state-local outlays of, for example, $1.64 for education. It seems clear that this state-local fiscal response should be placed in the stimulative class, although we cannot say that the federal aid *caused* this sharp increase in state-local expenditures between 1958 and 1966. Other forces, such as increased enrollment, were also present.

The amounts of $.67 and $.53 for health and welfare, respectively, suggest a stimulative effect. Before jumping to this conclusion, however, we must recall that the state-local matching amounts necessary to obtain the grants are buried in the state-local own-source outlays for these functions. For example, let us make the reasonable assumption that the average matching ratio for the two functions just named is 1:2. That is, $.50 of state or local own-source money will secure $1.00 in federal aid for health and welfare. Given these ratios, our initial

---

16. Thomas O'Brien, "Grants-In-Aid: Some Further Answers," *National Tax Journal,* 24 (March 1971): 65–77.

judgment requires cautious qualification. Only a figure (coefficient) showing an increase above $.50 can be classed as stimulative. The effects of federal grants to health between 1958 and 1966 appear slightly stimulative—by about $.17 on the dollar. For welfare, federal grant funds are almost exactly additive.

The highway figure is instructive. Remember that the state/federal matching ratio for a major segment of highway aid (the interstate system) is 1:9. The exceptionally low figure of $.04 forces the conclusion that federal highway aid was strongly substitutive during the period studied: A great deal of state resources leaked or shifted away from highway spending. The figure for "other" expenditures cannot be interpreted easily because this is a composite category, so a reasonable matching ratio is difficult to estimate. The figure for total general expenditures (the sum of the five types of expenditures) can be sensibly judged if we use a 1:2 matching ratio for aggregate federal grants. The conclusion follows that during the period examined the aggregate effect of federal aid was additive.

Evidence from several other research studies covering different periods tends to confirm this conclusion. Although many particular programs or functions show clearly stimulative effects, federal grants, in the aggregate, are additive.[17] It should be mentioned that little research covers the period of the late 1960s and 1970s. Nevertheless, we can hypothesize that the large increases in federal aid funds have either sustained the additive effect or have shifted perceptibly toward a substitutive effect. Future research will confirm or correct this hypothesis.

Policy Choice Effects. We leave the fairly precise realm of quantified fiscal data and enter a qualitative and judgmental one: We now attempt to assess how the policy choices made by state and local decision makers are affected by grants. Although no single broad-scale, validated hypothesis has yet been made or confirmed, several hypotheses of narrower scope seem promising, and are indeed accepted by most IGR practitioners and scholars. They are as follows:

1. Because an aided program can be pursued at less of a financial sacrifice than an unaided one, state and local officials are encouraged to alter their agenda of issues. Subsidizing home repair loans, providing

---

17. For a review and evaluation of some of this research as well as original analyses and results see two articles: Russell Harrison, "Federal Categorical Grants and the Stimulation of State-Local Expenditures," and Laura Irwin, "Expenditure Effects of Federal Aid: Data Aggregation and the Risk of Uncertainty," in *Publius: The Journal of Federalism* 5 (Fall 1975): 123–136 and 137–160 respectively.

rural fire protection, and other activities might never seem feasible to officials unless the availability of outside support prompted them to pose a fundamental policy question: Why not?

2. Grants alter the scheme of priorities that state-local decision makers implicitly or explicitly hold when making a choice on programs or policies. By, in effect, lowering the "price" of a public good or service, a grant can influence the preferences of state or local officials with respect to that good or service. It may even be a "free good," as is the case with nonmatching, block grant manpower (CETA) and community development (CD) funds allocated on a formula basis to cities and counties. One observer, speaking at a roundtable session on block grants, described these effects:

> many local jurisdictions now receiving manpower and community development funds were not really involved in these programs before. All block grants have a precise eligibility formula compared to most of the categoricals. We're putting cities and counties in a ball game they never heard of and didn't ask to be in. What does that do to the generalists? For them, in a sense, it is new money which might confer some discretion compared with the position of others who have been in the HUD or Labor Department pipeline before. Yet, these cities and counties often don't have the professional staff to counteract the influence of the line agency people.[18]

3. Grants have the potential to alter the decision-making hierarchy in state and local governments. In the quote above, the observer notes that even block grants, which are aimed in part at giving more discretion to generalist officials, may not have that effect. Because all grants are conditional and have a functional focus, they engender a powerful programmatic emphasis among the specialists in any field receiving grants. This effect, of course, is largely a reiteration of the "picket fence" phenomenon of vertical functional autocracies, balkanized bureaucracies, functional feudal federalisms, etc. One of the most succinct descriptions of altered power relationships was given at the same roundtable session just quoted from. The speaker was discussing the "opening up" of social-service activities under the 1974 block grant program (Title XX).

> Title XX prescribed for the first time that this planning process be open to public review. The welfare bureaucracies in the states are pretty much closed

---

18. ACIR, *Block Grants: A Roundtable Discussion*, pp. 24–25. Quoted statement of Dr. David Walker.

systems (as was HEW for many years). They are vertical power systems with a lot of federal-state interaction. There were many times the state directors would have the federal regulations come out so that governors and other controlling people would have to do certain things. Welfare directors at the county level would go to county supervisors and say they needed a lot of money to do these things because the state required it, because the feds had made them do it that way.[19]

Potent centrifugal forces propel program specialists toward greater autonomy from legislators, executives, etc. And block grant reforms of old categoricals are no assurance that such "picket fence" tendencies will automatically be held in check.

4. Related to the prior point is the policy consequence of giving federal administrative officials powers of review, oversight, and approval over state and local elected officials. The national administrators have assumed such a crucial role because they control, to a large extent, both the funding approvals and the detailed regulations under which the grant programs operate. The shift toward block grants allocated on a formula basis is designed to restrain federal administrative discretion and allow state and local officials more flexible policy choices. Another set of observations made at the block grant roundtable—although addressed specifically to HUD's plan approval under the community development program—are relevant here:

> . . . I have heard from HUD officials in the area offices and local officials frequently enough so that I believe it was a common assumption that the burden of proof in terms of acceptability of the application has shifted. Under the categoricals, it was up to the community to prove that its application satisfied the spirit and the letter of the law, whereas now the HUD area office must prove that the application is not satisfying the Community Development Act.
>
> I think the communities going into this, at least for the first time, and the HUD area people really did operate in a way indicating that they did believe there was a shift. I think HUD's approval of all but three applications indicates that they were really willing to let the communities go the first year.[20]

5. Linked to the preceding point is the issue of whose policy preferences will prevail. Federal grants bring about a direct confrontation between conflicting national and state or local policy preferences. The constituency of national decision makers is entirely different from that

---

19. Ibid., p. 7. Quoted statement of Mr. Jerry Turem.
20. Ibid., p. 16. Quoted statement of Dr. Sarah Liebschutz.

to which state or local officials respond. Federal statutory and administrative requirements concerning, say, health policies or highway location, interject policy objectives that may conflict sharply with state or local views of what is desirable or necessary in a given program area.

6. Grants normally carry a number of procedural "strings" that can, and often do, have important policy consequences for a receiving unit. For example, although requirements for public hearings and for administration by a single agency may be intended only to set the procedural framework for grant-aided programs, in practice they can be critical to the program's outcome.

7. Finally, grants may restructure the hierarchy of influence within a state or a local community, producing not only gains or losses in influence among executives, legislators, and administrators, but also significantly changing the power potential of interest groups and associations.

The aforementioned effects of federal grants emphasize the noise and conflict that can occur in IGR; they underscore the "picket fence," competitive phase of IGR more than the creative and cooperative phases. Changes in the presidency and in the attitudes of officials in the Congress, in state capitols, county courthouses, and city halls produced a readiness to examine new options on federal aid policies. The national policy toward IGR was in a state of flux in the early 1970s. Categorical and project grants had lost their glitter, and there was a lively, wide-ranging search for changes and improvements.

The Advisory Commission on Intergovernmental Relations and many other participants trained their rifles on middle-range reform targets. Among these were improved grant program information, periodic grant review (a type of "sunset" legislation on grant programs), joint funding, improved financial management, program coordination, and block, or consolidated, grants. Many misses and a few bull's-eyes perhaps best describe the tally on IGR policy shifts. But the big guns promoting IGR policy changes had also trained their sights on larger game. As might be suspected from prior discussions in the local and state chapters, General Revenue Sharing (GRS) was their prize trophy.

GENERAL REVENUE SHARING

General Revenue Sharing (GRS) is seen by many as the main jewel in the New Federalism crown of the Nixon administration. Despite the tarnish suffered by that administration, GRS remains a notable, if controversial and impermanent part of a diversified federal aid policy that covers categorical grants, block grants, and unconditional aid (GRS). The significant, variable impacts of GRS on states and local units and officials were examined in chapters 4 and 5. With respect to national public policy making, three aspects of GRS are pertinent to IGR: its origins, its purposes, and its extension (renewal).

The Origins of GRS

The first modern-day tax sharing bill was introduced by Congressman Melvin Laird (Rep.–Wisconsin) in 1958. It provided for the return to each state of a fixed percentage of the federal income tax collected from that state. Patterning the bill after an income tax sharing scheme in Wisconsin, Laird offered it as a replacement for the growing number and variety of categorical grants. The bill gained little serious consideration. Then, in 1964, revenue sharing received top billing when it was articulately advocated by Walter Heller, Chairman of the Council of Economic Advisors. A task force within the Johnson administration gave GRS serious study, and it was a plank in the Republican party platform of both 1964 and 1968.

What national factors contributed to the rising national attention to, and ultimate passage of GRS? And why is it on the statute books today? Several factors can be briefly noted.

Fiscal Factors. Several fiscal factors pushed GRS to the fore. There was the mismatch between national revenues and state-local expenditures, as illustrated and discussed in the preceding chapters. There was concern over the inadequate supply of public goods and services, for example, education, health, sanitation, police and fire protection. There was even apprehension that the national government would have a surplus of "fiscal dividend." That condition would exert a fiscal drag on the economy unless provision for its allocation was anticipated.[21]

Partisan Politics. Revenue sharing was favored and pushed strongly

---

21. For development of this and other pertinent IGR points see Walter W. Heller, *New Dimensions of Political Economy* (Cambridge, Mass.: Harvard University Press, 1966), esp. pp. 117–172.

by several prominent Republicans. Its support by many (though not all) conservatives (both Democratic and Republican) made liberal Democrats wary of supporting GRS. An unpublished, favorable task force report on GRS was delivered to President Johnson shortly after his smashing victory in 1964. He chose to reject that report and opted for the array of categorical and project grants—largely, it was claimed, at the urging of labor and the public school lobbyists. By the late 1960s and early 1970s a substantial number (but not a majority) of Democrats, among them Senator Muskie, were ready to support some form of GRS.

Decline of Party Politics. A strong case has been made that GRS could be pushed and finally passed because discipline and issue-orientation had declined within the two major political parties. This decomposition of party allegiance, cohesion, and commitment to issues in the Congress paved the way for GRS. In this party vacuum GRS could become a prominent policy issue.[22]

Intergovernmental Politics. If party decay was not enough, by itself, to bring GRS into being, into the power vacuum it created stepped the "intergovernmental lobby." This lobby is simply another term to describe the Big Seven or the Public Interest Groups (PIGs). Because this lobby was spearheaded by governors, mayors, and county executives it has also been called the "executive coalition." During 1971 and 1972 "jet-ins" by several hundred city and county officials from "back home" were arranged at critical legislative junctures. These officials, accosting their representatives and senators both individually and collectively, raised more than a few eyebrows on Capitol Hill. More importantly, they altered congressional views on GRS.

As an illustration, one episode can stand for many: A confrontation between big-city mayors and the House Democratic leadership occurred over GRS on March 10, 1971. As reported later, the small group of no more than two dozen men were sparring verbally when New York City Mayor John Lindsay began a persuasive plea for GRS. Then, unexpectedly, House Majority Leader Hale Boggs (Dem.-Louisiana)

> suddenly slammed his fist on the desk and shouted: "You don't need to make any points. Revenue sharing is dead. I'll see that it never passes. So let's get

---

22. Samuel H. Beer, "The Adoption of General Revenue Sharing: A Case Study in Public Sector Politics," *Public Policy* (Spring 1976): 127–195.

on to something else." Flabbergasted, Lindsay slid back into his seat. There was a moment of embarrassed silence—and then a rolling Southern drawl rang out from the back of the room. "Hale," said New Orleans Mayor Moon Landrieu, "that's the rudest treatment I have ever witnessed, and I think you better talk about revenue sharing and you better listen. Because, Hale, if you don't start thinking about helping the cities, I want you to know you'll never be welcome in the city of New Orleans again." Now it was Boggs' turn to be flabbergasted.[23]

Among status-seeking and protocol-conscious Washington this upbraiding of a powerful veteran legislator by a first-term mayor was far more than merely a momentary shock. (Boggs's district, incidentally, included New Orleans.)

Influence of Prominent Persons. Walter Heller's 1964 endorsement of GRS was already mentioned. In the late 1960s and early 1970s it had the support of other prominent and powerful national officials. Foremost in pressing for GRS was President Nixon. He launched an opening public flurry in August 1969 and persevered through backstage bargaining sessions prior to GRS passage in October 1972.

Other central actors were John Connally, testifying on GRS as Secretary of the Treasury; Senator Russell Long, Chairman of the Senate Finance Committee; and Wilbur Mills, Chairman of the House Ways and Means Committee. Long and Mills chaired the two committees through which GRS was required to pass. Mills was an implacable opponent of GRS from the start.

On January 25, 1971, Mills emerged from a meeting with Nixon and acknowledged that he had agreed to hold hearings on revenue sharing bills. Yet Mills added, "I am perfectly willing to have hearings, but not for the purpose of promoting the plan—for the purpose of killing it."[24] Mills later called GRS "a Trojan Horse," "bad in principle because it separates the spending function from the revenue-raising responsibility," and a "no-strings-attached proposal that I am strongly and utterly opposed to."[25]

By December 25, 1971, Christmas Day, Mills had done what appeared to be a 180-degree turn: One of Governor Nelson Rockefel-

23. Quoted in Richard E. Thompson, *Revenue Sharing: A New Era in Federalism?* (Washington, D.C.: Revenue Sharing Advisory Service, 1973), p. 70.
24. Ibid., p. 67.
25. Ibid.

ler's aides flew to Mills's Arkansas home to pick up a letter Mills had written to the Governor. It said, in part:

> I want to give you and the leaders of the New York State Legislature my assurance that HR 11950 will be my top priority as soon as Congress resumes its work on January 18.
>
> The Ways and Means Committee plans to go into Executive Session on this Bill and related proposals as soon as the Session opens, and I am confident we can bring a bill out of Committee promptly and to the House Floor.
>
> In view of the broad support demonstrated for providing for Federal funds to localities, for high priority purposes and for providing funds to the states to encourage more effective use of their revenue sources, I am also confident that we will have a favorable vote in the House. Many House Members have talked to me about HR 11950 and other proposals and have told me they are in favor of passage early in the new Session.
>
> It is my belief that great understanding has developed in the Congress about the fiscal problems facing states, cities, counties and local communities throughout the Nation; and we who have the responsibility for leadership in Congress will assist in resolving these problems.[26]

What prompted Mills to reverse his stand on revenue sharing may never be known. It was reputedly his growing presidential aspirations for the 1972 nomination that altered his outlook on GRS.

Administrative Practicalities. GRS became an attractive policy option for two practical administrative reasons, one negative, the other positive. On the negative side, Congress, the president, the Office of Management and Budget, executive branch agencies, the ACIR, and almost any casual observer, had become acutely concerned over the tremendously complex operations that the proliferation of grants had generated. A variety of epithets were trotted out to describe the difficulties: administrative jungle, management morass, intergovernmental impotence, organized chaos. Whether or not these are overstatements, the terms, and the attitudes that generated them, made the apparent neatness and simplicity of GRS attractive. The idea that a $30-billion program could be administered by twenty clerks and a computer made a persuasive point for administrative practicality.

---

26. Ibid., p. 83.

It has, in fact, taken more than twenty clerks. The Office of Revenue Sharing, located in the Treasury Department—more by accident than by design—employs around 100 persons on an operating budget of about $3 million.[27] Much of that budget maintains a computer and massive data file on 39,022 units of government. The data file on each unit must be updated regularly for current calculations involving population, taxes, expenditures, etc. Every quarter the computer spews out thousands of checks that are addressed and slipped into waiting envelopes; these head for the waiting treasuries of those 39,022 cities, counties, townships, and states across the nation. Oh yes, the checks also go to 346 Indian tribes and Eskimo villages. Without the capacities of a computer, GRS in its present form would be impossible.

Public Popularity. Attention to the politics and practicalities of GRS should not cause us to forget that the $30 billion poured into state-local coffers from 1972 through 1976 was intended to do something beneficial for people—the public. How did the public feel about GRS? Or did they even know what it was?

In virtually all instances the public was spared having to identify or describe GRS. The opinion survey questions usually asked: "How do you feel about a plan that would return some of the federal tax money to the states and their localities for them to spend as they see fit?" Nevertheless, GRS struck the public's fancy. In national opinion polls presenting the question at varying times between 1965 and 1975 the proportion favorable to GRS rarely dropped below 60 percent, and usually hovered around 70–75 percent. Did the supporters know what they were supporting? No one knows how clearly or vaguely the respondents perceived GRS. We should not, however, chide the citizenry too much for uncertainty about GRS. A look at the stated aims or purposes of GRS posed problems for the Congress, recipients, researchers, and students of IGR.

GRS Purposes

What did the Congress intend when it passed GRS on October 13, 1972? For what purposes did the House and Senate create this largest of all federal aid programs? One standard means of determining legisla-

---

27. *The Budget of the United States Government, Fiscal Year 1978, Appendix* (Washington, D.C.: Office of Management and Budget, 1977), pp. 592–593.

tive intent is to examine the statute. Often there is a series of "whereas" clauses indicating why it is necessary for legislative action on a problem. And almost without fail there is a set of statements expressing the purposes to be achieved by the programs and processes set in motion by the legislation. (For an illustration of congressional purposes for a block grant program—Community Development—see Appendix G.)

A reading of Public Law 92-512 (the 1972 act) and its successor, P.L. 94-488 (the 1976 act extending GRS) provides an IGR researcher-analyst with a complete vacuum. There is no statement of purpose(s). GRS passed both houses of Congress without explicit purposes! This was not because the members of Congress lacked views about what GRS could, would, or should do. On the contrary, there were so many diverse and intensely held views about GRS that no single rationale or short statement of purposes appeared workable to legislative leaders guiding the fate of GRS.

The tremendously varied political quarters from which GRS drew support were nicely captured by two members of the House. Rep. John Anderson, Chairman of the House Republican Conference, led off debate for Republicans supporting GRS with purpose-oriented appeals to both wings of his party (and the House), "To my conservative friends . . . [here is a chance] to conserve federalism. To some of my liberal friends . . . [here is a chance] to ease the plight of our cities." Later in the debate House Speaker Carl Albert acknowledged the broad sources of support for GRS with comments that the bill "is not a Republican or a Democratic bill, neither is it a conservative nor a liberal bill."[28] If it was none of these, what was GRS? If support for the bill was broad, it was also uncertain. What were the diverse aims and purposes behind GRS that enabled its advocates to construct a winning coalition?

Most, if not all, of the identifiable purposes that supporters saw embodied in GRS can be grouped, somewhat crudely, along a liberal-conservative political spectrum.

Liberal
Help the poor and disadvantaged, especially in cities.
Provide cities with more funds to combat urban problems.
Equalize or redistribute funds to lower-income areas.
Finance more public goods and services.
Rely more on income taxation for public service financing.

28. As quoted in Beer, "Adoption of General Revenue Sharing," p. 193.

Moderate, Middle of the Road
Stimulate the use of state income taxes.
Promote the reform and modernization of state-local government.
Encourage innovation and experimentation at the state and local levels.
Ease the fiscal crunch on the cities and states.
Stabilize or reduce property taxes.
Strengthen generalists' control over functional bureaucrats.
Conservative
Decentralize power.
Contain or restrain the growth of the national government.
Cut "handling costs" of dollars entering and leaving Washington, D.C.
Substitute GRS for grants.

The purposes or probable results of GRS can be classified another way: the views held by different IGR participants as to what the probable effects of GRS would be. Three highly simplified outcomes of GRS can be posited: (1) a plague, (2) a panacea, and (3) a placebo.

Plague
Fiscal irresponsibility—"a kind of cancer";
local government boondoggle;
promotion of state-local waste, inefficiency, and corruption;
encouraging state-local *FTC* outlays (*F*rivolity, *T*hievery, and *C*hicanery);
buying mayors' reelection tickets;
giving governors senatorial nomination chits;
the greatest diversionary invention since the milking machine and the cream separator.
Panacea
Relieving fiscal drag;
bridging the revenue-expenditure gap;
saving cities from bankruptcy;
curing the categorical grant disease—"hardening of the categories";
restoring power to the generalists;
rescuing the hard-pressed state-local taxpayer;
reforming local government;
returning power to the people;
simple, neat, and correct.

Placebo
An insignificant financial dose;
a false fiscal fix;
a bandaid in place of an operation;
sugar water instead of a laxative;
conducive to incremental impotence.

Clearly, it was no easy task to sort out and sharpen the central issues on which GRS might stand or fall. To key strategists, putting together a winning coalition must have seemed like trying to build a ski slope out of Jell-O.

The range of views on GRS narrowed significantly, however, when the respective House and Senate committees completed many days of testimony and deliberations. The committees, required to justify favorable recommendations to their respective chambers, in their committee and conference reports, condensed the formal statements of purpose to meeting two needs: (1) the need to provide fiscal assistance to hard-pressed states and localities, and (2) the "need for a new type of federal aid."[29]

Justifying GRS as meeting state-local fiscal needs and as being a different kind of federal aid policy brought GRS a full 360 degrees back to its formal start. In his message of August 13, 1969, Nixon outlined and justified his proposal, "Federal Revenue Sharing with the States." He argued that "The fiscal case for Federal assistance to States and localities is a strong one." But the ardor in his phrases was strongest when he asserted, "we have hampered the effectiveness of local government by constructing a Federal grant-in-aid system of staggering complexity and diversity. Many of us question the efficiency of this intergovernmental financial system which is based on the Federal categorical grant."[30]

The president referred to six negative features of categorical grants that were to be avoided by GRS:

- Overlapping programs at the state and local level.
- Distortion of state and local budgets.
- Increased administrative costs.

---

29. *State and Local Fiscal Assistance Act of 1972,* House Committee on Ways and Means, 92nd Congress, 2nd Session, House Report 92-1018 (Part I), April 26, 1972, pp. 4–8.
30. "Text of President Nixon's Message on Revenue Sharing," *Congressional Quarterly Almanac,* Vol. 25, 91st Congress, 1st Session, 1969 (Washington, D.C.: Congressional Quarterly, Inc., 1970), p. 74–A.

- Program delay and uncertainty.
- A decline in the authority and responsibility of chief executives, as grants have become tied to functional bureaucracies.
- Creation of new and frequently competitive state and local governmental institutions.

There is no way to know what purposes of GRS persuaded which members of Congress to vote Yea or Nay on GRS. The crucial vote came in the House on June 21, 1972, and involved voting to consider GRS under a closed rule (no amendments). The vote was 223–185 in favor of the closed rule (pro-GRS), with Republicans voting 113–57 and Democrats 110–128. Two-thirds of the House Republicans and nearly half the House Democrats supported GRS. The Senate adopted it nearly three months later (September 12) by a large margin, 65–20.

GRS Extension

GRS had been made possible partly by the influence of the IGR executive coalition that encompassed mayors, county executives, governors, and the president. GRS was due to expire at the end of 1976, and a persistent question from 1973 through 1976 was whether the executive-based intergovernmental lobby could sustain its effectiveness and secure the extension (*and* expansion) of GRS.

It was anticipated that the renewal of GRS would hinge on two factors: the results of the five-year, $30-billion experiment, and the political muscle that the Big Seven public interest groups could exert as the time for extension approached. The first factor was amenable to research, evaluation, and reasonable approximation. The second could only be ascertained at the moment of critical executive and legislative decisions. Evidence is available chiefly on the first factor as it affected renewal prospects. Before that evidence is summarized a few features of GRS should be noted.

First, a relatively small number of jurisdictions received a major portion of the money. For example, the 465 largest cities (population over 50,000) received 52 percent of the $2 billion distributed annually to cities. (They contained about 47 percent of total city populations.) Second, the formula for allocating the funds was exceedingly complex and was poorly understood by most legislators. Indeed, during the House debate one Ways and Means Committee member opposed to GRS explained the problem in this half-sarcastic fashion:

We finally quit, not because we hit on a rational formula, but because we were exhausted. And finally, we got one that almost none of us could understand at the moment. We were told that the statistics were not available to run the [computer] print on it. So we adopted it, and it is here for you today.[31]

Third, heavy criticism had been trained on GRS by civil rights, social welfare, and social action groups. These criticisms ranged widely but clustered around three fundamental policy concerns:

1. the insensitivity of state and local governments to the needs of the poor and disadvantaged in the use of GRS funds;
2. basic distrust of the honesty, integrity, and leadership shown (or not shown) by state and local officials;
3. lack of expertise, professionalism, and management capacity to make reasoned decisions with unfettered resources such as GRS.

A sampling of press articles and editorial opinions suggests the sentiment against GRS:

- "Revenue-Sharing a Trap After All—Fire Trucks Before Mental Health" (March 1973).
- "Revenue Sharing: Too Much for Brick, Mortar" (July 1973).
- "Revenue Sharing: The Grandest of Boondoggles" (January 1975).
- "Revenue Sharing Record Shows Glaring Inadequacies" (February 1976).
- "Revenue Sharing Record Flawed" (March 1976).
- "U.S. Revenue-Sharing Program Attacked as Defect-Ridden by Public Interest Units" (March 1976).
- "Revenue Sharing Evil Here to Stay" (June 1976).[32]

When the 1976 renewal moved through the House in June 1976 without a major overhaul the *New York Times* commented critically:

The Washington lobby of elected local officials has been telling the House of Representatives that, in effect, almost nothing in the General Revenue Sharing program should be changed. Their argument flies in the face of intelli-

31. As quoted in Paul R. Dommel, *The Politics of Revenue Sharing* (Bloomington: University of Indiana Press, 1974), p. 158.
32. Clippings in author's files from *Raleigh News and Observer, Durham Morning Herald,* and *Wall Street Journal.*

gent analysis, for it suggests that in spending $30 billion over a five-year period the nation has learned nothing of value. That is clearly not the case.[33]

What was learned from experience with GRS? During 1974–1975 the National Science Foundation (NSF) funded eighteen research projects, totaling more than $3 million in outlays, on GRS. Nine of the projects dealt with various features of the intricate formula; the other nine centered on issues involving civil rights, fiscal impacts, effects of inflation, public and community leaders' views of GRS, planning and citizen participation, and city or state decision-making impacts. A ninety-eight-page "synthesis" of the latter group of studies presented a distillation of findings from the evaluation research effort.[34] The major features and findings of that research were reported in chapters 4 and 5 on local and state impacts of GRS.

A less ambitious, more interpretive, and federally oriented evaluation of GRS was conducted by the ACIR late in 1974. The Commission report presented sixteen findings on GRS based on approximately two years' experience with the program.

1. Despite the presence of certain Federal conditions on the use of revenue sharing funds, state and local policymakers have enjoyed wide discretion in the use of the dollars.
2. General revenue sharing tends to equalize fiscal capacities of rich and poor states.
3. General revenue sharing provides far more financial aid to the nation's major central cities than to rich suburban communities.
4. The equalizing thrust of the revenue sharing allocation formula is blunted by the provision that no county area or municipal or township government shall receive less than 20 percent nor more than 145 percent of the average local per capita entitlement.
5. General revenue sharing is gradually being eroded by inflation.
6. General revenue sharing appears to be gaining public support.
7. Since the enactment of the revenue sharing program, total Federal aid outlays have continued to increase in absolute

33. *New York Times*, June 12, 1976.
34. National Science Foundation/Research Applied to National Needs, *General Revenue Sharing Research Utilization Project*, Vol. 4, *Synthesis of Impact and Process Research* (Washington, D.C.: Government Printing Office, December 1975). See also Vol. 2, *Summaries of Impact and Process Research* (September 1975).

terms but have declined somewhat in relation to total state and local expenditures.

8. While there is no legal mandate calling for citizen participation in decisions on the use of revenue sharing funds, the publicity attending the enactment of the program and the distribution of the funds along with the requirement that recipients publish Planned Use and Actual Use Reports stimulated some additional citizen participation and concern in determining local budget priorities.

9. Because revenue sharing dollars can be substituted for equal amounts of state and local revenue from their own sources, many of the conditions on the use of revenue sharing funds are largely cosmetic in character, and the Planned Use and Actual Use Reports are of little value for analysis of the ultimate impact of the program.

10. At this time it is virtually impossible to determine on an aggregate basis how revenue sharing funds have been spent.

11. Although revenue sharing has come under fire for short-changing the poor there is no way to prove or disprove this allegation because the requisite data do not exist.

12. The use of Federal general revenue sharing to stabilize or to reduce state and local taxes precipitated a debate at the beginning of the program over the propriety of tax stabilization action but now that the adjustments have been made this issue has become moot.

13. Revenue sharing tends to prop up certain duplicative, obsolete, and/or defunct units of local government.

14. A basic conflict arises as to the means of reconciling *no strings* Federal aid with Federal enforcement of the anti-discriminatory provision of the revenue sharing law. Thus, while the inclusion of the non-discrimination provision in the general revenue sharing law has extended the ability of the Federal government to combat discrimination in the state-local sector, the Office of Revenue Sharing does not possess sufficient staff to launch a vigorous affirmative action program.

15. The long lead time required to update local population and per capita money income data delayed realization of the Congressional intent to distribute funds to local general purpose governments on the basis of current need and effort.

16. To date, the incentives for greater state use of the personal income tax have not proved strong enough to accomplish their objective.[35]

Passage of the GRS extension was anticlimactic; other issues of major IGR import had crowded onto the congressional stage during 1975 and 1976. A bill containing $1.25 billion in anti-recession fiscal assistance for cities worked its way through the turmoil of executive-legislative conflict, energy-environmental clashes, and a high-unemployment, high-inflation economy. Precedent and pressures by the PIGs (Big Seven) worked on a supportive president and a more pliable Congress to extend GRS beyond 1976. GRS was renewed with no formula changes: the only alterations were deletion of the priority expenditure categories, modification of eligibility requirements to exclude "paper" or single-function governments, some citizen participation requirements, more comprehensive financial reporting and publicity mandates, and greatly strengthened nondiscrimination provisions in which the burden of proof rests with the recipient to demonstrate that state-local officials have not used GRS monies in a discriminatory manner. Appendix H provides more detail on the comparison of provisions in the 1972 and 1976 enactments.

SUMMARY

The federal aid policies of the national government affect state and local governments in numerous and direct ways. This chapter has emphasized these direct effects by exploring policy issues and problems associated with federal loans, grants-in-aid, and General Revenue Sharing.

Federal loans to state and local governments are minuscule in terms of net outlays but they are substantial (over $1.5 billion) in gross disbursements to loan recipients. The federal loan to New York City has been the most-publicized and most controversial example of this type of federal aid. The long-term significance of federal loans to state and local governments is neither clear nor certain. Nearly all state or local loans favor physical, durable goods, as do, to a lesser degree,

---

35. Advisory Commission on Intergovernmental Relations, *General Revenue Sharing: An ACIR Evaluation* (Washington, D.C.: Government Printing Office, October 1974, A-48), pp. 1-16.

the federal loans discussed here. The study of IGR finances could benefit from a more extensive, systematic analysis of federal loans.

The grant is a long-standing, firmly established, major IGR fiscal mechanism. In the last several decades grants have grown greatly in number, fiscal amounts, and variety of type. They have had diverse purposes and varying fiscal effects and policy consequences for recipient units.

Both policy and managerial difficulties associated with categorical grants surfaced in the 1950s and produced a crescendo of complaints in the 1960s. Block grants and revenue sharing were offered and enacted in part as reform measures in the 1970s. National IGR fiscal policies are more diverse or balanced in the 1970s. But they appear to be in a greater state of flux, partly because it is not certain what policies produce what results, but also because the larger political and economic setting is unstable. The absence of clear, firm political and economic alignments can be seen in vacillating IGR fiscal policies. GRS is due to expire again in 1980. Block grants show mixed results and generate tepid political support.

There are stirrings of regional or sectional battles over federal aid programs generally and over the formulas that spread funds among the states (or localities). Aspects of regional-sectional splits are discussed in the next chapter. The chief success story of IGR finances in the mid-1970s was probably the continuation of GRS. It signaled the consistent strength of the public interest groups, a presidential-congressional yielding of discretion to state-local officials, and a greater balance among federal aid funding policies.

National Finances:
Other IGR Policies

7

INTRODUCTION

In the preceding chapter we analyzed federal aid—the flow of money between the federal treasury and the treasuries of state and local governments. Other components of federal finances have less direct and deliberate IGR effects than does federal aid. For convenience we shall refer to these other components as having *secondary* IGR effects— secondary only in the sense that they do not involve the *direct* transfer of funds from the national government to the states or to local units.

In this chapter two such other components of the federal fisc are discussed: direct spending and taxation. The national government directly spends monies for the purchase of goods and services—for example, defense procurement, salaries of military and civilian federal-government employees, expenditures on cancer research, dam building. In these examples (and thousands of others that could be offered) services or materials are purchased for use by the national government.

How state and local governments are affected by these purchases and/or their use is, from the federal government's point of view, secondary or incidental to the basic purpose of the transaction(s).

Secondary effects can also be felt from federal taxation policies. Two illustrations of such tax policies with indirect IGR effects are: (a) state-local taxes are deductible from the taxpayer's federal income tax and (b) interest earned from investments in state-local government bonds are totally exempt from federal income tax.

In both these instances, when either establishing or maintaining federal fiscal policy, the national government gives IGR considerations little or no weight. Because non-IGR decision criteria preponderate, such policies fall in the category of secondary effects.

These two groups of policies, direct national expenditures and federal taxation, are the topics for discussion in this chapter. To get some idea of the fiscal magnitudes under discussion, see table 7-1. Because these policies are classified as having secondary IGR effects, the amounts substantially overstate the apparent impacts on state and local governments. The total of direct national expenditures in 1970 was estimated at nearly $176 billion; the total for federal tax policies was estimated at about $160 billion. We address detailed analyses of each of these two amounts in the next two sections.

DIRECT NATIONAL EXPENDITURES

In chapter 5 reference was made to the "second war between the states"—the competition among regions of the country for federal outlays. The controversy, which tended to be drawn around a Snowbelt-Sunbelt split, signifies a deeper set of issues involving differential income, wealth, employment, population growth, and general well-being among states and regions. And the issue that has gotten most attention is how much the national government consciously or unconsciously favors one region over another in deciding *where* to spend its money.

Few of us need to be reminded that where and how the federal government spent $176 billion in 1970 greatly affected the lives and fortunes of most if not all Americans. By 1976 the figure for direct national outlays had risen to $310 billion. Escalating political interest in where such massive amounts are spent is not surprising, and it came into sharper focus during the economic difficulties of 1974-1975 and

Table 7–1. *Intergovernmental Financial Policies of the National Government in 1970: Secondary IGR Effects (in billions of dollars)*

I.	Direct National Outlays	
	A. Personnel Compensation	
	1. Civilian	$ 29.5
	2. Military	20.7
		50.2
	B. Transfer Payments	
	1. Interest	14.0
	2. Subsidies	4.6
	3. Other Transfers (e.g., social security)	56.5
		75.1
	C. Purchases of Goods (including capital outlays)	50.6
	Total	$175.9
II.	Tax Policies	
	A. Tax Sources (1970 Tax Revenues)	
	1. Income (personal and corporate)	$123.2
	2. Sales and Excises	18.3
	3. Other	4.4
		145.9
	B. Tax Overlapping (taxpayer benefits)	
	1. Deductability of State-Local Taxes	8.5
	2. Tax Exempt State-Local Bonds	2.0
		10.5
	C. Tax Credits (estate and employment tax offsets)	3.3
	Total	$159.7

Sources: *Special Analyses: Budget of the United States Government Fiscal Year 1972* (Washington: Government Printing Office, 1971), Sections A, H, and P; Bureau of the Census, *Government Finances in 1969–70*, Series GF 70-No. 5 (Washington, D.C.), Table 2.

the harsh winter of 1976–1977. Regional-sectional battle lines were more clearly drawn, however, by a well-publicized study published by the *National Journal* in June 1976.[1] The analysis of "winners and losers in the contest for federal spending," headlined its main con-

---

1. "Federal Spending: The North's Loss Is the South's Gain," *National Journal*, June 26, 1976 (Washington, D.C.: Government Research Corporation), pp. 878–891. See also, William H. Miernyk, "The North Isn't What It Used to Be" (Morgantown, W. Va.: Regional Research Institute, West Virginia University, Reprint Series X, No. 5, 1975), pp. 19–48.

clusion, "that there is a massive flow of wealth from the Northeast and Great Lakes states to the faster-growing West and South."[2]

The study covered both sides of the fiscal ledger—the state-by-state (and regional) sources of federal tax revenues, and four classifications of federal spending:

1. civilian and military salaries,
2. transfer payments to individuals,
3. purchases of goods and commodities, and
4. federal aid to state and local governments.

The first three correspond to the categories of national direct outlays in table 7-1; the last is the direct equivalent of our primary impact category.

Responses to the *National Journal* study and the several deeper issues noted above seem to fall into three categories. First, there is the analytic response, best demonstrated by an extensive research study produced by two visiting scholars with the Office of Economic Research in the Economic Development Administration. The analysis was a rejoinder to the *National Journal* study under the title, *A Myth in the Making: The Southern Economic Challenge and Northern Economic Decline.*[3]

Paragraphs from that essay summarize its conclusions and interpretations while simultaneously confronting policy choices involving the secondary IGR impacts of national spending.

It is evident that, by almost any measure used, the Northern Industrial Tier possesses a significant lead in the level of economic development both in aggregate and per capita terms.

It is also evident that the Northern Tier States presently confront serious economic difficulties. The degree to which these are critical for both the region and the Nation should in no way be minimized.

The improving economic performance of the Sunbelt-South indicates only that the wide disparities between the two regions are diminishing to some degree. The bottoming out or divergence in regional per capita incomes as a percent of the national average in 1975 suggests that the relative position of the South declined in that one year.

---

2. *National Journal,* p. 878.
3. C. L. Jusenius and L. C. Ledebur, *A Myth in the Making: The Southern Economic Challenge and Northern Economic Decline* (U.S. Department of Commerce, Economic Development Administration, November 1976).

The United States is emerging from the worst recession since the Great Depression. It is inevitable that the highly industrialized regions of the economy would be impacted more heavily in the course of this recession. Therefore, conclusions on the relative performance of these two regions recently should be regarded with some caution. It may well be that the relative improvement of the Southern States is, in part, a cyclical phenomenon which may not be sustained through the full recovery of the economy.

Policy decisions based on the assumption that the experience of 1970 through 1975 represents a new trend may be ill-considered and counterproductive in the longer run.

An implicit and often explicit premise or goal of public policy in the United States has been to attempt to redress the imbalance in the distribution of economic welfare among regions. Undoubtedly, the Northern Industrialized States are undergoing economic difficulties which are unprecedented in a period of relative economic prosperity. *However, it is not clear that the situation of these States today is more adverse economically than that which the Southern, less developed, States have experienced historically even though they are now experiencing an increasing rate of income, employment and population growth.* At best, the evidence is mixed and fails to support the unequivocal claim that the Northern Industrialized States should benefit from a reallocation of Federal program benefits which diminishes the flow of benefits to States in the South.

The regional economies of the United States are highly interdependent. Rhetoric and biased studies which encourage a growing sense of economic competition between these two regions do a disservice to the overall goal of balanced economic growth for both regions. The economic futures of the two super-regions are inseparably intertwined. A balanced and carefully conceived approach which mitigates economic distress in particular regions and harmonizes regional growth is essential. The current debate which focuses on the rate of growth of the Sunbelt as a partial explanation of the economic difficulties of the Northern States is detrimental to the goal of achieving National policies that facilitate overall growth among all regions of the United States.[4]

A second response to rising interstate and interregional tensions is attitudinal—at the level of the individual citizen. The widespread concerns over economic conditions, environmental threats, and energy shortages have, not surprisingly, affected most citizens deeply—apparently encouraging among them growing beggar-thy-neighbor attitude. For example, during recent energy shortages strong anti-eastern sentiments surfaced in energy-producing states like Texas, Louisiana, and

---

4. Ibid., p. 34–35. Italics in original.

Oklahoma. Bumper stickers urged fellow citizens to keep and use their oil, gas, and electricity at home. Two examples were: "Take a bath and freeze a Yankee" and "Let the Yankee bastards freeze in the dark."

The third response to Snowbelt-Sunbelt cleavages has been political: Officials from the aggrieved northern tier of states have organized. Sixteen states stretching from Iowa and Minnesota to Maine and Pennsylvania formed the Northeast-Midwest Economic Advancement Coalition. The coalition was officially founded in September 1976 under the leadership of representatives Henry Reuss of Wisconsin and Michael Harrington of Massachusetts. The avowed aim of the group is to shift more federal spending to their states. Also reported to have been established about the same time was the Council for Northeast Economic Action, an organization composed of persons from government, industry, labor, and financial institutions in the northeast. This association, headed by a Boston banker/economist, was expected to receive a grant of $500,000 from the Economic Development Administration for research on the northeast's economy, tax structure, transportation, energy, industrial base, and federal funding.[5]

Two other organizations entered the IGR fray on the federal spending issue. In June 1976 the governors of seven states formed the Coalition of Northeastern Governors and listed three top aims for the group: joint representation in Washington, regional economic planning, and creation of a Northeastern Economic Development Corporation. The fourth organization to be heard from on the issue was the New England Congressional Caucus, a group of twenty-five members in the House of Representatives from the six New England states.[6] This group, formed in 1973 before the energy and fiscal "crises," operates the New England Economic Research Office in Washington. The executive director of the caucus, Jill A. Schulker, said of the federal flow-of-funds controversy: "Awareness is the key. For 20 years they've been discriminating against New England. Now we're trying to heighten sensitivity to this problem through the Caucus."[7]

---

5. "Southern Growth: Problems and Promise," newsletter of the Southern Growth Policies Board (Research Triangle Park, N.C.) 4, 2 (Winter 1976–1977): p. 3.

6. Ibid.; also, *National Journal,* pp. 889–891.

7. *National Journal,* p. 991. For somewhat skeptical appraisals of the Sunbelt versus Snowbelt controversy see the following *Wall Street Journal* articles: "The Rise of the Sunbelt," October 5, 1976; "Seven Northeast States Propose to Create U.S.-Backed Concern to Help Economies," November 15, 1976; and "Sunbelts and Snowbelts," December 27, 1976. For counterpoint articles see: Neal R. Peirce, "Targeting Aid to the Areas Hit Hardest," *Washington Post,* January 18, 1976; and Felix Rohatyn, "Reviving the Northeast," *Washington Post,* April 17, 1977.

Such charges have not gone unheeded or unchallenged by Sunbelt officials. One means for such rejoinders is the Southern Growth Policies Board, an action- and research-oriented agency formed in 1972 to foster balanced growth and development among fifteen states stretching from Virginia through Texas. The board has pushed, successfully, the holding of an official mid-decade census count.[8]

Controversy over the geographic distribution of federal spending may be a persistent issue for some years to come. Five facets of the controversy should be borne in mind when drawing conclusions about the "war" for federal funds:

1. The three categories of direct national outlays have a relatively fixed geographic distribution: for example, location of federal workers, the residence of welfare and social security beneficiaries, the place of businesses and industries from which government buys weapons systems.

2. The easiest kind of spending to change is what we have called primary IGR impact funds—federal aid.

3. The controversy has moved toward a polarization of positions approaching a zero-sum game situation (any gains by one region will come at the expense of another). This is most evident in the *National Journal* analysis of "winners versus losers." Unless the overall U.S. economic picture brightens appreciably in the near future, the positions may harden, and pitched battles may be fought over grant-in-aid formulas within the U.S. Congress.

4. It is ironic, but perhaps fortuitous, that the escalation and political adjustment of this issue occur at a time when the first southern president in over a century occupies the White House.[9] A president from the allegedly most advantaged region *may* have more room to maneuver and to compromise than a nonsouthern president.

5. Research, data dissemination, interpretation, and recommendations on the several issues involved in this controversy may be important in defining the lines around which different positions are taken and also the grounds on which compromises may occur.

8. *The Southern Growth Policies Board* (Research Triangle Park, N.C.: Southern Growth Policies Board, 1972). For another brief discussion of this organization see Thad L. Beyle, "The Southern Growth Policies Board: A New Beginning or a Last Chance?" *The Southern Journal* (Spring 1972), pp. 1–2, ff.

9. This theme and others are developed in James P. Gannon, "Northern States Start Drive for Federal Aid for Slack Economies—But South Girds to Guard Its Interests, Leaving Carter as Man in Middle," *Wall Street Journal,* January 17, 1977.

On this last point it is pertinent to cite research and findings on the distribution of federal spending in the late 1950s and early 1960s. The figures are drawn from a study performed for Senator Muskie's Subcommittee on Intergovernmental Relations and published in 1966. Table 7–2 presents coefficients that express relationships between per capita income in the fifty states and the per capita federal expenditures for several categories of federal outlays. The last category, aid to states and localities, covers the federal aid amounts discussed in chapter 6 as having primary IGR effects; all others are those with secondary IGR effects. Coefficients are calculated for three different years, and for 1963 the percentages are shown for the $88.6 billion subjected to the expenditure analysis. A negative sign means that more money per capita is going to or is spent in states with lower personal income levels.

Only three categories, all small in percentages of outlay, are redistributional or equalizing. That is, in per capita terms, they tend to go more to the lower-income states. The three largest components of federal spending are strongly or moderately favorable to the higher-income states. Even the federal aid category is only mildly equalizing, and that pattern declined slightly over the three years. Because these

Table 7–2. *Product Moment Correlation Coefficients Relating Per Capita Personal Income and Per Capita Federal Expenditures in the 50 States by Type of Outlay*

Type of Outlay	1957	1960	1963	Percentage Distribution for 1963 Outlays
Military Reserves and Civil Works	–.26	–.36	–.34	2.1
Defense Research and Development	.51	.48	.40	6.3
Defense and NASA Procurement	.69	.68	.65	25.7
Transfer Payments	.52	.52	.51	27.7
Civilian and Military Wages and Salaries	.13	.16	.15	27.0
Aid to Individuals	–.27	–.26	.03	1.8
Aid to States and Localities	–.29	–.20	–.14	9.4
Total Outlays	.38	.42	.43	100.0%
Amounts of Expenditures Allocated (billions of dollars)	56.3	70.0	88.6	

Source: *Federal Expenditures to States and Regions: A Study of Their Distribution and Impact,* Subcommittee on Intergovernmental Relations, U.S. Senate, 89th Congress, 2nd Session, Committee Print (Washington: Government Printing Office, 1966), pp. 12, 59.

primary impact funds are the ones most subject to manipulation, considerable research is likely to be done on federal aid distribution and continued political attention given to its fiscal effects.

NATIONAL TAX POLICIES

Tax policies are important elements in the secondary IGR impacts of national fiscal policies. The three discrete segments into which these impacts are divided are tax sources, tax overlapping, and tax credits. Taken as a group, these tax policies of the national government are normally evaluated and changed not primarily or exclusively because of IGR consequences but because of non-IGR decision criteria. For example, decisions by the Congress and the president to increase or cut federal income taxes are influenced by the condition of the economy, the economic effects of more (or less) federal borrowing, and national revenue requirements. The fact that higher (or lower) federal taxes will affect the tax options, decisions, and revenues of state and local governments is incidental, if not irrelevant, to national decision making on tax matters. For example, although a tax cut will have IGR consequences, those consequences will rarely if ever critically affect the national decision.

Tax Sources

Local, state, and national governments derive tax revenues from three basic sources: income, consumption, and wealth. The respective levies on these three economic factors are income, sales, and property taxes. How much of the three tax domains does each governmental jurisdiction occupy? Figure 7-1 shows us. The national government is dominant in the income tax arena and collected nearly 90 percent ($123.2 billion) from this source in 1970. Of all income taxes collected, state governments garnered about 9 percent and local governments barely 1 percent. Comparable proportions for state and local units in 1975 were, respectively, 13.3 and 1.4 percent—showing the relative rise in state income taxation. National tax policy has not preempted the income tax arena, but the federal presence is so large that it has been criticized as hampering more vigorous state and local entry into the field.

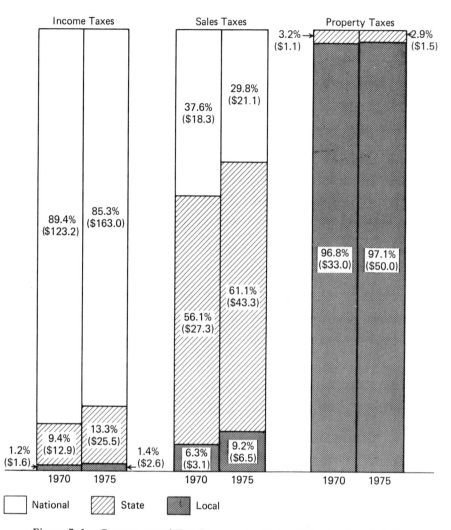

Figure 7-1. *Governmental Tax Revenue by Type of Tax by Level of Government, Fiscal Years 1970 and 1975 (in percents and billions of dollars)*

Whether correct or not, this claim invites for consideration the significant issue of intergovernmental tax competition and the question whether there should be a conscious policy of separation of tax sources in IGR. When it reported to the president and the Congress in 1955 the (Kestnbaum) Commission on Intergovernmental Relations argued that a "greater separation of tax sources is desirable."[10] Behind such

10. Commission on Intergovernmental Relations, *Report to the President for Transmittal to the Congress* (Washington, D.C.: Government Printing Office, June 1955), p. 103.

a recommendation rest several premises about the nature of IGR and IGR fiscal policies. One such premise is that the exercise of tax powers by one jurisdiction negatively (or undesirably) affects the tax options of other governments' actions in the same tax arena. It revives the familiar zero-sum-game IGR relationship as applied to tax policy issues.

Another look at figure 7-1 reveals that there is in fact a high degree of separation in income and property taxes. National dominance in securing income taxes has been noted, but local governments have even more dominance over controlling property taxes. In 1970 they collected nearly 97 percent of more than $34 billion in property tax revenues. As figure 7-1 also shows, by 1975 the comparable proportion exceeded 97 percent of more than $51 billion in property tax collections.

Only in sales and excise taxes is there a marked overlap. All three jurisdictions have jockeyed for a larger share of these revenues. State governments garnered more than 56 percent of all sales tax revenues ($48.7 billion) in 1970; local governments took only 6 percent, the national government less than 38 percent. By 1975 the states took 61 percent of the $71 billion, the local share was 9 percent, and the national 30 percent.

What are the IGR policy consequences of partially overlapping but substantially separated revenue sources among U.S. governing entities? Several stand out:

1. Policy autonomy is fostered by the separation of tax sources. The more dominant jurisdiction in each tax field can make its policy decisions with less concern about how its tax actions affect other jurisdictions.
2. Tax separation, when combined with the revenue elasticities of the three types of taxes, produces a bias toward the national government's greater expansion.
3. The revenue benefits from economic growth accrue chiefly to the national government.
4. The political pains of raising tax rates and revenues are felt chiefly by state and local governments.
5. That there should be separate tax sources is the first premise in a set of assumptions leading to the conclusion that the pleasure or benefits of spending money should be directly associated with the pain of raising it. (The opposite precept is that the best tax revenue to spend is that which others have raised.)

Tax Overlapping

These policy consequences show the results of an IGR policy process that blends separation and competition with overlapping and collaboration in the field of taxation. Overlapping has produced a plethora of proposals for tax comity—concessions that promote harmony rather than competition in IGR tax policies. Only two such tax comity features were noted as secondary impacts in table 7-1. These are provisions of the federal revenue code permitting individuals and corporations to deduct state-local taxes and to exempt interest income from state-local bonds.

The primary beneficiaries of these deductibility and exemption provisions are of course the individual and corporate taxpayers, not state or local governments. In 1970 the value of these taxpayer benefits totaled $10.5 billion—the estimated amount of revenue thereby lost to the U.S. treasury. Their dollar value to taxpayers increased rapidly. By 1975 the deductibility provision saved taxpayers $13.8 billion, the exemption of interest income an additional $3.8 billion.[11]

How do state and local governments benefit from these clauses in the internal revenue code? The advantages are secondary and indirect, although they are no less eagerly sought and defended by state and local officials. These officials accept one IGR policy premise behind the deductibility feature, that is, the greater tolerance or acceptability of state and local tax levels (and tax increases) by taxpayers. The validity of this premise has not been confirmed by any known empirical evidence. In the absence of evidence, state and local officials seem to hold these opinions even more tenaciously.

Other secondary IGR policy impacts flow from the deductibility feature:

1. It may ease or temper complaints against state-local taxes by high-income individuals: being in high tax rate brackets, they benefit most from the deduction.
2. It may ease or foster the enactment of state income taxes with high marginal rates (higher tax rates for successively higher income brackets) because such rates capture for state treasuries

---

11. *Special Analyses, Budget of the United States Government, Fiscal Year 1977* (Washington, D.C.: Office of Management and Budget, 1976), Special Analysis F, "Tax Expenditures," pp. 116-137. See also *Tax Expenditures: Compendium of Background Material on Individual Provisions,* U.S. Senate, Committee on the Budget, 94th Congress, 2nd Session, Committee Print, March 17, 1976.

money from high-income persons that would otherwise be paid in federal income taxes.

3. It produces perceived (though not specifiable) advantages to state-local officials because no federal controls or direct interventions affect state or local decisions.

4. The power to eliminate the provision rests exclusively in the hands of the national government, yet the provision has been viewed as a matter of right by some state-local officials, these same ones who are most active, vocal, and articulate in lobbying for and preserving that "right."

The income exemption feature of state-local bond interest has been defended with even greater zeal by state-local officials than has the deductibility provision. The intergovernmental policy issues surrounding the exemption are numerous and complex, and produce conflict that is intense to the point of bitterness. Nevertheless, if there is a single matter on which all sides to the controversy agree, it is that the exemption makes state-local bonds attractive to investors. The approximate cost to the federal treasury in lost revenues was $2.0 billion in 1970; $3.8 billion in 1975.

The tax exemption of interest from bonds produces other IGR impacts:[12]

1. Exemption of state-local debentures is a stimulus to borrowing and capital construction by states and local governments. More specifically, it lowers the interest rate on state-local bonds from one-half to as much as one full percentage point. The 530 percent rise in state-local debt from 1954 to 1974 partially confirms this stimulus effect.

2. Another by-product of tax exemption is the greater stimulus toward borrowing rather than taxation. New York City carried the borrowing bent or bias to an extreme: It borrowed to fund current operating costs. Debt as a substitute for current taxation is further encouraged by the economic and political rigidities of property and sales taxes. Up to a point, it is easier to float loans and pay current interest costs than to face the ire of taxpayers if large tax increases were enacted.

3. A related policy consequence of the preceding point is a twofold tendency toward: (a) the issuance of revenue bonds rather than

---

12. For a concise, descriptive discussion of state-local borrowing see Advisory Commission on Intergovernmental Relations, *Understanding the Market for State and Local Debt* (Washington, D.C.: Government Printing Office, May 1976, M-104), 56 pp.

general obligation bonds, and (b) the creation of special districts and "paper governments" to circumvent state-imposed bonding limitations.

4. Governmental fragmentation not only leads to popular confusion and political complexity, it also alters the nature of political responsibility. The constituency that limits and defines policy alternatives is not that of the voters or of other public officials but the market for tax-exempt bonds. For better or worse, Wall Street and the investors are the crucial constituencies for New York City, the New York Port Authority, and numerous other cities, counties, school districts, and special district governments choosing to rely on debt financing.

5. The tax-exemption feature leaves bond-funded allocation decisions entirely in the hands of state and local officials contingent on the acceptability and salability of the bonds.

6. A final IGR policy consequence stems from continuing differences over the constitutional issues. Local and state officials have sometimes questioned whether efforts to tax income from state-local bonds was worth the risk of confronting head-on the traditional constitutional immunity dating from *McCulloch* v. *Maryland*. Success in persuading the Supreme Court to adopt the separatist model of IGR on this issue seems highly unlikely.

Tax Credit

The tax credit, or tax offset as it is sometimes called, is the 100 percent reduction (or subtraction) of a partial tax liability from a total tax liability. (Use of a state tax credit against the federal tax liability on telephone service was proposed—to no avail—by the Joint Federal State Action Committee: See chapter 3.) There are two prime examples of the tax credit usage in federal-state relations: (1) death tax credit and (2) the unemployment insurance tax credit.[13] The former was enacted in 1924 and expanded in 1926 to an 80-percent offset of the state tax at the urging of a majority of the states. Florida and Nevada had eliminated their taxes on estates in an effort to attract wealthy retirees.

---

13. From an IGR standpoint the definitive work on this topic is James A. Maxwell, *Tax Credits and Intergovernmental Fiscal Relations* (Washington, D.C.: The Brookings Institution, 1962).

The unemployment insurance tax offset (of 2.7 percent against the federal levy of 3.0) was enacted during the New Deal. The tax credit device was used in place of a direct, totally national program for two reasons—one legal, the other political, and both pragmatic. The first involved creating a program that had the appearance if not the actuality of national-state cooperation to make it more palatable to a hostile Supreme Court. The second, or political, reason was to secure the support of congressional members desiring an effective program with a minimum of federal controls.

In 1970 the death tax credit amounted to $350 million. Tax credit revenues to the states under the payroll tax provisions were about $3 billion. The experience with two uses of the tax credit provides a basis for several observations about its actual and probable intergovernmental policy impacts.

1. It is first and foremost a means of securing almost immediate response from the governments that benefit from the credit. The response may be either a positive action to establish a nationally desired program (unemployment compensation) or a restraint in acting in a way judged destructive to intergovernmental comity (death tax).

2. No geographic redistribution effect is achieved by the tax credit. The absence of redistributional effects was dramatically demonstrated by the abortive proposals of the Joint Federal-State Action Committee to allow a tax credit against the federal telephone tax in exchange for state assumption of vocational education and waste-treatment construction programs.

3. Efforts of the Joint Action Committee confirmed the political impossibility of substituting the tax credit for one or more categorical grant-in-aid programs. The shifting of functions or programs to the states, if it is to be achieved, must measure not only economics and politics but the interaction between the two.

4. The tax credit can be a potent constraining (or coercive) device. This may be either a virtue or a vice depending on how the use of the instrument fits one's policy preferences.

A few years ago the Advisory Commission on Intergovernmental Relations (ACIR) proposed to allow up to 25 percent of an individual's federal income tax liability to be offset by state income taxes. The proposal had three discernible policy aims: (a) improved tax coordination, (b) immediate revenue stimulus in several states together with some revenue maintenance in others, and (c) long-term "improvement" in state tax structures through use of the income tax.[14] Politically speaking, however, the credit lacked appeal because many states did not have broad-based personal income taxes. The ACIR proposal, if adopted, would virtually force these states to adopt such taxes. The coercive character of the credit device was formally noted in U.S. Supreme Court dissents in *Steward Machine Co.* v. *Davis* upholding the unemployment tax legislation.[15]

At this juncture of the twentieth century the tax credit seems destined to generate political rather than legal repercussions. There were, for example, dissents from among the ACIR membership on the income tax credit proposal.[16]

5. An important feature of the credit device is its high visibility to the taxpayer. The federal income tax law and form are so arranged as to highlight taxpayer benefit from having paid a state or local tax that is an eligible credit.

The two uses of tax credits in IGR are indications of the practice, but not the promise, of this technique of intergovernmental fiscal coordination. Indeed, a capsule history of the actual and proposed uses of the credit suggest its unlikely prospects for subsequent adoptions.

    1920s: death tax (adopted)
    1930s: unemployment compensation (adopted)
    1950s: telephone tax—Joint Action Committee (rejected)
    1960s: state income tax —ACIR (rejected)

Special circumstances led to the two adoptions of tax credits four and five decades ago. If the credit device is ever again employed in national-state fiscal relations, the conditions leading to such action are also likely to be exceptional rather than an outgrowth of usual IGR patterns and policies.[17]

---

14. Advisory Commission on Intergovernmental Relations, *Federal-State Coordination of Personal Income Taxes* (Washington, D.C.: Government Printing Office, October 1965, A-27).

15. *Steward Machine Company* v. *Davis,* 301 U.S. 548 (1937), esp. pp. 610–618.

16. ACIR, *Federal-State Coordination,* pp. 13–19.

17. The tax credit device at the state-local level has recently enjoyed more extensive usage, albeit under a different name: the property tax "circuit breaker." This technique is best illustrated by the case of Bill West in Chapter 1; part of his local property tax bill was offset by a state tax *credit.* As of 1975 twenty-five states had some type of "circuit breaker" or tax credit legislation on their statute books. See Advisory Commission on Intergovernmental Relations, *Property Tax Circuit-Breakers: Current Status and Policy Issues* (Washington, D.C.: Government Printing Office, 1975, M-87).

SUMMARY

Other federal policies besides federal aid have IGR consequences. These other policies, national expenditures and national tax policies, are called secondary because they do not involve the direct transfer of funds from the federal treasury to state and local accounts. The fiscal aggregates associated with these other (secondary) IGR policies are large. For example, direct national expenditures totaled $176 billion in 1970 and rose to $310 billion in 1976. The precise effects of these expenditures on state and local jurisdictions are not easy to specify.

The lack of clearly specified effects on localities, states, and regions has in part contributed to a rising controversy over whether federal expenditures favor one region over another. The battle lines for this "second war between the states" have been drawn largely between the "Snowbelt" and the "Sunbelt." Officials from the Snowbelt contend that federal revenues come chiefly from their section while federal outlays tend to favor the Sunbelt. Not surprisingly, officials from the latter region challenge the claims that the secondary IGR effects of national expenditures disproportionately favor Sunbelt states.

National tax policies are also loaded with consequences for state and local governments, even though the effects are termed secondary or indirect. Three broad types of tax policies were singled out for analysis and identification of IGR: tax sources, tax overlapping, and tax credits.

The bulk of all income taxes (85 to 90 percent) are collected by the national government, and an even larger proportion (97 percent) of all property taxes are claimed by local governments. Federal dominance of the income tax has led to contentions that it preempts these revenues and discourages state-local use of this tax source. It does appear that the national government's income tax dominance gives it an immensely stronger revenue position over the states and their local units. The states, in turn, are in a stronger revenue position than localities despite state reliance on a diversified revenue structure that involves IGR competition with the national and local levels for income, sales, and property taxes.

Tax overlapping is a not-infrequent occurrence in IGR. Two examples of overlapping are deductibility (of state-local taxes) and exemption (of interest on state-local bonds). Both arrangements have generated considerable controversy over how much they benefit state and local units, especially in comparison with revenues lost to the U.S. Treasury. Whatever the specific, identifiable benefits to state and local governments from these tax policies (and there are some), state and local officials are vigorous opponents of change that would eliminate the deductibility and tax-exemption provisions.

The tax credit is a device to foster IGR fiscal coordination. Unique circumstances led its adoption in the 1920s (death tax) and 1930s (unemployment compensation). Unique conditions also prompted proposals to extend its use in the 1950s (telephone tax) and 1960s (state income tax)—the first an effort to link the tax credit with a return of two functions (categorical grants) to the states, the second an effort to promote more extensive use of the income tax by the states. Both recent proposals failed adoption for various reasons, making future expanded use of the tax credit for IGR fiscal coordination improbable.

Having drilled the financial strata of local, state, and national jurisdictions it is time to change our probing techniques. Instead of using drill bits with dollar calibrations we need to shift our method, and now listen for reverberations through the IGR strata below us. We shall ask IGR participants to tell us what they think, what they like, and what they do. These "participants' perspectives" will command our attention for the next four chapters.

Local Officials:
Actions and Attitudes

8

ADAPTIVE BEHAVIOR IN THE 1970s

In the spring of 1976 Ms. Ann Michel, Director of the Office of Federal and State Aid Coordination (OFSAC) for the city of Syracuse, New York, spoke to a large group of students enrolled in the public administration program of Syracuse University. Her talk was entitled "Intergovernmental Aid: A Local Perspective."[1] An equally appropriate title might have been: "The Dependent City." Ms. Michel directs a staff of eighty persons engaged in a wide variety of grant-seeking, grant-administering, and grant-operating activities. Her agency's efforts produced $55 million from state and federal sources in 1976. This was 45 percent of Syracuse's annual budget!

---

1. Ann Michel, "Intergovernmental Aid: A Local Perspective," in James D. Carroll and Richard W. Campbell (eds.), *Intergovernmental Administration: 1976—Eleven Academic and Practitioner Perspectives* (Syracuse, N.Y.: Maxwell School of Citizenship and Public Affairs, Syracuse University, 1976), pp. 241–257.

Consider the significance of these selected remarks as Ms. Michel describes the actions and aims of her agency:

> Our first function is to manipulate the system to get as much of the money as we can into the City of Syracuse, in the first instance, at least, to be used to meet city priority needs. That includes grant negotiations, most heavily in the categorical grants and block grant systems; it includes the preparation of our applications, some of them more intelligible than others. It also includes the development of a state legislative program and the follow-up lobbying effort, which has become a much more important aspect of our activities than it used to be and takes a great deal of my own time. . . .

> An additional activity related to procuring maximum outside aid is fairly active participation in federal legislative lobbying efforts, though that tends to be less intense than the state process. (If for no other reason than it seems to take two years to get any sizeable piece of federal legislation passed.) So, what at the state level requires week after week persistence, at the federal level may take two years and only require quarterly trips to Washington as the bills make their way through the Congressional process. . . .

> Finally, this effort of procuring outside aid includes city-county negotiations. As cities become less able to support functions with their own revenues you will see increasing efforts on the part of city governments to try to get the county governments with their broader suburban-financed tax base to pay for a larger share of services. . . .

> The second category of activity within O.F.S.A.C. is fiscal management and oversight. The quickest way to lose credibility with funding sources is to have an audit exception. If we are going to retain our reputation the city must manage its monies well and demonstrate a capacity to effectively use state and federal resources. . . .

> The third category of activity in O.F.S.A.C. is a function we've only recently added, a division of program evaluation. It is done for several reasons. Partly it's an attempt to stay one step ahead of the funding sources, because if we discover the problems before they do and get them corrected then we continue to have the reputation we feel we need to strengthen our negotiations. . . .

> Finally, O.F.S.A.C. is also responsible for human services planning and program operation. In most communities your human services program operation effort is in a separate department, and that is generally the way it ought to be done. But in Syracuse that's not possible because of the general attitude that local government should be small, invisible, and not involved in extraneous issues. Thus, we operate our human services efforts under the state and federal aid umbrella. . . .[2]

2. Ibid., pp. 250–252.

Although these statements raise numerous points for discussion, we shall concentrate on how they illustrate two themes permeating this chapter and the ones to follow: the attitudes and the actions of local, state, and national officials as they function in a complex, bargaining-oriented, exchange-based intergovernmental context.

By *attitudes* we mean the opinions, views, or perspectives of these officials. How do they see each other? How do they perceive the problems they face? We base our attention to this theme on the two previously discussed IGR perspectives of national, state, and local officials (see figure 3–4).

By *actions* we mean the specific behaviors and efforts of public officials as they function in an IGR context. The "picket fence" federalism pattern of IGR (see figure 3–3) implies not only attitudes but actions as well; we will examine these here and in chapters 9, 10, and 11. We have also implied a good bit about officials' IGR actions when discussing models of IGR in the United States (chapter 2, figure 2–1). A fair inference from the overlapping-authority model is that officials' actions are guided by decisions that emphasize interdependence and patterns of bargaining: Consider, for example, the verbs in Ms. Michels' talk: "get," "manipulate," "procure," "lobby," "negotiate," "manage," "evaluate," etc.

LOCAL OFFICIALS AND IGR INFLUENCE

The actions of which local officials are important and influential in IGR? In theory, the actions of all local officials are. Although the elected mayor of What Cheer, Iowa, for example, may never have contact with a federal grant official, the mayor may still have an impact, however small, on IGR. By never having applied for a federal (or state) grant, the town of What Cheer, and its mayor, have left more money available for those who did apply and receive intergovernmental fiscal aid. Such impact, of course, is minor, even insignificant. And in actuality different local officials have widely varying impacts on IGR. We suggest some of the reasons for these varying impacts after first identifying the broad categories of local officials who are IGR participants.

Table 8–1 provides a summary listing of the various actual and potential IGR participants by the type of local jurisdiction in which they

Table 8-1. *Categories of Local Officials as IGR Participants*[a]

Municipalities (18,000)	*Counties (3000)*
Mayors	Board chairpersons
Council members	Board members (or commissioners)
City managers (or chief administra- tive officers)	Elected agency heads (sheriff, treasurer, auditor, clerk)
Staff generalists (budget, personnel, planning, IGR coordinators)	Elected executives (usually large urban counties)
Department heads	Appointed executives (e.g., county managers)
	Agency heads
	Administrative boards
School Districts (16,000)	*Special Districts and Regional Bodies (25,000)*
School board members (elected or appointed)	Chairpersons, governing board
School superintendent	Governing board members
Central staff personnel	Chief administrators (directors, councils of governments)
Program specialists (vocational edu- cation, science education, psychologists)	*Townships (17,000)*
	Elected supervisors
	Elected and appointed administrators (clerks, attorneys, assessors)

[a]Numbers in parentheses indicate the approximate number of jurisdictions (not officials) for each type of local government unit.

operate. The approximate number of each kind of jurisdiction is shown in parentheses. As indicated earlier, the total number of full-time local government employees is over 7 million. If we arbitrarily figure that 1 percent of this total represents important or influential IGR participants we would have 70,000 major actors on the IGR stage. In addition, there are over 500,000 popularly elected part-time local officials across the nation. If we acknowledge that perhaps 10 percent of these are important or influential in IGR, then we must add 50,000 more key actors. In short, there are millions of *potential* IGR participants in local government, and there are tens of thousands of officials who are probably important and influential actors involved in writing (or ad-libbing) the scenarios for IGR in the United States.

Obviously, no one "audience" could compile and edit the total play or the numerous plots, subplots, and scenarios produced on such a far-flung and populous stage. The actions and attitudes of local officials must therefore be sampled and described selectively. "Importance" and "influence" being ambiguous and elusive terms, how can a representative sample be selected? Some criteria to help us assess the importance and influence of IGR actors can be listed:

- What are the legal powers of the position held by an official?
- What is the informal, extralegal political base of an official?
- How much expertise, skill, or specialized knowledge does the official have?
- What leadership abilities, innovative ideas, and policy foresight does the official possess?

These questions tap the four bases for the potential exercise of power in an IGR bargaining context—position, political acumen, expertise, and leadership. In the 1950s and 1960s, for example, Mayor Lee of New Haven, Connecticut, would have scored high probably on all four power criteria, and they contributed greatly to his successes in securing millions of dollars for urban renewal and rejuvenation efforts in downtown New Haven.[3] Robert Moses was the legendary (and actual) "power broker" who controlled the spending of an estimated $250 billion in the New York metropolitan area over a forty-year period. A large proportion of this sum came from federal and state governments. Although not an elected official, Moses combined several appointive and honorary posts with unusual expertise, a cultivated popular image, and a political base composed of powerful interest groups.[4] The late Mayor Daley of Chicago, on the other hand, relied chiefly on his political clout, that is, votes, to secure concessions on IGR problems—sometimes from the Illinois state legislature but more often from the federal government by tapping his influence with Democratic presidents.[5]

City managers gain intergovernmental influence chiefly through ex-

3. Robert A. Dahl, *Who Governs? Democracy and Power in an American City* (New Haven, Conn.: Yale University Press, 1961). For a series of articles on community politics and political power that incorporate extracommunity or IGR influences see "Community Politics," *Southwestern Social Science Quarterly*, 48 (December 1967): 267–450.

4. Robert A. Caro, *The Power Broker: Robert Moses and the Fall of New York* (New York: Random House, Vintage, 1974).

5. Edward C. Banfield, *Political Influence* (Glencoe, Ill.: The Free Press, 1961). An action-based, model-oriented, comparative analysis of mayors in twenty large U.S. cities that explicitly incorporates IGR features is John P. Kotter and Paul R. Lawrence, *Mayors In Action: Five Approaches to Urban Governance* (New York: John Wiley and Sons, Wiley Series in Urban Research, 1974). For a popularized but perceptive exposé of Mayor Daley see Mike Royko, *Boss: Richard J. Daley of Chicago* (New York: New American Library, Signet, 1971).

pertise, formal control over budget and personnel, and a reputation for achievement or implementation—getting done what a community deems desirable. Indeed, these factors can combine to allow an aggressive city manager to build or exploit a political base.[6] For example, in the mid-1960s a city manager in a midwestern city of about 100,000 was faced with an awkward policy and political situation stemming from IGR problems. The city had a half-dozen large federal grant programs underway, for example, in highways and bridges, urban renewal, public works, sewage treatment. On numerous occasions the manager had implored the mayor to intervene with both congressional and state legislators to assist the city in expediting the grants. The manager's efforts were to no avail. The mayor, though not hostile, was totally uncooperative with the manager. The city council frequently sought progress reports on the grant projects. Frustrated by slow progress, the city manager, in a fit of exasperation, announced at the close of one council meeting, "Gentlemen, I've had it! Either the mayor goes or I go!" The council immediately convened in executive session, where the manager explained the need for and importance of mayoral "push" with federal and state elected officials. The next day the *mayor* resigned!

Mayors and city managers generally occupy key positions as IGR actors. However, although these two categories of local official are important, there are substantial power differences among individual occupants according to variations in city characteristics: its size, its political complexion, its geographic location, its metropolitan status, and the like. The official's personal characteristics—among them age, experience, partisan identification, negotiatory skill, general knowledge, intelligence—also affect that official's IGR importance. For example, from 1970 to 1974 Richard Lugar, Republican mayor of Indianapolis, Indiana, was labeled, somewhat derisively, "Mr. Nixon's favorite mayor"—because of the apparent ease with which Indianapolis secured federal grant funds.

But mayors and city managers are far from being the only powerful and influential local IGR actors. Within cities of moderate to substantial size department heads, budget and finance staffs, and even personnel administrators have notable leverage and much leeway with which to produce IGR results.[7] Another central set of IGR city ac-

6. Ronald O. Loveridge, *City Managers in Legislative Politics* (Indianapolis: Bobbs-Merrill, 1971); Deil S. Wright, "Intergovernmental Relations in Large Council-Manager Cities," *American Politics Quarterly,* 1 (April 1973): 151–188.
7. Douglas M. Fox, *The Politics of City and State Bureaucracy* (Pacific Palisades, Calif.: Goodyear, 1974).

tors are IGR coordinators—persons like Bonnie Brown (mentioned in chapter 1) and Ann Michel.

Beyond city boundaries county officials have IGR significance. Counties have varying political, legal, and administrative autonomy, but county size is, to some extent, also a determinant of IGR impact. In many states, however, counties are administrative subdivisions of the state government.

Despite the subservience that might be inferred from the term *administrative subdivision,* counties (and their officials) in most states are influential and must be reckoned with in state capitols. Since county officials normally have responsibility for the provision of three major functions—health, highways, and welfare—they often have considerable leverage with state officials on important policy decisions. In several states this has produced a political environment in which county officials have greater access and impact at the state level than do city officials. The disenchantment and even disgust with state government expressed by many city officials (especially those from large cities) is a partial reflection of such a distribution of influence in state capitols. A much-discussed issue is whether reapportionment has made any appreciable difference in how state legislatures favor (or disfavor) cities.

The IGR significance of two other sets of local officials should be noted: school superintendents, and directors of regional councils of government (COGs). Within most localities, educational functions are organized into "special districts"—that is, more or less nearly autonomous school districts. Although variable, that autonomy is highly resistant to encroachment. School district officials, especially superintendents, are important determinants in protecting the much-debated integrity and effectiveness of the elementary-secondary educational function.[8]

School officials are often at loggerheads with city and/or county officials over such issues as school site planning, recreational programs (especially use of school facilities for "city" recreation), and, above all, taxation and finances. The last-named issue is perhaps the most tense because in most states schools, cities, and counties all rely heavily on revenues from property taxes. This competition for one finite resource

---

8. An analysis of the actions and attitudes of local school officials involving intergovernmental finances is David O. Porter et al., *The Politics of Budgeting Federal Aid: Resource Mobilization by Local School Districts* (Beverly Hills, California: Sage Publications, 1973). For an extension of Porter's IGR action and policy themes that incorporates citizen-official relationships see also his "Responsiveness to Citizen-Consumers in a Federal System," *Publius: The Journal of Federalism,* 5 (Fall 1975): 51–78.

can produce much heat among local officials. A city manager, irked at the regular electoral defeat of municipal bond issues in contrast to school bond successes, was once heard to exclaim: "If I had known earlier that the school people had this town all locked up, I probably wouldn't have taken this job!"

The second-named category of official, the executive director of a regional Council of Government (COGs), is an actor of considerable significance to IGR. The number of COGs, and of executive directors, has grown from zero to approximately 500 in the last two decades. The first COG was organized in 1954 as a voluntary association of officials from the six counties of the southeastern Michigan (Detroit) area. Its organizational leader and moving force, one Edward Connor, was both a Detroit city councilman and a member of the Wayne County governing board. This association evolved into a formal corporate entity, the Southeast Michigan Council of Governments. Subsequent developments in other parts of the nation, chiefly in metropolitan areas, resulted in similar associations. COG officials formally represent their respective local units, the governing body of which usually has designated them.

As late as 1969 there were only ninety-one COGs. That number increased dramatically (to about 500) in the 1970s for a combination of reasons, but two were most prominent: (1) the availability of federal grant funds for staffing regional planning activities under the HUD 701 program; and (2) federal legislative provisions, enacted in 1966 and 1968 and subsequently implemented by OMB Circular A-95, which required that all local applications for federal grants undergo a co-ordinated review and comment process at regional and state levels.* COGs, then, have been created in large numbers to perform, among other things, this federally mandated regional review function.[9]

---

*See Appendix I for a description of A-95.

9. The literature on regional councils and "substate regionalism" is already extensive and still growing. The ACIR published six volumes on substate regionalism in 1973-1974 and recently provided a summary-introduction to those works: ACIR, *Regionalism Revisited: Recent Areawide and Local Responses* (Washington, D.C.: Government Printing Office, June 1977, A-66). Two short, well-focused, but time-bounded analyses of COGs in the metropolitan context are: Charles W. Harris, *Regional COGs and the Central City* (Detroit: Metropolitan Fund, Inc., March 1970); and Melvin B. Mogulof, *Governing Metropolitan Areas: A Critical Review of Council of Governments and the Federal Role* (Washington, D.C.: The Urban Institute, 1971). Descriptive data on the growth and activities of COGs appear in: Urban Data Service, "Councils of Governments: Trends and Issues," Vol. 1, No. 8 (Washington, D.C.: International City Management Association, August 1969); Urban Data Service, "Areawide Review of Federal Grant Applications: Implications for Urban Management," Vol. 4, No. 2 (Washington, D.C.: International City Management Association, February 1972).

Executing the grant review function and others—for example, comprehensive planning, intergovernmental cooperation, and program or policy implementation—requires a modest to substantial COG staff normally headed by an executive director. This appointed official is responsible to a governing board varying widely in size (from fifteen to seventy-five members) but composed almost universally of elected officials from local units—mayors, councilmen, county commissioners, etc. A COG director is set in a web of federal mandates and regulations and copes with the vicissitudes of state agency programs and politics, yet must satisfy a Hydra-headed local board that is at best diverse and sometimes is uncertain in quality, concern, and cohesiveness.

In sum, a COG director holds an exciting and challenging job, as would a tightrope artist performing without a balance pole. One COG in North Carolina, well known to the author, has a budget of $2.1 million. Of that amount, however, less than $200,000 (or 10 percent) comes from local units in the form of local dues and contributions. The remainder is all federal grant money for more than a dozen projects, programs, and studies.

LOCAL OFFICIALS' ACTION RULES

Psychologists and sociologists tell us that nearly all human behavior is patterned, goal-directed, and predictable. Our purpose will be neither to prove nor disprove such grand claims, but rather to catalog a set of IGR action or decision rules by which the behavior of *some* local officials is guided *some* of the time. And rather than specify which local officials follow which IGR action rules under what conditions, we present only succinct summaries of the rules. The rules are grouped in two categories: *pervasive,* those by which nearly all local officials are guided; and *particularistic,* those that are specific to one particular arena of local action—seeking and securing federal (or state) grants-in-aid.[10]

---

10. In addition to the author's own experience and contacts, these behavioral rules are stimulated by two articles written by IGR practitioners: See David J. Kennedy, "The Law of Appropriateness: An Approach to a General Theory of Intergovernmental Relations," *Public Administration Review,* 32 (March/April 1972): 135–143; James L. Garnett, "Bureaucratic and Party Politics in an Intergovernmental Context," in Carroll and Campbell (eds.), *Intergovernmental Administration,* pp. 83–110.

Pervasive IGR Rules for Local Officials

1. Maximize federal and state dollar revenues and minimize local taxes. (This action rule is similar to the Law of Fiscal Appropriateness: The level of government most appropriate to finance a governmental program is a level *other* than the one the official currently serves.)
2. Maximize local flexibility and discretion while minimizing federal/state controls, regulations, guidelines, etc. (This rule resembles the Law of Administrative Appropriateness: The level of government by which one is currently employed is the one most appropriate to administer a program.)
3. Accept the IGR Law of Gravity: "The buck drops *down* to local officials." (This law is also known as the Law of Program Sedimentation: Operational responsibility for a program is delegated downward to local officials, beyond whom no delegation can take place.)
4. Maximize public participation and satisfaction while implementing an efficient and effective grant program—otherwise known as "Get everyone in on the action but get *action.*"
5. Maximize respect and gain the confidence of other IGR participants by using the following subrules:
   a. demonstrate honorable and decent intentions;
   b. develop evidence of capable personnel and program performance; and
   c. package and "sell" agency (or unit) accomplishments.
6. Mobilize marginal resources, that is, those resources that:
   a. provide the highest returns for the effort committed to securing them;
   b. allow the greatest flexibility of usage; and
   c. can be preserved as "slack" or "money in the bank" to meet emergencies and future uncertainties.
7. Retain and enhance political/organizational "clout" by:
   a. using favorable constituencies and contacts;
   b. neutralizing hostile interests;
   c. trying not to appear greedy; and
   d. husbanding power as if it were a finite currency, like "green stamps," confident that modest clout used today will leave more for future use.

Particularistic IGR Rules for Local Officials

The following rules are particularistic in being restricted to two facets of federal (or state) grant-related behaviors. The first set is appropriate to grant-seeking or grant-searching efforts; the second to grant-acquisition or grant-approval activities.

Grant-Search Rules. The rules for grant-hunting include:

1. Know the regulations (the rules of the game).
2. Know the application deadlines. (This is similar to knowing it's your turn at bat.)
3. Know what the grantors want to hear. (This is frequently referred to as "knowing the language—and the various dialects.")
4. Know where the dollars are. (Sometimes compared to hunting for buried treasure: The map is the current *Catalog of Federal Domestic Assistance.*)
5. An alternative rule to number 4 is: Know who knows where the dollars are. In more common parlance, "Hire a consultant, preferably an experienced one." (This is equivalent to hiring a guide with a good, detailed map.)
6. Know the best matching ratios or formulas. This rule is important because one local dollar (cash or in-kind) can produce from one to nine federal or state dollars. This rule is a special case of pervasive rules 1 and 6: maximize outside resources and mobilize marginal resources (and sometimes called the "Elastic Dollar Principle," or, "Getting the Biggest Bang for the Local Buck").

Grant-Acquisition Rules. Once the preceding rules are satisfied by local officials a formal grant application will probably be prepared for processing. A set of grant-acquisition rules now becomes operative. (These rules might be called "Boy Scout" rules, since they are all preceded by the motto "be prepared.") In the acquisition/approval process local officials should be prepared to:

1. Have the grant rejected.
2. Learn that the grant regulations have been changed.
3. Resubmit the grant in a revised form (the revision may be slight, moderate, or substantial).
4. Lobby with the grantor agency using legislative, executive, and professional contacts (this is frequently termed "Having friends

call"—a more effective but rarer strategy is called "Having a godfather").

5. Call in your own experts (if the grantor agency raises questions or has doubts about the grant proposal, produce character witnesses).

6. Show past or potential results that look good (this rule is probably preferable to rule 5 but is more demanding: Officials must do the nitty-gritty work rather than merely pay for an expert's opinion).

7. Work on a short fuse! Like fighting fires, rapid response times are critical. Developing a 100-page proposal for a $100,000 grant in one month (including all local clearances and sign-offs) is a suitable dry-run test for assessing the adequacy of local response time. (The short-fuse rule results, in operational terms, in such behavior as all-night work sessions, and such by-products as cigarette butts and coffee cups, frayed nerves, and special-delivery couriers sent on the early-morning plane.)

Intergovernmental Games

The thoughtful reader is already well aware of the "gamesmanship" involved in IGR behavior—and among all participants, not just local officials. This juncture is a convenient place to briefly identify—and not exhaustively—the different types of games that are played in the IGR arena. Several of these games may be played in IGR at the same time with numerous participants engaged simultaneously in two, three, or more games. It is easy to see, then, why IGR has been referred to as "mild chaos," a "menagerie," a "can of worms," a "zoo," and "crisis baseball." This last "game" is played exactly like regular baseball with one exception: When the ball is pitched to a batter, any player can pick up any *base* and run with it in any direction!

Intergovernmental Games Officials Play

Name of IGR Game	Brief Description
Liberty	Don't tell *us* how to spend *your* money.
Equality	Distribute the dollars evenly.
Fraternity	Program professionals stick together (or, Remember the picket fence!)

(continued)

Intergovernmental Games Officials Play (continued)

Name of IGR Game	Brief Description
Beggar Thy Neighbor (Also, Lure the Big One and, disparagingly, Smokestack Chasing)	Give tax breaks to attract industry.
Covet Your Brother's Birthright	Get an earmarked share of another government level's tax revenue.
Hustle the Buck	Play the grantsmanship game.
We Are All in the Same Mess	Appeal for intergovernmental cooperation and coordination.
End Run	Bypass the states.
Medicine Ball	The General Accounting Office audits a grant.
Hang Together or We Will Hang Separately	Strategy of the Big Seven public interest groups (PIGs) in pushing general revenue sharing.
Turf Protection	Defending the program against all attacks and challenges, especially from elected officials.
Project Perfectionism	Defining project grant requirements so strictly that only "angels" can qualify.
Snowballing	Growth in the number, specificity, and complexity of grant program regulations as the program acquires: (a) more money, (b) greater age, and (c) more constituents and applicants.
Einstein's Law of IGR Relativity: $E=MC^2$	E = energy invested in the number, specificity, and complexity of regulations M = mass of dollars available for expenditure C = conservative, cautious speed of the officials writing regulations
Bump and Run	What the national government does with general revenue sharing money: It gives a tap or touch (with money) and leaves. (This is also called "Putting the money on the stump and running.")

LOCAL OFFICIALS' ATTITUDES

The difficulty of obtaining a representative sample of all local officials poses a modest but not insurmountable problem in reaching conclusions about attitudes relevant to IGR. Data availability determines to a large extent which local officials' attitudes are part of the analysis. The perspectives of city and county chief executives will therefore be predominant. These local chief executives are the balance wheels around which IGR games revolve in cities and counties. The formal positions they hold and the other power bases they may have developed make their attitudes important elements in understanding IGR at all levels. The many surveys provide us much data for describing several IGR attitude dimensions of these officials.

Cognition (Salience)

How important and significant are IGR to local executives? Are they aware of interjurisdictional effects on local government? Where do they rank IGR in the hierarchy of local problems? Relevant to these questions was a 1973 survey by the National League of Cities (NLC), which generated responses from over 500 mayors across the nation.[11] A large number of "urban problems," twenty-eight in all, were presented to the mayors under eight broad categories. One of the eight was intergovernmental relations, which covered four problem areas: relations with county, regional, state, and federal governments. Depending on city size, this overall IGR category ranked second, third, or fourth among the eight categories in importance. Somewhat surprisingly, it ranked second in smaller cities (under 100,000) and slightly lower in larger cities. Among the twenty-eight specific problems, the following four IGR problems were ranked as indicated by the mayors (the percentages in parentheses are of mayors mentioning the item as a major problem):[12]

Relations with county:	4th	(53%)
Relations with state:	15th	(30%)
Relations with national gov't:	16th	(25%)
Relations with regional gov'ts:	21st	(22%)

IGR ranks in the middle to upper ranges in the cognitive map of mayors surveyed by the NLC.

11. Raymond L. Bancroft, "America's Mayors and Councilmen: Their Problems and Frustrations," *Nation's Cities,* 12 (April 1974): 14-24.
12. Ibid., p. 15.

Two further sidelights on the significance of IGR for mayors might be noted. First, IGR was one of eight topics allocated a half-day session in a 1975 Harvard seminar for fifteen new mayors of large (over 100,000) cities. A postseminar evaluation by the mayors indicated that "Intergovernmental relations . . . between city, state, and federal levels needed more attention."[13] Second, the extensiveness of IGR among small cities is revealed by a survey of intergovernmental service agreements. From one-half to two-thirds of cities ranging in size from 2500 to 25,000 persons had service agreements with other governmental units. Most of these contractual exchange agreements were with counties and/or other municipalities, but nearly one-fourth of the cities had service agreements with state governments, special districts, and school districts.[14]

The mayors surveyed by the NLC also identified "the use of general revenue sharing funds" as a major problem. It ranked eleventh as a problem and was mentioned by 38 percent of the mayors. The survey was conducted in 1973, one year after the 1972 enactment of the IGR program, and thus while the new program was very much on the minds of most mayors. But on the "problem" of revenue sharing one *councilman* remarked: "As long as federal programs continue along the lines of general revenue sharing and elimination of categorical grants, the entire responsibility for program development will shift from the Congress and federal administrators to local legislatures and local bureaucrats."[15] Note that he omitted mention of mayoral responsibility for program development!

Issues

A more dominant IGR theme among the mayors (and councilmen) in the NLC survey was the shifting of power away from local government. They saw an erosion of home-rule powers by state legislatures as a present and future dominant issue. One mayor observed that "if present trends continue with state and federal bureaucrats making

13. Institute of Politics and The United States Conference of Mayors, *Seminar on Transition and Leadership for Newly Elected Mayors—Final Report* (Cambridge, Mass.: Harvard University, John F. Kennedy School of Government, May 1976), p. 17.

14. Urban Data Service, "Intergovernmental Service Agreements for Smaller Cities," Vol. 5, No. 1 (Washington, D.C.: International City Management Association, January, 1973).

15. Bancroft, "America's Mayors and Councilmen," p. 24.

more decisions then local government will become little more than a 'clerical function' or a 'debating society.'" Another mayor asserted, "Local government is in jeopardy," and still another, "Control has shifted away from the elected official to the administrative official. . . . this is disastrous."[16] The chief corrective actions urged were: (1) to mobilize "cooperative efforts by cities and their counties" and (2) to generate more influence at state and national levels through the various statewide municipal leagues. More specifically, the following percentages of officials concurred that the NLC and state leagues of cities should act in the following ways:[17]

Activity	NLC	State League
	(% favoring)	
Disseminate information on state &		
federal programs	35	31
Assume aggressive stance with:		
a. state legislature		39
b. Congress and executive branch	33	

Although notable percentages of these officials favor using these city-based associations as means for exercising influence on IGR issues, it is perhaps slightly surprising that the percentages are so modest—about one-third of all respondents. There are two possible explanations.

First, most associations of municipalities are not like-minded and cohesive; they are often sharply divided, especially according to city size. Hence the existence of the U.S. Conference of Mayors (USCM), an organization restricted to mayors of cities above 30,000 in population. Second, the nonspecific nature of issues on which state leagues (or the NLC) should take an "aggressive stance" could depress apparent cohesiveness. Some issues, such as home rule and General Revenue Sharing, may tend to pull cities (and counties) together; other issues may split them badly. A few issues can exemplify the full range of convergent and divergent issues.

The General Revenue Sharing (GRS) law enacted in 1972 expired in 1976. During 1974 and 1975 several research studies examined the effects of GRS with respect to a core issue: Should GRS be continued? Exceptionally high percentages of the city and county chief

---

16. Ibid., p. 22.
17. Ibid., p. 21.

executives (and also their key fiscal officers) surveyed were strikingly consistent in "very strongly" supporting the continuation of GRS. From 80 to 90 percent of the city and county officials gave this most favorable response. When the responses were analyzed by type of unit (city or county), by type of official (elected or appointed), and by size of unit, there were no significant differences in the views of these local officials on the continuation of GRS. Additional questions on whether GRS should be expanded and by how much, and whether GRS should be adjusted for inflation also produced remarkably uniform opinions among these various local officials.[18]

In contrast with these consistently favorable attitudes on GRS are the varied views of local officials about the first large block grant program—the 1968 Omnibus Crime Control and Safe Streets Act. In addition to creating the Law Enforcement Assistance Administration (LEAA) to administer the program, the act gave state governments a central role in criminal justice planning and in making decisions on the distribution of funds within the states. The USCM and NLC were united in official opposition to the block grant approach and to control over funds by state government. They favored a direct grant program between the national government and cities and in early 1969 published a scathing attack on the basic design and initial execution of the LEAA block grant program.

During the summer of 1969 the International City Management Association sponsored a survey of city executives' views on the Safe Streets Act.[19] Over 600 executives responded to a mail questionnaire sent to the 859 cities over 25,000 population. One surprising general finding was that two-thirds of the executives *supported* the block grant approach; the remaining one-third preferred a categorical grant approach. It should also be noted that more than two-thirds of the respondents favored a block grant approach with direct grants to localities, that is, bypassing the states. But the most distinctive finding from the survey was the variation in officials' attitudes by city size: Only 40 percent of the officials from cities over 500,000 supported the block grant principle; nearly three-fourths of the officials in cities of from 25,000 to 100,000 favored the block grant.[20] City size was

---

18. F. Thomas Juster (ed.), *The Economic and Political Impact of General Revenue Sharing* (Washington, D.C.: National Science Foundation/Research Applied to National Needs, April 1976), pp. 6–9.
19. Urban Data Service, "The Safe Streets Act: The Cities' Evaluation," Vol. 1, No. 9 (Washington, D.C.: International City Management Association, September 1969).
20. Ibid., p. 20.

associated with a substantial split in IGR attitudes; officials from larger cities were more skeptical about block grants and more fearful of state decisions in allocating LEAA funds.

In sum, then, depending on the issue, the particular position, and the type of jurisdiction, local officials' IGR attitudes may be convergent or divergent, and may demonstrate consensus or cleavages.

Involvement

Within what patterns of IGR knowledge and contacts do local executives operate? How do they view their relationships with county, regional, state, and national governments? Again, it is impossible to map more than a tiny fraction of the terrain.

A 1965 survey of forty-five city managers in cities of over 100,000 in population revealed that only five of the managers did *not* belong to some type of formal or informal intergovernmental association.[21] In the Detroit metropolitan area at the time of the survey there was a group of twelve north-suburban city managers, self-styled the "Dirty Dozen" (because they initially met to discuss areawide sanitation and sewage problems). They convened monthly to compare and coordinate any of their respective cities' activities that had larger area significance and that crossed municipal boundaries. Later, in the western part of the Detroit metropolitan area, a baker's dozen of managers (calling themselves the "Clean 13") organized for essentially similar purposes.

Formal as well as informal IGR involvement is extensive and includes numerous officials besides city managers. The 1965 survey found that over half of the managers belonged to two or more interjurisdictional associations. But it was equally noteworthy that over three-fourths of the mayors and two-thirds of the councilmen in the surveyed cities belonged to one or more multijurisdictional associations.[22]

These intergovernmental links reveal that each type of official tended to have a specialized pattern of contact. The managers mostly contacted other *appointed* officials at the local, state, and national levels. Mayors, however, were the clear leaders in contacting *elected* officials at the local and national levels (for example, other mayors, councilmen, and members of Congress). The significant exception to these pairings occurred with respect to state legislators; contacts with

21. Wright, "Intergovernmental Relations," p. 160.
22. Ibid.

these legislators was about evenly divided between mayors and city managers.

Which major programs or functions did city managers perceive to be critical in involvement with national, state, county, and school governments? Critical city-national contacts clustered around three functions: urban renewal, welfare, and highways. City-state relationships focused most on highways, financial matters, and general legal issues (such as the authority to perform certain activities). City-county relationships revolved around highways, health, and financial matters. Somewhat surprisingly, the range of city-school involvements on critical functions was the most extensive: parks and recreation, financial matters, police (law enforcement), planning, streets, traffic, and educational policies. Clearly, city managers perceive other jurisdictions to be critically involved with basic local programs and services.[23]

In addition to assessing the managers' perceptions of how other units are involved with city activities, it would be useful to learn about their participation in various IGR activities. Fragmentary data are available from two surveys done in 1965 and 1972. The first drew on the large-city study of managers and provided gross measures of how regularly managers contacted officials from other levels on the "critical involvement" functions just noted. The figures below indicate what percentage of the managers had such contacts once a month or more often. (Percentages in parentheses indicate weekly contacts.)

Jurisdiction	Percentage of Managers with Monthly (or Weekly) IGR Contacts
National	61 (7)
State	68 (15)
County	62 (17)
Schools	44 (11)

Substantial percentages of these managers of large cities had fairly frequent involvement with officials in other jurisdictions, a modest percentage appeared to have intensive intergovernmental involvement.

The second survey (1972) on managers' IGR involvement includes responses from 98 city managers (from a universe of 148) located in

23. Ibid., pp. 164–68.

four midwestern states.[24] The survey focused chiefly on knowledge of and involvement with federal grant-in-aid programs in cities under 100,000. The study was designed to explore the "information-participation gap"—the alleged absence of information about grant programs that was necessary for securing federal aid—thought to surround the numerous federal categorical grant programs. The study identified fifty-seven grant programs available to all the cities surveyed and sought the manager's awareness of these programs.

A majority of the managers (54 percent) indicated that the *Catalog of Federal Domestic Assistance* was their most frequently consulted first source of information on grants. Less than one-third relied initially either on representatives of federal agencies or on other city managers. State municipal leagues were a significant but less used source of information, while private consulting services were the least mentioned source of initial grant information—named by about one in ten managers. Managers were asked questions that enabled the researchers to develop involvement/knowledge scores, which were then analyzed by federal agency, grant size (in dollars), city size, and such personal characteristics of the city manager as education.

Managers were most knowledgeable about, and most involved with, grants administered by HUD (an expected finding considering HUD's urban mandate), and were least knowledgeable about and least involved with programs administered by HEW and OEO. Between the dollar size of grants and the managers' knowledge of and involvement with the grant, there was a positive and statistically significant relationship—although it was not as strong as anticipated. It did, however, confirm the general proposition that managers know about and tend to participate in grant programs where the dollar payoffs tend to be large. (See the IGR action rules, especially in the pervasive category, rule 6, on mobilizing marginal resources.)

The association between managers' educational attainment and grant knowledge was positive and significant; the more advanced the education, the greater the knowledge of and involvement with grants. No link was found, however, between length of the manager's experience and knowledge of grants. Possibly the most significant finding of the study was a very strong positive relationship between city size and

---

24. F. Ted Hebert and Richard D. Bingham, *Personal and Environmental Influences Upon the City Manager's Knowledge of Federal Grant-In-Aid Programs* (Norman: Bureau of Governmental Research, University of Oklahoma, 1972).

managers' knowledge of and involvement in grant programs.[25] When analyses controlled for other variables such as education, experience, and use of a part-time or full-time person charged with coordinating grant efforts, this strong association remained. Larger cities (among those under 100,000) with greater staffs apparently have an advantage in the grantsmanship game.

Another survey, a 1969 Urban Data Service study, provides more findings on the character of local executives' involvement in the grantsmanship process on a wide array of IGR matters. Five specific questions focused on how city executives were involved with various participants in the grant application and approval processes. Table 8-2 tabulates responses to the five survey items by sources of assistance on whom the local executive may call. (The sources of assistance are not mutually exclusive categories.)

The table describes the shifting nature of executive involvement and strategies through the successive stages of the grantsmanship game. Grant information and application efforts are clearly centered on federal regional offices, involvement with any of the other participants being incidental. But to expedite or promote a grant application or to bring about a change in guidelines involves drastically different strategies and sources of assistance. The role of regional offices clearly declines, while the roles of congressional and senatorial members become predominant; approaches to agency headquarters in Washington, D.C., also increase; and use of national associations or of a city's own lobbyist is minuscule. Following grant approval, a city executive, faced with administrative complications, appears to rely on diverse types of support; the regional office, however, is again the focal point.

An analysis of the responses by city size, geographic region, and city type (central, suburban, independent) disclosed no appreciable variations. The grantsmanship process appears to be particularistic in the way local executives perceive their involvement. But it may be more pervasive, uniform, and systematized than is suspected.

Impacts

How do local officials view the impacts of IGR on themselves and on the programs, policies, and administrative operations of their juris-

---

25. Ibid., p. 24.

Table 8-2. *Sources of Contact and Assistance in Connection with Federal Grants-In-Aid for City Executives, 1972*

Source of Contact and Assistance	Initial Source Contacted	Completing Grant Application	Expediting Grant Application	Change in Federal Guidelines	Administrative Problems in Approved Grant
	(percentages of city executives: N's=704-782)				
Federal regional offices	85	94	34	49	63
Agency headquarters in Wash., D.C.	5	3	11	15	13
Congressmen/ staff	13	3	60	40	34
Senators/ staff	7	3	43	27	22
National assoc.	5	1	1	6	2
Own D.C. office	—	—	1	1	1
Governor's office	2	2	5	3	2
State legislator	3	1	6	3	4

Source: Urban Data Service, "Federal, State, Local Relationships," International City Management Association, Vol. 1, No. 12 (Washington, D.C.: December 1969), pp. 30-35.

dictions? What, for example, have been the perceived effects of grants-in-aid on local fiscal efforts?

A major data base for analysis of perceived impacts at the local level is an extensive ACIR-ICMA survey conducted in 1975.[26] Executives of cities and counties above 10,000 and 50,000 in population, respectively, were sent questionnaires on federal and state aid programs. The survey instruments requested factual information on the two aid sources and posed queries on a wide range of grant effects. Response rates for cities larger than 50,000 varied from 45 to 67 percent and for counties over 100,000 from 26 to 56 percent. Response rates from the smallest cities and counties were lower.

The receipt of federal grants, one measure of impact, was highest among counties—over 80 percent for the responding counties, slightly under 75 percent for responding cities. There was a strong relationship

26. Advisory Commission on Intergovernmental Relations, *The Intergovernmental Grant System as Seen by Local, State, and Federal Officials* (Washington, D.C., Government Printing Office, March 1977, A-54). The following reported findings are in tables and text of Chapter II, pp. 3-81.

between jurisdiction size and receipt of federal aid: Only about 60 percent of the smallest cities and counties indicated receipt of federal grants, compared to virtually 100 percent among the largest cities and counties. The impact of state grants-in-aid to cities and counties was not drastically different from that of federal aid; the positive relationship between size and grant receipt was evident, although the percentages for state aid were generally somewhat lower than those for federal aid in both cities and counties.

About one-third of all federal grants to cities were block grant funds for health, law enforcement, employment training, and community development. The remaining two-thirds were categorical aids. Counties obtained only about one-fifth of their federal grant funds through block grants. The remainder came from categoricals. The average *number* of individual federal grants received by the responding cities was 9.3; for counties, 20.6. Larger cities obtained about fifteen grants each while the larger counties averaged thirty-five grants each. Large cities and counties are obviously big-league players in the grantsmanship game. For a concrete illustration of the grantsmanship game see Appendix J, "How You Play the Game."

Similar data on the number of state grants to cities and counties are not available. State aid, however, differed notably as to the predominant *type* of grant to cities and counties: General, nonrestrictive grants made up over half the state aid to counties but less than 40 percent to cities, which received over 60 percent as categorical assistance. In this respect, federal and state grants are somewhat offsetting in the presumed discretion they allow cities and counties to employ in using the funds.

A central aim of most if not all federal and state categorical grants is to affect local decisions on the overall priorities and funding levels for the aided program. What effects do federal and state aid in fact have on local decisions? Do they induce spending patterns or allocations that differ from what would occur if there were none of the restrictions normally accompanying categorical grants? The answer appears to be a resounding yes. When asked whether they would allocate categorical funds differently if program restrictions were removed, 66 percent of the city executives and 81 percent of the county executives said yes. A follow-up question revealed that over three-fourths of the executives in both groups would have made moderate or substantial allocational shifts.

When the two executive groups were asked the same questions with respect to state categorical grants similar patterns emerged: One-half of the city executives and 72 percent of the county executives declared that they would allocate the categorical monies differently, and over 80 percent of those so answering said the shift would be moderate or substantial. Jurisdictional size was positively related to reallocation responses for federal and state categoricals to counties and for federal categoricals to cities. Central-city and metropolitan county executives exhibited the strongest tendencies to reallocate federal categoricals. Metropolitan and northeastern county executives were also more inclined to reallocate state categorical aid. Categorical grants, then, do have moderate to substantial effects on how local funds are spent.

What fiscal effects do federal and state categorical grants have on the amount of money raised by the recipient jurisdiction in excess of the required matching amounts? In other words, are specifically targeted grants a stimulus to the aided program? Most city and county executives believe that both federal and state categorical aids have such a stimulative impact. By margins of greater than three to one, varying somewhat by program area, these executives "saw Federal categorical programs affecting the spending of local funds, and that effect was seen as overwhelmingly stimulative, and more so by the city than the county officials." For state categorical aids there was also "a more stimulative than substitutive effect on local spending; yet, it was not nearly as pronounced a stimulative effect as in the case of the Federal aids. . . ."[27]

Additional data could permit the examination of local perceptions of other IGR impacts on local governments: for example, efforts to improve federal grants management, changes in local administrative capabilities and service levels, impact on administrative supervision. Sufficient evidence has been provided, however, to confirm that the impacts of state and federal actions are explicitly recognized and taken into account by local officials. And local officials, like all IGR participants, have jurisdictional interests to protect, policy preferences to push, and personal likes and dislikes. These arrays of attitudes emerge when the officials are asked to rank or judge various IGR events, policies, procedures, or participants, as we shall see.

Evaluation of IGR by Local Officials

A major responsibility of local governments is to provide public goods and services. Everything said and documented about IGR, how-

---

27. Ibid., p. 80.

ever, has emphasized the extensive influence of state and federal officials in this delivery process. How do local officials evaluate the involvement of these IGR "others"? How do they compare the performance and assistance rendered by the national and state governments? Again the analysis is confined mainly to city executives.

In the 1965 (Wright) survey managers of large cities were asked to evaluate the results of IGR contacts with national and state officials on the three major functions specified as most critical by the manager. Managers indicated "excellent" results for 31 percent of their national IGR contacts and 18 percent of their state IGR contacts.[28] This favorable evaluation of federal over state results is consistent with a later, more extensive study, a 1969 Urban Data Service survey.[29] Thirty-eight percent of the 800 city executives indicated that the federal government was more helpful than state government in dealing with city problems; only 21 percent found the state more helpful; and 27 percent indicated that *neither* jurisdiction was helpful.[30] Again, size influenced this IGR evaluation. Over half the executives from cities above 50,000 found the federal government more helpful, while only one-third of small-city executives did so. These findings show clearly and explicitly the higher ratings given to the federal government (and lower ones to state government) by executives from larger cities. To clinch the point, data from the Urban Data Service Safe Streets survey (also in 1969) disclosed that nearly 60 percent of the executives in cities over 250,000 "seldom" or only "occasionally" found state government officials helpful and sympathetic.[31]

Among the many sources of large-city disenchantment with state government, one of the longest-standing complaints was underrepresentation. Urban representation in the form of battles over reapportionment was an issue in state legislatures and the courts before and after the *Baker* vs. *Carr* Supreme Court decision in 1962. By 1969 over half the responding city executives indicated that reapportionment had already made state legislatures more helpful and sympathetic to urban problems.[32] This figure varied little by city size and included more than half the executives from central cities. (One wonders if such high proportions would still hold today.)

---

28. Wright, "Intergovernmental Relations," p. 168.
29. Urban Data Service, "Federal, State, Local Relationships," Vol. 1, No. 12 (Washington, D.C.: International City Management Association, December 1969).
30. Ibid., pp. 4, 12.
31. Urban Data Service, "The Safe Streets Act," p. 14.
32. Urban Data Service, "Federal, State, Local Relationships," p. 40.

When asked to rate the important barriers to state assistance in solving urban problems, city executives offered and judged several means of state response and areas of reform. Major state barriers were evaluated and ranked in descending order of importance:[33]

1. lack of state fiscal resources;
2. lack of legislative leadership;
3. political traditions favoring rural areas;
4. constraints in state law;
5. lack of gubernatorial leadership;
6. lack of leadership in state agencies;
7. lack of professional administrators.

An economic factor (1) and political forces (2-5) stand out as the chief stumbling blocks to effective state responses on urban problems. The first factor, which is in fact political as well as economic, is not easily manipulated. Barriers 2-5 are all subject to influence by city (and county) political leaders with IGR bargaining skills. Items 6 and 7 are administrative in a straightforward sense. A major change in one or more of the preceding barriers, especially 5, could pave the way for positive shifts in 6 and 7. Altered state-city relationships, then, hinge on basic political forces and influences. Once these are properly aligned according to the perspectives and values of local officials, it should be possible to induce appropriate administrative behavior in state agencies.

But from the perspectives of local officials, administrative recalcitrance, complications, and even confusion are still present in IGR, as selected data show. For example, over one-fourth of the city executives indicated that federal regional officials were "seldom or never flexible" in adjusting federal programs to the special conditions of a locality, while nearly another half indicated that the federal administrators were only "occasionally" flexible.[34] This finding may seem to contradict the earlier-noted favorable rating of federal over state helpfulness, but it does not. The earlier ranking was only *relative*. Furthermore, this low evaluation of federal regional officials is consistent with views expressed by more than one-fourth of city executives that neither federal nor state governments were helpful on urban problems.

If additional evaluations of IGR administrative features are needed, the 1975 ACIR survey on grants provides ready samples. From a list of twenty-four "problem areas" city and county executives were asked to

---

33. Ibid.
34. Ibid., pp. 36-37.

identify the five most serious involving the design and administration of federal categorical grants. Two sentences from the ACIR report will adequately summarize city and county executives' evaluations of federal grant administration:

> . . . problems which have been the focus of grant administration reform ef-
> forts of the past decade still are viewed as the key sore spots. The complexity
> and volume of paper work, the time involved in processing project grants, the
> complexity of reporting, accounting, and auditing requirements, variations
> in reporting, accounting, and auditing requirements—these read like a litany
> of the problems that the Federal Assistance Review (FAR) program and the
> related management circulars were designed to cure.[35]

Equally devastating are responses to the question whether each problem area had improved or worsened in the past five years. All of the five problem areas identified separately by city and county executives—volume of paperwork on project grants; time involved in grant process; getting prompt policy interpretations; complexity of reporting, accounting, and auditing requirements; inadequate consultation in developing regulations and guidelines—had become *worse* in the past five years.

SUMMARY

The fiscal analysis of local units within IGR (chapter 4) revealed substantial and increasing dependence on state and national governments, especially by cities. In this chapter the analysis of the actions and attitudes of local officials supports that conclusion. But these discrete, microlevel data on individuals permit a wider range of inferences about the way IGR works in local government.

If asked point blank, "Are you dependent on the national (or state) government?" most local officials would probably give a prompt "Yes." But the inquiry should not—and probably would not—stop there. As the sampling of opinions and actions in this chapter indicates, local officials would add several other points about their IGR roles:

- While local officials may be *dependent* on state and national officials, these latter officials are dependent on the locals—for

---

35. ACIR, *The Intergovernmental Grant System*, p. 37.

the implementation of programs fostered and funded by the other jurisdictions.

- The net result is a set of interdependent relationships in which each participant is important to the successful or satisfactory conduct of programs.
- The interdependence produces a set of nonsubservient, non-hierarchical relationships best described as bargaining-negotiation patterns.
- Local officials feel free to complain, criticize, and chastize state and national officials on policy and procedural concerns.
- Many local officials aggressively voice their views to other IGR participants, although a substantial number undoubtedly comply when pressured by national and state officials.
- Mayors and city managers occupy featured IGR roles, sometimes as a team and sometimes in separate, and disparate, scenarios. Of mayors it has been said, "They come from nowhere and go nowhere"; of city managers, "They come from anywhere and will probably go anywhere." But in their IGR capacities neither their prior nor their future positions make much difference in what they think or how they act. Mayors and managers are not, I suggest, "beggars-in-chief" (although a few may be). Most are better described as "IGR bargainers-in-chief."

State Officials:

Actions and Attitudes of Governors and Legislators

9

THE STATES AS MIDDLEMEN

"The states are in the middle." "The states are keystones in the federal arch." "The states are sick, sick, sick." "State government is the tawdriest, most incompetent, and most stultifying unit of the nation's political structure." "The states move ahead." "The states are powerful." These quotes are a minute sampling of perspectives on the states. There are more ways of describing and judging the states than there are states. To U.S. and foreign observers the states may invite varying blends of fascination and awe, confusion and contempt. Seldom, however, have the states been given unqualified praise or respect.

Even the writers of *The Federalist* papers, the classic apologia of the U.S. Constitution, were inconsistent about what role and respect the states would enjoy in the new system that was "in strictness neither a national nor a federal Constitution."[1] On the one hand, *Federalist*

---

1. *The Federalist* papers, No. 39 (New York: New American Library, Mentor 1961), p. 246.

papers Nos. 17 and 45 spell out the strengths of the states based on their capacity to govern and the loyalty they command because of their proximity to the populace. On the other hand, *Federalist* papers Nos. 3, 46, and 82 reveal more skeptical views of the states, best summarized by Jay's assertion in No. 3 that "the administration, political counsels, and judicial decisions of the national government will be more wise, systematical, and judicious than those of the individual states."[2]

We will not try here to resolve the love-hate relationship that the states have been in the midst of for the last 200 years. It is sufficient to note that the difficult and sometimes confounding conditions facing the states are not attitudinal but *institutional*. State governments are in the middle of a three-player game of political "tag." Being between local units and the national government, they are forever "it." They are intermediate politically, fiscally, and administratively. And, as one writer has contended, "decisions made at the two ends of the [governing] process are more significant than those made in the middle."[3] The states have some kind of role and some influence, however indirect, in almost all governmental activities. But there are relatively few issues in contemporary affairs for which the state has exclusive responsibility unfettered by formal national constraints or potent local pressures.

The states, then, are pushed toward secondary roles in the governing process—roles that might best be described as facilitative and instrumental rather than forceful and integrative. To the degree that these observations are accurate we could infer that decision-making powers in IGR have gravitated away from the states and into the hands of local and national officials. Imagine a seesaw occupied at one end by the national government, the other end by localities; the states stand in the middle near or at the fulcrum. But shifts in the states' weight around the fulcrum have far less leverage than shifts at either end of the teeterboard.

But the states' position in IGR is actually more complex than the teeterboard and three-player game analogies suggest, as the model in figure 9–1 shows. At the center of the model is the state decision-making system. This system operates under a set of constraints that derive from three major external sources: national government, other states, and local governments. These constraints affect state officials

2. Ibid., p. 43.

3. York Willbern, "The States as Components in an Areal Division of Powers," in Arthur Mass (ed.), *Area and Power: A Theory of Local Government* (Glencoe, Ill.: The Free Press, 1959), p. 82.

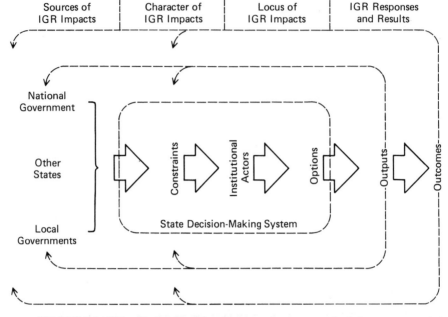

Figure 9-1. *The State Decision-Making System and Intergovernmental Relations (IGR)*

(labeled "institutional actors"). These officials perceive various options. Selection of options produces outputs (for example, highway or hospitals) that impinge on citizens *and* other governments in the form of outcomes—a safe trip, medical care, lower taxes for elderly persons. The outputs and outcomes produce feedback loops (the broken lines and inward-turning arrows) that affect these other IGR participants and the state decision-making system directly.

For our purposes in this chapter, then, this model not only clarifies the IGR network in which the states function but it emphasizes (through the feedback loops) that state actions are reflexive. Moreover, the model pinpoints the central role of state officials, whose actions and attitudes with respect to IGR are the subject of this chapter and the following one.

GOVERNORS AND IGR

It was not by happenstance that the originator of "picket fence federalism" was *Governor* Terry Sanford. Caught in the matrix of expanding federal programs of the 1960s, Sanford and his staff found the analogy a handy way of describing the scene of activity. It is debatable whether the picket fence model is a sufficiently precise guide to policy and administrative actions.[4] Yet the model dramatizes the need for powerful assertions of gubernatorial influence if state policies and programs are to be more than a hodgepodge of independent professional and functional fiefdoms.

But suppose a governor does get an effective grip on those directing and controlling these centrifugal programmatic forces. What has been gained? Which of two broad contentions is most compelling depends on one's preferences and values:

1. The governor has restored the integrity, strength, and coordinating capacities of the state, or
2. The governor has succeeded in becoming the "chief federal systems officer."

This last phrase, sometimes expressed quietly in the corridors of the annual Governors' Conference, has a suspect quality. Are top accolades and awards given to governors for their ability to manage programs initiated and financed largely under national aegis? From what little we know about governors' interests, aims, priorities, and proclivities we know that management is *not* near the top of any list of such concerns.[5] Policies and programs, however, are near and dear to most governors' concerns. Yet comparatively few governors apparently perceive and pursue management, staffing, organization, etc., as instruments for influencing policy and controlling programs.

Whatever approach or posture a governor adopts, one fact seems certain: A governor cannot escape from entanglement in a web of IGR political, policy, and administrative relationships. They impinge upon any governor from the farthest nooks and crannies of our intricate political system. For example, Robert Wood, former Secretary of HUD, reports that in 1967 an operational simulation (that is, a model) of the Model Cities program "identified the governor as a key figure in

---

4. The predominance of "vertical" or functional perspectives over "horizontal" or state-oriented views among the heads of state administrative agencies is supported by analyses presented in Alfred R. Light, *Intergovernmental Relations and Program Innovation: The Institutionalized Perspectives of State Administrators,* unpublished doctoral dissertation, Department of Political Science, University of North Carolina at Chapel Hill, 1976.

5. Coleman B. Ransone, Jr., *The Office of Governor in the United States* (University, Ala.: University of Alabama Press, 1956). See also National Governor's Conference, *On Being Governor* (Washington, D.C.: Governor's Office Series, No. 1, November 1976). The latter publication reports the results of a 1976 survey of fifty-two former governors in which only ten mentioned "day-to-day management of state government" as one of eleven "most difficult and demanding aspects" of the governor's job.

the delivery program.''[6] It should be emphasized that Model Cities was primarily a direct federal-local program in which it was expected that state government would have only an incidental role. How, then, could a governor have a critical role? A major reason was that state legislative actions were needed, and hence so was gubernatorial involvement in getting legislation passed.

The Model Cities illustration provides a starting point for discussing the actions and perspectives of governors on intergovernmental relations in general and on grants-in-aid in particular.[7]

Discrete and Collective Actions and Perspectives

Grants-in-aid are a major subset of all intergovernmental relationships experienced by governors (although precisely what proportion of a governor's IGR contacts are prompted by grant matters is impossible to specify). One consequence of grant-induced relationships is the governor's increased orientation toward Washington, D.C. (In more informal parlance, governors expand their "Potomac pipelines.") Three brief items reveal the nature and expanding scope of these state-national linkages.

First, former governor (of Florida) Farris Bryant testified that:

> The next to the last year I was in office, I sent the executive director of our State board of health to Washington on a year's leave of absence, badly as we needed him, just so he could learn how to operate with Federal people. He has been a great help to us since that time. But you ought not to have to do that kind of thing to learn just how to get along and through this morass.[8]

Second, about half the states have offices and permanent staffs in the nation's capital, there largely for the purpose of acquiring grants and virtually every state has an IGR coordinator; all but a few of these are located in governors' offices. In the late 1960s, however, a proposal, by North Carolina's Democratic governor, that a state-federal relations

---

6. Robert C. Wood, "Needs and Prospects for Research in Intergovernmental Relations," *Public Administration Review,* 30 (May/June 1970): 267.

7. The following section draws heavily on Deil S. Wright, "Governors, Grants, and the Intergovernmental System," in Thad Beyle and J. Oliver Williams (eds.), *The American Governor in Behavioral Perspective* (New York: Harper and Row, 1972), pp. 187–193.

8. *Grant Consolidation and Intergovernmental Cooperation,* hearings before the Subcommittee on Intergovernmental Relations of the House Committee on Government Operations, 91st Congress, 1st Session (Part 2), June 1969, p. 241.

agency be created and located in Washington, D.C., generated criticism from state legislators of both parties. The matter was resolved by creating the office but keeping it "at home" in Raleigh, the state capital. In 1973, under a Republican governor, the office was moved to D.C. as part of the new governor's announced aim of securing "all the federal funds to which North Carolina is legitimately entitled." At the same time a Raleigh-based Office of Intergovernmental Relations was created to, as one staff member said, "chase federal aid dollars." In subsequent years the governor annually announced to the press how much more federal money was coming into the state; for example, "Average per capita [federal] spending in North Carolina jumped from $203 to $279 per person—a 37 percent increase which far exceeds the national average increase of 11 percent."[9]

The third piece of evidence about expanding Potomac pipelines appeared in 1966, when a separate, permanent staff for the National Governor's Conference (NGC) was created and located in Washington, D.C. Previously the NGC had been served by the staff of the Council of State Governments with offices in Chicago (now in Lexington, Kentucky). The NGC staff is professional, aggressively active, and attempts to inform state chief executives on federal policy developments affecting the states, and to provide leverage for the governors' effective reactions to those policies.[10]

The NGC provides another source of gubernatorial perspectives on IGR: the resolutions passed at its annual sessions. Table 9-1 presents the results of using a fivefold classification scheme to examine the formal, substantive resolutions passed at the Governors' Conference from 1946 through 1969.[11] A total of 298 identifiable substantive resolutions (called "policy statements" after 1968) were coded, but 373 assignments to the intergovernmental action categories were made, since a single resolution often called for more than one type of action. The tabulation is also subdivided into three periods that correspond to particular break points in federal-state relations. (These points are explained below.)

The distribution for the entire 1946–1969 period reveals that

9. Press Release, Office of the Governor, State of North Carolina, January 16, 1976.

10. Jonathan Cottin, "Washington Pressures: National Governors' Conference," *National Journal*, February 28, 1970, pp. 454–459.

11. Resolutions on policy questions adopted annually by the National Governor's Conference appear in *State Government*. The author is indebted to Mr. David Stephenson for assistance with coding and check-coding the resolutions. Coding reliability was 84 percent agreement. This research was supported in part by the University Research Council of the University of North Carolina at Chapel Hill.

Table 9-1. *Resolutions of the Governors' Conference by Type of Intergovernmental Action Recommended and Period, 1946-1969*

Type of Action	Numbers (and percentages)			Total Numbers (and percentages)
	1946–1957	1958–1964	1965–1969	1946–1969
Less (or opposed to) national action	14 (11)	13 (10)	13 (11)	40 (11)
More (or favorable to) national action	38 (31)	55 (40)	54 (47)	147 (39)
More state action	43 (35)	52 (38)	36 (31)	131 (35)
More interstate action	20 (16)	12 (9)	5 (4)	37 (10)
More local action	8 (7)	4 (3)	6 (5)	18 (5)
Total actions	123 (100)	136 (100)	114 (100)	373 (100)
Total resolutions	90	109	99	298

Source of resolutions: *State Government* (Council of State Governments), annual articles on the Governor's Conference.

the governors' collective policy concerns were nearly two-fifths for more positive action by the national government and slightly over one-third for more state responses to public problems. Opposition to national action was about as frequent as resolutions urging interstate efforts, that is, "horizontal" federalism. Recommendations urging local action (such as improved local law enforcement) were infrequent.

One conclusion from the long-term tabulation is the limited extent to which the Governors' Conference has been a forum for formal verbal blasts against the national government. Only a states' rights "tithe" of about 10 percent of the governors' resolutions calls for a reduction in national government activities or policy initiatives. This finding confirms that "the governors have not invariably sought to turn back the invading national government at the borders of the states."[12] Indeed, a plurality of their recommendations are for greater national action and funding.

A breakdown of the resolutions by the three periods shown in table 9-1 permits further comments and conclusions. Rationales for the two dividing points are easily stated: In 1957 President Eisenhower made his historic Williamsburg speech urging a "return" of functions to the states; 1964 was the year of the last Governors' Conference prior to the flood of grants under the Great Society and creative federalism policies.

The marked feature of the percentages across the three periods is the rise in proposals for greater national action—from less than one-third in the first period to nearly half in the last period. This rise was at the expense of attention paid by governors to interstate matters. The Governors' Conference had in effect become increasingly "nationalized." In the late 1960s nearly 60 percent of its policy statements were beamed toward Washington with about half of all statements asking for affirmative national responses.

A 1960 study reported that perhaps 20 percent of a governor's time was occupied by national problems and relationships.[13] If the proportion of Governors' Conference resolutions relating to national action only roughly reflect the time governors spend on their potomac pipelines, then in the 1960s gubernatorial-national relations made a quantum leap.

12. Glenn E. Brooks, *When Governors Convene: The Governors' Conference and National Politics* (Baltimore, Md.: The Johns Hopkins Press, 1961), p. 167.
13. Ibid., p. 167.

Federal Grants: Payoffs and Problems

The actions and attitudes of governors in relation to grant-in-aid programs are anomalous and ambiguous. Because grants supply a major portion of state budgets it would border on political suicide for governors to oppose or refuse them. Politically a governor benefits greatly from obtaining as much federal aid as possible. Federal grants help meet demands for services and, as at the local level, they are generally regarded as a way of keeping taxes down.

But grants have disadvantages because they restrict a governor's range of policy choices. General constraints and specific restrictions accompany virtually every grant—not only between programs, but also within any programs that include several detailed grant categories or prescribe administrative standards sharply limiting flexible and effective use (from the governor's viewpoint) of grant funds.

A governor is further restrained by a combination of two factors: pressure groups, either the traditional private lobbies or those composed of public officials, and the commonly used device of a board or commission that partially insulates grant-supported fields from gubernatorial control. For example, policy control over highways usually rests less with governors than with alliances of highway engineers at all levels plus construction contractors and cement and equipment manufacturers. The administrative consequences of grants-in-aid tend to reinforce the dispersion of powers away from the chief executive. In short, the governor's policy-coordinating role is often diluted or effectively blocked.

One succinct analysis of these cross-pressures raised a central question asked by most governors: "Are grants a bane or a boon?" Two conclusions were:

> In practice, therefore, the governor finds that his policy decisions are conditioned by the policy decisions which have been made in Washington. . . .

> The governor, to a considerable extent, is bypassed in the line of communication and finds that his control over both policy and management of the agencies which administer these (grant) programs at the state level is weakened considerably.[14]

Grants-in-aid, then, paradoxically contribute to the governors' political and administrative headaches at the same time that they can serve as aspirin to alleviate state fiscal pains.

---

14. Ransone, *Office of Governor,* pp. 249–250.

Earlier Perspectives on Grants

What do governors think about grant problems? Unfortunately, the data are exceptionally limited; there has been no systematic analysis of the frequency, or of the content, of governors' testimony before congressional committees or their interactions with the president and cabinet officers. However, surveys in the 1950s and 1960s solicited governors' views on a range of questions on grants-in-aid. The first survey, sponsored by the House Subcommittee on Intergovernmental Relations in 1957, asked detailed questions in four functional areas: employment security, highways, public health, and welfare. The number of responses from governors ranged from twenty to thirty.[15]

Regarding program adequacy, expansion in all four functional areas was favored by most respondents. Clear majorities were satisfied with federal supervision, but in three areas a notable minority indicated dissatisfaction. A substantial minority favored some transfer of responsibility, mainly to the states. Questions regarding the need for legislative or administrative changes pointedly demonstrated that governors were ambivalent about grant programs. Almost uniformly, the governors noted that improvements were needed—*at the federal level.* These views stood in sharp contrast to their support for program expansion and their general satisfaction with distribution of program responsibilities and with federal supervision. The response pattern, although out of date and limited in scope, described a situation that could be summarized as: policy pleasing but administratively messy.

A second survey, undertaken by the Senate Subcommittee on Intergovernmental Relations in 1963, queried 6000 state and local officials, including all governors.[16] The response rate was very poor (8 percent), and only nine of the fifty governors responded. Not surprisingly the responses repeated the pattern revealed by the earlier House subcommittee survey. For example, six of the nine governors mentioned additional functions that should receive grant assistance, and

---

15. *Replies from State and Local Governments to Questionnaire on Intergovernmental Relations,* Sixth Report by the House Committee on Government Operations, Subcommittee on Intergovernmental Relations, 85th Congress, 1st Session, House Report No. 575, June 17, 1957. For more detailed data see *Staff Report on Replies from State and Local Governments to Questionnaire on Intergovernmental Relations,* Intergovernmental Relations Subcommittee of the House Government Operations Committee, 84th Congress, 2nd Session, Committee Print, August 1956.
16. *The Federal System as Seen by State and Local Officials,* a study prepared by the staff of the Subcommittee on Intergovernmental Relations, Senate Committee on Government Operations, 88th Congress, 1st Session, Committee Report, 1963.

the same number wanted some responsibilities reassigned under grant programs to the states. Conversely, five felt that grants distorted the emphasis of state and local programs, and eight of the nine agreed that federal grant requirements hampered the organizational flexibility of the states and localities.

In short, the governors acknowledged both the political and programmatic advantages of grants and the financial and administrative problems that accompanied them. These views, however, were voiced before the grant explosion and proliferation in the mid-1960s.

Recent Attitudes and Actions

The six years from 1957 to 1963 produced no sharp differences in governors' views on federal grants. But the passage of another six years from 1963 to 1969 raised substantial questions about the distribution of gubernatorial opinions on grants. Did governors still support the expansion of grant programs? A clue to a change in attitudes came early. In 1965 the Governors' Conference became the first public interest group to go on record in favor of General Revenue Sharing legislation. Endorsement and active promotion of GRS was an early indicator of softening support for categorical aids. However, governors did not necessarily favor a reduction in existing aid, but rather that no new aid should be in the form of categoricals.

The governors' aims first met with modest success in the Partnership for Health Act of 1966, which consolidated several categorical disease grants into a small block grant for health. Somewhat greater political and policy success was achieved in 1968 with the larger law enforcement ("Safe Streets") block grant program. But because categorical aid continued to expand and revenue sharing was getting no closer to enactment, governors intensified their advocacy of reform and redirection of the total federal aid non-system.

In 1969 two governors, Nelson E. Rockefeller of New York and Calvin L. Rampton of Utah, testified before the House Subcommittee on Intergovernmental Relations on pending grant reform legislation. They spoke as representatives of the National Governors' Conference and of their own states. Excerpts from their statements to the subcommittee convey the substance and the strength of the attitudes of governors in general.

Governor Rockefeller:

I would like to concentrate on two fundamental questions:

Is the present system of categorical grants-in-aid effectively meeting today's needs?

And, two, if given more flexibility, can, and will, the States and localities use Federal funds more effectively?

There is a maze of programs—420 Federal grant-in-aid programs. In the five years between 1963 and 1967 alone, some 240 new programs have been added, an average of about 48 programs a year. . . .

The splintering of grants produces a maze of plans, regulations and rulings. The 17 grants in welfare alone have led to 5,000 pages of Federal program operating requirements. In the case of education grants, a State is required to submit 20 separate plans.

Now, I would just like to make a comment parenthetically regarding this, if I may. The complexity and number of these rules and regulations require a tremendous amount of skilled manpower just to conform to the regulations. Thus we are siphoning off skilled manpower to follow the detailed regulations. . . .

It is my feeling that the categorical grants system is not geared to today's needs. The failure to meet today's needs is far more critical than the concern for administrative waste, which, of course, is a very real concern.

The need for a more comprehensive approach and for greater flexibility to meet functional requirements is vital, as is the need for flexibility to help State and local governments meet their fiscal crises. . . .

Historically, Federal grants were used to prod and push States and localities to begin specific new programs. I think this was an eminently justified and farsighted point of view on the part of the Congress, and it has had very good effect. However, with rare exceptions, Federal programs are not available for the everyday burdens, the on-going services I mentioned before—police, teachers, fire, sanitation, et cetera, with a shortage of funds, the moneys have to be taken from basic services to be used for matching for fringe-benefit services. In fact, due to Federal matching requirements, State and local funds must be used for the new programs. State and local fiscal crises are due, however, to the rapidly rising cost of day-to-day public service.

The basic need today is for Federal support, not Federal stimulation.

Governor Rampton:

Mr. Chairman, I have very little to add to what Governor Rockefeller said, except that the problems encountered by New York State in responding to Federal programs are probably magnified in a small State. Our State government is smaller and considerably more simplified than either the government of the State of New York or the Government of the United States, and for the limited number of State departments that we have that have to respond or who have the opportunity to respond to so many Federal programs, it is very difficult.

We have another problem, too, in regard to categorical grants. The standards and guidelines of categorical grants, which are often rigid and very detailed, are set forth to meet the needs of the typical State, and the typical State, of course, is generally a larger State. Often these rigid guidelines will not meet at all the requirements of a smaller State with substantially different problems. . . .

I prepared a bill and had it introduced into the last legislature to make a single department of State government administer all manpower programs and consolidate them. Well, about halfway through I got cold feet for fear that I was going to lose some Federal money by using this consolidating procedure, and so we substituted a bill providing for a coordinating committee to try to coordinate them.

But, of course, coordination, while it is sometimes the only answer that you can get, is never as successful as actual consolidation into a single department, which we could do if all of these 17 grants that we have . . . come to us in a single block grant.[17]

In each of these statements there are significant features that should be emphasized. Governor Rockefeller makes four points concerning grants:

1. The growth in grants had produced a situation bordering on administrative chaos.
2. Criticism of grants extends beyond mere administrative difficulties.
3. Categorical grants (according to Rockefeller) fail to meet "today's needs."
4. Categorical grants are out of phase because they finance "fringe benefits" rather than basic state-local services and because they are stimulative rather than supportive.

Governor Rampton concurs with these points and adds a few other significant ones:

1. Grants pose greater problems for small states than for large

---

17. *Grant Consolidation and Intergovernmental Cooperation*, pp. 87, 89, 93–94, 97.

ones; grant guidelines and standards geared for the "typical state" are really designed for a large state. Implicit in this observation about typical states is a second point.

2. There is an underlying diversity, and even divisiveness, among the states (for example, in size); there is a hint of interstate competition over grants and also the more openly expressed feeling that grant distribution favors the large states.

3. Governors have difficulty asserting a policy-coordinating role. (Rampton spoke of manpower programs but numerous other program fields could be named.)

4. Block grants are a promising solution to many of these problems.

The two initial block programs already mentioned—Partnership for Health and LEAA—were followed by the passage of three others in the 1970s, and with GRS in 1972. Although gubernatorial attitudes and actions were not singularly responsible for these shifts in the strategies of fiscal assistance to state and local governments, their energies were nevertheless indicative of widely shared sentiments concerning intergovernmental fiscal relationships.

In the 1970s have governors further changed their outlook toward grants? A wide-ranging survey of governors' policy views on grants is not available, but recent experience shows that organizational and administrative problems associated with grants are matters of major continuing concern. At the 1976 National Governors' Conference (NGC) the NGC Committee on Executive Management and Fiscal Affairs met with James T. Lynn, Director of the (U.S.) Office of Management and the Budget. At that meeting the governors emphasized their concerns that state and local governments could not effectively administer intergovernmental programs because of excessive federal requirements, restrictions, paperwork, duplication of reports, etc. Director Lynn asked the governors to provide specific documentation of the states' most significant intergovernmental management problems. The result was a NGC report, *Federal Roadblocks to Efficient State Government*, which identified (and gave examples for) six general issues:

1. Lack of coordination among federal departments or agencies limits the effectiveness of programs in solving problems and increases the administrative burden on the States.

2. The federal executive branch exceeds its proper authority in some areas, encroaching on matters which are within the proper jurisdiction of the States.

3. Federal regulations are prescriptive in methodology rather than oriented toward results.
4. Excessive reporting and paperwork requirements must be met by States participating in federal programs.
5. Funding and program implementation are delayed by lengthy approval procedures, absence of program guidelines, and other administrative practices which cause serious dislocation and inequities at the state level.
6. Lack of federal coordination and consistency in implementing indirect cost determination procedures creates continuing administrative confusion for States.[18]

A grants-based intergovernmental economy has created problems that have had multiple effects on state government. Two major effects have been the ascendancy of program professionals in state government and the stimulus for common attitudes and sometimes cohesive actions on the part of governors. These two developments in turn raise two general issues.

One consequence of the increased professionalism is that the governor is encouraged to be the grand coordinator, controller, connector, and compromiser of the executive branch. These administrative and managerial demands require time, energy, resources, and skills that are notably different from the political and policy-leadership skills normally required by high elective office. Do we want or need governors who are managers—chief federal systems officers? Can governors be capable managers without costs to their other functions? It seems clear that IGR impacts have posed new dilemmas for our state chief executives, and that they have not yet arrived at a role resolution that reflects common attitudes or consistent actions.

A second issue arising from this analysis involves the question: How broad and firmly fixed is a consensus among governors? Governor Rampton's testimony touched only lightly on the issue of interstate diversity.[19] Often the diversity in state interests combines with drastically different governors' attitudes to produce intense interstate con-

---

18. National Governors' Conference, *Federal Roadblocks to Efficient State Government*, Vol. 1, *A Sampling of the Effects of Red Tape* (Washington, D.C.: 2nd printing, February 1977). p. vii. See also *Federal Roadblocks to Efficient State Government*, Vol. 2, *Agenda for Intergovernmental Reform* (Washington, D.C.: National Governors' Conference, February 1977).
19. See Robert E. Smylie (Governor of Idaho), "Difficulties of a Small State in the Federal System and Suggestions for Dealing with Them," *State Government*, 37 (Spring 1964): 96–102.

flict. An example of this occurred briefly at the 1963 Governors' Conference, one that featured intense political maneuverings by Governor Rockefeller in anticipation of the 1964 battle for the Republican presidential nomination. Civil rights was a prominent national and state issue in 1963, the year that saw, for example, Martin Luther King's summer "March on Washington." Rockefeller pushed for a Governors' Conference resolution committing each of the states to protect the civil rights of its citizens. He argued that the fifty states acting in concert could do more to guarantee civil rights than national or individual state actions.

His argument may have been correct, but the prospect of securing the firm commitments of fifty governors, much less of their respective legislatures, was as promising as trying to douse a fire with gasoline. Rockefeller's proposal got nowhere. Indeed, his resolution produced so much tension amid the usual comity of the conference that the governors voted that year to abolish their resolutions committee: Columnist Richard Wilson commented harshly on what he believed to be the sorry circumstances of the Governors' Conference.

> Time has passed by the older concepts of state sovereignty, and it is only a presumption that some governors still cling to it.
>
> The governors could look about them and see a practical effect of the changed atmosphere. Once the conference of governors was the spawning ground of presidents. But not for more than 30 years has a governor become president, and it will probably be some years more before one does.
>
> A few of the governors go to the U.S. Senate, to Cabinet or sub-Cabinet positions, but most of them fade into obscurity, possibly because they have not grasped the irreversible domestic and international forces which have created a strong U.S. central government.
>
> As the governors left their pleasure grounds at Miami Beach they could see exposed the pretense that they can act collectively. It would be better if they could just enjoy themselves and exchange views at their future meetings.[20]

By 1969, six years after the 1963 donnybrook, another columnist, David Broder, observed dramatically different attitudes at the Governors' Conference. Broder traced part of that change to a different political climate. President Nixon addressed the conference and pushed

---

20. Richard Wilson, "Governors' Myth of State Sovereignty," *Des Moines Register, July 28, 1963.*

his "New Federalism" program. Commenting on the Nixon speech Broder said:

> His was a very different message from the one President Lydon B. Johnson had given the governors in 1968. Looking back on the vast growth of federal programs from the New Deal through his own Great Society, President Johnson told the governors that it all stemmed from the failures of the states. "At no time," he said, "was the federal government eager to take on increasing responsibilities. . . . Responsibility was passed to the federal government by default—after, and only after, it became clear that the states would not or could not solve the problems that pressed in on all sides."
>
> Mr. Johnson gave the governors scant hope for a reversal of the trend. . . .
>
> Either the states and the federal government together would find jobs for the unemployed, make a success of model cities, protect children's health and make a college education possible "for every boy and girl who want it," Mr. Johnson said, or the federal government would have to do it alone. . . .
>
> Mr. Nixon, in his address, rejected Mr. Johnson's "either-or" approach, with its explicit reliance on Washington's ability to rescue every situation.
>
> "As we look ahead to the '70s," the new President said, "we can see one thing with startling clarity. There is far more that needs to be done than any one unit of government, or any level of government, could possibly hope to do by itself. If the job is to be done, a greater part of it must be done by states and localities themselves, and by the people themselves." [but]. . . Mr. Nixon said, "I can assure you . . . we are not simply going to tell you the states have a job to do; we are going to help you find the resources to do it."
>
> . . . if there has been a change in the attitude of the national administrations between 1968 and 1969, the change in the governors' own thinking is even more dramatic. . . .
>
> In every major problem area—transportation, the environment, crime control, welfare and revenue-sharing—the message from this Governors Conference was the same:
>
> Mr. Nixon's initiatives are steps in the right direction, but the country has the financial capacity and the urgent necessity to do more. Implicitly as a group and explicitly as individuals, they suggested that Congress avoid the temptation to purchase easy popularity by cutting federal taxes while the states and cities are forced to raise theirs.[21]

The Governors' Conference comes closer than any other institution to representing both the temperament and the power position of

---

21. David S. Broder "Governors Reverse Field," © 1969 *The Washington Post.*

the states. On the former, the conference can display either divisiveness or cohesiveness on major policy issues. On the power position of the states the conference reveals itself subject to potent nationalizing influences. The conference is far from subservient, as shown by recent criticisms of national policies on energy and environmental matters. But the conference (as a surrogate for the fifty states) cannot *bargain* as a collective entity. That capacity rests with individual governors using their intrastate political strength, part of which rests with another major institutional actor in the state decision-making system—state legislatures.

STATE LEGISLATURES: ATTITUDES AND ACTIONS

Legislative Image

In 1840, in an attempt to stall a bill by preventing a quorum, state representative Abraham Lincoln jumped out of the window of the Illinois House of Representatives. This escapade is tame and relatively respectable in comparison to descriptions of personal dissipation and organized corruption in the annals of state legislative behavior. An article in a popular magazine in the mid-1960s noted the "Symptoms of Decline in State Legislatures: Drunken Speeches, Fistfights, Barbershop Singing, Hoots, and Catcalls."[22] In both popular and informed opinion state legislatures and legislators would probably rank at the top of any scale of political seaminess.

Contrast such images of disrepute with two isolated but illustrative events from the mid-1970s. First, less than three weeks after his succession to the office, President Gerald Ford met with the officers of the National Legislative Conference, an association of state legislators from all fifty states. The purpose of the meeting was to explore "ways in which the relationship between state legislatures and the Office of the President can become even more productive."[23] The Legislative Con-

---

22. Trevor Armbrister, "Octopus in the Statehouse," *Saturday Evening Post,* February 12, 1966. See also "The Sick State of the State Legislatures," *Newsweek,* April 19, 1965, pp. 29–32.
23. Letter to the author from Earl S. Mackey, Executive Director, National Legislative Conference, August 29, 1974.

ference had a Washington-based professional staff of four operating with the following IGR premise and strategies:

1. that state legislators, like governors, have recognized the tremendous need and value of a Washington presence,
2. to assure that communication between the nation's state legislatures and Congress and the federal agencies is maintained, and
3. to formulate and articulate state legislative concerns with respect to federal-state policy issues.[24]

The meeting with the president was designed to further stabilize IGR strategies for state legislators.

The second event was the creation, in 1975, of the National Conference of State Legislatures (NCSL), a consolidation of three predecessor organizations (one being the National Legislative Conference). Its autonomy, financing, staff, and location in Washington, D.C., have contributed to an improved image for state legislatures and legislators. The 1976 conference of NCSL was viewed to have sufficient political significance that the vice-presidential candidates from both major parties addressed it.[25]

Among the themes stressed in Senator Mondale's speech was a "return of more power to the states and for meaningful communication between the President and State Legislatures." Curiously, the main reported theme of Senator Dole's speech was to urge state action on a constitutional amendment giving the president the item veto power—a power that forty-four governors enjoy. Among the resolutions passed by the NCSL was one calling for state legislative control of all federal funds passing through state treasuries. Another IGR issue commanded the attention of NCSL participants—the questionable solvency of local and state pension systems. A special task force and staff study was commissioned with the announced aims of proposing and promoting state reforms and opposing federal action.

As one of the Big Seven public interest groups the NCSL is a Johnny-come-lately. It is apparent, however, that state legislatures are increasing their visibility and respectability. Whether these helpful but nonquantifiable factors can be translated into effective leverage on IGR decisions is an open question. This question is considerably different

---

24. Ibid.
25. Council of State Governments, "Legislators Seek Federal Role," *State Government News,* 19 (October 1976): 8. For information about the formation NCSL see "Forging a New Legislative Voice," *State Government,* 47 (Autumn 1974): 252–256.

from, and has more optimistic implications than, one posed a few years ago by Professor Duane Lockard: "Whether the legislature can be saved is in my opinion an open question."[26]

Institutional Position

In *Baker* v. *Carr* Chief Justice Earl Warren wrote, "State legislatures are, historically, the fountainhead of representative government in this country."[27] In relation to IGR it has been commonly charged that as fountainheads state legislatures have been rusted shut, and the main task is to get them flowing freely and effectively. Extensive energies have been invested and numerous approaches pursued to reform, if not revolutionize, the functioning of state legislative bodies. Spearheading much of the reform effort has been the Citizens Conference on State Legislatures (CCSL), now renamed LEGIS-50. It was founded in 1965 as a nonprofit, nongovernmental organization, the explicit purpose of which is to "revitalize state legislatures" on the grounds that:

> The legislature is at the heart of the state governmental system. The quality of state government is no better than that which the legislature permits it to be. The legislature is the funnel or the bottleneck through which the development of state government must flow.[28]

It is difficult to challenge these claims about the centrality of state legislative institutions even if one were disposed to do so. And the legislature's importance within the state decision-making system emphasizes

---

26. Duane Lockard, "The Legislature as a Personal Career," in Donald G. Herzberg and Alan Rosenthal (eds.), *Strengthening the States: Essays on Legislative Reform* (Garden City, N.Y.: Doubleday, Anchor, 1972), p. 14.

27. Baker v. Carr, 369 U.S. 186 (1962).

28. Larry Margolis, "Revitalizing State Legislatures," in Herzberg and Rosenthal, *Strengthening the States,* p. 27. Margolis has served as the executive director and major moving force behind CCSL, now LEGIS–50. The CCSL gained special visibility and precipitated substantial controversy with its sponsorship of a study and book that ranked the fifty state legislatures on how they measured up "to minimum standards of legislative capability." See *The Sometime Governments: A Critical Study of the 50 American Legislatures,* written by John Burns for the Citizens Conference on State Legislatures (New York: Bantam Books, 1971). The IGR significance of state legislatures was noted by Senator Muskie at the apex of the "Creative Federalism" phase. See "The State Legislatures in an Age of Creative Federalism," address to the American Assembly on State Legislatures in American Politics, April 30, 1966, *Congressional Record,* May 17, 1966, p. 10275–10277. For a more recent view see Walter H. Plosila, "State Legislative Involvement in Federal-State Relations," *State Government,* 48 (Summer 1975): 170–176.

its significance for IGR. How have legislatures dealt with IGR issues in the past? What patterns of actions and attitudes have been dominant in recent years? Data on legislative dealings with intergovernmental affairs are largely institutional and aggregate rather than individual and discrete. We will deal with them in the context of two perspectives: state-local and state-federal.

State-Local Relations

Perhaps the chief intergovernmental problem that confronts a state legislature is state-local relations. In approximately half the states the legislature is relieved from the burden of numerous specific enactments by the existence of a substantial degree of home rule. Home rule is the legal power, either constitutional or statutory, of a unit of local government to frame, adopt, and amend the basic charters of governance and to exercise governing powers on matters of local concern within the limits of the constitution and general laws of the state.

Home rule for cities has been a century-long struggle and an article of faith among local officials since Missouri adopted a constitutional provision in 1875. Home rule for county governments has followed a very different course; major home rule concessions to counties have taken place only since 1960. Between 1960 and 1974 fourteen states provided home-rule powers to county governments either selectively or statewide.[29]

In the absence of home rule state legislatures provide for the structure and powers of local units by three alternative legal strategies: (a) special act, (b) general law, and (c) optional law. The special act strategy is virtually Dillon's Rule in pure form. A unit's entire governmental structure and the detailed powers it can exercise are passed (or amended) as a special bill in the legislature. Approval of the legislature would be required for something as minor as increasing the number of members on a city's planning board from its original authorized size.

General law strategies usually specify a uniform structure of government and set of governing powers for all cities in a broad category, usually specified by population size. For example, in cities of from 10,000 to 25,000 in population the mayor might be popularly

29. *The Municipal Yearbook 1974* (Washington, D.C.: International City Management Association, Vol. 41, 1974), pp. 43-44. A classic and, for its time, definitive study of state-local relations was conducted in 1946. See *State-Local Relations: Report of the Committee on State-Local Relations* (Chicago: Council of State Governments, 1946).

elected, the council could consist of seven members, and the town could operate a water system, create and staff police and fire departments, etc. Under general laws the local units accept the legislature's statutory decision about what structure and powers are appropriate. The one consolation is that all other similar units are in the same boat, to suffer and/or benefit together. In some states the general law strategy tends toward attrition by special acts; for example, although the Iowa constitution provides that for local units "all laws shall be made general and of uniform operation throughout the state," the Iowa legislature regularly passes laws that apply to a single city. The enactment merely specifies that it applies to all cities over 150,000—of which there is only one, Des Moines.

In the optional law strategy (which might best be likened to how a cafeteria is run) state law provides for two or more basic governmental structural arrangements and accompanying powers that the unit may exercise. The voters in a community, upon incorporation and by a referendum, then vote for one among these alternatives. Subsequent referenda may be held to change to a different governmental structure or set of powers—say be switching from a mayor-council to a council-manager or commission form of government.

Whether a local unit is governed under home rule or one of the three alternative provisions just described, two essential points about legislative state-local relations must be made clear: First, we are discussing statutory or *legal* relationships, not political or administrative relationships. Although legally subservient, in whole or in part, officials of local units can and do carry heavy clout on some (or even many) state legislative actions. Also, administrative controls and regulations offer distinct opportunities for dependent, autonomous, or bargaining patterns to emerge between state and local officials.

Second, legislation applicable statewide may supplement or supersede the arrangements broadly specified under any of the four legal strategies. Within broad limits defined by state and federal constitutions as interpreted by the courts (either state or federal), state legislatures may enact laws that apply to some or all of its local jurisdictions. These laws may be permissive, prohibitory, or mandatory, and as long as they cannot be shown as arbitrary or unreasonable they are likely to be sustained in courts when challenged by a citizen or local jurisdiction.

Permissive Legislation. Permissive legislation allows some or all local units to exercise a specified power or to pursue a particular activity. For example, public housing developed across the nation at such a slow rate in large measure because in many states there was no permissive, or enabling legislation. Without permission—that is, an authorizing statute—local units, and cities in particular, could not legally undertake this activity. One classic case of permissive legislation was Pennsylvania's so-called Tax Anything Act passed in 1947. Under this law local units were granted power to levy any tax that the state government was not already levying. This permissive authority led, as one might expect, to a profusion and confusion of local taxation. Since the state did not tax incomes, local units could, and, by 1965, 45 cities, 450 boroughs (town), 430 townships, and 1070 school districts were levying an individual income tax.[30]

Prohibitory Legislation. Taxation and bonding are areas abundant with legislative prohibitions. For example, in North Carolina the Local Government Commission Act (of 1931) prohibits any local unit from proposing, issuing, or incurring a bonded indebtedness without the review, evaluation, and approval of North Carolina's Local Government Commission.[31] This commission supervises all aspects of the debt-issuance process for local units. A proviso in the law allows a local unit, in the face of an adverse action by the commission, to override the commission by a favorable vote of the people in the jurisdiction proposing to issue the bonds. But in its nearly half-century of existence that escape hatch has not been employed, and the Local Government Commission has earned the widespread respect and support of local officials throughout the state.

State controls on the taxing and spending powers of local units are long-established features of state-local relations (and they are sore points in those relations). Such restrictions include limits on property tax rates, debt ceilings, and flat prohibitions against certain types of taxes. On property taxes, for example, as of 1974 twelve states imposed a levy (dollar amount) limit and twenty-six states imposed a rate limit. A study evaluating the effectiveness or impact of these limits concluded that "property tax bills and property tax burdens tend to be lower in

---

30. Advisory Commission on Intergovernmental Relations, *Tax Overlapping in the United States: Selected Tables Updated* (Washington, D.C.: Government Printing Office, January 1967, a supplement to Report M–23), p. 37.
31. Harlan E. Boyles, "Local Government Debt Administration in North Carolina," *Popular Government,* 38 (June 1972): 10-13.

local governments affected by state imposed tax rate or levy limits, *ceteris paribus* [other things being equal]."[32]

Mandatory Legislation.   Mandatory state legislation is the subject of considerable debate and state legislative action. Most of the current controversy centers on the costs that local units are forced to meet when a state law requires the unit to provide a service or remit a tax obligation, or imposes a constraint that raises local costs. Not all mandated legislation, however, has direct dollar implications. Open meetings and ethical behavior by local officials are two nonfiscal areas filled with state mandates; so-called sunshine laws compelling open meetings, open records, etc., are normally binding on all local government officials, as are competitive bidding on contracts and hiring employees under civil service regulations, in some states.

Twenty state legislatures have adopted codes of ethics that, in most of those states, apply to local as well as state officials. In New York the legislature concluded that the state-adopted code was too rigid to be applicable to the diverse conditions faced by the thousands of local officials in the state's nearly 2500 local units. Therefore, a 1969 law mandated that each local unit must adopt its *own* code of ethics and file a copy of the code with the State Department of Audit and Control. As of January 1976, forty-six towns, forty-two villages, and sixty-one school districts had failed to file a copy of the code. The vast majority of New York local units adopted verbatim a model code of ethics jointly developed by the Department of Audit and Control and the State Office of Local Government.[33]

State statutes that mandate added local costs have been a special irritant. In one recent analysis it was noted that "It would be difficult to find an issue that sparks more resentment among local officials than that caused by state mandated expenditures."[34] State mandates of maximum weekly hours that can be worked by firemen have raised the

32. John Shannon, Michael Bell, and Ronald Fisher, "Recent State Experience with Local Tax and Expenditure Controls," *National Tax Journal,* 29 (September 1976), p. 279. For an excellent summary and analysis of tax and expenditure controls, accompanied by policy recommendations, see Advisory Commission on Intergovernmental Relations, *State Limitations on Local Taxes and Expenditures* (Washington, D.C.: Government Printing Office, February 1977, A–64).

33. Management Information Service, "Ethics in Local Government," Vol. 8, No. 8 (International City Management Association, August 1976), p. 2.

34. John Shannon and L. Richard Gabler, "Tax Lids and Expenditure Mandates: The Case for Fiscal Fair Play," *Intergovernmental Perspective,* 3 (Summer 1977), p. 9.

ire of many city and municipal league officials against legislative intervention: Fireman appear to be very adept at state capitol lobbying, more so than they have been in scores of city halls. But state mandating and efforts to resolve state-local conflict have probably reached their greatest sophistication in California. A 1972 property tax relief act required that any new or increased service "mandated by legislative action after January 1, 1973 shall . . . provide an amount sufficient to cover the total cost of the mandated program as estimated by the Department of Finance."[35] An obvious problem was how to determine the increased local costs, especially how to allocate the local unit's overhead expenses between the mandated and nonmandated activities. A staff unit of nine analysts prepared over 800 mandated-cost estimates in 1973 and over 1000 in 1974.

State legislatures are clearly in the thick (or thicket) of IGR. State-local relations are probably more divisive and potentially more volatile than state-national relations. There are least five principal areas of state-local conflict:

1. taxation;
2. incorporation, annexation, and consolidation procedures;
3. regulatory authority in the fields of land use, health, building, traffic, and utilities;
4. organization and jurisdiction of local courts; and
5. conditions attached to the provision of major public services—education, public safety, sanitation, housing.

Is there an underlying attitude or underlying policies that state legislatures bring to their dealings with local matters? One participant observer, a governor, concludes that "On their attitudes toward their political subdivisions—particularly the cities—both governors and legislatures are apt to share the belief that these subdivisions are errant stepchildren whose needs are properly relegated to a second echelon of priorities."[36] Two other close observers, the second a former legislator, contend that:

> State legislatures, with only a few exceptions, have been more recalcitrant. In the past they proved negligent in recognizing the problems of the cities. . . .

35. Joseph F. Zimmerman, "State-Local Relations: The State Mandate Irritant," *National Civic Review* 65 (December 1976): 548–552.
36. Harold E. Hughes, "From the Governor's Chair," in Herzberg and Rosenthal, *Strengthening the States,* p. 114.

> Although the functions of the legislature have actually expanded in the past
> fifty years, its relative capacity for initiative, for creativity, and for author-
> itative control over government has diminished.[37]

These are harsh judgments. They might be qualified or modified but
to refute them would be a difficult task.

State-Federal Relations

With what patterns of actions and attitudes do state legislatures
relate to the federal government? Ignorance and indifference might be
one answer. Few legislatures, for example, directly and deliberately
consider federal aid in their budgetary decisions. An ACIR study
found that:

> When a state match is required for the aid programs, it is often absorbed into
> appropriations bills for state agencies and is not separately designated as a
> "match" for federal funds. In addition, approximately 13 percent of the
> federal-state grant dollars require no state match—thus these dollars can
> circumvent the state appropriations process completely.[38]

The study did find, however, that state legislators were becoming more
interested in and actively involved in the problem of federal (and state)
budgetary control. The reasons for this rise in attentiveness are:

1. the size of federal aid in relation to the state budget;
2. increased latitude in the use of some federal funds, for example, block grants and GRS;
3. increased professionalization of legislatures, as seen in larger
   staffs, higher salaries, more frequent sessions;
4. growing fiscal conservatism, prompting tighter control; and
5. executive-legislative disagreements.

It may be that congressional activism has its analog in increased state
legislative assertiveness.

A second legislative theme relevant to state-federal relations is reorganization and reform. How well state executives and legislatures are
able to cope with and control federal impacts is affected by how the

---

37. Herzberg and Rosenthal, *Strengthening the States,* pp. 98 and 13.

38. Advisory Commission on Intergovernmental Relations, "State Legislatures and
Federal Grants" (Information Bulletin No. 76-4, November 1976), p. 1.

state is organized and how reliably both these institutions operate. According to the ACIR, since the mid-1960s there has been "a dramatic movement toward modernizing and restructuring state governments to make them more manageable and responsive to citizen needs."[39] While reorganization and other changes in the executive branch are often viewed as increasing the governor's influence, power is not necessarily a zero-sum condition: A better-functioning executive branch can enhance a legislature's influence.

A few brief data points from a 1974 survey of state agency heads will specify some configurations of legislative-executive influence in state government.[40] Asked how much influence the governor and legislators (evaluated separately) exercised over important agency decisions, 50 percent of the agency heads responded that the governor was "highly influential," while 32 percent answered that the legislators were. Asked whether the governor or the legislature exercised greater control and oversight of their agency, 45 percent of the top administrators said it was the governor; 26 percent said it was the legislature; and another 26 percent said each exercised about the same influence. As expected, the governor is clearly the prime actor, but the legislature also must be reckoned with both at the state level directly and indirectly in state-federal relations.

A third theme, hostility, also must be acknowledged in legislative state-federal relationships. Says a former governor (who also makes evident that legislatures have no monopoly on this attitude): "The chief executive and the legislature are also likely to share the same attitude toward the federal government: that it is an alien and essentially hostile power."[41] This attitude has found both mild and extreme forms of expression, and in diverse places. One especially potent expression, in a formal resolution passed by the Indiana General Assembly in 1947, produced no known results but displayed two elements of irony: The same legislative session approving the resolution did *not* refuse to accept further federal funds; it also denied greater home-rule powers to local units in Indiana.

> Indiana needs no guardian and intends to have none. We Hoosiers—like the people of our sister states—were fooled for quite a spell with the magician's

---

39. Advisory Commission on Intergovernmental Relations, *State Actions in 1975* (Washington, D.C.: Government Printing Office, July 1976, M–102), p. 3.

40. Unpublished data from Deil S. Wright, American State Administrators Project, Institute for Research in Social Science, University of North Carolina at Chapel Hill, June 1976.

41. Harold E. Hughes, "From the Governor's Chair," p. 114.

trick that a dollar taxed out of our pockets and sent to Washington, will be bigger when it comes back to us. We have taken a good look at said dollar. We find that it lost weight on its journey to Washington and back. The political brokerage of the bureaucrats has been deducted. We have decided that there is no such thing as "Federal" aid. We know that there is no wealth to tax that is not already within the boundaries of the 48 states.

So we propose henceforward to tax ourselves and take care of ourselves. We are fed up with subsidies, doles, and paternalism. We are no one's stepchild. We have grown up. We serve notice that we will resist Washington, D.C., adopting us.

Be it resolved by the *House of Representatives of the General Assembly of the State of Indiana* (The Senate concurring), That we respectfully petition and urge Indiana's Congressmen and Senators to vote to fetch our county courthouses and city halls back from Pennsylvania Avenue. We want government to come home.[42]

A fourth theme involving state legislatures and IGR is aggressiveness, as was recently demonstrated, in 1977, in a potentially pivotal case in Pennsylvania. The state legislature asserted its right to appropriate and to control all federal money entering the state's treasury. It argued that neither a state agency nor the governor could spend money, regardless of its source, unless the funds had been specifically appropriated by the state legislature. Pennsylvania Governor Milton Shapp and executive branch agencies challenged this claim on the grounds that federal funds can be appropriated only by the U.S. Congress. They contended that when these monies are granted by federal agencies to Pennsylvania (or any state) for a specific purpose the state legislature cannot intervene to reject or redirect the funds.[43] But legislative leaders, citing uses of federal grants to establish or continue programs specifically rejected by the legislature, argued that the governor and the "bureaucrats" thus use federal monies to make a mockery of the legislative body. So strongly did the leaders feel on this point that they refused to include a routine sentence in appropriation bills that gave administrative agencies blanket authority to spend any federal money they could obtain.

42. Quoted in William Anderson, *The Nation and the States, Rivals or Partners?* (Minneapolis: University of Minnesota Press, 1955), pp. 6-7.
43. For descriptions of this case and discussions of its implications see Neal R. Peirce, "Legislators v. Bureaucrats: Who Will Spend the Money?" *The Washington Post,* February 7, 1977; Richard Hickman, "Pennsylvania Case Highlights Increased Legislative Role in Overseeing Federal Grants," *ASPA News and Views,* Vol. 27, No. 3 (Washington, D.C: American Society for Public Administration, March 1977), p. 3.

The controversy produced a state court case involving legislative versus executive power over spending authorizations. A Pennsylvania lower court held against the governor, but the case is likely to be appealed, perhaps ultimately to the U.S. Supreme Court because, as one observer noted, "It now appears that only a clear-cut Supreme Court decision favoring executive branches over legislatures can stem a rising tide of legislatures seeking to gain control of federal money spent in their cities."[44]

The president of the National Council of State Legislatures, Minnesota House Speaker Martin Sabo, offered strong views on the subject:

> . . . state legislatures are convinced they must take firm control of the federal funds in their budgets or face increases in the cost of state government and in the power of state bureaucracies. Both the U.S. Constitution and our state constitutions delegate the power for controlling the purse strings to the legislative branches of government. It is outrageous that we stand by and allow that power to be usurped.[45]

More temperate but equally revealing were the responses of twenty-five Florida legislators to survey questions about federal grants-in-aid some years earlier, in 1963:

> Over one-fourth thought all grants should be terminated and half favored the termination of certain grants. One-half were of the opinion that no new grant programs should be enacted and two-thirds mentioned some grant program that should be turned back to the states. Three-fourths of the legislators favored the repeal of some federal taxes as the means for state financing of "returned" programs. Finally, about half felt that grants produced distortion and/or substitutive effects by asserting that state matching of federal grants took funds away from programs not receiving federal aid.[46]

The views expressed by these state legislators were negative toward federal aid and also critical of federal and state administrative officials. State legislators' attitudes on IGR range from negative to assertive, and their actions range from obstruction to reform. Thus no single, summary observation about state legislatures and IGR can be made. We cannot determine whether Daniel Elazar's judgment is correct when he said, "the least effective way for the states to influence the

---

44. Neal R. Peirce, "Legislators v. Bureaucrats."
45. Ibid.
46. Summary of tabular results presented in Vincent V. Thursby and Annie Mary Hartsfield, *Federal Grant-In-Aid Programs in Florida* (Tallahassee: Institute of Governmental Research, Florida State University, 1964), pp. 149–154.

direction of [intergovernmental relations] . . . is through the formal institutions normally considered the bulwarks of state autonomy, particularly the state legislatures."[47]

STATE IGR COORDINATORS: FUNCTIONS AND VIEWPOINTS

Federal grants and the "picket fence" pattern of IGR tend to diminish the governor's control over state programs and operations. But legislative control also appears to be drastically reduced, especially when the governor and agency administrators form a coalition against legislators. Who, then, does exercise effective control over federal funds? In many states one person exercising a major oversight function is an IGR coordinator, the state-level counterpart to a coordinator at the local level.

The dollar and policy impacts of federal funds on the states is of such a magnitude that in virtually every state one or more persons, and agencies, directly monitor and/or control the flow of these funds. Most such agencies are located in the governor's office or in a budget unit. As at the local level, the functions of state IGR coordinators vary widely, but the most highly developed IGR offices cover the following: direct control over the outlay of federal money, general grant coordination, information on grant applications and funds, calculation of indirect costs on grants, policy analysis, program and policy clearance, policy control, and lobbying in Washington, D.C. In short, these IGR coordinators fit the category of administrative generalists perfectly.

For each of the IGR functions the candid observations of Robert Greenblatt, Coordinator and Chief, Federal Relations Unit of the Budget Divison of the State of New York, are illuminating. Mr. Greenblatt described his position, his activities, and his perspectives to a graduate class in public administration, at the Maxwell School of Syracuse University.[48] His descriptions have been organized into categories of activity.

---

47. Daniel J. Elazar, *American Federalism: A View From the States* (New York: Thomas Y. Crowell, 1966), p. 153.

48. Robert Greenblatt, "A Comment on Federal-State Relations," in James D. Carroll and Richard W. Campbell (eds.), *Intergovernmental Administration: 1976—Eleven Academic and Practitioner Perspectives* (Syracuse, N.Y.: Maxwell School of Citizenship and Public Affairs, Syracuse University, 1976), pp. 143-171.

Fund Control. After describing the general sources of federal funds and the approximate amounts received by New York State, Mr. Greenblatt commented:

> Many . . . state legislatures . . . "appropriate" the federal funds that come in. In effect the legislature controls the federal money as it does its own state money. By appropriating it, the legislature directs that the money be spent in such and such a way or for such and such a program. That doesn't happen in New York State, although our legislature would probably like it to. They would like to have more control over the money. What happens is that the money comes into the state, into the general fund, and the Comptroller's office parcels it out. In effect, we contemplate that money in advance in developing the budget every year. We spell out in the budget, per program, how much federal money is coming in. In effect, the Division of the Budget, for the Governor, is controlling that federal money. It's allocated according to the way the Division of the Budget lets it go.[49]

Grant Coordination. The major mechanism for grant coordination and review derives from Budget Circular A-95. How this review is conducted in New York is characterized somewhat caustically.

> The federal government issues circulars. They number them consecutively. The one I'm going to tell you a little bit about is called A-95. (They're up into the A-120s now, and they'll probably go on forever.) The A-95 is supposed to be a management tool to let local and state officials as well as regional planning organizations be aware of who is applying for federal grants. One section in the federal relations unit is what's called the State Clearinghouse. Every person, every entity, non-profit, profit-making, local government, whatever, who is applying for federal programs and a good number of the human service, educational, and research programs, has to send a notice of intent to apply to the Regional Clearinghouse and to the State Clearinghouse. The purpose is to let interested officials, be they public or planning, be aware that somebody is going to do something with federal money somewhere in the state. It's an attempt to better coordinate the use of federal money, so that you don't have two groups applying to build two sewers on parallel streets in the same town or so that the federal government itself doesn't decide to expand an airport right across a new highway that the state is building.
>
> Believe me, it doesn't always work because people still go ahead and do what they please. But we get this notice, we get thousands of them every year. Not only are they reviewed in the Division of the Budget, but they are also reviewed at the state level by an appropriate state agency which, if it has any objections or comments, makes them known. The local applicant usually is

---

49. Ibid., p. 146.

not successful in his grant application if there's an objection from the state.[50]

Information Systems. Knowledge is a potential basis for exercising control, and the New York State Federal Relations Unit developed and operates an extensive information system on all applications filed for any federal program by every state agency and every local unit of government.

> By virtue of state law enacted in the late 1960's, the state agencies also notify us, not just for programs covered by A-95 but for any federal program. To manage all this information, we've developed a computer system in my unit called the Federal Aid Control System. We keep track of all the applications in the entire state, and there are many thousands every year. All the applications for federal money, all the modifications of those applications, whether or not grants are awarded or disapproved—if they're awarded, how much, for how long; any renewal applications, whatever—it gives us a small handle on one piece of the federal money coming into the state. It doesn't give us any control over it but at least we know what's coming in.[51]

Indirect Costs. The action rule, maximize federal funds, is nowhere more evident than with respect to the indirect costs of acquiring, receiving, and administering a federal project or categorical grant. Responsibility for this task in New York rests with the Federal Relations Unit.

> One other program that we run is called the Statewide Cost Allocations System which is another attempt to maximize federal funds. The federal government, in most of its programs, allows the grantee to include what's called overhead costs, and in many programs, to be reimbursed above the amount of the grant for these overhead costs. Limiting it to the state government, which is the part we run, the state agencies are required by us to apply for their indirect costs when they apply for a federal grant. We have various control forms to try to make sure that they're doing it.

> These indirect costs, for instance, my salary, we throw in. We charge a little piece of it to everybody. We calculate central costs, the Budget Division, the Department of Law, that is, the Attorney General's office, the Comptroller's Office, what, in general, could be called the central support service of state government. We come up with a cost figure each year representing the percentage of the combined central costs that are chargeable to the federal government, a portion of which is charged to every state agency, depending

---

50. Ibid., p. 148.
51. Ibid., p. 149.

on a number of factors—its size, how much federal money it gets, and the like. The agencies take this statewide cost allocation, which is a dollar amount we give each of them, and include in every grant they apply for, a percentage of that cost plus their own indirect costs. That includes their commissioner's costs, their deputy commissioner's costs, and the administrative costs that otherwise are state costs. We try to get back from the feds whatever we can.[52]

Policy Analysis.   Before working in the New York State government Mr. Greenblatt was with the Human Resources Administration in New York City. He described his policy analysis role there and also his transition to the state agency.

My responsibility was . . . the Division of Legislative and Policy Analysis. We were responsible for monitoring and analyzing all of the federal and state legislative activity in the entire field of human services and to prepare the subsequent policy analyses and options for program implementation. The State of New York, believe it or not, had no centralized operation under which it monitored federal legislative activity. It was done, as best it could be, by one or two people, kind of haphazardly, but with all good intent, in the Division of Budget.

When the new administration came in and a new budget director, the need was apparent and the will was there to do something about it. So they spirited me away from New York, brought me to Albany and asked if I would set up the kind of legislative analysis that we had been doing in New York City. The difference is that for the state, we review everything across the board from a fiscal perspective as opposed to a program perspective. In the City of New York, we really didn't have to care how much it cost or who it was going to cost. If we liked it, we were for it.

The state is not like that. We measure everything in how much it's going to cost and whether we are going to have to put in anything and, if so, how much it is worth to us. Legislative analysis, anticipation of legislation, is a major part of our work. We have a staff which is now broken down into several broad functional areas—human services; transportation; housing; and so on. Their primary responsibility is to closely follow what's happening in Congress with regard to their area of interest.

The Governor has a Washington office—in effect, a staff of lobbyists who desperately need information as to what a particular bill or formula or formula change will do to New York. It's our [The Federal Relations Units] job to find it out.[53]

52. Ibid., pp. 149–150.
53. Ibid., pp. 153–154.

Program and Policy Clearance. State department heads or commissioners, as noted, have a programmatic bias and strong expansionist tendencies. Governors and their staff units attempt to contain or constrain these centrifugal forces. One means is policy clearance:

> Traditionally, in New York State, any legislator, any federal legislator, any federal agency wanting to know where the State was on a particular subject would write to the commissioner of that agency: "Dear Commissioner Lavine," (in former times) "What do you think about welfare reform, what do you think about Medicaid, what do you think, what do you think?" Each department, independently, would tell Congress or its favorite legislators or its own federal counterpart what it thought about a particular legislative proposal. Nine times out of ten, the Governor didn't have the faintest idea what his commissioner was saying. If the Governor subsequently wanted to take a policy position, it was very often embarrassing to find out that his commissioner had said something very much the opposite either in personal testimony or official correspondence or whatever.
>
> Well, we're set up to try to coordinate the whole thing. If an agency wants to take a position on any federal issue, be it a policy issue, a legislative issue, a fiscal issue, it has to be cleared through my office. They send us the draft of their testimony, the draft of their position paper, the draft of their response to a proposed federal regulation, and we review it. We review it for overall policy implications and for fiscal implications.[54]

Policy Control and Coordination. An agency's policy statement must be cleared not only for its consistency with the governor's position, but also with the positions taken by other agencies. This requires interagency coordination and control. In New York State this function is well developed.

> Most federal issues cut across a single agency's jurisdiction. Particularly in human services, almost every federal program initiative not only affects the Department of Social Services but also affects the Department of Health, the Department of Mental Hygiene, the Office for Aging, the Division for Youth. It is true that all four or five of these agencies separately took their positions in the past and really couldn't care less what the other had to say or how it would affect any other agency. We have tried to take all of their separate and very often disparate positions and meld them into one state position. We sent out these communications either from the Governor's office or from the Budget Director or from the lead agency, the agency that is most impacted by a particular policy initiative. It's harder than it sounds—to get two state

---

54. Ibid., pp. 154–155.

agencies to agree on anything is a difficult proposition. They all have their own program interests. Those of you who go into public service, you'll find it out. Everybody protects his own, seeks to enhance his own, couldn't care less for anyone else. So we do our best. It's fun to try. It's fun to be a middle man in this instance and to negotiate and sometimes to impose your will—we enjoy that part of it.[55]

Washington Lobbying. Looking out for how a state's best interests are affected by Washington actions is a final IGR function. Historically, this was often left to federal legislators or, collectively, the state legislative delegation in Washington, D.C. Demands on congressional time, lack of information, divisions within delegations, and other forces have shifted the state self-interest efforts to specialized IGR agencies in the states. Often, as in New York's case, they work hand in glove with the state's full-time lobbyist (or unit) in Washington, D.C. Greenblatt describes and reflects on this activity.

> We run, as I said, the Federal Aid Control System, and the State Clearinghouse and, to some extent, do some lobbying work. We try to assist both the budget examiners and the state agencies in maximizing the federal aid that comes into the state and it's usually done by formula manipulation rather than merely applying for federal grants. The place to get in is on the ground floor when Congress is reviewing the program or initiating a program and deciding how it's going to allocate the funds. We have some good people and enough experience to know, as I said in the beginning, which formula elements will be most beneficial to New York State and which ones will be most harmful. We've had some successes in recent months working with various congressional committees to alter formulas which had been proposed that would have hurt New York. I won't go into the details but it's kind of an exciting thing for us to get something changed before it goes into effect, so that New York benefits rather than loses. That's a tough thing because the whole trend in Congress today is to route money, as I said, to the south and southwest, and away from the older, industrialized northeast. . . .
>
> I'd like to tell you a little bit about formulas and what they do to New York. Formulas are nothing more than ways to distribute money, and if you understand that formulas are created by a political body, that is, Congress, then you'll understand how the money is directed to meet political ends.[56]

Obviously, not all states have agencies with the size and sophistication of New York. But selected features of these several activities exist, sometimes in embryonic form, in the IGR units in many state govern-

---

55. Ibid., pp. 155–156.
56. Ibid., pp. 156–157, 144.

ments. Debates over the utility of such an agency have failed to stem their proliferation.

A recent survey of state IGR coordinators obtained responses from twenty-seven of these officials—all of whom were ultimately responsible to the governor.[57] They were asked two sets of questions, one set about the functions they performed, the other about their views on IGR issues. The following proportions of the twenty-seven IGR coordinators performed these tasks:[58]

Review federal legislation	96%
Write to members of congressional delegation	89
Meet counterparts from other states	89
Handle contacts with NGC on state-federal issues	88
Write to members of Congress from other states	86
Locate additional federal aid opportunities	82
Analyze amounts of federal aid received	81
Review proposed federal regulations	74
Assist local governments with federal programs	74

Most of these IGR coordinators fulfill nearly all of the IGR functions described by Robert Greenblatt.

How do these coordinators assess the current state of IGR? What opinions do they hold on several IGR issues? The issues and the percentage of all twenty-seven coordinators agreeing are shown below.[59]

Washington decision makers do not understand well the impacts of federal programs on state and local governments	96%
The balance of power in the American federal system has shifted too strongly toward federal dominance	89
Low-level federal bureaucrats often take the position that they can tell a governor what to do on a federal program	78
Too many federal programs have direct federal/local ties and deny the states an appropriate role	70

(continued)

57. National Governors' Conference, Center for Policy Research and Analysis, *State-Federal Relations in the Governor's Office* (Washington, D.C.: Governor's Office Series-No. 10; November 1976).
58. Ibid., p. 8.
59. Ibid., p. 11.

(continued)

Congress is more responsive to the views of local officials than to those of state officials	30%
The state's congressional delegation is more responsive to local officials than to state officials	19
The state's senators are more responsive to local officials than to state officials	16

That federal officials do not understand federal IGR impacts is a near-unanimous view held by these coordinators. Almost as many view the federal government as too dominant. Low-level bureaucrats receive majority criticism, as do federal/local programs that bypass the states. Only modest proportions of these IGR generalists feel that congressmen and senators give local officials better treatment than they give state officials. Rather than being surprising, the views of these actors in the state-level vortex of IGR fit quite logically the mold of the generalist-oriented administrator attempting to contain and perhaps effectively control the vertical functional alliances of federal-state-local program officials.

SUMMARY

Governors, legislators, and IGR coordinators are three sets of institutional actors in state decision-making systems. They operate in a larger intergovernmental setting that affects, and constrains, their freedom of action. Because of IGR these state officials find their policy choices restricted. Their actions and opinions on IGR are summarized below.

Governors labor mightily, sometimes, to gain control of an otherwise fragmented policy-making process at the state level. One strategy used to achieve this aim is to strengthen a governor's Washington connection, or Potomac pipeline. The National Governors' Conference (NGC) staff, located in Washington, furthers that purpose. The annual meeting of the NGC is also a vehicle for exerting pressures on the federal establishment—president, Congress, the bureaucracy.

Governors' views on IGR issues have undergone some transformation in recent decades. They have shown some nationalizing tendencies and have sought, with notable assertiveness, to become masters of their respective state households. These changing, ambiguous, sometimes contradictory views expressed by governors are characteristic of the anomalous positions they occupy. On the one hand, they lead fifty significant, even powerful political entities; on the other hand, they are often typecast as chief federal systems officers for the implementation of most federal domestic policies.

State legislatures have had "image" problems throughout their sometimes tumultuous histories. Significant efforts have been made since the 1960s to raise their low prestige by performing responsibly. It is too soon to judge whether state legislatures (and legislators) will achieve stronger, more visible roles in IGR decision making. Yet legislators now seem to be making their influence felt more vigorously in IGR than at any time in the past half-century. State legislatures were once the bastions of recalcitrance and obstructionism on IGR policies. More recently they have reasserted the prerogatives of state government and of legislative bodies in general.

A new breed of official has entered the arena of state decision making in recent years—the IGR coordinator. He or she is an administrative generalist attempting—usually on behalf of the governor—to contain and control the powerful programmatic forces that threaten to turn state government into administrative chaos. No easy judgment can be given on how successful IGR coordinators, either singularly or collectively, have been. But two points can be made about their roles and performance: First, if Robert Greenblatt's operations in New York state are at all representative, IGR coordinators try *very* hard; second, the collective views of these coordinators fit the classic pattern of *generalist* officials in the states.

State Officials:

Administrators' Actions and Attitudes

10

Compared to scholarly and popular attention to state politics and to governors and legislators, the attention devoted to state administrators is minuscule. Ira Sharkansky declares that, "The quantitative revolution in political science has passed by many features of public administration. . . . Until we have more information, we can claim only superficial knowledge about the functions of administration in the state policy-making process."[1] This discussion of administrators and administration at the state level is not intended to fill the gap to which Sharkansky refers. But it does attempt to plot several action and attitude orientations of state administrators. Their several bases of power are primarily at the state level but, of necessity, these officials function in the larger complex and changing setting of IGR. If state gov-

---

1. Ira Sharkansky, "State Administrators in the Political Process," in Herbert Jacob and Kenneth N. Vines (eds.), *Politics in the American States: A Comparative Analysis* (Boston: Little, Brown, 1971), p. 270.

ernment is indeed in the middle, then a strong case can be made that state administrators are in "the middle of the middle."

Sharkansky's comment that the "quantitative revolution" has bypassed the study of state administration is taken to heart in this chapter. What follows is an analysis of state administrators that is empirically based and heavily quantitative. After establishing who "state administrators" are and something of their importance, we examine three major aspects of their links to IGR. First, we describe the IGR *actions* of state administrators—their contacts with officials in other jurisdictions, their receipt of federal aid. Second, we explore the *attitudes* these administrators hold on a range of IGR issues—their views on state-local policy questions, their outlook on the authority relationships between the national government and the states, their opinions on federal aid impacts on the states and on aid funding levels. Third, we analyze those state administrators (about 1000 strong) who head agencies receiving federal aid. The views of these recipients are organized around three topics: federal aid effects on the states, satisfaction with aid programs, and preferences for changes in aid programs.

STATE ADMINISTRATORS: IDENTIFICATION AND IMPORTANCE

Who are state administrators and why are they of more than minor importance in IGR? For purposes of this discussion state administrators are the appointed or elected executive heads of state departments, agencies, boards, and commissions: They are, in short, the operational directors of any major organizational unit in the executive branch of state government. Much of the data discussed below come from one or all of three successive mail surveys of state administrators conducted in 1964, 1968, and 1974.[2] The administrators were listed in the bi-

---

2. Much of the data and findings reported in this chapter are only partially extant in published form. To minimize repetitive citations of diverse, and frequently unpublished, sources a few chief sources are noted here: Deil S. Wright, American State Administrators Project (ASAP), unpublished data, Institute for Research in Social Science, University of North Carolina at Chapel Hill, June 1976; Deil S. Wright, "Executive Leadership in State Administration," *Midwest Journal of Political Science,* 11 (February 1967): 1-26; Deil S. Wright et al., *Assessing the Impacts of General Revenue Sharing in the Fifty States: A Survey of State Administrators* (Chapel Hill: Institute for Research in Social Science, University of North Carolina, 1975); Deil S. Wright and Elaine Sharp, "State Administrators and the Intergovernmental Grant System," a discussion paper prepared

Table 10–1. *Policy Roles of State Agency Heads*

1. *IGR Entrepreneur*
   a. Establishes IGR contacts
   b. Plays IGR games
   c. Gets grants

2. *Program Promoter*
   a. Cultivates clientele
   b. Builds power base
   c. Gains autonomy

3. *Fiscal Aggrandizer*
   a. Desires bigger budgets
   b. Asks for more money
   c. Obtains earmarked revenues

4. *Professional Programmatic Expert*
   a. Develops program expertise
   b. Holds civil service status
   c. Is active in professional associations

5. *Program Innovator*
   a. Deals with changing program priorities
   b. Gets new ideas for improvement of programs
   c. Spends time on policy-making activities

ennial publication of the Council of State Governments, *State Administrative Officials Classified by Function.*[3] A recent edition of that document contained the names of approximately 3000 state administrators who headed 70 different types of departments, agencies, boards, and commissions.

The policy importance of state administrators (or agency heads) can be supported in varied ways with diverse data. In 1976 they helped set priorities for and influenced the expenditure of $102 billion in direct state expenditures. They direct the several thousand agencies that employed 2.8 million (full-time equivalent) state employees in 1976. On the average, they spend about 25 percent of their time in policy development and in presentations to governors, legislators, or

for the Advisory Commission on Intergovernmental Relations (Chapel Hill: Department of Political Sciences, University of North Carolina, August 1975). The Wright-Sharp paper appears in revised and condensed form as Chapter IV, "Survey of State Administrators," in Advisory Commission on Intergovernmental Relations, *The Intergovernmental Grant System as Seen by Local, State, and Federal Officials* (Washington, D.C.: Government Printing Office, March 1977), pp. 111–176.

3. Council of State Governments, *State Administrative Officials Classified by Functions* (Lexington, Ky., biennial, Supplement II to the *Book of the States*).

boards and another 20 percent building public support for their agency's programs among clientele and interest groups.[4] Still another indicator of their importance to both state policy and IGR is their role in originating legislation. In a 1974 survey they were asked what proportion of all legislation related to their own agency "originates or is initiated from within your agency?" The average indicated was 70 percent. A great deal of policy action begins and ends with state administrators.

The data cited above are little more than fragmentary items about the policy roles of American state administrators. To put those and other data about state administrators into a larger, more informative context, we must identify the administrators' major policy-making roles. These roles cover considerably more than IGR, as the identifications in table 10-1 and subsequent short discussions make clear. The roles can and should be seen, however, as interrelated and reinforcing: Effectiveness as a program innovator and fiscal aggrandizer can strengthen a state administrator's capacity as an IGR entrepreneur. We shall examine each of the five roles in table 10-1 (see page 248), giving the IGR entrepreneur role most of our attention.

POLICY ROLES OF ADMINISTRATORS

Two preliminary facts may be noted. First, among state administrators responding, in 1974, to a set of questions on their IGR contacts, about 60 percent indicated that they had daily or weekly contacts with officials in other governmental jurisdictions. Second, nearly two-thirds of the administrators indicated that they headed agencies receiving some type of federal aid, whereas in 1964 only one-third reported receiving aid.

Administrators as Program Promoters

As a program promoter the state agency head is expected to find a clientele or constituency, cultivate it, and build a power base with which to gain some degree of autonomy from the governor and legislature on policy decisions. Clientele support and interest groups are facts of administrative life. An active, cohesive clientele group (or

---

4. Wright, ASAP (unpublished data), 1976.

groups) can add measurably to an administrator's power base. No neat, simple, or precise measure of such a power base has yet been devised, but one rough estimate on the influence of clientele groups is available. When state agency heads were asked in 1974 to say how important clientele group influence was on major agency decisions, exactly half of the respondents said they were either moderately (41 percent) or highly (9 percent) influential.

The autonomy of the program promotional role can be linked to the IGR entrepreneurial role. In the 1974 survey recipients of federal aid were asked whether receiving it made their department or agency *less* subject to supervision and control by the governor and legislature. Nearly half (47 percent) of the agency heads claimed more autonomy thereby.

Administrators as Fiscal Aggrandizers

The fiscal aggrandizer desires and requests large increases in the agency budget. Doing so is of course one more way in which state agency heads affect the policy process. In the 1974 survey administrators were asked whether they thought the programs and expenditures of their agencies should be increased. Eighty-two percent said yes (notably more than the 72 and 76 percent who said so in 1964 and 1968 respectively). Responses to an identical follow-up question in the 1964, 1968, and 1974 surveys revealed progressive increases in the proportion of administrators opting for expenditure expansions of 15 percent or more. The respective percentages were 31, 38, and 44 percent.

Another indicator of the fiscal aggrandizing tendencies within the state administrative establishment are earmarked funds: monies received by a state agency that are pledged, nearly always by statute, to a specified or restricted use. The classic example of earmarking involves revenues from gas taxes—funds mandated, sometimes in the state constitution, for use on streets and highways. Earmarked revenues enhance administrative discretion on fiscal matters, and the three surveys of state administrators showed that nearly half of the agency heads' organizations received earmarked revenues.

Clearly, substantial segments of top state bureaucrats are fiscal aggrandizers. Their success as such is inversely related to the containment capabilities of governors and legislators. A single-state study, in

Illinois, emphasized how powerfully administrative-bureaucratic factors propel budgetary expansion in state government. It aptly conveyed the governor's apparent inability to contain overall growth:

> In this respect the budget document may be compared to a huge mountain, which is constantly being pushed higher and higher by underground geologic convulsions. On top of that mountain is a single man, blindfolded, seeking to reduce the height of the mountain by dislodging pebbles with a teaspoon. That man is the Governor.[5]

Another study (covering nineteen states) arrived at two broad conclusions about the fiscal initiative of administrators:

a. When we examine the response of governors and legislatures to the budgets of individual agencies, we find some evidence for the administrators' domination of the expenditure process.

b. . . . only the acquisitive agencies come out of the legislature with substantial increases over their previous budgets; there are strong positive relationships between the percentage increase requested by the agency and the percentage growth in agency expenditures.[6]

Administrators as Program Professionals

Data from the 1964, 1968, and 1974 surveys show that increasing proportions of state administrators have higher levels of education as well as more specialized education. For example, in 1964 less than 40 percent of the agency heads held graduate degrees, but by 1974 over 50 percent held them. Data on these administrators' personal backgrounds suggest that they are more professionalized than municipal and federal administrators are.[7]

In his analysis of bureaucracy and the role of experts, Max Weber early and lucidly demonstrated that expertise places power in the hands of appointed administrators. State administration, our analysis indicates, is heavily populated at the top with professional persons in command of much expertise.

---

5. Thomas J. Anton, *The Politics of State Expenditure in Illinois* (Urbana: University of Illinois Press, 1966), p. 146.

6. Sharkansky, "State Administrators," p. 258.

7. Deil Wright, "The States and Intergovernmental Relations," *Publius: The Journal of Federalism,* 1 (Winter 1972): 7–68.

Weber pointed to another contributor to the influence of administrators—their official appointive position, particularly their civil service status. Data from the three surveys show that consistently increasing proportions of the agency heads were appointed to, and hold, their posts under civil service status: 28 percent in 1974 compared with 21 percent in 1964.

Other data from the surveys help document appointed state agency heads' policy-making role in general and their professional-programmatic role in particular: About 30 percent of the state agency heads were appointed by plural-member boards or commissions. This type of appointment is often, of course, a buffer or barrier to policy control by the governor and legislature. In place of these two usual, primary sources of policy cues for the administrator are several alternative sources of policy guidance; among them are: federal agencies (especially if federal aid is provided), clientele or interest groups, the appointing board or commission, units of local government (or associations of local officials), and, perhaps preeminently, the administrator's own professional values and standards—as influenced by membership in a professional association or associations.

State administrators appear to be extensively and intensively involved with professional associations. First, 85 percent of the state agency heads responding to the 1974 survey reported that they belonged to a professional association. Second, and probably more significantly, one-third belonged to *four* or more professional associations. Third, over 60 percent had held an office in at least one association, and fourth, the agency heads attended an average of three out-of-state professional association meetings per year. Finally, over 40 percent of the administrators were formally licensed (or certified) by a licensing body or professional association. Top-level state administrators, then, are not unprofessional clods or pure political hacks.

Administrators as Program Innovators

The last policy role identified in table 10-1 is the program innovator. Program innovation is especially difficult to measure. Our measures are far from foolproof but the three suggested in table 10-1— changing program priorities, new ideas for program improvement, and time spent on policy making—are a start. A datum cited earlier could also be relevant: Because 70 percent of all agency-relevant draft legislation originates in the agency, innovation-minded administrators have substantial opportunities to innovate.

Changing priorities among programs within an agency are both an opportunity for and the result of program innovations. To what extent have there been shifts in program priorities in state agencies in the past four to five years? Responses to the 1974 survey showed the following extent of changes in program priorities; major shifts, 42 percent; moderate shifts, 37 percent; minor shifts, 17 percent; no shift, 3 percent. That about 80 percent of the agency heads report moderate or major recent changes in program priorities suggests that a great deal of program innovation *may* be occurring in state agencies. (Clearly, not all shifts in priorities are necessarily innovative.)

What are the sources of state administrators' innovative proposals for improving agency programs? In the 1974 survey the first-ranked sources were:

	First-ranked
Sources within the agency	57%
Sources from other states	13
Professional associations	11
National government	10
Governor	3
Legislators	2

Innovative ideas come predominantly from within state agencies, but about one-third of all administrators indicate that officials in other states, professional associations, or the national government are the primary sources of new ideas. (Recipients of federal aid are far more likely to rank the national government first as a source of new ideas.) Most noticeable, perhaps, are the tiny proportions of respondents citing the governor or legislators as sources of innovative proposals. These two institutions of representative democracy are not viewed as major originators of constructive program change.

The third and final indicator of an agency head's innovative role is the amount of time spent on policy-making activities. Actually, this measure is a rough indicator of the overall policy role of the state administrator and is only an indirect approximation of the administrator as innovator.

Regardless of which role we generalize about, the data show a substantial, self-acknowledged role in policy making by state agency heads. In 1974, 34 percent indicated that they spent one-third or more of their time on policy-making matters—such as contacting, and making presentations to, governors, legislators, and boards. (Over one-fourth of the agency heads had weekly or daily contact with the governor of their state and 50 percent had similar frequencies of contacts with legislators.) State administrators' self-described policy-making involvement has remained fairly constant in the past decade: In 1964 and 1968 one-third of the agency heads spent one-third or more of their time in policy-making activities.

This overview of the policy roles of state administrators is important to IGR for two reasons: First, agency heads' IGR activities increase their role in the policy process at the state level; second, the state-level contacts, activities, and relationships have a direct bearing on how influential and effective the agency head can be in an IGR context.

In both direct and indirect ways the policy roles of state administrators are played at the forefront of the IGR stage. Furthermore, the agency heads play somewhat differing roles depending on position, programs, policies, and other factors. In this book, for example, the most common roles are those previously described as administrative generalists and program specialists. Representative of the former group are administrators heading such agencies as budget, personnel, planning, and finance; illustrative of the latter are heads of departments such as agriculture, corrections, education, health, highways (transportation), insurance, parks, police, and welfare.

TYPES OF IGR INVOLVEMENT

How are state administrators involved in IGR? To what extent and in what ways are they a part of the great grantsmanship game? How regularly are they involved in contacts with federal and local officials, or with officials from other states? Data bearing on these questions are available chiefly from the 1974 administrators' survey with selective comparisons extending back to 1964.

In 1964, 34 percent of the responding agency heads indicated that their agency received some type of federal aid; by 1968, 49 percent did so; and by 1974 over 60 percent did so. The extent of the agency reliance on federal aid is an added indicator of increased involvement. In 1964 barely 10 percent of all responding state agencies relied on federal aid for 50 percent or more of their agency's budget. By 1974 nearly 20 percent did so. Among those agencies actually receiving federal aid nearly 30 percent were dependent on it for half or more of their budget, including 13 percent that were 75 percent or more dependent on federal aid.

Dependency on federal aid is of course one measure of state agency involvement in the federal aid process. Two other measures are *diversity,* the number of different federal departments from which state agencies receive funds; and *complexity,* the different types of grants received. A brief tabulation shows the proportions of all grant-receiving agencies that obtain funds from one, two, or more different federal departments.

One	36%	Four	8%
Two	27	Five	3
Three	16	Six or more	8

Over 60 percent of the aid-receiving agencies follow what might be termed a "bullet" strategy, concentrating their fund acquisition efforts on only one or two agencies. But more than a third of the agencies are what might be loosely called "scramblers." They obtain funds from three, four, or more federal departments. (This approach has also been called, "living dangerously.")

By complexity of aid involvement is meant, again, the types of federal aid received by a state agency. Six types of aid can be listed, with percentages of aid recipients securing each type:

Project grants	70%	Block grants	29%
Formula grants	55	Nonmatching grants	20
Contracts	35	Loans	4

Some of these types, of course, are not mutually exclusive. That is, a project grant could also be a nonmatching grant. The first four types are practically mutually exclusive. A tabulation of the number of different types of aid received gives an additional indication of the complex aid involvements by state administrators. The proportions of agencies receiving different types are:

One	39%	Three	18%
Two	26	Four or more	16

Most agencies, then, rely on one or two bread-and-butter types of aid. But one-third adopts a multiple-risk, entrepreneurial strategy in securing several types of aid.

About state administrator or agency involvement in the federal aid process four major points can be made:

1. Aid involvement is extensive.
2. It is concentrated for a majority of administrators and agencies.
3. It is varied, complex, and strategic for a substantial segment of administrators and agencies.
4. Actions appear to be guided by rules of IGR games.

Additional insights into the game-directed behavior of state agency heads come from an analysis of the frequency and patterns of these administrators' contacts. Federal aid money may grease the wheels of IGR but officials have their hands on the throttles and control the switches. What tracks do they follow and at what speeds?

Table 10-2 presents findings on the frequency of IGR contacts by state administrators with a wide array of local, national, and other-state officials. The figures reveal the deep involvement of state agency heads in a varied and dense network of IGR interactions. The frequency, content, and scope of the boundary-spanning behavior of these administrators undoubtedly varies by type of agency and by other variables. But even in the aggregate, the evidence reveals that state administrators are firmly fixed "in the middle" of IGR and their contacts extend in many directions with variable strengths.

The aggregate patterns in table 10-2 do not describe contact configurations for individual agency heads. How many administrators, for example, have daily or weekly contacts with local officials *and* peers in other states *and* federal regional personnel? The frequencies of other discrete patterns are also of interest. Using "up," "down," and "horizontal" terms for federal, local (appointed), and other-state contacts, respectively, we can identify the distribution of daily or weekly con-

Table 10-2. *Contacts of State Administrators with National, State, and Local Officials**

Type of Official Contacted	Frequency of Contact					
	Daily	Weekly	Monthly	Less than Monthly	Never	Not Ascertained
Locally:	(percentages)					
County						
Elected	8	23	21	34	9	6
Appointed	8	21	20	31	9	12
Municipal						
Elected	7	21	22	38	9	4
Appointed	8	20	19	35	8	10
School						
Elected	3	7	13	45	27	6
Appointed	4	8	13	43	23	10
In Other States:						
Administrators of						
similar agencies	3	23	38	34	1	2
Administrators of						
different agencies	2	8	19	53	16	3
Other states'						
legislators	0	0	2	41	55	2
National Officials:						
Agency heads	2	10	21	47	16	4
Regional personnel	7	29	30	27	4	4
U.S. senators	0	10	24	52	12	2
U.S. representatives	0	10	24	52	11	3
Exec. office/OMB	0	1	2	27	66	4

*N = 1581.
Source: Deil S. Wright, American State Administrators Project, University of North Carolina at Chapel Hill (1976); see also, Advisory Commission on Intergovernmental Relations, *The Intergovernmental Grant System as Seen by Local, State, and Federal Officials* (Washington, D.C.: March 1977), p. 121.

tact patterns for nearly all respondents (about 15 percent of the sample was excluded for lack of data).

The tabulations below show that 60 percent are intensely involved IGR game players in the sense of having daily or weekly IGR contacts. The remaining 40 percent are either fringe players or isolates that have one chief characteristic in common: Their agencies receive no federal aid. Among the IGR game players there are significantly varying patterns of contact.

	Number of Administrators	Percent
Down only	167	12
Horizontal only	93	7
Up only	135	10
Down-horizontal	55	4
Up-horizontal	74	6
Up-down	141	11
Up-down-horizontal	139	11
Other (limited contacts)	539	40

The first three categories in the list, constituting nearly 30 percent, might be called single-level specialists; their daily or weekly contacts are restricted to a single vector, either up (national), down (local), or horizontal (officials of other states). The next three categories are dual-directed administrators; they have daily or weekly contacts along two intergovernmental dimensions. The largest of these three is the "up-down" group with contacts concentrated along the vertical dimension, that is, daily or weekly contacts with federal and local appointed personnel. Administrators in this category are pure representatives of the "picket fence" pattern of programmatic specialists. They are more than 10 percent of all administrators. Virtually identical in size to the vertical specialists is the highest-intensity contact group, those administrators who have daily or weekly contacts through all three IGR spaces. Their involvements best exemplify the case of "IGR person" in the purest generic sense.

Do the IGR contacts of state administrators vary by the type of agency they head and by particular personal attributes?[8] One obvious expected variation would correlate with the agency's dependency on federal aid. If an agency receives no federal money, we would expect its administrator to have far fewer contacts with national officials than the administrators of an agency that has 75 percent or more of its budget coming from federal aid. Analysis of contact frequencies (daily or weekly) with categories of national officials reveals sharp differences. For example, three-fourths of administrators heading highly dependent agencies were in daily or weekly contact with federal regional officials,

---

8. Wright and Sharp, "State Administrators"; see ACIR *Intergovernmental Grant System* for published data on variables that explain the IGR contacts and perspectives of state administrators.

whereas less than one-fourth of all administrators from nonrecipient agencies were. Similar differences were found in contacts with other national officials, such as senators.

The aid and nonaid differences extended beyond variations in contacts with national officials. High dependency on federal aid was associated with distinct differences in contacts with officials from other states, especially those in a similar agency, and with all types of local officials. More evidence, and more analysis, would be required to demonstrate that federal aid "causes" more-intense IGR contacts beyond direct state-federal interactions. Indeed, the causality might flow in the opposite direction: A state administrator who has more contacts with local officials may be pressured to secure more money—for the state agency *and* the local. This condition leads to more contacts with the "feds," which in turn produce greater aid dependency. Regardless of the causal direction explaining *why* aid dependency is linked to higher contacts, catalytic forces are at work around and through the federal aid process, producing interdependency and multiple linkages.

Other characteristics are associated with higher levels of IGR contacts. The functional focus of an agency is one variable. Listed below are groupings of agency heads by general function and an indication of where these officials' contacts (daily or weekly) are significantly higher. Three categories of agency head are distinguished: (1) elected, (2) functional administrators (heads of *line* agencies), and (3) staff generalists (budget, finance, personnel, etc.).

Administrator Categories	Higher Contacts with Officials from
Elected:	city, elected/appointed
	county, elected/appointed
Functional:	
Education	national, department/agency heads
	national, congressional/senatorial offices
	other states, similar agency
Health	county, appointed
Highways	national, regional
	national, congressional/senatorial offices
	other states, similar agency
	city, elected/appointed
	county, elected/appointed

(continued)

(continued)

Administrator Categories	Higher Contacts with Officials from
Welfare	national, regional national, congressional/senatorial offices county, appointed
Staff generalists:	none (with respect to every type of official, staff-generalist agency heads had consistently and significantly *lower* IGR contacts.)

More frequent contacts with officials in nearly all categories were positively associated with the following variables:

1. agency size,
2. earmarked revenues,
3. federal aid diversity,
4. federal aid complexity,
5. administrator's desire for agency expansion,
6. high assessment of clientele influence, and
7. appointment by the governor.

In sum, there are patterns of regularities by which IGR processes are ruled. There is order in spite of claims that there is "chaos." The ability to discern or identify segments of that order is all the more impressive because of the presumed fragmentation, complexity, interdependency, and indeterminacy posited as present in state government and in state administration.[9]

VIEWS ON IGR ISSUES

Being at the hub of IGR, state agency heads are in an exceptional position to provide assessments and opinions on a range of IGR issues. We shall examine four clusters of such issues:

1. state-local policies,
2. state-national authority relationships,

---

9. The phrase "indeterminate government" as applied to the states is from Jospeh A. Schlesinger, "The Politics of the Executive," Jacob and Vines (eds.), *Politics and the American States*, p. 211.

3. federal aid policies, and
4. federal aid funding levels.

State-Local Policy Issues

Legislative actions and attitudes highlighted the critical role of state-local relations in IGR. For state agency heads the frequency of their regular contacts with local officials serves as an added reminder of state-local relations as a critical dimension of IGR.

In 1974 state administrators were asked five specific state-local policy questions, involving financial and authority relationships. Distributions of the responses are presented in table 10-3. There is overwhelming agreement that the states should become substantially more involved in resolving urban problems; only 6 percent voiced disagreement. On three more narrowly focused policy questions (issues 2 through 4 in the table) with specific implications for urban problems, only bare majorities of state agency heads expressed concurrence, and about 25 percent of the respondents disagreed or strongly disagreed.

In the abstract, then, state administrators favor affirmative state action on local and especially urban problems (issue 1) by a ratio of 12:1. But on three policy actions—two (issues 2 and 3) involving financial aid and the other (issue 4) involving service performance standards—the ratio in favor is only about 2:1.

The issue (number 5) of increased power to regional grant review agencies discloses a sharp split in the opinions of state administrators—those favoring stronger regional agencies (37 percent) only modestly exceeding those disagreeing (29 percent). Over one-fourth are undecided. Administrators' views on this issue apparently have not crystallized sufficiently for there to be a majority sentiment. It may be that the issue of substate regionalism is one of low salience to these respondents, but it clearly causes mixed feelings among those who have an opinion.

On all three administrator surveys from 1964 to 1974 a "home rule" question was replicated, asking whether the administrators agreed or disagreed on the granting of greater home-rule powers to local units. Support for more home rule was fairly constant at around 65 percent, opposition of about 25 percent. The concept of home rule as it is viewed by state administrators has a positive valence.

Clearly, state administrators differ in opinions on how state gov-

Table 10-3. *State Administrators' Views on State-Local Issues* *

State-Local Issue	Agree or Strongly Agree	Unde-cided	Disagree or Strongly Disagree	Not Ascer-tained
	(percentages)			
1. The involvement of the states in finding solutions to urban problems should be substantially increased.	76	11	6	7
2. State financial assistance to local units should be substantially increased.	52	17	24	6
3. The state should provide substantial relief from local property taxes.	53	16	26	7
4. Strict standards should be set by the state for the performance of local government services.	54	14	25	7
5. The state should give regional grant review agencies more power over applications for federal grants.	37	26	29	8

*N = 1581 respondents
Source: Wright, American State Administrators' Project; see also, Advisory Commission, *Intergovernmental Grant System,* p. 122.

ernments should deal with localities. Are there variables that help explain some of these variances? An extensive analysis of several administrator and agency variables yielded only modest results.[10] We expected, for example, that prior career experience in local government would be strongly related to administrators' policy attitudes. Only on property tax relief was this so—but even then it was not strongly so. Agency heads with experience in local government work were moderately more inclined to favor substantial property tax relief. Thus, career patterns in the form of IGR mobility failed to explain attitude differences; where the agency head sits *now* seems to control how he or she "stands" on an issue.

For the four policy issues other than property tax relief one variable showed consistent and moderately significant relationships. State administrators scoring high on agency expansionism (that is, who want their agencies expanded by 15 percent or more) were consistent in favoring increased state action on the four policy questions. These

10. Wright and Sharp, "State Administrators."

consistent associations lend support to the view that an activist, assertive role by administrators within the framework of state government is accompanied by similarly aggressive inclinations in an IGR context.

Are agency characteristics associated with particular response patterns on these policy issues? Agency size, use of earmarked revenues, and the functional category of an agency disclose no distinct or consistent differences. But the three federal aid measures of dependency, diversity, and complexity present a very different picture: All three variables are positively associated with agreement on all five of the state-local policy issues. For example, less than half of the agency heads not receiving federal aid want state aid to local units increased, whereas more than three-fourths of the administrators scoring highest on aid diversity and complexity want state aid increased. These associations reflect the wider linkages, interdependencies, and contingencies that the federal aid variable represents for the entire IGR system. The more an agency head is involved as an IGR "player," the more inclined he or she is to realize and favor IGR approaches or strategies.

State-National Authority Issues

On issues of state-national authority the responses of state agency heads reflect substantial agreement with a view that state government is a critical, central link in the federal system. There is a strong tendency toward asserting what might be termed "state prerogatives" (see table 10-4).

This pattern is clear in responses to the first question: should national-local contacts be channeled through the state? Four-fifths of the respondents said yes. But while support for channeling suggests a more central role for the states, it leaves many questions unanswered as to the further specifications of that role. For example, a more central state role might be associated with a lesser national role, or it might be seen as a more balanced state-national relationship, or as simply more state activism regardless of the national role. Channeling may also suggest a facilitative role for the states rather than an assertive or initiating role. Finally, channeling may, for some administrators, imply active policy intervention, that is, exerting a major influence on programs as they are channeled through the state.

Whatever the interpretation of "channeling," it is a prominent

Table 10–4. *State Administrators' Views on Issues of State-National Authority Relationships**

State-National Authority Relationships	Agree or Strongly Agree	Unde-cided	Disagree or Strongly Disagree	Not Ascer-tained
	(percentages)			
1. National-local contacts should be channeled through the state	80	8	7	5
2. Should be greater decentralization from national government to the states	83	6	6	6
3. Programs should be assigned (or separate) rather than shared	46	16	32	6
4. National government should set strict performance standards	46	8	41	6

* N = 1581 respondents.
Source: Wright, American State Administrators' Project; see also, Advisory Commission, *Intergovernmental Grant System*, p. 124.

and persistent issue in national-state-local relationships, one on which state agency heads have shared a consensus for over a decade. In 1964 and 1968 surveys of state administrators, a question similar to the first in table 10–4 was asked. Those in agreement made up 88 percent and 90 percent, respectively, of the total; those disagreeing make up 8 and 5 percent respectively. Clearly this issue for state administrators is one that approaches an article of faith—and the heretics are few.

The same issue can be viewed in the context of other state-national authority relationships. For example, as question 2 in table 10–4 poses, should there be greater decentralization of authority and responsibility from the national government to the states? The percentages make it clear that there is widespread agreement on decentralization. As on the issue of channeling this response pattern suggests that administrators desire an assertive state role. Decentralization, of course, may be interpreted in one of at least two ways: the first would mean granting responsibilities to administrative districts that are subcomponents of central government agencies; the second, more common meaning is "devolution," the delegation of power and authority (by a polity or a constitution) to an internal political jurisdiction. The wording of the question in table 10–4 suggests the latter interpretation.

Questions 3 and 4 of the table might further clarify what decentralization means to state administrators. Responses to question 3, on assigning (or separating) rather than sharing programs, show a plurality (46 percent) approaching a majority for assignment, but a substantial minority (32 percent) dissents. Thus, despite widespread endorsement of decentralization, there is far from a consensus on whether programs (or functions or responsibilities) should be discretely assigned to either state or national governments, or whether the concept of shared functions should be pursued. If the New Federalism represented a concerted effort to "sort out" roles, responsibilities, and programs, then a cleavage existed among state agency heads over this policy issue in intergovernmental relations.

Question 4, on national performance standards, also reflects on the issue of decentralization. Should the national government set strict performance standards for federal programs administered by the states? There is another marked split in administrators' opinions. Nearly half (46 percent) agree with strict standards, but nearly as many (41 percent) disagree.

It seems strikingly inconsistent that 46 percent of the administrators would concur with strict national performance standards while 83 percent agree that authority and responsibility should be decentralized to the states. One possible explanation for this apparent inconsistency may lie in the overwhelming agreement among these administrators on the state role in channeling national-local contacts via the states. Administrators may see national performance standards as a means for exerting leverage on local governmental units, clientele groups, and/or other state officials. Strict standards may be perceived positively from a programmatic or professional standpoint rather than as a constraint upon self-performance. That conjecture is the more plausible since similar proportions agree that there should be strict national performance standards for the states and, as seen in item 4 of table 10-3, strict state performance standards for local units (46 percent for the former, 54 percent for the latter).

Another less Machiavellian interpretation can be placed on the response pattern to the issue of strict national standards. As posed to the administrators, question 4 (of table 10-4) contains a qualifying phrase: "for federally-funded programs administered by the states." A respondent could simply concur that if the national government is prepared to pay for programs it has a legitimate claim to specify standards of execution. (As the old adage goes, "He who pays the piper calls the tune.") This interpretation derives additional support from an analysis of several variables that might explain variation in administrators' views on issues of state-national authority. The only variables moderately associated with attitude variations were the dependency, diversity, and complexity of federal aid. For example, those administrators most dependent on federal aid were more in favor of channeling and of strict national standards, and less in favor of assigning or separating functions.

Administrators' responses to questions 3 and 4, on state-national authority relationships, clarify the concept of decentralization so warmly endorsed in answers to question 2. In fact, with a slight inferential stretch, question 1 has a bearing on decentralization. When the federal government does agree to channel national-local contacts or programs through the states, federal officials are, in fact, recognizing the prerogatives of the states and acknowledging that power is not centralized.

The question (number 3) on sharing or separating programs, however, is more directly about decentralization. The sorting out of programs is part of the process by which decentralization would occur. The Joint Federal-State Action Committee proposed this route in the late 1950s, and that approach, as posed in question 3, moves in the direction of the separated-authority model. State autonomy in the determination of policies and the conduct of programs is the result of decentralization implicit in question 3.

Not so with question 4, the setting of strict performance standards by the national government. Responses to this question have a dual bearing on decentralization. On the one hand, administrators who give affirmative responses reject decentralization in favor of firm national control in IGR affairs. Alternately, these respondents may concede a strong, even dominant national presence, yet feel their position at the state level benefits from the leverage they gain over other state or local officials. In either case, positive responses to question 4 suggest the inclusive-authority model. More than a hint of hierarchical authority relationships seems present in a "yes" response on whether the national government should set strict performance standards.

Federal Aid and Funding Level Issues

The significance of federal aid as an influence on the IGR attitudes of state agency heads has been well established in several ways and on several issues. Table 10-5 displays response distributions of the

Table 10-5. *State Administrators' Views on Federal Aid Issues and Funding Levels**

Federal Aid Issues	Yes	No	Not Ascertained
	(percentages)		
1. Federal aid should be channeled thru state	81	13	6
2. Federal aid leads to interference in state affairs	75	17	8
3. Federal aid skews or unbalances state programs	74	17	9
4. Federal aid stimulates state programs	90	3	7

	Funding Level Is:		
Federal Aid Type	Too Little	About Right	Too Much	Not Ascertained
---	---	---	---	---
	(percentages)			
1. Categorical grants	29	27	24	20
2. Block grants	42	26	10	22
3. General revenue sharing	40	26	10	24

*N = 1581.
Source: Wright, American State Administrators' Project; see also, Advisory Commission, *Intergovernmental Grant System*, p. 124.

administrators' replies to questions focused on federal aid processes, effects, and funding levels. Item 1, a revisit to the channeling issue, makes the activist stripe among the administrators clearly evident. That assertiveness is confirmed in item 2, as resistance, to "national interference in affairs that are the appropriate domain of the state." The third item, on the skewing effects of federal aid, also reveals the dominance of one view: Three-fourths of the responding agency heads concurred that federal aid produced national interference in state affairs and tended to unbalance the overall character of state programs.

What are the long-term trends in state administrators' views on these two federal aid issues—"interference" and "skewing"? Surveys employing these questions were conducted in 1928 and 1948.[11] The respondents then were state agency heads in charge of federally aided activities in the forty-eight states. In 1928 only 6 percent of about 250

11. "Report of the Committee on Federal Aid to the States of the National Municipal League," supplement to the *National Municipal Review,* 17 (October 1928): 619–659; *Federal Grants-In-Aid* (Chicago: Council of State Governments, 1949), pp. 273–281.

respondents indicated federal aid led to "interference," but by 1948 the percentage increased to 36 percent. The 1974 figure for federal aid recipients is 80 percent. However fundamentally ambiguous the term "interference" (used in all three surveys) might be, the dramatic rise in the proportion of agreeing administrators nevertheless signals an important shift in attitudes among these central IGR actors.

Administrators receiving federal aid have manifested a similar opinion shift with respect to the statement that federal aid "tends to unbalance or skew the overall character of state programs": from not quite one-third (29 percent) agreeing in 1948, to more than four-fifths (83 percent) in 1974. Although hard evidence proving the "skewing effect" of federal aid remains elusive (despite persistent controversy surrounding the issue), state administrators nevertheless *think* that federal aid alters and unbalances state spending patterns.

As item 4 of table 10–5 indicates, opinions of the national establishment and of federal aid are not uniformly one-sided and negative. Nine out of ten administrators agree that federal aid has helped the states provide programs that would not otherwise be offered. This near-consensus has remained remarkably stable over nearly a half-century; in 1928 and 1948 the same overwhelming consensus prevailed on the stimulus effects of federal aid.

The response in 1974, however, is somewhat less encouraging when juxtaposed to the majority (74 percent) indicating that federal aid skews the character of state programs. Evidently, a substantial proportion of the agency heads think federal aid provides or promotes programs that should not be offered or should not be given the priority ranking fostered by federal aid. In short, aid creates added competition for limited resources.

Dollars are the fuel that powers the intergovernmental grant system. Respondents in 1974 were asked to evaluate the adequacy of the funding levels of categorical, block, and revenue sharing aids available to state and local governments generally. Two-fifths or more of the respondents see General Revenue Sharing (GRS) and block grants as inadequately funded; less than one-third see categorical grants as inadequately funded. Correspondingly, administrators who see categorical grants as too heavily funded outnumber by more than two to one those who see block grants and GRS as overfunded.

From administrators' views on the adequacy of the three federal funding strategies a scale or typology can be constructed.[12] Three

---

12. Wright et al., *Assessing the Impacts,* chap. 2, pp. 11–15. Daniel Silver and Michael Karpinski were responsible for developing and analyzing the federal aid postures.

response categories to each of three different questions yield twenty-seven different possible combinations. These were condensed into the five broad "federal aid postures":

1. *Acquisitive aggrandizers:* administrators whose uniform or dominant response pattern was "We want more of everything." They indicated that two or all three of the federal aid items were "too little" funded.
2. *Antifederalists:* administrators who thought that all three forms of federal aid should be cut back or who wanted GRS and categorical aid reduced.
3. *Complacent neutralists:* administrators who were satisfied with the existing aid levels for virtually all three forms of aid. They tended to give "about right" responses on all three aid items.
4. *New Federalists:* administrators who favored GRS over categorical grants; that is, they think GRS is too little and categorical aid is too much.
5. *Traditionalists:* administrators who thought that categorical aid was too little and that GRS was too much. In other words, they tended to favor the past predominant pattern of heavy reliance on categorical grants.

Among the more than 1000 administrators who responded to all 3 funding level items, all but 4 percent could be classified into these 5 dominant response clusters. Their distribution is as follows:

Acquisitive aggrandizers	34%
Antifederalist	4
Complacent neutralist	22
New Federalist	27
Traditionalist	8

The distribution is indicative of policy trends with respect to both federal aid and broader IGR issues. Over one-third of the state agency heads are fiscal aggrandizers. This percentage conforms closely to the high-expansionist group, noted earlier, who want their agency budgets increased by 15 percent or more. The size and apparent strength of this group suggests that something more than mere bureaucratic imperialism (growth for growth's sake) may be at work. Rather, there may be objective conditions, needs, and demands for enlarging the programs and expenditures of state agencies.

The contrast between expansion and retrenchment is clear and sharp in the minuscule proportion for the Antifederalist category. A "states' rights" posture, if that designation is accurate, holds insignificant sway among state agency heads. A far commoner opinion is one of basic acceptance of federal aid arrangements as they are. The neutralist position is perhaps best described as: "We'll take what we have and be satisfied."

The issue of federal aid policy is most directly confronted in the contrasts between the New Federalists and the traditionalists. The latter favor the standard, traditional categorical aid over GRS. The New Federalists, who prefer the reverse, are far stronger in numbers (by more than three to one) than the traditionalists.

The traditionalist posture, then, commands only slight support among state administrators (provided the complacent neutralists' stand-pat posture does not make them traditionalists). Change in federal aid policy receives majority endorsement, if the New Federalists and acquisitive aggrandizers are combined. Their natural affinity, or outright alliance, suggests the general proposition that change is most likely when those who *think* they will be helped combine with those who *know* they will be helped.

What variables might explain, in whole or in part, why state agency heads vary in their evaluations of funding levels? Do personal and organizational features play any such distinctive role? One "personal" variable is the administrator's attitude on agency expansion. Those agency heads favoring the greatest expansion of their agencies' programs and outlays were far more disposed to answer "too little" for funding levels for categorical and block grants. Also, agency heads appointed by governors were *less* inclined to favor increased categorical aid and *more* inclined to favor block grants than administrators appointed to their posts by other methods. These relationships pinpoint some of the evident tension between the generalists and the specialists over federal aid policy.

Personal attribute variables revealed little or no association with views on GRS funding levels—with one exception: partisan preference. State agency heads who identified themselves as Democrats were notably less favorable toward GRS than those who identified themselves as Republicans. This difference held both for GRS funding levels and for agreement versus disagreement with GRS as a federal aid policy. For example, over two-thirds of the Republicans agreed or strongly agreed with GRS as a policy, slightly more than one-half of the Democrats were favorable to GRS.

Partisanship also disclosed expected differences in federal aid postures. Significantly more Democrats than Republicans were acquisitive aggrandizers, and significantly more Republicans than Democrats were New Federalists. On the national level GRS was a Republican proposal that eased through a Democrat-dominated Congress. Although partisan differences over both GRS and federal aid policies carried over to state administrative officials, the degree of difference seems to have moderated.

Agency characteristics revealed more numerous and stronger associations with attitudes toward funding levels. Agency size was strongly linked to one funding level variable—block grants. Over three-fourths of the administrators from the largest agencies favored increases in block grants, compared to considerably less than half of those heading the smallest agencies. Likewise, the agency head's functional category made a significant difference in his views toward block grants.

Administrators heading education, health, and welfare agencies were highly favorable toward increased block grant funding; over three-fourths of each functional group indicated block grant levels were "too little." These agency heads gave pronounced support of more flexible federal funding. Except for health officials, however, none were exceptionally favorable to increased funding via GRS. State officials heading human resources agencies were inclined toward new federal aid policies, but only with respect to block grants; they were neither more nor less supportive of GRS funding levels than other agency heads.

The three variables—federal aid dependency, diversity, and complexity—were consistently, and usually strongly, associated with differentiating administrators' attitudes on funding levels of categorical grants and block grants. There was little or no association between the three variables and opinions on GRS funding levels. The relationship between block grant funding and the three aid measures was positive: The greater the dependency, diversity, and complexity, the more favorable were administrators toward block grant funding. For example, arrayed according to four categories of the complexity variable (ranging from none to five or more types of grants), those indicating block grants were "too little" made up, respectively, 40, 52, 64, and 81 percent. The more agency heads must scramble for different types of grants the more they prefer to have funds come from the national government in broad categories that, presumably, would reduce the scrambling.

For categorical grant funding a *negative* relationship was found between the three aid variables and the level of categorical grants. The more dependent, diverse, and complex the agency involvement with federal funds, the less inclined were the agency heads to favor expansion of categorical grants. Disenchantment with categorical aid policies is greatest among the administrators whose agencies are most deeply involved with federal aid processes. This finding, combined with the positive associations for block grants implies that state administrators might well consider block grant money as a substitute for categorical grant funds. Whether that is the case cannot be determined from existing data.

What is evident, however, is that federal aid policies are significant on a wide range of issues confronting state agency heads. Those fiscal policies extensively and pervasively affect state administrators' actions and attitudes. How agency heads perceive the impacts of these aid policies, and how they evaluate policy changes, we now examine.

AID IMPACTS AND EVALUATIONS

The preceding discussion of state administrators' actions and attitudes included, for the most part, all respondents to the 1974 and earlier surveys—whether or not they received federal aid. But the analysis has shown that federal aid plays central, significant roles in agency heads' thought and behavior. We must therefore examine only aid recipients' views on federal aid processes and impacts. More specifically, the state administrator surveys ask agency heads receiving federal aid several questions dealing with: (1) estimates of federal aid effects, (2) evaluations of policy and administration in the distribution of federal aid, and (3) preferences on proposed administrative and policy changes.

Precisely 1000 administrators headed agencies receiving federal aid. Their responses to questions on aid effects, satisfactions, and preferences are indicated in table 10-6.

Federal Aid Effects

Measuring the impact of federal aid on the states is an elusive and involved undertaking, and one that easily arouses controversy. State agency heads administering federal aid were asked what they *perceived* to be the impacts on their state. It was assumed that these respondents would be persons "most likely to know" the effects of

Table 10-6. *Opinions of State Agency Heads Receiving Federal Aid on the Effects, Satisfactions, and Change Preferences on Federal Aid* *

Federal Aid Impacts and Evaluations	Response Categories			
	Yes	No	No Effect	Not Ascertained
Federal Aid Effects	(percentages)			
1. Are federal aid monies subject to the same financial controls as other state funds?	86	12		2
2. In practice, is your department/agency less subject to supervision by the governor and legislature in federally financed activities than in activities financed solely by the state?	47	51		2
3. Does federal aid seem uncertain, making it difficult to estimate revenues for the next fiscal year?	76	22		2
4. With respect to the amount of money raised by your state, do you think federal aid has increased or decreased the level of funds raised by your state?	49	13	34	4
5. Has federal supervision of grant programs improved standards of administration and service?	46	18	33	3
Federal Aid Satisfactions				
6. Do you feel that federal grant administrators are sufficiently flexible in applying federal standards to programs operated by your agency?	42	55		3
7. Are existing provisions on matching arrangements satisfactory?	65	29		6
8. Are existing provisions on the apportionment formulas for funds among the states satisfactory?	45	47		8
Change Preferences				
9. Should federal aid monies be subject to the same financial controls as other state funds?	87	11		2
10. In place of categorical aids, if your agency were given an equal amount of money without "strings" attached, would you allocate the money differently from the way federal aid funds are now being allocated?	65	29		6
11. Should federal aid be expanded to include support of new programs for your agency?	76	20		4
12. Should federal aid for existing programs be:				5
increased	68			
decreased	6			
stay the same	21			

*N = 1000
Source: Wright, American State Administrators' Project: See also, Advisory Commission, *Intergovernmental Grant system,* p. 128-129.

federal aid on their state and agency. The reported results are what the agency heads *think* apply or prevail.

Responses to the first item in table 10-6 reveal high agreement (86 percent) that regular state financial procedures apply to federal aid. That only 12 percent of the respondents indicate otherwise could grossly understate the fiscal autonomy over federal aid in state budgets. The financial controls could be merely procedural and accounting in nature and not the types of controls that affect policy decisions.

What administrators see as a fact corresponds closely to what they feel *should* be the policy in controlling grant funds, as answers to question 9 of the table shows. The correspondence of affirmative percentages on questions 1 and 9 is no mere coincidence. Further analysis of the data revealed that virtually all administrators who report federal funds to be under standard state fiscal controls also agree that they should remain there. Preference for greater autonomy from state fiscal controls is negligible.

Responses to question 2 in table 10-6 suggest that the state's financial control over federal aid is in fact narrowly restricted—for example, to such devices as accounting and auditing. Thus, the policies for which federal funds are used may be independent of conventional state control channels; and indeed nearly half (47 percent) the administrators acknowledge that in practice their agency is less subject to supervision by the governor and legislators in federally financed activities than in activities financed solely by the state.

The planning and effective execution of public programs normally require a substantial measure of predictability of funding. All three state administrator surveys (1964, 1968, 1974) asked aid recipients whether federal funds seemed uncertain and made revenue-estimating difficult. Those answering affirmatively were 39 percent (1964), 68 percent (1968), 76 percent (1974). The 1964–1974 decade, then, was one in which uncertainty (real or imagined) nearly doubled for state administrators relying on federal aid. The increases in federal aid dollars and the greater number of program authorizations undoubtedly contributed to actual and perceived uncertainty. In addition, a substantial number of federal grant programs on the statute books have not been funded. The number of unfunded programs in fiscal year 1975 was over 100! It seems clear that the negative effects produced by aid uncertainty have not been fully appreciated by the Congress or by national aid administrators. The passage of GRS with the motto "more money with greater certainty" could be construed as a partial response to the revenue uncertainty that traditional forms of federal aid convey.

Judgments about two other effects of federal aid were sought: fiscal and programmatic. As to the former, was federal aid viewed as providing a fiscal stimulus? Almost half (49 percent) of the aid respondents in 1974 said yes. It is unclear, however, whether this fiscal stimulus was equal to or exceeded the funds necessary for matching the federal aid. That is, it was not possible to distinguish whether the fiscal effect was stimulative (generating more than matching funds) or merely additive (generating only matching funds), according to the definitions in chapter 6. While one-third reported there was no stimulative effect, 13 percent thought that federal aid had substitutive effects. That is, they replied that the federal aid allowed the state to *decrease* the amount of money raised. Combined with the 1974 percentage, trend data from 1964 and 1968 surveys, 49 and 56 percent respectively, show little shift in administrators' perceptions of federal aid fiscal effects over the ten years. The ten-year increases in federal aid appear to have altered state administrators' perceptions of fiscal impacts in only one respect: They have perceived reduced substitutive effects, from 24 percent (1964), to 16 percent (1968), to 13 percent (1974).

As to the final impact variable, question 5 asked administrators whether federal supervision of grant programs had improved standards of administration and services. Again, nearly half of the agency heads (46 percent) gave an affirmative response. Comparable long-term trend data are, for 1928, 67 percent, and, for 1948, 70 percent—a drop, then, in nearly fifty years from over two-thirds of assenting state-level aid administrators to less than half.

It is not surprising that a decline has occurred. We might visualize degree of improvement as describing a curve of diminishing arc. That is, as improvements in administrative and service standards occur and are realized, the *need* for improvement, and the area in which is is possible, correspondingly diminish. So, then, does the percentage of those who see still further improvement.

Federal Aid Satisfactions/Dissatisfactions

The acceptability of federal aid controls and standards are mediated by how they are applied. Aid recipients were asked (question 6) whether they were satisfied with how federal administrators applied standards to state agency programs; more specifically, how flexible or inflexible were these federal grant administrators? Over two-fifths of the state agency heads felt that federal grant administrators are sufficiently flexible, but more than half felt that they were not flexible enough. It may be encouraging that over 40 percent of the state agency heads thought federal grant administrators sufficiently flexible. There may be considerable overlap of those state agency heads who perceive flexibility and those state agency heads (46 percent) who agree with strict national performance standards. Nevertheless, a majority of state agency heads find federal administrators unsatisfyingly inflexible.

Administrative rigidities may be either a major or a minor irritation, but the commanding concern is acquiring the desired fiscal resources. Two important determinants of fiscal resources are the matching requirements necessary to obtain aid and the apportionment formulas for distributing it among the states. In answer to question 7 of table 10-6 nearly two-thirds of the aid recipients found matching arrangements satisfactory; to an identical question in 1948, nearly three-fourths of the state administrators expressed satisfaction. There has been only a slight drop in satisfaction during a quarter century.

The same is not true, however, for satisfaction levels and trends in opinion on apportionment formulas (question 8 of the table). Whereas in 1948 over three-fourths of the state respondents were satisfied with how funds were spread among the states, in 1974 less than half were. One factor contributing to the dissatisfaction with apportionment formulas may be their proliferation—146 different formulas are used to spread federal aid among the states and their localities. Here is another issue of policy concern and opinion shift that deserves attention by the Congress and federal agencies responsible for aid programs.

Federal Aid Change Preferences

What changes in the federal grant process do aid recipients desire? We have already noted the near consensus (question 9 of table 10-6) that federal aid should be under regular state financial controls. Less agreement exists on what might be called the "reallocation" question (number 10 of the table). Nearly two-thirds of the responding administrators indicated that if their agency were given an equal amount of money without "strings" they would allocate the money differently. Asked how different the reallocation would be, 27 percent declared they would initiate substantial or radical changes in spending patterns.

In recent year percentages of state agency heads preferring to reallocate federal aid have been on the increase—from 53 percent in 1964 to 57 percent in 1968, and then, a rise to 65 percent in 1974. These findings emphasize a larger trend persistent through the federal aid findings. There has been a steady rise in the proportions of state agency heads expressing dissatisfaction with and desiring changes in federal aid policies.

The final two items on preferences were designed to tap opinions of the aid recipients on broad funding shifts. Questions were posed on the amount of federal aid for new programs (question 11) and for existing programs (question 12). Not surprisingly, significant majorities of the respondents want both—about two-thirds wanting more support for existing programs and about three-fourths wanting aid expansion to new programs. Acquisitive aggrandizers are a strong segment among grant recipients.

While the percentage favoring an increase is large, it is remarkable that 27 percent of the respondents (question 12) said aid for existing programs should stay the same or be decreased. On the other hand, more agency heads (76 percent) favor extension to new programs than want aid to existing programs increased (68 percent). In 1948, by contrast, those favoring extension to new programs were 52 percent of respondents, and those wanting more funds for existing programs were 78 percent. The trend, then, is increasing favor of new programs, and slightly decreasing favor of better-funded existing programs. The reasonable inference would be, again, that state agency heads' spending priorities and preferences are not those specified by recent federal aid categorizations; hence, state administrators are receptive to shifts in federal aid policies.

Are some administrators more disposed to these shifts than others? What are the relationships between administrator or agency variables and these views on impacts and change preferences involving federal aid?

The standard measures of federal aid involvement show significant associations with several of the impact and evaluation items. The more diverse and complex is the administrator's aid involvement:

1. the greater the perception of stimulus effects;
2. the greater the perceived policy autonomy from the governor or legislature;
3. the greater the perceived uncertainty of federal aid;
4. the lower the perceived flexibility of federal administrators;

5. the lower the satisfaction with matching arrangements and apportionment formulas;
6. the greater the inclination to make major reallocations if "strings" were reduced; and
7. the higher the preferences for more aid to existing programs and to new programs.

The agency heads most deeply enmeshed in the federal aid process reveal a curiously conflicting and varied set of outlooks. They are in deep and want in deeper (that is, more funds), but they want to spend funds differently. They are more dissatisfied with matching and apportionment arrangements than in the past and have greater complaints concerning aid uncertainty and the inflexibility of federal administrators. Finally, they acknowledge the fiscal stimulus effects of aid and the policy autonomy that aid seems to engender. This combination of perspectives may appear chaotically inconsistent. Consistency and order, however, are not always the leading qualities of administrators' views and are far from hallmarks of the federal aid process.

An agency's functional category is also associated with the particular constellation of views among its administrators. By far the most distinctive set of views was expressed by welfare administrators, who were:

- highest in perceiving stimulus effects;
- lowest in seeing greater policy autonomy;
- lowest in indicating that aid was uncertain;
- least satisfied with federal administrators' flexibility;
- least satisfied with both matching and apportionment formulas;
- highest in wanting to reallocate aid if "strings" were reduced; and
- highest in desiring more aid for both existing and new programs.

Clearly, the public has no monopoly on dissatisfaction with the "welfare mess"; the state agency heads responsible for this function are among those most disposed toward changes. From the perspectives of both the public and state welfare administrators it was understandable that "welfare reform" was part of the "New Federalism" of the Nixon administration and was also one of the earliest major domestic policy initiatives of the Carter administration.

One other group of agency heads deserves comment: The opinions of fiscal and staff generalists were exceptional in two areas. First, they perceived federal aid to have the least stimulative effects fiscally but to have promoted policy autonomy the most. (In these two respects they were at polar opposites from the welfare administrators, and also from health officials.) Second, these generalists were least in favor of more aid for existing and new programs. In short, the analysis clearly discloses the contrasting views and tensions between generalist agency heads and functional, programmatic specialists.

Several personal attributes and perspectives of the agency heads were examined for their possible link to contrasting assessments of federal aid impacts and changes. Only two personal-attribute variables disclosed clear, consistent links to administrators' impact judgments and evaluations. First, as expected, an exceptionally strong positive association existed between the desire for agency expansion and preference for more federal aid to existing and new programs. Second, administrators who accorded high influence to clientele groups were much more likely to see federal aid as (a) providing a fiscal stimulus and (b) promoting policy autonomy from the governor and legislature. In addition, these administrators were more inclined to see federal aid as uncertain and were less ready to make any major reallocation of aid funds even if fewer "strings" were attached. These relationships highlight an often neglected influence in IGR—namely interest groups that may be effective both within and across the boundaries of governmental units. The administrator may purchase actual or perceived autonomy from the governor or legislature at the price not only of formal federal constraints, or "strings," but also of informal, less explicit constraints set by the clientele, or interest, groups. Evidence of such forces is the finding that, where clientele influence is high, a relaxation in formal aid constraints is not followed by program or expenditure shifts. Although the symbiotic relationship between federal aid and interest groups is often mentioned, it is seldom so clearly specified in the perceptions and actions of participants.

SUMMARY

The attention devoted in state politics to governors and legislators has overshadowed the significant roles of state administrators in policy decisions. At least five major policy roles of state agency heads—IGR entrepreneur, program promoter, fiscal aggrandizer, professional expert, and program innovator—have been identified and described with empirical data.

The IGR entrepreneurial role, the primary focus of this chapter, both affects and is affected by the other four roles. Much data support the view that state agency heads are central actors in state policy making. Their influence at the state level is increased by their involvement in IGR.

A majority of state administrators are extensively and intensely involved in IGR activities. As one rough indicator, over 60 percent of the administrators' agencies receive federal aid. The agency heads have frequent contacts with officials in diverse roles in numerous other governmental jurisdictions. Administrators' IGR contacts and types of involvement are strongly and positively associated with measures of federal aid dependency, diversity, and complexity. Thus, federal aid is a variable that contributes a great deal to our understanding of state administrators' IGR actions.

Likewise, federal aid helps explain state administrators' attitudes on a broad range of IGR issues, such as: state-local policy problems, state-national authority relationships, and federal aid impacts and funding levels. Those agency heads scoring higher on measures of federal aid dependency, diversity, and complexity tended to favor (1) a more activist state involvement in local issues, (2) an assertive but shared-function approach by the national government, and (3) more federal funds of a block grant, discretionary type.

State administrators receiving federal aid expressed various views on the effects of federal aid, on satisfaction with aid arrangements, and on preferences for change in federal aid policies. Nearly half of the aid recipients agreed that federal aid improved standards of administration and services, increased the amount of funds raised by the state, and made the agency heads less subject to supervision and control by the governor or legislators. One sore point over federal aid surfaced —over three-fourths of the agency heads thought federal aid was unpredictable. About two-thirds of the administrators were satisfied with matching arrangements for federal aid, but less than half thought formulas apportioning funds among the states were satisfactory. Also, less than half viewed federal aid administrators as sufficiently flexible in their dealings with the state agency heads. Finally, from two-thirds to three-fourths of the agency heads favored expansion of federal aid for existing programs and the extension of federal aid to include new programs. Yet at the same time nearly two-thirds of them indicated they preferred greater discretion in the use of federal aid. (Sixty-five percent would use federal aid funds differently if there were no "strings" attached.)

The measures of federal aid dependency, diversity, and complexity were significantly associated with the attitude items on aid effects, satisfactions, and change preferences. More specifically, those state agency heads with more diverse and complex federal aid involvement tended to:

1. see greater stimulus effects of aid;
2. say that they had more autonomy from the governor and legislature;
3. think that federal aid was more uncertain;
4. think that federal administrators were not sufficiently flexible;
5. be less satisfied with matching and apportionment arrangements;
6. desire more discretion to reallocate federal aid funds; and
7. be more in favor of expanding federal aid to existing and new programs.

State administrators are important actors in IGR. Their actions and their attitudes show certain regularities or patterned and cumulative "working relationships" previously identified (chapter 1, table 1-1) as one of the distinctive features of IGR. Further, the variables showing the strongest and most consistent associations with administrators' actions and attitudes are measures of federal aid. Federal aid may not *cause* these patterns, but it appears to be so closely linked to IGR actions and attitudes that it can be thought of as muscles, which give an organism movement and direction. For state agency heads that movement is at a fast pace and, currently, inclined toward greater self-direction.

National Officials:
Actions and Attitudes

11

One set of IGR actors remains to be discussed: officials of the national government. What are their actions and attitudes on intergovernmental policies and programs? We have noted the IGR role of the Congress in authorizing and expanding grant programs and in passing revenue sharing. And we have occasionally noted the IGR policy postures of various presidents—Eisenhower, Johnson, Nixon. In this chapter we pursue a more focused, in-depth examination of national officials' approach to IGR. Our point of departure is this assertion by the Kestnbaum Commission, more than two decades ago: "Policy making authorities of the national government are for most purposes the arbiters of the federal system."[1]

We shall see that, in fact, there are many "policy making authorities" on IGR in the national government. So numerous and diverse are the national-level IGR actors that no one of them can function as

---

1. The Commission on Intergovernmental Relations, *Report to the President for Transmittal to Congress* (Washington, D.C.: Government Printing Office, June 1955), p. 59.

an "arbiter." Indeed, it is doubtful that all the national actors discussed below, despite their common presence within the executive branch of government, can act as a collective arbiter. The absence of a single unifying purpose among these national actors enhances the bargaining powers and influence of states and local units.

In this chapter we look first at the presumed pinnacle of the national executive hierarchy, the president. We will note, however, the limits of presidential power on IGR matters. We will then focus on executive staff agencies, especially the Office of Management and Budget. Particular attention is given to an OMB-sponsored study on policy management assistance as a means of strengthening the management aspects of IGR. Third, we examine the IGR activities of two commissions—the Civil Service Commission and the Advisory Commission on Intergovernmental Relations. Fourth, and finally, federal aid agencies and their administrative heads are discussed from the standpoint of their roles as leaders of the powerful vertical functional alliances of local, state, and national program administrators.

PRESIDENTS AND IGR

President Woodrow Wilson called the relationship between the nation and the states "the cardinal question of our constitutional system." Every president in this century has paid some attention to IGR issues. It has been argued, however, that IGR is in such a poor state because presidents have been either insufficiently attentive or wrongheaded in this field. Although presidents are far from being the only national officials who have devoted time, energy, and imagination to IGR, theirs is the only elective post with a national constituency and it is often the focal point for IGR questions.

Woodrow Wilson emphasized the importance of federal or IGR questions. Yet his presidency is seldom remembered for IGR innovations or initiatives. Coincidentally, he was president when the Sixteenth Amendment, instituting the federal income tax, was added to the Constitution and also when the first modern grant-in-aid programs were enacted. But the contrast between Wilson's classic assertion and his practical actions is perhaps prophetic: Whereas he spoke of IGR matters as being in the first rank, in practice he relegated them to insignificance amid international and other national concerns.

There may be a lesson in this irony. Most later presidents have spoken self-approvingly of their approach to federalism or IGR matters, but rarely have they found it simple to confront IGR concerns directly—or extensively or effectively. A brief review of one recent president's IGR policies and administrative strategies will illustrate the point.

The New Federalism of the Nixon administration was ostensibly aimed at returning power to state and local governments ("the people"), although it was actually meant to undo much of the Great Society. Nixon was attempting to reverse a march of programs and power to Washington that began chiefly with the New Deal policies of Franklin D. Roosevelt during the Great Depression. New Federalism crashed on the rocks of Watergate but even if Nixon's administration had been ethically flawless there is every reason to believe that his IGR policies would have been, at best, modest in accomplishment. The several reasons for positing such an outcome do not apply only to the special conditions of the Nixon presidency.

Time is a primary reason why a president can have only limited impact on IGR matters. Foreign affairs and domestic economic policies command prime time on the president's decision-making agenda. Policies on domestic programs, of which IGR issues are a subset, tend to be relegated to a lesser status. As it was aptly expressed: "The domestic policy arena is one to which all recent Presidents have devoted limited attention, while within it, new legislation—not program operations—has been the most significant concern."[2]

Of course, some domestic programs are exceptions to this observation of presidential inattention to IGR: for example, federal aid to education (Truman, Kennedy, and Johnson), federal aid to highways (Eisenhower), mental health (Kennedy), economic opportunity and civil rights legislation (Johnson), and General Revenue Sharing (Nixon). But presidential attention span and priorities in the early 1970s were such that $1 billion was the estimated threshold below which the president did not normally devote his valuable time. Most IGR issues, programs, and policies tend to be below that threshold even though the aggregate amounts of federal aid are currently around $70 billion and constitute more than one-fifth of the domestic budget.

---

2. Advisory Commission on Intergovernmental Relations, *Improving Federal Grants Management* (Washington, D.C.: Government Printing Office, February 1977, A-53), p. 167.

Other reasons why presidents have restricted impact on IGR issues include:

1. the weakness of party allegiance and discipline;
2. the localism prominent, if not predominant, in the Congress;
3. the expertise and professionalism of functional specialists in IGR program fields;
4. the political strength and strategic access of grant-related interest groups within the "triple alliance" (see chapter 6);
5. the comparatively modest political payoffs and pride accruing from most IGR accomplishments;
6. the unexciting administrative and managerial features of IGR; and
7. the degree of decentralization in the U.S. political system.

The most recent efforts by a president to reshape IGR in his own image were Nixon's in early 1973. In 1972, through the promise of GRS enactment and broad hints of favorable White House treatment, Nixon was better able to politicize federal aid funding than had hitherto been done. These promises and hints gained him the support of many Democratic big-city mayors. But early in 1973, despite a smashing victory at the polls, Nixon could not turn his presumed electoral success into sustained effective IGR policy making. Quite apart from Watergate, he lost strength with mayors and many other state-local officials when he attempted to reduce or eliminate federal grant programs. He rubbed salt in these officials' wounds when he suggested that they use GRS money to replace the grant reductions. Nixon alienated the Congress, disastrously for his own cause, when he attempted to impose many cuts in the spending of federal agencies by his impoundment of funds. Quite naturally, he lost the little remaining support and trust he had among agency managers and administrators. Finally, he lost the unilateral cuts he attempted when states and localities successfully sued and federal courts compelled release of federal aid funds.[3]

The Nixon "experiment" in IGR policy redirection is a flashing beacon warning subsequent presidents. Similarly, the major policy initiatives and "successes" of the Johnson administration stand as monuments to the proposition that legislation and dollars alone are

---

3. An outstanding analysis of impoundment law, practice, policies, and politics, as well as other executive spending issues is Louis Fisher, *Presidential Spending Power* (Princeton, N.J.: Princeton University Press, 1975).

insufficient for assured accomplishment in IGR. In a telling phrase quoted by James Sundquist, one top Johnson administration official said: "We have no organizational philosophy; only a program philosophy."[4] Sundquist, the ACIR, and many others have pointed to the imperative need in IGR programs for an organizational-managerial philosophy.

The originator of such a philosophy, most believe, should be the president. Morton Grodzins, one of the most respected observers in the field, contended in 1960 that "The centrifugal force of domestic politics needs to be balanced by the centripetal force of strong presidential leadership. . . . simultaneous strength at the center and periphery exhibits the American system at its best, if also at its noisiest."[5] Nearly a decade later, in the wake of "strong presidential leadership . . . at the center," Sundquist a sympathetic analyst of the Johnson years, observed, "Somewhere in the Executive Office [of the president] must be centered a concern for the structure of federalism—a responsibility for guiding the evolution of the whole system of federal-state-local relations, viewed for the first time as a *single* system."[6] Have presidents, as they have been urged to do, assumed leadership in IGR? And what have been the long-term results of presidential actions?

IGR POLICY AND MANAGEMENT

An October 1976 report by the National Academy of Public Administration, prepared for use by either the Ford or Carter administration, offered advice on both policy and management issues of IGR. The report emphasized that "Difficult as the task may be, only the President is in a position to chart a course for bringing order and direction to this multitude of grant programs and associated objectives."[7] The analysis provided a brief historical sketch of presidential attention (and inattention) to IGR and observed that, "If any lesson has been learned in recent years, it is that intergovernmental problems

---

4. James L. Sundquist with the collaboration of David W. Davis, *Making Federalism Work: A Study of Program Coordination at the Community Level* (Washington, D.C.: The Brookings Institution, 1969), p. 13.

5. Morton Grodzins, "The Federal System," *Goals for Americans* (Englewood Cliffs, N.J.: Prentice-Hall, Spectrum, 1960), p. 282.

6. Sundquist, *Making Federalism Work*, p. 246.

7. National Academy of Public Administration, *The President and Executive Management: Summary of a Symposium* (Washington, D.C.: October 1976), p. 42.

are not separable from general problems of federal organization and administration."[8] Finally, the report posed a series of IGR-related questions to both the president and the Congress:

1. On what basis are the relative merits of one grant program to another evaluated?
2. What attempts are being made to unify the application, reporting, and review procedures for the hundreds of programs now classified as Categorical Grants?
3. Who has the responsibility to simplify and streamline the volumes of regulations which are written to implement Congressional enactments?
4. How is the effectiveness of these federal grants measured?
5. To whom do state and local officials turn for recourse when they believe their authorities and responsibilities are clearly being ignored?
6. What formal mechanism can be established to provide input by state and local officials into the federal budget and management process, including the writing of regulations?
7. How do we develop a national fiscal policy which takes into account the effect of federal tax decisions on state and local governments?
8. What is a national growth policy, how does it relate to the question of national planning, and how does it impact on the machinery of government?[9]

These questions guide us to the major dimensions of IGR on the national scene. First, although no doubt policy and management are inextricably intertwined, questions dealing chiefly with policy can be sorted out from those dealing mainly with management, even if only for discussion. Policy questions are predominant in questions 1, 7, and 8; management matters in questions 2, 3, 5, and 6. Question 4 best illustrates the inseparability of both policy and management issues.

In broad, slightly simplified terms, policy issues are of *what* or *why* something should be done; management issues are of *how* a policy is to be implemented. Although question 7, for example, is a "how" question, it rests on the policy premises that there *should* be a national fiscal policy and that it *should* take into account its own effects on state and local governments.

The eight questions above are useful for extracting, from IGR on the national scene, three subsidiary management issues, which can also be put as questions:

1. How can the national government organize itself and "put its own house in order" in dealing with state and local governments?

---

8. Ibid., p. 43.
9. Ibid., p. 44.

2. How can national officials and agencies build into their thinking and operations an awareness of the state-local effects of
their actions?
3. How can state-local officials be offered (or assured) an opportunity for input and influence on the national decisions that
affect them?

These cross-cutting issues of policy and management should be kept in
mind in the discussion that follows: though they are not always explicit, they are only barely below the surface. In that discussion, IGR
participants are grouped into two categories: first, executive staff
agencies and advisory groups; and second, line agencies and bureaus
responsible for administering grants and other IGR-related programs.
Discussion of the second group, line agencies and bureaus, also includes
a general analysis of these participant's influence on national policy
making. Two other sets of participants involved with the bureaus in
policy making are clientele groups and professional associations.

EXECUTIVE STAFF AGENCIES
AND ADVISORY GROUPS

Several staff and advisory units have been linked to IGR policy
and management responsibilities. Among these are units of the Executive Office of the President (White House staff, Domestic Council,
Office of Management and Budget), the Civil Service Commission, and
the ACIR. In addition, there have been numberless special task and
study groups and interagency coordinating committees, and more
recently the Federal Regional Councils (FRCs). We neither need nor are
able to discuss this many IGR participants. Furthermore, an excellent
and thorough contemporary analysis of the executive branch and IGR
has been produced by one of the participants.[10] The ACIR publication
is top-priority reading for anyone who desires to understand in some
depth IGR in the national government. In the following discussion we
attempt only to identify some of the participants, to clarify their roles,
and to point to a few of the perennial policy and management issues

---

10. Advisory Commission on Intergovernmental Relations, *Improving Federal Grants
Management* (Washington, D.C.: Government Printing Office, February 1977, A-53).

that have confronted the national government. Both the actors and many events may be put in temporal context by consulting Appendix K— a twenty-year chronology of major events involving IGR management.

Executive Office of the President

The Bureau of the Budget (BOB, now the Office of Management and Budget: OMB) is probably the executive unit with the longest-standing interest in IGR. After it was placed in the president's executive office in 1939, the bureau's first director organized a Council on Inter-governmental Relations. On the council were representatives from local and state governments as well as federal agency personnel and scholars. World War II crowded it out of existence but it left a legacy of ideas and issues that are still current.

One idea was to have an IGR liaison—a mechanism for communication among local, state, and national officials. A second was a concern for management strategies that would bring about coordination among the programs and policies of federal agencies as they made their impact on state and local governments. This was essentially a field operation conducted under BOB field office leadership until 1953, when the bureau's field offices were eliminated. The story of one region's efforts and qualified successes can be read in an article on the Pacific Coast Board of Intergovernmental Relations, (PACBIR).[11]

Another legacy of BOB's interest in IGR was organizational. Every administration since President Eisenhower has acknowledged the significance of IGR issues by making some organizational arrangement to deal with them. Acting largely on the Kestnbaum Commission's recommendations in 1955, Eisenhower designated a White House staff member, former Governor Howard Pyle of New Mexico, as his deputy assistant for IGR. Among his assigned duties were:

1. advice and coordination in the executive office on policy matters affecting either states or local governments,
2. liaison with state and local government associations, and
3. the promotion of coordination among federal departments and agencies on IGR problems.

A sidelight on the IGR policy orientation of the Eisenhower

---

11. Stanley K. Crook, "The Pacific Coast Board of Intergovernmental Relations," *Public Administration Review,* 11 (Spring 1951): 103–108.

administration is instructive. On the Kestnbaum Commission urban interests and policy perspectives were not significantly represented. Urban interests were further alienated by Pyle's appointment and still further so by Eisenhower's opposition to most of the grant programs that a Democratic-dominated Congress (1955–1961) pressed upon him. These policy differences and Eisenhower's rural-military backgrounds once prompted the executive director of an urban lobbying group to comment to the author, "Ike wouldn't know what a city was until one reached out and clobbered him to get his attention!" In the 1950s the public interest groups (PIGs) had very little muscle to gain presidential attention.

Presidential staff continued to handle IGR duties during the Kennedy administration, and Johnson gave the issue greater visibility in some respects but with dubious results. Under Johnson IGR responsibilities were divided between Vice-President Humphrey, a former mayor, who handled liaison with local government officials, and two former governors, first Buford Ellington and later Farris Bryant, who served successively as liaison with the states. That two persons performed liaison duties presented some difficulties, but more than mere communication with state and city officials was involved. There were fundamental problems of policy, management, and coordination.

The Great Society programs burst on local and state officials and on the existing federal establishment with such force that no policy and control mechanisms were adequate to keep programs, procedures, grants, etc., in phase or sequence. In late 1966 Democratic governors mounted a "revolt," charging LBJ and the White House with poor communication on programs and policies. Mayors and many other local officials were also up in arms over federal sponsorship and support of community action agencies and other autonomous entities, derisively called "paragovernments." But for the Johnson administration and its top officials the most critical cries were those coming from the Congress.

Three weeks of congressional hearings in 1966 on the federal role in urban affairs produced condemnations of fragmented federal assistance. Senator Abraham Ribicoff, who chaired the hearings, was more specific as he "excoriated the BOB for negligence and culpability" in allowing policies and programs to get out of control.[12] The Senator said:

---

12. ACIR, *Improving Federal Grants Management*, p. 162.

I trust that in the months ahead, before a new Federal budget is submitted, this question of coordinating Federal programs for our urban areas will receive sharper and more devoted attention. This task of coordination and a unified view had been sadly ignored in our headlong rush to adopt bigger and newer programs. And this failure must be laid squarely on the doorstep of the Bureau of the Budget—because that is the traditional function as an arm of the Executive Office of the President.

For too long, this agency has abdicated its responsibilities in this area. I suggest a detailed re-examination of the role of the Bureau of the Budget so this vital function of government does not continue to languish unattended.[13]

In some respects BOB was taking a "bum rap," since the policy initiatives and organizational configuration of the Great Society programs had bypassed the bureau. But the BOB took these and other criticisms seriously. Among its efforts were:

1. attempting to identify grant programs suitable for consolidation;
2. developing legislation to simplify procedures when two or more federal agencies could jointly fund a common-interest project;
3. formalizing procedures by federal agencies to assure state and local executives an opportunity to review and comment on federal regulations;
4. consolidating several agency-based catalogs of available federal grants; and
5. reviewing the bureau's own internal organizational arrangements.

The bureau was reorganized in 1967, ostensibly to strengthen its management capacities. That change was short-lived; the Nixon administration not only undid that structure but, with Reorganization Plan number 2 in 1970, further changed the bureau's framework, name, and mission. IGR actions had not languished from 1967 to 1970. In 1968 and 1969 ten common standard regions were encouraged and instituted for most agencies in eight Cabinet departments, and Federal Regional Councils were created in the ten regional center cities. In addition, starting in 1969, a three-year Federal Assistance Review (FAR) program began with multiple policy, management, and procedural goals. Among the IGR objectives of FAR were:

1. promoting common regional boundaries;
2. strengthening regional councils;

---

13. Ibid., p. 163.

3. cutting red tape and reducing grant-processing time;
4. decentralizing administrative agency authority to regional and
   district offices;
5. joint funding; and
6. consolidating grants.

The Reorganization Plan of 1970 was intended to strengthen management and budget-related operations (hence the name change to Office of *Management* and Budget). The same plan also created the Domestic Council (an intended domestic analog of the National Security Council), which would be the policy body with primary attention to substantive issues, or the *what* of government. The OMB would concentrate on operations and evaluation, the *how* and *how well* features. There seemed to be reasonable grounds for drawing these distinctions but there were doubts and objections, especially about the presumption that policy and administration can be neatly divorced.

The skeptics carried the day—but not entirely because policy and administration are inseparable. Rather, the reasons seem traceable to leadership and to traditional organizational routines and goals within OMB, as succinctly summarized by the ACIR:

1. the lack of a strong, continuing White House interest in managerial issues;
2. the concentration of the attention and resources of OMB's leadership on budget preparation and review;
3. a high level of turnover among those in policy positions in OMB and other agencies;
4. tension between the budget and management divisions within OMB;
5. differences of workflow and style in the budgetary and legislative areas on the one hand and management improvement on the other.[14]

The ACIR has also provided an excellent overview of OMB's attempts to cope with IGR complexities:

The Office of Management and Budget has, to date, had limited success in improving the management of the intergovernmental grant system. Despite repeated reorganization and a change in name, budgetary issues and problems continue to predominate. The agency has a lengthy history of involvement in

---

14. Ibid., p. 169.

intergovernmental relations. It was among the first to perceive the growing problems of intergovernmental and interagency management which emerged in the mid 1960s, and developed a full agenda for improvement. However, this has still been only partially implemented.

In the period 1973–75, the agency's formal responsibilities for many aspects of intergovernmental management were considerably reduced. Many of its management procedures were transferred to the General Services Administration and Treasury Department, although the OMB retained policy oversight. In 1973, the Executive Director of the Domestic Council was designated as the President's liaison with state and local governments, although this function might have been given to the OMB, as the Ash Council had recommended. Hence, though the budget office was among the first Federal agencies to become involved in the intergovernmental arena, its role in this area did not grow, but was fragmented and divided.

By action of Congress, some of these former responsibilities have now been returned to the OMB, but with reduced resources and organizationally distributed within OMB in four separate divisions. These new functions, clearly, will challenge the agency to strengthen its capabilities in the management area. The past record provides little basis for optimism in this regard.[15]

From 1969 to 1973 presidential liaison with state and local officials had been consolidated in an Office of Intergovernmental Relations (OIR) within the vice-president's office. This liaison role was only part of the vice-president's expanded and formalized role in national-state-local relations; also included were duties to serve as a clearinghouse for the resolution of intergovernmental problems and to identify recurring federal interdepartmental and interprogram problems. For a variety of reasons, including lack of leadership, the OIR fell far short of its potential and was abolished in late 1972.

One problem endemic to OIR was the pressure and proclivity to become involved in details, for example, in particular projects or one-city complaints. I recall visiting OIR offices and waiting in the anteroom with a mayor who had procedural problems with a grant and two county commissioners who wanted to mobilize some high-level clout favorable to a pending project grant. OIR, in short, tended to get lost in operational trivia at the cost of attention to broader issues involving management and policy.

The Domestic Council was intended to be the policy-oriented spear carrier of the executive office under Nixon. That role never

---

15. Ibid., p. 171.

materialized despite the reputed power that John Erlichman exercised from 1971 to 1973. Although there are several somewhat conflicting explanations for this failure, it seems fair to conclude that the Domestic Council never effectively decided what should be the overall policy posture of the Nixon (or Ford) administration on IGR. General Revenue Sharing, for example, was handled by a special task force as an *ad hoc* issue, as were welfare reform, model cities, special revenue sharing, etc. The Domestic Council seldom initiated policy proposals but instead concentrated on reviewing and reacting to proposals coming from agencies.

This *ad hoc* reactive role of the Domestic Council was not confined to IGR policy questions. Like the pressures on OIR, members of the Domestic Council staff were importuned to intervene in specific circumstances that were unproductive in a larger sense and often trivial, even humorously so: One Erlichman vignette (see Appendix L, "The Federal System and a Sewage System") describes a sequence of institutional, personal, and circumstantial relationships that resulted in a federal grant to a Michigan city for experimental sewage treatment. It reveals not only White House influence but also the constituency payoffs that grants have.

The larger significance of this single minor episode should not be lost. There is a great, almost irresistible, temptation for White House staff members and others in positions of great influence to become involved in such minutae. Such involvement subtracts from the time and energy to deal with larger, more significant policy and management issues. The end result is what former Secretary of HUD Robert Wood calls the "policy inversion process":[16] Details and small case problems are drawn to the executive office and crowd out attention that should be devoted to policy planning, program innovations, and management strategies. Policy initiative is then left to—or lost to—the bureau chiefs, program administrators, and middle management in the operating departments and agencies.

Other IGR Participants

Although they are not executive staff agencies, two commissions—the Civil Service Commission and the Advisory Commission on Inter-

---

16. Robert Wood, "When Government Works," *The Public Interest,* No. 18 (Winter 1970),; 39–51.

governmental Relations—must be given some recognition of their roles in IGR. The first-named has recently (1970) assumed important IGR duties, most prominent among them is administering the Hatch Act of 1939 as it applies to state and local governments. That legislation prohibited federal employees from engaging in certain types of political activities; these prohibitions were later extended to state or local government employees paid in whole or in part from federal grant funds. (The constitutionality of such restrictions was sustained by the Supreme Court in 1947.)[17] The Civil Service Commission now monitors the compliance of states and localities with those provisions for 29 grant-in-aid programs covering 300 state agencies. In this respect the commission is like a police officer, supervising and reviewing state compliance with federal merit system requirements in these grant programs.

But the commission has other responsibilities and has sought to avoid a negative policelike image by encouraging and assisting states in developing comprehensive statewide merit systems. The commission's capacity to project this positive image was helped immensely by passage of the Intergovernmental Personnel Act (IPA) of 1970 (Public Law 91–648). That legislation authorized the commission to make grants to state and local governments for personnel-management improvement, for training, and for government-service graduate study fellowships. IPA appropriations for these grants have been about $15 million annually. The commission has also launched an aggressive technical-assistance consultation service.

In addition, the IPA authorized an intergovernmental personnel mobility program to permit short-term (two-year) loans or exchanges of personnel between governments. In the first five years of the program there were more than 3000 IPA mobility assignments. And in fiscal 1976 alone over 800 intergovernmental moves took place, with about 500 persons shifting *to* federal agencies from local or state governments or institutions of higher education. About 300 full-time federal agency employees made temporary moves to local or state governments or educational institutions.[18] These changes were made under the act without loss of salary, fringe benefits, etc.

The five-year mobility patterns are worth noting in two respects.

17. See *Oklahoma* v. *Civil Service Commission,* 330 U.S. 127 (1947).

18. U.S. Civil Service Commission, Bureau of Intergovernmental Personnel Programs, *Intergovernmental Personnel Notes,* July/August 1976, p. 1. Subsequent mobility data from: "Fact Sheet: IPA Mobility Program," Cumulative Data, May 1, 1971-June 30, 1976, USCSC, Bureau of Intergovernmental Personnel Programs, September 2, 1976.

First, a nearly equal number of assignments were made to and from the federal government, about 1600 each way; second, the largest single type of assignment, more than 1000 moves, was *from* institutions of higher education *to* federal agencies. The two next largest categories were *from* federal agencies: 750 going to state governments, 500 to local governments. The nearly 300 shifts from federal agencies to higher education made the academic-practitioner two-way flow the major feature of the IPA mobility program. While 40 different federal agencies had participated in IPA assignments, two agencies, HEW and Agriculture with about 550 and 450 respectively, were involved in nearly one-third of all mobility agreements.

The mobility resulting from the IPA can be interpreted in several ways, some of them unfavorable. For example, was the act *intended* to foster the high degree of mobility between educational institutions and the federal government? (A major effect of the legislation seems to have been to offer interim employment to nontenured academics.)

More critical to the short- and long-range success of IPA mobility, however, is its use by federal agencies. Are the federal administrators who seek and receive IPA assignments persons of outstanding ability, or are they "spares" from the federal agency's standpoint? Even granting that federal IPA mobility assignees are of the highest quality, it is also important to pose the career risk problem for those taking an IPA assignment. What costs does a federal career official incur by being absent from his own post and agency for one or two years? Might not an IPA assignment confirm the potentially embarrassing fact that the assignee is dispensable?

Clearly, there are many nuances and ramifications to this one prominent IGR activity of the Civil Service Commission. They complicate efforts to arrive at simple, easy judgments about the IGR effects of commission programs.

The IGR activities of the Civil Service Commission can be summarized:

- grants
- technical assistance
- mobility assignments
- state-local participation in federal training sessions
- cooperative recruiting efforts
- administration of merit system standards for grant programs

The responsibilities of another commission, the Advisory Commission on Intergovernmental Relations, can also be summarized. Created in 1959 to review and recommend IGR policies, the ACIR is given statutory mandates:

1. To bring together representatives of the Federal, State and local governments for the consideration of common problems.
2. To provide a forum for discussing the administration and coordination of Federal grant and other programs requiring intergovernmental cooperation.
3. To give critical attention to the conditions and controls involved in the administration of Federal grant programs.
4. To make available technical assistance to the executive and legislative branches of the Federal Government in the review of proposed legislation to determine its overall effect on the Federal system.
5. To encourage discussion and study at an early stage of emerging public problems that are likely to require intergovernmental cooperation.
6. To recommend, within the framework of the Constitution, the most desirable allocation of governmental functions, responsibilities, and revenues among the several levels of government.
7. To recommend methods of coordinating and simplifying tax laws and administrative practices to achieve a more orderly and less competitive fiscal relationship between the levels of government and to reduce the burden of compliance for taxpayers.[19]

The ACIR and its staff have compiled an impressive record of activities and accomplishments. More than any other agency or entity, it has made visible and has sharpened focus on IGR issues on the national scene. It has achieved these and other tasks while laboring under two major constraints: (a) a small staff with modest budget, and (b) diverse and disparate commission membership.[20]

Through most of its organizational life the staff has never ex-

---

19. Public Law 86–380; 86th Congress, H.R. 6904, September 24, 1959.
20. The background and creation of the ACIR and its distinctive features and policy orientation during its early years are discussed in Deil S. Wright, "The Advisory Commission on Intergovernmental Relations: Unique Features and Policy Orientation," *Public Administration Review*, 25 (September 1965): 193–202. For a contemporary view of the policy orientation of the ACIR, with a special focus on urban problems, see the following report based on the commission's research and recommendations: Advisory Commission on Intergovernmental Relations, *Improving Urban America: A Challenge to Federalism* (Washington, D.C.,: Government Printing Office, September 1976, M-107).

ceeded fifteen professionals and a total of fewer than forty persons. The commission's total budget, coming almost exclusively from congressional appropriations, did not break the $1 million barrier until 1973. Yet the staff has produced for commission consideration and action more than fifty major policy reports, which normally have required extensive staff research, report drafting, formulating alternative policy recommendations, and so on. In addition, the staff has produced over 100 additional research studies, information reports, major staff papers, etc. This output has been prodigious, and it has been exceeded only by the care, depth, and excellence of analysis.

In submitting the ACIR's fifteen-year report to the U.S. Senate in 1974, Senator Muskie gave the ACIR high commendation:

> The Fifteen-Year Report of the ACIR summarizes an impressive record of activities. In numerous, well-documented reports, the ACIR has frequently pointed the way to more rational approaches to intergovernmental cooperation. Because it is merely an advisory body which must rely on others to implement its recommendations, the Advisory Commission does not have —nor should it have—high political visibility. Its strength lies in its reputation for thoroughness and nonpartisanship and in its proven ability to assemble vast bodies of factual information, define salient intergovernmental issues, and recommend appropriate policy decisions. Perhaps its most outstanding achievement in this respect is the general revenue sharing program, first recommended and vigorously supported by the ACIR nearly a decade ago.[21]

This outstanding record has been compiled by the staff and by a twenty-six member bipartisan commission composed of six members of the Congress, three private citizens, three officials of the executive branch, four governors, three state legislators, four mayors, and three county officials. Congressional members—three representatives and three senators—are appointed by the leadership of their chambers. Congressman Fountain and Senator Muskie, both charter members, head the respective House and Senate Subcommittees on Intergovernmental Relations.

The president appoints the chairman and all remaining ACIR members (except staff), subject to a rule of bipartisan representation and special circumstances surrounding state and local government representatives. The president's powers of appointment of the private

---

21. *Advisory Commission on Intergovernmental Relations: 15-Year Report,* Subcommittee on Intergovernmental Relations, Senate Committee on Government Operations, 93rd Congress, 2nd Session, Committee Print, October 1974, p. vi.

citizens and executive branch members are unrestricted. But governors, legislators, mayors, and county officials must be chosen from a panel of two names submitted to the president by the NGC, the NCSL, NLC/USCM, and NACO, respectively. In short, the president's appointive power is considerably circumscribed and cannot easily be used to control or dominate the ACIR. The PIGs have formal representation in an official, national-level forum. There have been times when state-local interests have dominated commission deliberations. This tendency has been increased by the poor attendance record of representatives of the executive branch.

The policy reports of the commission contain over 400 recommendations for action by national, state, and local governments. The recommendations may be broad or specific, fiscal or structural, management- or policy-oriented, minor or major. Issues on which the ACIR has made one or more recommendations include:

- reapportionment of state legislatures
- reduction in the number of popularly elected state administrative officials
- allowing governors to succeed themselves
- prohibiting public employees from striking
- investment of state-local idle cash balances
- state collection and administration of local sales or income taxes
- state income tax as a credit against federal income tax
- repeal of federal documentary stamp tax
- balanced federal aid policy of categorical grants, block grants, and revenue sharing
- decentralization of decision making on grant programs to regional office directors
- channeling of federal aid for urban development through the states (conditional on state matching money)

A substantial proportion of the ACIR recommendations (an official list of which exceeds forty printed pages) has been implemented by the national government and by many states and localities. Although one unit of the ACIR devotes full time to implementation, the two major staff components are research sections; one focuses on taxation and finance, the other on governmental structure and organization.

There is one external indicator that the states are aware of the ACIR and its performance. In the 1974 survey, state administrators were asked whether they had heard of the ACIR.[22] Over half (55 percent) indicated that they were familiar with the ACIR, a dramatic increase from the 16 percent who knew of the ACIR in 1964. Of those who had knowledge of the ACIR in 1974 two-thirds had read one or more ACIR reports and more than one-third had had contact with ACIR staff or commission members. The ACIR had become far better known among one constituency—state administrators—than it had ten years earlier.

Which state agency heads were most aware of or attentive to the ACIR and its activities and reports? A few notable variables were significantly and positively related to high ACIR awareness/attentiveness scores:

1. amount of administrator's time devoted to policy development;
2. staff generalist position as contrasted with a line, functional agency head;
3. federal aid complexity, diversity, and dependency

From these and other results we can draw a profile of the state administrator most likely to be aware of ACIR: a generalist who, through involvement in policy development, participates in an active communications network with a variety of officials outside the agency. Administrators most aware of the ACIR come from agencies that participate in IGR programs involving federal aid, or they have had personal exposure to that system through work experience at other levels of government.

Awareness was not the only aspect of ACIR pursued in the 1974 survey. Two evaluation-oriented questions on ACIR were put to the agency head respondents:

1. Had the ACIR been useful in connection with the agency head's work?
2. How did the state administrator rate the ACIR on a scale from poor to excellent?

More than one-third of the agency heads had found the ACIR's work useful to their agency and nearly two-thirds rated ACIR performance either good or excellent. These results are, a vote of confidence in what has been achieved by the ACIR over its relatively brief lifespan.

---

22. The following discussion relies on the analysis and findings of Mary Wagner, "The Advisory Commission on Intergovernmental Relations and the Council of State Governments: State Administrators' Perspectives," unpublished master's thesis, Department of Political Science, University of North Carolina at Chapel Hill, 1976.

The ACIR is the only agency of the national government whose sole mission is to focus on IGR. It has done so extensively and intensively. The ACIR's annual reports are an insightful chronical of nearly two decades of significant issues, tensions, proposals, and progress in IGR. The ACIR, however, has influence largely in proportion to the expert, persuasive, and timely character of its recommendations. Lacking size, program responsibilities, political clout, and other strengths, it cannot compel the adoption of its policy choices. That capability is reserved for more potent agencies.

Study Committee on Policy Management Assistance

We have examined the IGR role of OMB and its potency (or impotence) from historical and organizational standpoints. It is also useful to review a special initiative mounted by OMB and other federal agencies in the mid-1970s. The focus of the initiative is best described by the title of the report produced by a special study group: *Strengthening Public Management in the Intergovernmental System: A Report Prepared for Office of Budget and Management by the Study Committee on Policy Management Assistance.*[23]

The key phrase in the long title is "policy management." It was defined by the study committee as

> the capacity of elected officials to perform on an integrated, functional cross-cutting basis the needs assessment, goal setting, and evaluation functions of management; to establish priorities and to mobilize and allocate resources, to guide relations with the community; and to initiate and guide the planning, development, and implementation of strategies and programs that are related to sustaining or improving the physical, socioeconomic, or political conditions that have a bearing on the quality of life in a community.[24]

In slightly different terms, policy management "is a *process* that involves the *strategic* functions of *guidance* and *leadership* with respect to a governmental jurisdiction." Policy management was contrasted

---

23. Executive Office of the President, *Strengthening Public Management in the Intergovernmental System: A Report Prepared for Office of Management and Budget by the Study Committee on Policy Management Assistance* (Washington, D.C.: Government Printing Office, 1975). See also "Policy Management Assistance—A Developing Dialogue," *Public Administration Review,* 35 (December 1975): 693–818.

24. Philip M. Burgess, "Capacity Building and the Elements of Public Management," *Public Administration Review,* 35 (December 1975): 707. See also, Appendix A, "Policy Management."

with program management: "the performance of *administrative* functions and *tactical* requirements of executing specific policy by undertaking programs, activities, and services."[25]

These definitions and the extensive activities, reports, and publications that lay behind them evolved from a Federal Interagency Study Committee on Policy Management Assistance. The study committee, created in 1974 under OMB leadership, conducted during 1974–1975 one of the most significant, broad-based examinations of the management aspects of IGR ever executed. The study committee developed an array of findings and recommendations grouped under three broad categories of needs: (a) to reorient federal programs to meet state and local needs, (b) to expand and coordinate public management assistance to state and local governments, and (c) to improve the federal machinery for better intergovernmental management. Brief comments are helpful on the findings and recommendations in each category.

Reorienting Federal Programs. The need to reorient federal programs arose from three general findings of the study committee:

1. Federal assistance is fragmented, making it difficult to administer and use.
2. The regulations, guidelines, and practices governing categorical assistance programs frequently have been confusing and unresponsive to local needs and priorities.
3. Federal domestic assistance often goes directly to non-governmental or special purpose agencies, bypassing key state and local decision-makers and thereby, weakening their authority and management capacity.[26]

Evidence supported each finding. For example, fragmentation was noted in the health area, where 10 different federal agencies administered 230 separate grant programs and a comptroller general's report cited "substantial problems that occur when state and local government(s) attempt to identify, obtain, and use Federal assistance to meet their needs."[27] Mayor Lugar of Indianapolis was quoted as representative of local opinion on the confusion and unresponsiveness of federal programs: "If Congress had any idea of what a horrendous monstrosity the administration of these hundreds of billions of dollars has been,

---

25. *Strengthening Public Management,* pp. 4–5.
26. Ibid., pp. viii–ix.
27. Ibid., p. vii.

they would look more kindly on the deficiencies of local governments."[28] A survey of nearly 900 cities was also cited that indicated that only one-fourth of the local officials felt that federal agencies were more than "occasionally" flexible in adjusting their programs to meet local conditions.

According to the study committee, a reorienting of federal aid programs required five actions:

1. continued movement toward revenue sharing, block grants, grant consolidations, and other funding policies that permit more administrative flexibility by state and local leaders,
2. federal agency development of performance and evaluation criteria measuring the degree of accomplishment of basic national legislative purposes rather than the creation of detailed and narrow administrative guidelines,
3. expansion of grant notification and review procedures to cover all major domestic assistance programs with federal contributions to the cost of implementing such procedures,
4. insured compliance of federal agencies with requirements for simplified grant application and administrative procedures, and
5. increased use by federal agencies of integrated planning, awarding, and monitoring of grants based on experience gained under joint funding, integrated grant administration, planned variations, annual arrangements, etc.[29]

Expanding Public Management Assistance. The need to expand and coordinate public management assistance was identified as critical to improving IGR. The study committee pointed to the budget constraints on local or state personnel for policy management purposes and to the meager and misdirected efforts of federal resources to compensate for the inadequacies in policy management. About $500 million in federal aid (only one percent of all federal aid) went to states and local governments for use in management—and about 90 percent of this aid went for *program* management, not general policy management. Only two federal programs, amounting to less than $50 million, focused on across-the-board management needs: the HUD "701" planning and management grant program, and funds under the IPA act.

---

28. Ibid., p. ix.
29. Ibid.

The committee found strong but mixed support for policy management assistance among state and local officials. There was a strong
emphasis on the need for policy management but "understandable
concerns about possible Federal encroachment into local policy matters or the imposition of particular management structures or processes"
connected with federal support of this activity.[30]

From these findings and considerations the study committee
recommended several courses of action:

1. a firm commitment by the national government to management assistance for state and local governments;
2. a joint national-state-local effort to develop a delivery strategy
   for management assistance;
3. the tailoring of management assistance to the particular needs
   of a recipient unit based on a joint federal-recipient needs
   assessment process;
4. incentives for more intensive state efforts to strengthen local
   units' management capacities by removing legal, structural,
   and fiscal constraints;
5. expanded, coordinated resources for building state-local management capacity by using nonfederal sources, such as state
   community affairs agencies, public interest groups, university
   public service institutes, and professional associations;
6. increased federal aid for policy management assistance relative
   to program management assistance—accompanied by its evaluation by state-local elected leaders; and
7. the development of a better information base on all aspects of
   public management assistance provided by federal agencies.[31]

Improving Federal Machinery.   The study committee's third area
of concern was the existing and altered federal machinery for improved
intergovernmental management. The committee stated the problems
succinctly and pointedly.

> Perhaps the key missing element has been formal machinery in the Federal
> government for making on-going adjustments in Federal policy toward State
> and local government, and for persevering in the implementation of policy
> changes.

> Only one agency is charged with strictly intergovernmental mission: The

30. Ibid., p. x.
31. Ibid., p. x–xi.

Advisory Commission on Intergovernmental Relations. For all its outstanding work, however, ACIR is confined to research and recommendations. The temporary interagency committees and presidential commissions assembled to deal with intergovernmental problems also have lacked implementing power, or the organizational status and staff to goad others to action.

If the Federal government is to develop the capacity for ongoing analysis and improvement of public management at all levels of government, responsibility for conducting intergovernmental business should be clearly assigned to key agencies.[32]

The committee did *not* call for a new agency or for standard IGR units in all federal departments and agencies. "For the most part, the basic elements of such machinery are now in place...." That is, the Domestic Council, OMB, the Undersecretaries Group for Regional Operations, and the Regional Councils satisfy the structural necessities. But the committee aimed at infusing these entities and personnel with a strong commitment to "put the Federal house in order." Its recommendations included:

1. designating a *policy* focal point in the Executive Office of the President with responsibility for the overall direction, coordination, and evaluation of intergovernmental policies and programs, including capacity-building management assistance elements;
2. designating a separate *management* focal point in the Executive Office to oversee the implementation of intergovernmental policies;
3. requiring each federal domestic agency to clearly assign IGR responsibilities for:
   a. securing state and local inputs to agency program development,
   b. integrating, planning, management, and capacity-building programs in the agency,
   c. promoting IGR technical assistance and training activities in each agency, and
   d. providing a central contact point for state and local officials;
4. strengthening federal field operations administratively by:
   a. increased central office-field consultation in the formulation of agency policies and programs,

---

32. Ibid., p. xi.

    b. increasing the capacities of the Federal Regional Councils
to coordinate federal programs in the field.[33]

The aggregate activities and recommendations of the Study Committee on Policy Management Assistance were significant blends of the creative and competitive phases of IGR. The committee correctly diagnosed that IGR problems arose from a combination of two shortcomings, (a) political leadership and (b) administrative management. During the creative phase of IGR the U.S. political system was marked by strong political leadership but loose management. The competitive phase has tended to emphasize management on the presumption that political and policy leadership will be asserted by the appropriate elected local or state leaders—as, for example, in revenue sharing. In the creative phase the programmatic and functional specialists were given a loose rein; in the competitive period generalist concerns for "policy management" were reasserted. Thus, the study committee attempted to merge and resolve the IGR legacies of the 1960s and 1970s. Its clear generalist preferences did not obscure its unstated premise: In IGR it is *programs* that must be promoted; this can be done only if there is political will or leadership, which in turn can be effective only if there is administrative management. At one point the committee explicitly recognized a continuing functional emphasis: "it is essential that new policy management services or coordination mechanisms evolve along the lines of existing functional programs."[34] Because the basic functional structure and focus of the national government remain, we must examine the roles of federal aid agencies and their associated interest groups in IGR.

FEDERAL AID AGENCIES AND ADMINISTRATORS

The federal executive branch is a diverse, far-flung array of activities, programs, divisions, bureaus, agencies, and departments. Sprinkled liberally but unevenly throughout this establishment are the scores of federal aid programs. Most of these aid programs appear to be administered at the bureau, division, or middle-management level by

---

33. Ibid., p. xi–xii.

34. As quoted and discussed in Allen Schick, "The Intergovernmental Thicket: The Questions Are Still Better Than the Answers," *Public Administration Review*, 35 (December 1975): 721.

administrators who have tenure, who have usually come up through the ranks, and who are specialists in the particular function or program they direct.

The bureau or division has a relatively homogeneous structure designed to perform one or more closely related tasks. It is a hardy, highly stable unit that reorganization plans may move around but rarely abolish. The presumptive traits of middle-management persons responsible for federal aid programs are stability based on organizational integrity; tenure; training; experience; and program goals. In these respects federal aid administrators are probably not unlike fellow managers responsible for the numerous other federal programs that have little or no direct impact on IGR.

Actually, we know relatively little about the backgrounds or career experiences of federal aid administrators, or about their actions. Selective case studies provide suggestive and sometimes penetrating insights into the way they operate. Most observers take for granted that, as Grodzins suggests, the administrators are deeply woven into the fabric of programmatic politics.[35] That is, they find a constituency and mobilize its support both within the executive branch and on Capitol Hill. In vernacular terms it is often said, alliteratively, that aid administrators engage in the five Ps: programming, promoting, persisting, protecting, and producing. The administrator develops a *program* that is actively *promoted;* the administrator *persists* against all odds or obstacles by *protecting* the program so that it *produces* results.

Little is known about who the aid administrators are but somewhat more is known about their attitudes. In 1965 this group was circularized with a questionnaire from the Muskie Senate Subcommittee on Intergovernmental Relations.[36] All managers of the 109 aid programs responded. The program breakdowns by major departments were: Agriculture, 18; Commerce, 3; Defense, 4; HEW, 40; Interior, 17; Housing and Urban Development, 10; and Labor 4. The findings, interpretations, and recommendations from this survey make instructive reading despite its mid-1960s origin. Especially noteworthy is the chapter, "Bureaucracy and Federalism: Some Observations and Proposals,"[37] in which it is noted that

---

35. Grodzins, "The Federal System," p. 274.
36. *The Federal System As Seen By Federal Aid Officials: Results of a Questionnaire Dealing With Intergovernmental Relations,* a study prepared by the Subcommittee on Intergovernmental Relations, Senate Committee on Government Operations, 89th Congress, 1st Session, Committee Print, December 15, 1965.
37. Ibid., pp. 93–102.

Four behavioral themes recur throughout the questionnaire responses of nearly all of the 109 administrators . . . themes that both correspond to and expand on the . . . traits of middle management:

Functionalism, or the respondents' preoccupation with protecting and promoting the purposes of their individual programs; . . .

Professionalism, or the deep commitment to the merit system principle and to the technical and ethical standards of the specialized group to which they belong; . . .

Standpattism, or the rigid defense of traditional practices, procedures, and principles; . . .

Indifference, or the cavalier dismissal of serious (IGR) questions and topics as being irrelevant or unimportant.[38]

These sweeping conclusions may have reached beyond the supporting survey data, but they clearly show that administrator attitudes or perspectives must be reckoned with on IGR issues. Extended analysis of the 1965 data discloses that aid administrators' attitudes can be more precisely described, as summarized in the following ten points.

1. The Federal, State, and local governments are interrelated parts of a single governmental system; each level, however, must effectively discharge its mandated responsibilities if all of its rights as a member of this partnership are to be preserved.

2. Most domestic functions of government are shared, but the Federal Government, as the senior, most progressive, and most affluent member of this partnership, has been forced to assume a disproportionate share of this responsibility.

3. Policymaking in intergovernmental relations is a multilevel process, but obstruction—not collaboration—is as likely to be encountered from elected policymakers at the State and local levels.

4. The administration of joint action programs is a mutual—and, ideally, a professional—undertaking. Their authorizing legislation establishes them on a functional basis, and the vertical lines of communication and collaboration between and among the functional specialists in Washington and their counterparts in the field must be kept clear and unbroken if the bases of genuine cooperation are to be maintained.

5. The Federal grant and other aid devices are, and will continue to be, the most prominent and positive feature of contemporary federalism. They—not block grants, tax credits, or similar devices—provide the only time-tested techniques whereby the levels of government can collaborate effectively to fulfill common purposes and to meet certain national standards. . . .

6. Responsive and responsible State governments are vital for an ef-

---

38. Ibid., pp. 93–94.

fective federal system; yet most States do not possess these characteristics and are not likely to acquire them in the near future. . . .

7. General units of local government, when properly empowered and financially aided by the States, can act as effective partners in Federal-State-local and Federal-local joint action programs. Special-purpose districts and authorities grow out of particular local and areawide needs and of the States' failure to strengthen the fiscal base of general units of local government; as such, they serve a useful purpose in helping to implement certain Federal aid programs.

8. Rapid urbanization challenges traditional intergovernmental functional relationships; yet it is largely through strengthening these individual relationships, along with some increase in informal interagency contacts, that this challenge will be surmounted. Excessive preoccupation with regional or areawide principles and mechanisms can slow up the implementation of much-needed urban development and, in some cases, subject program administrators to additional political pressures.

9. Intergovernmental relations are primarily a vertical and diagonal system of financial, functional, and administrative arrangements; the primary purpose of each and all of these relationships is to meet the demands of the American people for better or new public services. Intergovernmental relations, then, function as the essential means to this great end, not as an end in themselves.

10. Successful intergovernmental relations are chiefly successful bureaucratic relations. Authorizing legislation, funds, and oversight come from legislative bodies. Policy directives, budgetary review and control, and administrative rules and regulations come from top management. And advice, assistance, and support, as well as complaints, criticism, and censure, come from officeholders at all levels, individual citizens, and interest groups. These basic forces of our pluralistic political system shape and sustain the broad, complex pattern of intergovernmental relations. The day-to-day conduct of these relations, however, falls to Federal middle management administrators, their field personnel, and their functional counterparts at the State and local levels.[39]

Have federal aid administrators' views changed since the mid-1960s? A survey of aid administrators conducted by the ACIR in 1975 provides selected bases for comparison but offers data on a wider range of IGR issues.[40] The ACIR began with a universe of 440 formula or project grant programs and received valid responses from administrators of 276 programs.

39. Ibid., pp. 97–99.
40. Advisory Commission on Intergovernmental Relations, *The Intergovernmental Grant System as Seen by Local, State and Federal Officials* (Washington, D.C.: Government Printing Office, March 1977), especially Chapter V, "Survey of Federal Administrators of Grant Programs," pp. 177–236.

The number of grant programs (and responses) from cabinet de-departments in 1975 is worth comparing with 1965. The 1975 figures (with 1965 figures in parentheses for comparison) are: Agriculture, 26 (18); Commerce, 18 (3); HEW, 112 (40); Housing and Urban De-velopment, 7 (10); Interior, 9 (17); Justice, 6 (0); Labor, 9 (4); Trans-portation, 12. In addition, the Environmental Protection Agency had 17. Both Commerce and HEW experienced rapid rises in the number of grant programs. HUD and Interior showed declines; the explanation for HUD is grant consolidation (the Community Development Act of 1974) and for Interior is, perhaps, mostly reorganization and program transfers, especially as illustrated by EPA's rise to prominence in the grant field. Other departments entering the federal aid field between 1965 and 1975 were Justice and Transportation.

Attitudes of 1965 and 1975 can be directly compared with re-spect to three specific areas: deficiencies in the personnel systems of state-local government; the significance of state-local personnel turn-over; and the channeling of grants to localities through state govern-ments. The sharp drop in perceived personnel-system deficiencies is indicated in the informal tabulations below.

	1965	1975
Low salaries	79%	25%
Inadequate training	69	16
Lack of a merit system	39	5

Far smaller proportions of aid administrators in 1975 than in 1965 perceived such deficiencies. Stated positively, state and local gov-ernments are perceived as making substantial improvements in their personnel systems. A similar finding was disclosed on personnel turn-over. Whereas in 1965 over 40 percent of the surveyed administrators reported a high turnover rate, in 1975 only 8 percent did so.

While aid administrators see state and local performance as im-proved, the mechanisms for dealing with recipients have changed drastically. For one, there has been the dramatic shift from formula grants to project grants—In 1965 project grants were less than half the total; in 1975 they were over 75 percent (208 of 276). At the same time, far fewer grant programs to localities are now channeled through the state—down from about 60 percent in 1965 to 36 percent in 1975. As a follow-up, administrators were queried in 1975 about how channeling affects participation. About 25 percent thought that channeling local government applications through the states either moderately or substantially reduced local participation.

The 1975 survey is rich with detail worthy of more attention and discussion if space permitted. A few summary observations must suffice. First, federal aid administrators are neither eager for nor optimistic about changes in IGR policies or management strategies. Second, aid administrators have not fully accepted the bargaining, nonhierarchical aspects of IGR that have been elaborated throughout this book. Third, some distinct attitude changes had come about between 1965 and 1975. These were summarized by Dr. David Walker, ACIR staff member and director of both the 1965 and 1975 surveys:

> Overall, then, the 1975 aid administrators addressed some of the behavioral norms of their predecessors. But, their lesser commitment to standpat positions, their greater flexibility in confronting broad managerial and interlocal issues, their much more moderate professional concerns regarding state and local counterpart personnel, their rejection of their predecessors' cavalier indifference toward certain basic intergovernmental management challenges, along with a certain skepticism regarding some efforts to reform grants management, clearly indicate changed attitudes. And, for the most part, these basic opinion shifts must be judged as for the better.[41]

SUMMARY

The president is frequently seen by local, state, and other national officials as *the* source of leadership on IGR matters. Anticipation of presidential leadership has regularly surpassed action, and IGR have seldom, if ever, commanded sufficient and sustained attention from any twentieth-century president. Among the many reasons for this general neglect of IGR are time limitations and the high priorities placed on other policy problems. Hence the tasks of trying to make the system work and to provide some semblance of order have fallen to other national actors, particularly agencies in the executive branch. The Office of Management and Budget (formerly Bureau of the Budget) is the unit that has given the longest-standing attention to IGR. Elsewhere in the executive office of the president other units assigned IGR

---

41. David Walker, "Federal Administrators and the Federal System: Current Attitudes and Perceptions," paper presented at the annual meeting of the American Political Science Association, Washington, D.C., September 1–4, 1977, p. 25.

duties have surfaced and then submerged—such as the Office of the Vice-President, White House staff, the Domestic Council.

The task forces, study groups, interagency committees, etc., created to deal with immediate and long-term IGR problems are nearly numberless and have had only short lifespans. One of the more recent and more thorough study groups addressing IGR issues was the Study Committee on Policy Management Assistance. Its report and extensive background papers highlight the difficulty of successfully merging political or policy leadership in IGR affairs with strategies of management to achieve the desired policy results.

Two commissions have, in recent years, been charged with major IGR duties, the Civil Service Commission (CSC) and the Advisory Commission on Intergovernmental Relations (ACIR). Assigned several IGR tasks under the Intergovernmental Personnel Act of 1970, the CSC offers grants-in-aid and technical assistance to state and local governments to improve training and personnel activities. Arranging and supporting mobility assignments between the federal and state-local governments is another CSC duty. Finally, the CSC is charged with enforcing the Hatch Act prohibition of political activities by state-local officials whose salaries are paid in part or whole by federal aid funds.

The ACIR is the only agency whose sole mission involves IGR. Created in 1959, the commission, as distinct from its staff, is a diversely representative body that includes legislative and executive officials from local, state, and national governments. The ACIR has established an admirable record in producing numerous thorough reports and thoughtful recommendations. Many of the latter have been adopted by the governmental units to which they were addressed. The ACIR is generally well-known and well-regarded. But its small size, its research emphasis, and its lack of political clout prevent it from producing wholesale or dramatic changes in IGR.

In the national government, the center of IGR "action" is lodged in the federal agencies, bureaus, or divisions that administer the myriad of categorical and block grant programs. These units are at the peak of the "picket" in the "picket fence" patterns of IGR. Little is known about the personal characteristics of those who administer these federal aid programs, but surveys in 1965 and 1975 provide data on their attitudes. The views held by federal aid administrators in 1965 were not hospitable toward the constructive resolution of IGR problems. Professionalism, functionalism, stand-pattism, and indifference were among the descriptives used for their attitudes.

A decade of change in IGR policies and problems has had an impact on federal aid administrators—or new and different administrators now hold somewhat different views. Professionalism remains a strong, even powerful strain among aid administrators. But views about the capabilities of state and local governments have taken a favorable turn, and the aid administrators are more attentive to IGR problems and noticeably readier to consider and accept IGR policy changes.

Orientations to IGR:
Looking Back and Looking Ahead

12

The central aim of this book has been to increase understanding of intergovernmental relations. Through two approaches to IGR, the conceptual-historical and descriptive-empirical, we have explored the nature and functioning of U.S. political and administrative systems. Those two approaches, however, have tended to subordinate several themes woven into the fabric of the essay. Actually, they are more than simply themes; rather, they are features or characteristics of governmental processes in the United States. Our approaches to IGR have exposed them, nine in all, and each shall now be briefly examined in turn.

RETROSPECTIVE FEATURES

Diversity/Complexity. The U.S. political system is composed of many and diverse jurisdictional entities. The system is made still more

314

diverse and complex by the immense number and variety of officials who are actual or potential participants in policy decisions, and by their differing and contrasting views.

Participants' Perspectives. Participants' perspectives play a prominent role in IGR. The study of political *behavior* has provided substantial advances in understanding how the American political system functions. In this book, by also emphasizing political, policy, and administrative *perceptions,* we have added another dimension to our understanding of the system. It is not enough to know, for example, that the Congress acted to include "priority categories" of expenditures in the 1972 General Revenue Sharing legislation. It is important, even critical, for observers and actors to know that these were generally perceived as cosmetic or "paper" categories of outlay—a facade that the acknowledged fungibility of funds confirmed to virtually all participants.

Citizens' Perspectives. In the few references in this book to citizens' views and their selective perceptions of IGR entities and officials, the citizenry has been treated as only a *partial* participant. Yet there is a body of data that would allow us to analyze citizens as *full* participants in IGR. (That we have not done so—that we have instead concentrated on public or official participants in IGR—might in fact open this book to charges of being "elitist.") We shall now examine citizens' perspectives in that light. Analysis reveals six dimensions to citizen perspectives on IGR, best identified by the following questions.

1. How much do citizens know about the governmental entities, and their officials, that are engaged in IGR? How attentive are citizens to events and trends in IGR?
2. How do citizens see government activities as affecting them— for good or for bad?
3. What problems and controversies do citizens see as appropriate to government intervention—and by which jurisdictions?
4. By what means, and how effectively, do citizens interact with government units or their officials?
5. How efficiently and effectively are government entities and officials perceived to satisfy the needs of the citizens (both individually and in the aggregate)?
6. How much trust and confidence do citizens place in govern-

ment units? That is, how secure is the formal, legal authority of these units in citizens' perceptions?

Pervasiveness of Financial Policies.   The public sector and the U.S. political system are powered by money, and fiscal imperatives are ever-present in most public policies. The fiscal flows and their effects documented in this essay are succinctly summarized by a close observer of the system.[1]

> The recent record reveals a greater "marbleizing" of the intergovernmental fiscal system than ever before. The budgets of all levels now involve a greater intergovernmental fiscal component. . . . Increasingly, each level will be more conscious of the fiscal actions of the other.

Interdependency.   Finances provide one way of measuring the increase of interdependency within the American political system. New York City's fiscal crisis, for example, threatened the solvency of New York State, adversely affected municipal credit generally, and even influenced the value of the U.S. dollar on international money markets.

In this book we have seen that interdependency is most visible at the state level. Their location "in the middle" subjects the states to powerful pulls and ties that restrict their autonomy, flexibility, and possible integrity. This "parceling out" of authority no doubt contributes to the image of states as having "indeterminate government"—and perhaps indeed they do.

The states' interdependent, nonautonomous role is not new. Nearly two decades ago a keen observer of the states noted:

> Very little remains of any exclusive concern by either national or state government in any governmental function.

> With a few exceptions, the present areal division of powers in this country is one in which certain decisions with regard to nearly all governmental functions are made at the state level and meshed with related decisions made at the central and local levels.

> The intermediate position of the states has led much of their decision-making power to be instrumental and facilitative and has been conducive to diffusion of political responsibility.[2]

1. David B. Walker, "How Fares Federalism in the Mid-Seventies," *The Annals,* 416 (November 1974): 25.
2. York Willbern, "The States as Components in an Areal Division of Powers," in Arthur Maass (ed.), *Area and Power: A Theory of Local Government* (Glencoe, Ill.: The Free Press, 1959), pp. 71, 72, 82.

State governments are merely special cases of a general pattern of interdependency that pervades government in the United States.

Bargaining-Exchange Relationships.   When Moon Landrieu, Mayor of New Orleans, upbraided Hale Boggs, a powerful congressional representative, there was clearly exposed for all to see (or infer) the absence of a clear, neat hierarchical relationship. In that incident, and in thousands of others, political (or administrative) officials meet more as equals than as unequals. In such situations interaction necessarily takes the form of bargaining, negotiation, and exchange. One of the clearest, most authoritative expressions of this pattern comes from a practitioner who for many years was in the vortex of IGR activities: Allen Pritchard, Jr., was Executive Vice-President of the National League of Cities when he asserted that the effective public administrator in IGR would be one

> . . . who comprehends that intergovernmental relations is not a seminar topic, an academic study, or a once-a-month dinner meeting. He will understand that intergovernmental relations are in fact intergovernmental "negotiations" in which the parties are negotiating in dead earnest for power, money, and problem-solving responsibility. He will be fully aware that in virtually every major public policy issue the elements of power, money, and responsibility are on the bargaining table.[3]

Competition/Cooperation.   The descriptive-empirical approach to IGR has focused attention on both the actions and attitudes of participants in the governing process. How can the *content* of the "working relations" between "human beings clothed with office" best be described? In the past these patterns ranged from highly competitive to highly cooperative. Grodzins' thesis of shared functions, when combined with Elazar's conclusions about IGR collaboration, built a strong case for the dominance of cooperative relationships. But recent research and events in the late 1960s and early 1970s suggested competition and cleavage rather than consensus. The analysis presented in this book points to two general conclusions.

First, cooperation and competition are not opposite ends of the same spectrum: Competition need not mean the absence of cooperation. For example, state water pollution officials may compete with each other for available funds but cooperate in challenging EPA pollution regulations and in pressing for larger federal appropriations. Similarly,

---

3. Allen E. Pritchard, Jr., Editorial, *Nation's Cities*, 10 (August 1972): 12.

the state officials may be cooperating with EPA on budget expansion while competing with EPA over legal jurisdicational responsibilities.

The second conclusion is that the absence of superior-subordinate relationships among participants eliminates the need to ask which tendency—cooperation or competition—is more prominent. More constructive results may be achieved if we instead assume that both cooperation and competition are present in IGR. Thus, national officials may compete with state officials to either assist or to control the policy choices of local officials. From local officials' viewpoints, the assistance or cooperation furnished by national officials may be only slightly more adequate than that provided by state officials. The most significant datum may be, however, that one-third of the local officials may report that "neither" national or state officials were cooperative in helping solve urban difficulties.

Centrality of Management/Administration. The growth of large bureaucratic organizations within major governmental units has elevated managerial and administrative skills to first-rank importance in IGR and in the overall functioning of public programs and policies—as we saw in discussing local and state IGR coordinators, state administrators, and the organization of the federal executive branch to deal with IGR.

There is little question that current politics and long-term political trends influence the shape and direction of IGR. Johnson's Creative Federalism and Nixon's New Federalism are recent illustrations of the point. But the lack of sparkling achievements under either of these "federalisms" shows that political slogans and presidential pronouncements do not produce effective policies or programs.

The acknowledged absence of an "organizational philosophy" within the Johnson administration was a candid admission of administrative and managerial blind spots. By way of contrast, the Nixon administration took pride in an aura of managerial efficiency. Some effects of emphasizing administration during the Nixon presidency (involvement in detailed operations as illustrated in Appendix L) were mentioned briefly in the prior chapter and are discussed in depth elsewhere.[4] The Nixon years, much like the Johnson years, were long on image and sometimes bold with ideas but were short on solid, sustained accomplishments in IGR.

---

4. See Richard P. Nathan, *The Plot That Failed: Nixon and the Administrative Presidency* (New York: John Wiley, 1975).

The moral is that effective programs or policies require both political will and administrative skill. The many participants and varying perspectives, the high interdependency, the bargaining patterns, and the simultaneous cooperation and competition make the effective conduct of IGR dependent on the successful management of complexity.

Public Sector Politics. As government has grown and its bureaucracies proliferated, more than managerial and administrative considerations have advanced to the forefront of public affairs: Public interest groups have introduced a new dynamic into the political system. Governors, mayors, county executives, city managers, and state-local legislators may or may not be cohesive in their positions on IGR issues. When these groups are in agreement, as on General Revenue Sharing, they are a political force to be reckoned with. But even when not together their separate points of view cannot be ignored or overridden by national officials without some cost, however slight.

The public interest groups have established themselves as an institution in Washington, D.C., where they have achieved access to many if not all decision makers, have contributed valuable ideas and information, and have had a decided impact—though not one as broad or profound as they would like. On the Potomac wheel of political fortune their number has come up occasionally (for example, in GRS, block grants, A-95, and ACIR representation). These are modest but nonetheless significant victories. These achievements have not revamped the total configuration of political influence on Capitol Hill or in the executive branch. But they have brought about some internal power shifts; for example, GRS legislation has been taken away from Ways and Means, and there is advance consultation on administrative regulations.

Although the public interest groups' common front is frequently fragile and occasionally one or more of the individual groups experiences internal disarray, their political leverage or clout will affect the future directions of IGR.

ALTERNATIVE IGR FUTURES

This book in general and the preceding section of this chapter dealt with the past—and of course have tried to come as close as possible to the present. It is logical to ask what is the probable configuration of IGR in the long-term future, say in the next fifty years. Although there is no crystal ball available, we can construct contrasting models of what IGR might be like at the end of the first quarter of the twenty-first century. The three alternative models of authority relations that were presented in chapter 2 can serve as precedents for speculating about three possible IGR futures. The three futures will be sketched briefly, after which we try to identify the major variables likely to produce one or another of them.

Implosion Model

In the implosion model there will have been massive consolidation and centralization in IGR. The consolidations may occur chiefly through formal structural change, but it is also possible that hundreds or thousands of governmental units—counties, townships, cities, school and special districts—may simply atrophy.

In conventional terms this model resembles what is called a *unitary* system; any surviving local boundaries would only demarcate administrative districts of a higher governing entity. State governments would, for example, be "hollow shells": Governors and legislators would still be elected but would only observe and criticize decisions of the national government. If any "state" administrative agencies exist, their members will be appointed and removed by national officials, probably under controls resembling those of today's civil service.

The formal governmental structure under the implosion model would be shaped as follows:

	Number of Units
Central (national) government	1
Regional governments	10
Metropolitan districts	400
Urban districts	2000
Rural districts	1000

Clearly, the governmental landscape would be drastically different from the one we have described in this book, and would look, to a contemporary IGR analyst, like the surface of another planet.

Explosion Model

Opposite to the implosion model is one that projects greater fragmentation or "explosion" of political power than exists today. Such decentralization might take various structural forms but at a minimum there would be a noteworthy increase in the number of politically significant local government units. Such an increase might occur from three prime sources: First, the currently emergent Councils of Government might accrue powers to tax, spend, and borrow, with important service responsibilities and selective controls over smaller units within their boundaries. Second, additional special districts would be created to meet particular service or regulatory needs in urban and rural areas, for example, for water supply, health and hospital services, air pollution control, energy consumption. Third, existing governments might become further localized or might even disintegrate. The "new era of localism" that swept across the United States in the late 1960s would pale beside such fragmentation. New York City, for example, might be subdivided into 90–100 political entities with significant self-governing powers.

The explosion model projects a growth in the number of governing powers and entities on two planes in relation to existing local governments: one at a level between state government and present local governments (counties, cities, etc.); the second "below" or within existing local units. Contemporary IGR arrangements in the United States are sometimes referred to as a four-tier pattern:

1. national
2. state
3. county
4. city, school/special district

In the explosion model six tiers are contemplated (the hypothetical numbers of units at each level are in parentheses):

1. national (1)
2. state (50)
3. substate regional (1000)
4. county (3000)
5. city, school, special (70,000)
6. subcity (40,000)

The numbers of units may not convey how dramatically different this IGR alternative is from what we know today. Two ways of emphasizing the difference can be used: First, conceptually, the explosion model projects a drastic dispersion of power to the periphery. (Recent political slogans such as "power to the people" and "neighborhood government" would become operational political premises); second, examples might be neighborhood (subcity) governments that control and administer health, welfare, education, and public safety services to, say, the Roxbury section of Boston, Cleveland Park in Washington, D.C., Back-of-the-Yards in Chicago, and Westwood in Los Angeles.

Incremental Adjustment Model

The incremental adjustment model projects only slight or modest alterations in the structure and functioning of IGR over the next half-century. Changes are expected to be marginal and piecemeal. Furthermore, they are apt to offset or counteract one another rather than be cumulative in a single power-centered direction: No uniform power shifts are anticipated.

Although this model allows for change, shifts will be more like swings in a pendulum through a relatively small arc. In other words, governing powers in the United States will remain relatively dispersed, but the national government will remain strong and active, there will be fifty variously effective and assertive middlemen, and tens of thousands of local jurisdictions.

A Rip Van Winkle among IGR scholars could nap for fifty years and wake up on familiar governmental grounds: Mayors and governors would be pressing for the continuation and expansion of General Revenue Sharing; the ACIR would be emphasizing the need for the national government to better manage its IGR affairs; and presidential candidates would still be bound by the time-honored practice of pledging to maintain and strengthen the *federal* system.

In short, the incremental adjustment model posits a continuation of "muddling through" practices and policies. There are no clear, long-term goals and no strategic design for proximate goals. The pragmatic adaptiveness of such IGR policies are justified in part by the following observations: "It is a little unfair to ask our governmental institutions to work at full efficiency in helping to produce the good life when we change its content so rapidly. . . . Our structures may be somewhat confused, but our value systems are themselves none too orderly."[5]

CRITICAL VARIABLES

The shape of IGR fifty years hence will be influenced by a wide array of economic, social, and political factors. Those political variables we will now identify and will speculate on how they will affect IGR.

No doubt international problems, economic affairs, and social forces will not remain constant for the next half-century; there will undoubtedly be shifts in social values, economic highs and lows, foreign tensions, and perhaps minor hostilities. Nevertheless, those changes, of assumed modest magnitude, will affect IGR in only minor or marginal ways.

This last assertion may seem untenable as such domestic concerns as energy become increasingly linked to international developments. But even if the past is only a partially accurate guide for the future, the claim may not be as outlandish as it seems. Consider fifty years ago: the late 1920s. Since that time there has been a worldwide depression, a world war, constant international tensions and lesser wars, revolutionary scientific developments, radical technological changes in transportation and communication, and significant value shifts in the East, the West, and third-world nations. Despite these events, the character of federal-state-local relations in the United States has not been revolutionized. Instead, IGR have evolved through five phases, and the competitive patterns prominent today are not radically different from the conflict phase of the 1920s. In short, IGR in the United States have been remarkably resilient and resistant to earth-shaking foreign and nonpolitical domestic forces.

In the remainder of this analysis it will be assumed that in the next five decades only *domestic political* variables will shape IGR. Six broad political variables are singled out for discussion: (1) preferences, (2) perceptions, (3) policy issues, (4) finances, (5) organization and management, and (6) institutions.

---

5. Willbern, "The States as Components," pp. 86–87.

Preferences

Future IGR will be largely shaped by the preferences of two broad groups of participants: the citizenry, and key political officials —political leadership. Citizens, or the public, seldom or never can be placed uniformly and consistently along the six dimensions for measuring public attitudes relevant to IGR (see pp. 315-316). The recent period of public distemper, of citizen disenchantment with and disgust for government and officials does not alter or contradict long-standing public attitudes. The American public has held a set of surprisingly long-term preferences that have favored neither the centralized concentration of power nor the radical localization of power into small fragments. There appear to be a few reasons, then, to expect dramatic or polarizing changes in public preferences on the distribution and organization of power.

Similarly, political elites, as in the past, may continue to hold varied and conflicting preferences as to the arrangements and dispersal of political power. Local, state, and regional interests are likely to remain diversified. Elected officials responding to those diversities— and rewarded for doing so—are likely to resist centralization. National domestic legislation may continue to be, in effect, treaties among diverse local, state, or sectional interests. In short, the preferences of both citizen and officials are expected to favor and sustain the incremental adjustment (muddling through) model.

Perceptions

This book has emphasized not only the actions of officials but their *perceptions* as well—how, for example, key groups of officials saw their roles, functions, and, most importantly, their relationships with other officials. How programs, policies, and other participants are *perceived* will significantly influence alternative IGR futures. One need only recall the example of advocates of the U.S. Constitution in 1787-1788 to appreciate the importance of how an issue is perceived. By calling themselves "Federalists" they created a perception of their position that was strategically significant.

This strategy of generating favorable (or unfavorable) perceptions persists to the present day in IGR. It underlies the image-creating, support-building aims of IGR such policies as Creative Federalism and

the New Federalism. Another illustration is a specific legislative enactment, the Demonstration Cities and Metropolitan Development Act
(P.L. 89–754, 1966). Although legally titled "demonstration cities,"
this legislation became, through informal but uniform administrative
means, the *model* cities program. The reason was simple: In the late
1960s the word "demonstration" was ill-favored, there being protest
demonstrations around college campuses, courthouses, and city halls.
Political support for this program, while never strong, could be nur-
tured and sustained under the term "model" cities; it would have suffered a quicker, harsher fate as "demonstration" cities.

The preceding illustrations document the general proposition:
"What it is is what you call it." Garrett Hardin, the scientist-ecologist,
calls it "Word Magic":[6] the designation attached to an event or to
someone's action or view determines how it will be perceived. Thus,
terminology fixes participants' perceptions of IGR and will undoubtedly
influence their future shape—*how* cannot be predicted since we cannot
predict who will employ "word magic" to achieve what results. (It is
not difficult to imagine a political slogan such as "Old Federalism"
being employed to foster a shift in power from the states to the national government.)

Policy Issues

The long-term pattern of IGR will be heavily influenced by the
number and types of policy issues that are pressed into the public agenda
for decision. From the 1930s to the 1970s health, welfare, and income
and economic security have been persistent issues on which the national government has exercised powers to centralize and make more
uniform numerous policies in these fields. In the past two decades
focal issues of civil rights, education, and economic opportunity have
jarred IGR. Their shock effects have produced dislocations but have
not fractured the system. There are differences of opinion on whether
IGR have been altered irrevocably toward a more centralized system.

Currently the policy issues commanding prime attention that have
major IGR implications are energy, environment, and economic stability (including inflation). Until the Supreme Court decision in *National League of Cities* v. *Usery* the issue of public employee unionism

---

6. Garrett Hardin, *Exploring New Ethics for Survival: The Voyage of the Spaceship
Beagle* (Baltimore, Md.: Penguin Books, 1972), p. 66.

might have been added to this list. For the near future that court decision appears to have shifted the major IGR implications of this issue to the domain of state-local relations.

It is difficult to predict policy issues in the decades ahead. The application of existing technology in the commercial communications field may generate major issues involving commercial codes, the right to privacy, etc. Such questions as abortion, women's rights, and family relationships may generate demands for uniform national legislation and policies.

On both historical and logical grounds the impact of policy issues on IGR seems predictable. Functional, programmatic, and policy questions have exerted nationalizing and centralizing pressures in the past. We would expect them to shift the character of IGR toward the implosion model in the future.

Finances

The preservation and extension of autonomous sources of revenue have been important means of sustaining balanced, bargained IGR patterns in the past. Increased reliance on the federal fisc has given national officials *relatively* more power and influence in IGR. Policy changes toward block grants and revenue sharing are noteworthy but rather modest adjustments to accommodate local diversity and discretion. The maintenance of own-source revenues by state-local governments is possibly *the* pivot around which the future of IGR will revolve. Those sources are apt to be jealously guarded and perhaps extended in the future, thereby encouraging the continuation of contemporary incremental IGR patterns.

But revenues are only one side of the ledger. Expenditures to meet public needs and demands are the other side. What programs, services, activities, and policies will various jurisdictions be called upon to provide? Will local and state governments still be expected to furnish a major portion of domestic public services? To answer these questions we would have to predict general demands for public goods and how citizens and officials prefer that they be provided. The demand for public goods will probably continue to increase, and preferences as to who provides public services are little likely to change. We might expect, then, that IGR fiscal transfers will become more numerous and more varied.

Organization and Management

Landing a man on the moon was a major success story. But behind it was another, *organizational* success story. The space program was organized and managed in novel, innovative ways. The traditional hierarchical patterns of bureaucracy were altered to more effectively and rapidly achieve both short-run and long-run objectives.

Similarly, how effectively organizational and managerial skills are mobilized will have a bearing on future IGR patterns. For example, if many states were to develop a policy management system that clarified, specified, and ranked their respective program priorities, these jurisdictions would have fairly potent power bases from which to bargain with federal agencies. Regardless of the priorities they establish or of how well or poorly they conform to those of available federal grant funds, the process of setting state priorities would strengthen the states' individual positions in dealing with federal officials. The state officials would know where they stand.

Knowing one's policy stance suggests two supplemental rules for playing IGR "games": To win an IGR game you must first, know you are in one, and, second, know your own position. Intelligent anticipatory and innovative organization and management skills can enhance the ability of one or all participants involved in IGR efforts.

The national government has enjoyed greater organizational and managerial skills than the other jurisdictions. More than two decades ago L. D. White observed that "the states, with some notable exceptions, do not command the administrative talent that is available to the general government."[7] There is evidence that the discrepancy between national and state administrators' education and experience has narrowed significantly. The IPA mobility program (described in chapter 11) has also allowed local and state governments to use federal administrators' skills and experience.

There is a side benefit to the IPA mobility program. Those temporarily transferred to positions in other units gain a better understanding of the perceptions of others involved in IGR processes. They also are required to think through their own perceptions and policy stances. Increased awareness of other participants' perceptions is important in shaping future IGR patterns. The officials most skillful in developing

7. Leonard D. White, *The States and the Nation* (Baton Rouge: Louisiana State University Press, 1953), p. 60.

those capacities are likely to hold the advantage in affecting IGR decisions—an advantage that seems likely to remain with national officials. Organizational and managerial variables will therefore tend to encourage an imploded model.

Institutions

By institutional variables we refer to five entities involved in national decision-making processes—the president, Congress, political parties, interest groups, and the federal bureaucracy. The first and last of these institutions have tended to be the sources of centripetal tendencies. From 1932 to the present only two presidents, Eisenhower and Nixon, have been cautious or unfavorable toward national actions. The functional orientation of federal agencies, or bureaucracies, creates centripetal forces that favor standardization and screen out or subordinate IGR considerations. A mid-level federal program manager volunteered a classic and concise expression of this orientation: "These people hung up on intergovernmental matters bother me; they want me to develop a policy on it but I've got a program to administer!"

The Congress and the political parties have usually been acknowledged as chief institutional protectors of the interests of localities and the states. But their inclinations and effects with respect to IGR have seldom been this simple or uniform.

The Congress is not only two houses but many centers of power, most of which are oriented toward functional or programmatic aims. Congressional influence on future alternative IGR will fluctuate between maintaining the incremental model and fostering the implosion model.

Grodzins's point that "The parties provide the pivot on which the entire governmental system swings"[8] seems either overdrawn or no longer applicable. The decline of party voting, in the Congress and among the voters, leads to the conclusion that parties, and the party system, will continue to exert extremely limited influence on the future shape of IGR. Major party realignment, however, could significantly alter this projection.

Like Congress, interest groups will probably have mixed influences on future IGR. As trade, professional, and other associations increas-

8. Morton Grodzins, "The Federal System," *Goals for Americans* (Englewood Cliffs, N.J.: Prentice-Hall, Spectrum, 1960). p. 272.

ingly concentrate in Washington, D.C., centripetal nationalizing tendencies toward the implosion model are encouraged. Of 15,000 such associations over 25 percent had their headquarters in Washington, D.C., in 1976 (up from 19 percent in 1971).[9] Of course, some associations locate there to protect against national legislation and activities that they prefer remained with state or local governments.

The public interest groups—the PIGs or Big Seven—are among the more recently visible of these associations. But as noted in the references to public-sector politics (in chapter 6 and this chapter) their alliance is fragile. Their ability to counteract powerful program or functional interests is also limited. We might use the successes and failures of the PIGs during the years ahead as an important trace variable to indicate the tipping or "tilt" tendencies in IGR. The PIGs' fortunes may tell us much about the preservation of balance within the IGR system, and about the system's rate of movement between the poles of the implosion and explosion models.

CONCLUDING COMMENT

IGR in the United States is like a huge, complex building that is under continuous construction and reconstruction. The edifice has no single deliberate overall design or consistent architectural motif. There is nonstop remodeling and renovation, plus minor and major interior repairs; there is even selective razing and often whole new floors and wings are added. But the old foundations of the original structure remain intact. They have been strengthened as well as extended with reasonable ease to support the many more occupants and the many new, varied uses to which the building has been put. Barring catastrophes or calamities, it appears that the structure will survive and remain useful in the foreseeable future.

---

9. *Wall Street Journal,* December 17, 1976.

A Guide to Commonly Used Terms, Abbreviations and Acronyms in IGR
Appendix A

Terms	Description
ACIR	Advisory Commission on Intergovernmental Relations. A permanent commission established by Congress (PL 380) in 1959 "to give continuing attention to intergovernmental problems." ACIR's mandate includes bringing together participants from Federal, State and local governments to consider common problems, to provide a forum for addressing issues related to the administration of Federal Assistance Programs, to provide technical assistance of proposed legislation and its overall effect on the Federal system, to encourage study of emerging problems that may require intergovernmental cooperation, and to develop appropriate recommendations pursuant to its statutory responsibilities.

Terms	Description (continued)
ANNUAL ARRANGEMENTS	A tool to facilitate coordination among grant programs and to increase a city's capacity to set priorities. Involves negotiations between HUD field offices and cities aimed at packaging categorical programs into community development activities. (See also HUD, Planned Variations).
ARC	Appalachian Regional Commission. Grants of the ARC, a Federal-State Compact, are directed to multi-county areas and to help Economic development. The eligible units of government are the Appalachian States and through them, multi-county organizations (local development districts) certified by the States. Funding for FY 1974 was $3.45 million.
BLOCK GRANT	A consolidation of functional programs into one grant in which grantees are eligible through formula or through very broad application process. (See CETA).
CAPACITY BUILDING	A term used to refer to any system, effort, or process —including a Federal grant or contract—which includes among its major objectives strengthening the capability of elected chief executive officers, chief administrative offices, department and agency heads, and program managers in general purpose government to plan, implement, manage or evaluate policies, strategies or programs designed to impact on social conditions in the community.
	For the purposes of this report, capacity building is used as a generic term to refer to programs, projects, services or activities designed to strengthen the capabilities of general purpose governments—national, State, regional, or local—to perform the functions associated with policy management (PM), resource management (RM), or program/operations management (OM). (See also Elected Official, Policy Management; Resource Management; Program Management; Technical Assistance; Federal Assistance Programs).
CATEGORICAL GRANTS	A grant-in-aid offering funding for limited use directed for a specific objective, usually requiring the recipient to match a fraction of the grant. (Also a conditional grant).

Terms	Description (continued)
CERC	Chief Executive Review and Comment. A process which allows local elected officials to review and comment on local grant applications. A city strategy statement of community development goals, objectives, problems and solutions is formulated by a committee made up of the major HUD grant recipients involved. After negotiation between the local chief executives and the HUD area office director, a memorandum of understanding is drafted. This process enables city executives to improve their coordination of HUD-funded programs and to increase their abilities to get local priorities as well as to receive reasonable assurance the funds will be provided during the year. Over 200 cities have participated in this program since it was initiated in December of 1970.
CETA	The Comprehensive Employment and Training Act of 1973. Establishes a broad-based block grant program of manpower and manpower-related activities including recruiting, training, and other manpower services. Chief executives or "prime sponsor" designees must appoint and staff a planning council with advisory and evaluative responsibilities which is responsible for developing a comprehensive manpower plan.
COG's	Council of Governments, COG's represent multi-jurisdictional cooperative arrangements to permit a comprehensive approach to planning, development, transportation, environment and similar problems that affect the region as a whole. They are comprised of designated policymaking representatives from each participating government within the region. COG's are substate regional planning agencies established by States and are responsible for areawide review of projects applying for Federal funds (A-95 Project Notification and Review) and for development of regional plans and other areawide special purpose arrangements.
COMPREHENSIVE PLANNING ASSISTANCE (701)	A categorical grant program based on Section 701 of the Housing Act of 1965. Grants are given to support a broad range of planning and management activities by HUD, including comprehensive planning, development and improvement of management capacity for plan implementation and development. All recipients must produce a plan with both a housing and land use element.

Terms	Description (continued)
CRP	Community Renewal Program. HUD's Community Renewal Program was among the earliest to provide comprehensive planning assistance to local governments.
CSG	The Council of State Governments is a joint agency of all State governments—created, supported, and directed by them. Its purpose is to strengthen all branches of State government and preserve the State governmental role in the American Federal system through catalyzing the expression of States' view on major issues; conducting research on State programs and problems; assisting in Federal-State liaison and State-regional-local cooperation; and offering training, reference and consultation services to State agencies, officials and legislators; and serving as a broad instrument for bringing together all elements of State government.
ELECTED OFFICIAL	A term used in this report to refer to elected and/or appointed officials who typically and on a continuing basis exercise policymaking and/or strategic (or policy) management functions. Accordingly, the term "elected officials" includes chief executive officers (CEO) or Chief Administrative Officers (CAO)— e.g., city managers, appointed officials whose principal tasks are to assist the CEO or CAO in the policymaking process; and legislators—including councilmen and commissioners of general purpose governments.
ELIGIBILITY	Refers to legislative and administrative criteria for determining which units of government (or other potential beneficiaries—e.g., Indian Tribes, non-profits, universities, individuals, etc.) are entitled to be recipients of Federal Assistance Programs. Federal entitlement procedures distinguish applicant beneficiaries from recipient beneficiaries, for they are sometimes different. (See also Federal Assistance Programs; Categorical Grants; Revenue Sharing; Block Grants).
EDA	Economic Development Administration, Department of Commerce. An FY 1974 obligation of $7,700,000 was used in the development of multi-county district (and redevelopment areas) planning capabilities with an emphasis on the creation of jobs for the unemployed and underemployed (Federal Catalog Code 11.302).

Terms	Description (continued)
ERDI (RDI)	The Experimental R&D Incentives Program (more commonly referred to as RDI) of the National Science Foundation was established in 1972 to provide evidence from real time field experiments concerning the likely effects of various incentives that the Federal government could invoke to increase the application and use of science and technology by the non-Federal public and private sectors. More specifically, the thrust of the program has been to identify and test incentives that would promote the increased utilization of new technology by the public and private sectors and which, in the long run, would stimulate greater non-Federal investment in R&D.
FEDERAL ASSISTANCE PROGRAMS	A term used to refer to the variety of Federal programs available to State and local governments including counties, cities, metropolitan, and regional governments; schools, colleges, and universities; health institutions; non-profits and for profit organizations; and to individuals and families. Current Federal Assistance Programs are listed in the annual *Catalog of Federal Domestic Assistance*. The 1974 *Catalogue*, for example, provides a comprehensive listing and description of 975 programs administered by 52 different Federal departments, agencies, commissions, and councils. Federal assistance programs provide assistance through grant or contractual arrangements and include technical assistance programs or programs providing assistance in the form of loans.
FAR	The Federal Assistance Review Program was launched in 1969 for a three year period by OMB and nine cooperating agencies. FAR was directed by the Secretary of HEW and included 14 major departments and agencies. Its work is guided by the Federal Assistance Review Steering Group, chaired by OMB. Its objectives included: (1) the development of standard boundaries for Federal administrative regions; (2) the development of the ten Federal Regional Councils; (3) decentralization—which included program and administrative delegations to Federal regional (and lower level) field officials to assure decisionmaking closer to point of delivery of services; (4) greater reliance on State and local government in the detailed administration of Federal programs; (5) a reduction

Terms	Description (continued)
	in grant application processing time and red tape cutting, by program; (6) increased consistency in Federal procedures for planing, accounting, auditing, statistical data, land appraisal practices, engineering data, and other practices that impact on the management environment of State and local governments; (7) a simplification of the procedures for joint funding and grant consolidation; and (8) the implementation of the Intergovernmental Cooperation Act.
FORMULA GRANT	Grant allocations based on specified formulas incorporated in the outlying statutes. (See Grant-in-Aid).
FRC	The Federal Regional Councils. FRC's were established under E. O. 11647 in February 1972. They are comprised of the chief regional offices of DOL, HEW, HUD, DOT, OEO, EPA, LEAA, USDA, and DOI, serving the ten standard Federal regions. Their primary charge is clearer working relations between Federal Grant-making agencies and State and local governments and to improve coordination in the categorical grant-in-aid system.
GAO	The General Accounting Office. GAO is an arm of Congress whose charge includes an evaluation function vis-a-vis Federal policies and programs. GAO efforts have included some attention to the intergovernmental relations process.
GENERAL REVENUE SHARING	A program which authorizes expenditures to be allocated as determined by recipient governments in the following priority areas: public safety; environmental protection; public transportation; health; recreation; libraries; social services for the poor and aged; financial administration.
GRANT-IN-AID	Federal transfers of payments to states or Federal or state transfers to local governments for specified purposes usually subject to a measure of supervision and review by the granting government or agency in accordance with prescribed standards and requirements.
GRANTS-IN-KIND	Donations of Federal surplus property or commodities to State and local governments.
HUD	The Department of Housing and Urban Development. HUD efforts, measured by dollars invested, constitute

Terms	Description (continued)
	major elements of current Federal capacity building programs. In addition, HUD "701" (the Comprehensive Planning Assistance Program) is one of the few existing sources of Federal support to State and local governments for developing Policy Management Capacity. (See also Policy Management).
HUD "701"	Refers to Section 701 of the Housing Act of 1954 (and subsequent amendments) which provides for grants to strengthen the "planning and decisionmaking capabilities of the chief executives of State, area-wide, and local agencies to promote more effective use of the Nation's physical, economic, and human resources." (See Comprehensive Planning Assistance).
ICA	The Intergovernmental Cooperation Act (1968). In part, this Act (1) provided for supplying grant information to governors and legislatures regarding Federal grant program activities within their states and (2) modified the "single state agency" requirement in many Federal grant statutes. (See single state agency).
ICMA	The International City Management Association. The ICMA is the professional society for the appointed chief executive officers in cities, counties, towns, councils of governments, and other local general purpose governments. Its primary objectives include strengthening the quality of urban government through professional management, and developing and disseminating new concepts and approaches to management through training programs, information services, and publications. (See Public Interest Groups).
IGA	Integrated Grants Administration. A process of consolidating individual grant applications and administrative procedures into a single application and process. There are presently 34 FRC administered pilot projects which allow applicants of multiple related grants to submit a single application with a single set of financial control, recordkeeping and auditing requirements. (See FAR).
IPG	Intermodal Planning Groups. Intermodal Planning Groups are bodies composed of DOT field-planning personnel and representatives of other Federal mission agencies charged with promoting integrated

Terms	Description (continued)
	planning, policy, and program development for highways, urban mass transit, airways, railways, etc., at the State, regional, and local level. Unified Work Programs are documents required by the DOT of its planning grant recipients, which integrate the urban, airways, and highway planning processes into a coordinated total transportation planning effort.
IPA	The Intergovernmental Personnel Act (See also Capacity Building; Mobility Programs) is administered by the Bureau of Intergovernmental Personnel Programs of the U.S. Civil Service Commission. IPA grants are for a broad range of personnel administration improvement activities including management capacity development, technical assistance, and training. One half of each State's allocation must be spent on local government needs. Twenty percent of the total allocation is discretionary and 80% is based on a population/public employee formula. Intergovernmental mobility assignments are also authorized under the IPA.
ISRU	The Intergovernmental Science Programs were initiated by the National Science Foundation in 1968 to assist State and local governments upgrading their capabilities to apply research and technology in solving their social, economic, and environmental problems. In 1972, the Office was given additional responsibilities for managing the utilization program for the NSF Program of Research Applied to National Needs (RANN). Over 100 grants have been made to State and local governments, legislatures, regional organizations, universities, private non-profit research organizations, national associations, and others, to support policy studies, demonstration projects, and technology transfer activities.
JOINT FUNDING	The Joint Funding Simplification Act of 1974 (PL 93-510) was signed into law on December 5, 1974. The purpose of this Act is to enable States, local governments and other public or private organizations and agencies to use Federal assistance more effectively by drawing upon resources from more than one Federal Agency, program or appropriation. The Act encourages Federal-State arrangements to combine State and Federal resources in support of projects of common interest.

Terms	Description (continued)
MISSION AGENCY	Any Federal Department or agency whose legislation gives it responsibility for promotion of some cause or operation of some system as its primary reason for existence (mission) and which is appropriated funds for the conduct of this mission.
MOBILITY PROGRAM	A type of executive development activity in which an employee of one governmental unit is temporarily assigned to another governmental unit, either within or outside his own agency, to develop management skills, and a perception of problems facing the other unit. The technique is also used, albeit rarely, to develop liaison between various governmental entities. It also is used to provide technical assistance and training on a short-term basis. The Program is authorized under Title IV of the Intergovernmental Personnel Act of 1970.
MODEL CITIES	Shorthand for the Demonstration Cities and Metropolitan Development Act (1966). The "Model Cities Act" provided the basis for (1) integrating the planning function with general policymaking for disadvantaged neighborhoods in those cities which were funded, and (2) for the recognition of metropolitan area-wide planning agencies. The Model Cities Program had a major impact on increasing local government's capacity to engage in more comprehensive planning activity. (See also Planned Variations; CERC).
NACO	National Association of Counties. NACO's membership includes 21,000 elected or appointed county governing officials and other management and policy officials. The association provides a research and reference service for county officials. Committees include roads and highways, natural resources, county planning, education, etc. (See Public Interest Groups).
NASPAA	National Association of Schools of Public Affairs and Administration. NASPAA, an affiliate of the American Society for Public Administration, is a national professional education association representing over 150 university programs, with a stated objective of advancing education and training in public affairs and public administration. It serves as a national center for information on programs and developments in this field, and represents the concerns and interests

Terms	Description (continued)
	of member institutions in the formulation and support of national policies for education in public affairs and public administration.
NCSL	National Conference of State Legislatures. In January, 1975, the NCSL formally came into existence, replacing three previously-existing organizations (National Legislative Conference, National Conference of State Legislative Leaders, National Society of State Legislators). The NCSL is the only nationwide organization representing all State legislators (7,600) and their staffs—approximately 10,000, and seeks to advance the effectiveness, independence and integrity of the State legislature as an equal coordinate branch of government. It also fosters interstate cooperation, and represents States and their legislatures with Congress and Federal agencies.
NGC	National Governors' Conference. Founded in 1958, the National Governors' Conference (NGC) is a membership organization that includes Governors of the States territories, and Puerto Rico. The NGC seeks to improve State government, addresses problems requiring interstate cooperation and endeavors to facilitate intergovernmental relations at the Federal/State and State/local levels.
NLC	National League of Cities. The NLC is a federation of 50 State leagues of municipalities as well as individual cities with population over 30,000, State capitals, and the ten largest cities in each State. The NLC seeks to develop and effect a National Municipal Policy, a statement of major municipal goals in the United States, in order to help cities solve critical problems they share in common. The NLC represents municipalities with Congress and Federal agencies, and maintains information and consultation services. (See Public Interest Groups).
NTDS	National Training and Development Service. NTDS is a non-profit organization that fosters new personnel training development techniques for public service employees at every level of government, and seeks to enhance the training capacity within governmental agencies. Its governing board is comprised of representatives from six major public interest groups.
OMB	The Office of Management and Budget in the Execu-

Terms	Description (continued)
	tive Office of the President. A number of efforts to rationalize, streamline, or otherwise improve the process of intergovernmental relations have OMB-administrative directives as their source—e.g., A-95. (See also Executive Order).
PLANNED VARIATIONS	Refers to an experimental effort within the context of the Model Cities Program to extend the program planning effort beyond the (disadvantaged) neighborhoods originally targeted by the Model Cities Program to the entire city and to provide chief executives with review and comment authority over all Federal programs in order to increase local policy management capacity. (See also CERC; Model Cities; HUD).
POLICY MANAGEMENT (PM)	A term used to refer to the capacity of elected officials to perform on an integrated, cross-cutting basis the needs assessment, goal setting, and evaluation functions of management; to mobilize and allocate resources; and to initiate and guide the planning, development, and implementation of policies, strategies, and programs that are related to sustaining or improving the physical, socio-economic, or political conditions that have a bearing on the quality of life in a community.

Thus, Policy Management is a process that involves the *strategic* functions of *guidance* and *leadership* from a jurisdictional or territorial perspective and the exercise of strategic management functions, including the capacity to relate these functions to other participants or entities whose policies or activities affect the performance of these functions. Accordingly, Policy Management capacity includes as well the ability to build or strengthen governmental institutions and area or "place" oriented structures that address and respond to community policy and program development issues and the ability to improve governmental systems—including intergovernmental processes for integrated needs assessment, goal-setting, management, and evaluation. (See also Program Management; Resource Management; Capacity Building; Elected Official; Policy Management Assistance). |
| POLICY MANAGEMENT ASSISTANCE (PMA) | Policy Management Assistance is a term used to refer to any system, effort, or process—including a Federal grant or contract—which has among its major objectives strengthening the capability of elected officials to exercise the strategic needs assessment, goal-setting, |

Terms	Description (continued)
	and evaluation functions of management on a jurisdictional or territorial basis. (See also Policy Management, Program Management, Elected officials, Capacity Building).
PROGRAM BUDGETING	A technique of budgeting by discreet objectives and tasks to be performed. The premise of the technique is output or performance, in contrast with line-item budgeting.
PROJECT GRANT	Grants made to governments for specific purposes or projects only which may range from 100 percent financing to partial support on a formula basis. (See also, GRANT-IN-AID).
PUBLIC INTEREST GROUPS (PIGS)	Refers to a national network of quasi-public voluntary associations. The so-called Big Seven include the Council of State Governments (CSG), the National Governors' Conference (NGC), the National Conference of State Legislatures, the National Association of Counties (NACO), the National League of Cities (NLC), United States Conference of Mayors (USCM), and the International City Management Association (ICMA). In addition to NGC, the CSG has several relevant affiliated organizations; associations of Attorneys General, Lieutenant Governors, State Budget Officers, State Purchasing Officials, and State Planning Agencies. The State leagues of municipalities are constituent bodies of the NLC. In addition, the American Society for Public Administration (ASPA), the National Academy of Public Administration (NAPA), and the National Association of Schools of Public Affairs and Administration (NASPAA) are the principal important inputs into the intergovernmental network. More specialized are the associations of planning, personnel, and finance officials.
RESEARCH AND DEVELOPMENT	That process which includes the discovery and application of new scientific knowledge, including the design, testing and evaluation of new materials, processes, products, and systems, whether physical, biological or organizational.
RANN	Research Applied to National Needs. Since its inception in 1971, this program of the National Science Foundation has sought to focus United States scientific and technological resources on selected problems of national importance, with the objective of contributing to their practical solution. Though its

Terms	Description (continued)

initial and primary emphasis has been in the areas of energy, environment and productivity, its programs include important pilot projects and demonstrations in intergovernmental relations and urban technology utilization.

RESOURCE MANAGEMENT (RM)

A term used for the purposes of this report to refer to the cross-cutting administrative and organizational *support functions* and their management. Resource Management includes personnel administration; property management—including facilities, equipment, and materials and supplies; information management; and financial management—including capital budgeting and insurance. Resource Management is related to the *core tools and support functions* of management and the *routine* requirements of *organizational maintenance*. Thus, Resource Management is concerned with policies, programs, and strategies designed to sustain or improve the *administrative support* systems that have a bearing on the capacity of the entire *organizational entity* and its constituent parts (a) to *perform prescribed* tasks and (b) *to adapt to a changing management environment* —changes resulting from events or situations internal (e.g., new priorities) or *external* (e.g., revenue short falls or new regulations) or the organization.

Thus, Resource Management is to be distinguished from *Policy Management* (concerned with the *strategic* functions of guidance and leadership) and *Program Management* (concerned with the *tactical* functions of executing policies in the form of concrete programs). Assessments of State and local government capacity continue to surface major deficiencies with respect to achieving adequate Resource Management capacity. Moreover, the extremely small Federal Technical Assistance investment which is not targeted on Strengthening Program Management Capacity is largely targeted on Resource Management (e.g., the HUD/USAC municipal management information demonstration)—with almost no TA allocated to Policy Management.

SITO

Service Integrated Targets of Opportunity and Partnership grants, SITO is an HEW pilot program to explore administrative innovations that are more responsive to local needs (See also FAR; Consolidated grants).

Terms	Description (continued)
STATE	Means one of the several States of the United States, the District of Columbia, the Commonwealth of Puerto Rico, Guam, the Virgin Islands, and American Samoa.
STATE MUNICIPAL LEAGUES	State associations of municipalities which offer a broad range of services to their constituents.
TECHNICAL ASSISTANCE (TA)	A term used to refer to the programs, activities, and services, provided by the Federal government, a Public Interest group, or another Third Party to strengthen the capacity of recipients to improve their performance with respect to an inherent or assigned function. The *delivery* of Technical Assistance requires serving one or more of three functions; (1) transferring information, (2) developing skills, and (3) developing and transferring products. The *tools* of Technical Assistance include counseling, training, statistical and other expert information, process innovations (e.g., new budgeting methods), equipment or facilities, goods or services—including advisory services.
	A review of current Federal TA programs indicates that the overwhelming majority (over 95% measured by Federal dollar investments) are contained *within* functional program categories administered on an agency basis and are designed almost exclusively to strengthen the capacity of State and local governments to manage Federal categorical programs. A partial exception is HUD 701 and a few other programs scattered among NSF, LEAA, HEW, and elsewhere. (See also Policy Management; Program Management, Resource Management, Capacity Building, HUD 701; NSF).
THIRD PARTIES	A term used to refer to recipients of Federal Technical Assistance (TA) dollars who are charged with delivering TA to State and local governments. Typical "third party" recipients include Public Interest groups —for example, Public Technology Inc. (PTI) and the National Training and Development Service (NTDS) —and universities who, in turn, develop training programs, information clearinghouses, or other services designed to strengthen one or more of the management capacity elements of general purpose governments.

Terms	Description (continued)
TITLE V REGIONAL ECONOMIC DEVELOPMENT PLANS	Planning grants to multistate commissions under *Title V* of the Public Works and Economic Development Act of 1965 (Department of Commerce). Grantees under Title V are the Regional Commissions—Coastal Plains, Four Corners, New England, Ozarks, Upper Great Lakes, Old West and Pacific Northwest.
USG	The Under Secretaries Group for Regional Operations is a committee composed of the Under and Deputy Secretaries of the agencies represented on the Federal Regional Councils, and which serves as a steering group of representatives designated by the member agencies. (See FRC)
USCM	Members of the U.S. Conference of Mayors are mayors of cities with a population exceeding 30,000. The Conference promotes improved municipal government by cooperation among cities as well as with State and Federal government. The USCM provides research, information, counseling and legislative reference services to cities, and maintains a specialized library. (See Public Interest Groups).

Source: Executive Office of the President, *Strengthening Public Management in the Intergovernmental System: A Report Prepared for Office of Management on Budget by the Study Committee on Policy Management Assistance* (Washington, D.C.: Government Printing Office, 1975), pp. 49–58.

Federalism: An Introductory Legal Analysis*
Appendix B

FEDERALISM

Federalism in the United States embraces the following elements: (1) as in all federations, the union of several autonomous political entities, or "States," for common purposes; (2) the division of legislative powers between a "National Government," on the one hand, and constituent "States," on the other, which division is governed by the rule that the former is "a government of enumerated powers" while the latter are governments of "residual powers"; (3) the direct operation, for the most part, of each of these centers of government, within its assigned sphere, upon all persons and property within its territorial limits; (4) the provision of each center with the complete apparatus of law enforcement, both executive and judicial; (5) the supremacy of the

*Source: *The Constitution of the United States of America: Analysis and Interpretation,* Senate Document No. 39, 88th Congress, 1st Session (Washington, D.C.: Government Printing Office, 1964), pp. 4–9.

"National Government" within its assigned sphere over any conflicting assertion of "State" power; (6) dual citizenship.

The third and fourth of the above-listed salient features of the American Federal System are the ones which at the outset marked it off most sharply from all preceding systems, in which the member states generally agreed to obey the mandates of a common government for certain stipulated purposes, but retained to themselves the right of ordaining and enforcing the laws of the union. This, indeed, was the system provided in the Articles of Confederation. The Convention of 1787 was well aware, of course, that if the inanities and futilities of the Confederation were to be avoided in the new system, the latter must incorporate "a coercive principle"; and as Ellsworth of Connecticut expressed it, the only question was whether it should be "a coercion of law, or a coercion of arms," whether that "coercion which acts only upon delinquent individuals" or that which is applicable to "sovereign bodies, states, in their political capacity."[1] In Judicial Review the former principle was established, albeit without entirely discarding the latter, as the War between the States was to demonstrate.

The sheer fact of Federalism enters the purview of Constitutional Law, that is, becomes a judicial concept, in consequence of the conflicts which have at times arisen between the idea of State Autonomy ("State Sovereignty") and the principle of National Supremacy. Exaltation of the latter principle, as it is recognized in the Supremacy Clause (Article VI, paragraph 2) of the Constitution, was the very keystone of Chief Justice Marshall's constitutional jurisprudence. It was Marshall's position that the supremacy clause was intended to be applied literally, so that if an unforced reading of the terms in which legislative power was granted to Congress confirmed its right to enact a particular statute, the circumstance that the statute projected national power into a hitherto accustomed field of State power with unavoidable curtailment of the latter was a matter of indifference. State power, as Madison in his early nationalistic days phrased it, was "no criterion of national power," and hence no independent limitation thereof.

Quite different was the outlook of the Court over which Marshall's successor, Taney, presided. That Court took as its point of departure the Tenth Amendment, which reads, "The powers not delegated to the United States by this Constitution, nor prohibited by it to the States, are reserved to the States respectively, or to the people." In construing this provision the Court under Taney sometimes talked as if it re-

---

1. 3 Farrand, *The Records of the Federal Convention of 1787,* 240, 241 (1911).

garded all the reserved powers of the State as limiting national power; at other times it talked as if it regarded certain subjects as reserved exclusively to the States, slavery being, of course, the outstanding instance.[2]

But whether following the one line of reasoning or the other, the Taney Court subtly transformed its function, and so that of Judicial Review, in relation to the Federal System. Marshall viewed the Court as primarily an organ of the National Government and of its supremacy. The Court under Taney regarded itself as standing outside of and above both the National Government and the States, and as vested with a quasi-arbitral function between two centers of diverse, but essentially equal, because "sovereign", powers. Thus in Ableman v. Booth, which was decided on the eve of the War between the States, we find Taney himself using this arresting language:

> This judicial power was justly regarded as indispensable, not merely to maintain the supremacy of the laws of the United States, but also to guard the States from any encroachment upon their reserved rights by the general government. . . . So long . . . as this Constitution shall endure, this tribunal must exist with it, deciding in the peaceful forms of judicial proceeding, the angry and irritating controversies between sovereignties, which in other countries have been determined by the arbitrament of force.[3]

It is, therefore, the Taney Court, rather than the Marshall Court, which elaborated the concept of Dual Federalism. Marshall's federalism is more aptly termed national federalism; and turning to modern issues, we may say without exaggeration that the broad general constitutional issue between the Court and the Franklin D. Roosevelt program in such cases as Schechter Corp. v. United States and Carter v. Carter Coal Co.[4] was whether Marshall's or Taney's brand of federalism should prevail. More precisely, the issue in these cases was whether Congress' power to regulate commerce must stop short of regulating the employer-employee relationship in industrial production, that having been hitherto regulated by the States. In Justice Sutherland's words in the Carter's case:

> Much stress is put upon the evils which come from the struggle between employers and employees over the matter of wages, working conditions,

---

2. *See* the words of Taney, C. J., in the License Cases, 5 How. 504, 573–574 (1847); and in The Passenger Cases, 7 How. 283, 465–470 (1849).
3. 21 How. 506, 520–521 (1859).
4. 295 U.S. 495 (1935); 298 U.S. 238 (1936).

the right of collective bargaining, etc., and the resulting strikes, curtailment and irregularity of production and effect on prices; and it is insisted that interstate commerce is greatly affected thereby. . . . The conclusive answer is that the evils are all local evils over which the Federal Government has no legislative control. The relation of employer and employee is a local relation. At common law, it is one of the domestic relations. The wages are paid for the doing of local work. Working conditions are obviously local conditions. The employees are not engaged in or about commerce, but exclusively in producing a commodity. And the controversies and evils, which it is the object of the act to regulate and minimize, are local controversies and exils affecting local work undertaken to accomplish that local results. Such effect as they may have upon commerce, however extensive it may be, is secondary and indirect. An increase in the greatness of the effect adds to its importance. It does not alter its character.[5]

We all know how this issue was finally resolved. In the Fair Labor Standards Act of 1938 Congress not only prohibits interstate commerce in goods produced by substandard labor, but it directly forbids, with penalties, the employment of labor in industrial production for interstate commerce on other than certain prescribed terms. And in United States *v.* Darby[6] this Act was sustained by the Court, in all its sweeping provisions, on the basis of an opinion by Chief Justice Stone which in turn is based on Chief Justice Marshall's famous opinions in McCulloch *v.* Maryland and Gibbons *v.* Ogden rendered more than a century and a quarter ago. In short, as a principle capable of delimiting the national legislative power, the concept of Dual Federalism as regards the present Court seems today to be at an end, with consequent aggrandizement of national power.

There is, however, another side to the story. For in one respect even the great Marshall has been in effect overruled in support of enlarged views of national authority. Without essaying a vain task of "tithing mint, anise and cummin," it is fairly accurate to say that throughout the 100 years which lie between Marshall's death and the cases of the 1930s, the conception of the federal relationship which on the whole prevailed with the Court was a competitive conception, one which envisaged the National Government and the States as jealous rivals. To be sure, we occasionally get some striking statements of contrary tendency, as in Justice Bradley's opinion in 1880 for a divided Court in the Siebold Case,[7] where is reflected recognition of certain results of the War between the States; or later in a frequently quoted

---

5. 298 U.S. 238, 308–309.
6. 312 U.S. 100 (1941).
7. Ex parte Siebold, 100 U.S. 371 (1880).

dictum by Justice McKenna, in Hoke *v.* United States, in which the Mann White Slave Act was sustained in 1913:

> Our dual form of government has its perplexities, State and Nation having different spheres of jurisdiction . . . but it must be kept in mind that we are one people; and the powers reserved to the states and those conferred on the nation are adapted to be exercised, whether independently or concurrently, to promote the general welfare, material and moral.[8]

The competitive concept is, nevertheless, the one much more generally evident in the outstanding results for American Constitutional Law throughout three-quarters of its history. Of direct pertinence in this connection is the doctrine of tax exemption which converted federalism into a principle of private immunity from taxation, so that, for example, neither government could tax as income the official salaries paid by the other government.[9] This doctrine traces immediately to Marshall's famous judgment in McCulloch *v.* Maryland,[10] and bespeaks a conception of the federal relationship which regards the National Government and the States as bent on mutual frustration. Today the principle of tax exemption, except so far as Congress may choose to apply it to federal instrumentalities by virtue of its protective powers under the necessary and proper clause, as at an end.

By the cooperative conception of the federal relationship the States and the National Government are regarded as mutually complementary parts of a single governmental mechanism all of whose powers are intended to realize the current purposes of government according to their applicability to the problem in hand. This is the conception on which the recent social and economic legislation professes to rest. It is the conception which the Court invokes throughout its decisions in sustaining the Social Security Act of 1935 and supplementary State legislation. It is the conception which underlies congressional legislation of recent years making certain crimes against the States, like theft, racketeering, kidnaping, crimes also against the National Government whenever the offender extends his activities beyond State Boundary lines. The usually cited constitutional justification for such legislation is that which was advanced forty years ago in the above quoted Hoke case.[11]

---

8. 227 U.S. 308, 322.

9. Dobbins *v.* Commissioners, 16 Pet. 435 (1842); Collector *v.* Day, 11 Wall. 113 (1870).

10. 4 Wheat. 316, 431 (1819).

11. For references and further details, *see* Corwin, *Court over Constitution,* 129–176 (1938).

It has been argued that the cooperative conception of the federal relationship, especially as it is realized in the policy of federal subventions to the States, tends to break down State initiative and to devitalize State policies. Actually, its effect has often been just the contrary, and for the reason pointed out by Justice Cardozo in Helvering v. Davis,[12] decided in 1937, namely, that the States, competing as they do with one another to attract investors, have not been able to embark separately upon expensive programs of relief and social insurance. Another great objection to Cooperative Federalism is more difficult to meet. This is, that Cooperative Federalism invites further aggrandizement of national power. Unquestionably it does, for when two cooperate, it is the stronger member of the combination who usually calls the tunes. Resting as it does primarily on the superior fiscal resources of the National Government, Cooperative Federalism has been, at least to date, a short expression for a constantly increasing concentration of power at Washington in the stimulation and supervision of local policies.[13]

The last element of the concept of Federalism to demand attention is the doctrine that the National Government is a government of enumerated powers only, and consequently under the necessity at all times of justifying its measures juridically by pointing to some particular clause or clauses of the Constitution which, when read separately or in combination, may be thought to grant power adequate to such measures. In spite of such decisions as that in United States v. Darby, this time-honored doctrine still guides the authoritative interpreters of the Constitution in determining the validity of acts which are passed by Congress in presumed exercise of its powers of domestic legislation—the course of reasoning pursued by the Chief Justice in the Darby case itself is proof that such is the fact. In the field of foreign relations, on the contrary, the doctrine of enumerated powers has always had a difficult row to hoe, and today may be unqualifiedly asserted to be defunct.

As early as the old case of Penhallow v. Doane, which was decided by the Supreme Court in 1795, certain counsel thought it pertinent to urge the following conception of the War Power:

A formal compact is not essential to the institution of a government. Every nation that governs itself, under what form soever, without any dependence

12. 301 U.S. 619 (1937).
13. In this connection, see Oklahoma v. Civil Service Comm'n., 330 U.S. 127, 142–145 (1947).

on a foreign power, is a sovereign state. In every society there must be a sovereignty. 1 Dall. Rep. 46.57. Vatt. B. 1. ch. 1. sec. 4. The powers of war form an inherent characteristic of national sovereignty: and, it is not denied, that Congress possessed those powers. . . .[14]

To be sure, only two of the Justices felt it necessary to comment on this argument, which one of them endorsed, while the other rejected it.

Yet seventy-five years later Justice Bradley incorporated closely kindred doctrine into his concurring opinion in the Legal Tender Cases;[15] and in the years following the Court itself frequently brought the same general outlook to questions affecting the National Government's powers in the field of foreign relations. Thus in the Chinese Exclusion Case, decided in 1889, Justice Field, in asserting the unlimited power of the National Government, and hence of Congress, to exclude aliens from American shores, remarked:

> While under our Constitution and form of government the great mass of local matters is controlled by local authorities, the United States, in their relation to foreign countries and their subjects or citizens, are one nation, invested with the powers which belong to independent nations, the exercise of which can be invoked for the maintenance of its absolute independence and security throughout its entire territory.[16]

And four years later the power of the National Government to deport alien residents at the option of Congress was based by Justice Gray on the same general reasoning.[17]

Finally, in 1936, Justice Sutherland, speaking for the Court in U.S. v. Curtiss Wright Corp., with World War I a still recent memory, took over bodily counsel's argument of 140 years earlier, and elevated it to the head of the column of authoritative constitutional doctrine. He said:

> A political society cannot endure without a supreme will somewhere. Sovereignty is never held in suspense. When, therefore, the external sovereignty of Great Britain in respect of the colonies ceased, it immediately passed to the Union. . . . It results that the investment of the Federal government with the powers of external sovereignty did not depend upon the affirmative grants of the Constitution. The powers to declare and wage war, to conclude peace, to make treaties, to maintain diplomatic relations with other

---

14. 3 Dall. 54. 74.
15. Knox v. Lee, 12 Wall. 457–555 (1871).
16. 130 U.S. 581, 604.
17. Fong Yue Ting v. United States, 149 U.S. 698 (1893).

sovereignties, if they had never been mentioned in the Constitution, would have vested in the Federal government as necessary concomitants of nationality.[18]

In short, the power of the National Government in the field of international relationship is not simply a complexus of particular enumerated powers; it is an inherent power, one which is attributable to the National Government on the ground solely of its belonging to the American People as a sovereign political entity at International Law. In that field the principle of Federalism no longer holds, if it ever did.[19]

---

18. 299 U.S. 304, 316–318.
19. See also Board of Trustees v. U.S., 289 U.S. 48, 59 (1933).

The Budget for Fiscal Year 1975: Federal Aid in SMSA

Appendix C

Federal Aid Outlays in SMSAs (in millions of dollars)

Function and Program	1961	1964	1969	1975 (estimate)
National defense	10	28	30	38
Agriculture and rural development:				
Donation of surplus commodities	128	231	313	299
Other	27	40	104	141
Natural resources and environment:				
Environmental protection	24	8	79	2,603
Other	30	10	101	249
Commerce and transportation:				
Economic development		158	104	331
Highways	1,398	1,948	2,225	2,678
Airports	36	36	83	232
Urban mass transportation			122	586
Other	1	5	5	117

(continued)

(continued)

Function and Program	1961	1964	1969	1975 (estimate)
Community development and housing:				
Funds appropriated to the President			432	183
Urban renewal	106	559	786	863
Public housing	105	136	257	1,023
Water and sewer facilities		36	52	104
Model Cities			8	209
Better Communities Act				560
Other	2	17	75	223
Education and manpower:				
Consolidated Education Grants				1,337
Elementary and secondary	222	264	1,262	556
Higher education	5	14	210	30
Vocational education	28	29	179	280
Employment security	303	344	449	315
Comprehensive Manpower Assistance				1,220
Manpower activities		64	530	369
Other	3	7	333	990
Health:				
Health services	47	82	219	458
Preventive health services				38
Alcohol, drug abuse, and mental health	4	8	77	530
Health resources	48	66	216	545
Medical assistance		140	1,731	3,989
Other		4	54	
Income security:				
Rehabilitation services	37	61	247	669
Public assistance	1,170	1,450	3,022	4,820
Child nutrition, special milk and food stamps	131	168	482	3,484
Other	3	16	148	429
General government:				
Law enforcement (including law enforcement assistance)			17	656
National Capital region	25	38	85	361
Other		9	27	65
Other functions		2		29
General Revenue Sharing				4,322
Total aids to urban areas	3,893	5,588	14,045	35,931

Source: *Special Analyses: Budget of the United States Government, Fiscal Year 1975* (Washington, D.C.: Government Printing Office, 1974), Special Analysis N, "Federal Aid to State and Local Governments," p. 212.

The Incremental Impact of General Revenue Sharing (GRS) on State Finances

Appendix D

GRS as a Proportion of New Tax Monies

(1) State	(2) State Tax Revenues: 1974	(3) State Tax Revenues: 1973	(4) 1974–1973 Difference (Col. 2 – Col. 3)	(5) General Revenue Sharing: 1974	(6) Incremental Impact of GRS (Col. 5 ÷ Col. 4)
	(millions of dollars)		(millions of dollars)		(percentages)
Alabama	1,017.4	931.0	86.4	34.7	40.2
Alaska	124.2	109.0	15.2	2.7	17.8
Arizona	743.2	682.0	61.2	20.6	33.7
Arkansas	605.5	523.0	82.5	22.8	27.6
California	7,971.7	7,323.8	647.9	219.0	33.8
Colorado	797.6	666.6	131.0	21.2	16.2
Connecticut	1,092.9	1,142.6	−49.7	25.4	
Delaware	308.1	265.4	42.7	6.7	15.7
Florida	2,786.6	2,487.8	298.8	58.5	19.6
Georgia	1,514.9	1,361.5	153.4	42.1	27.4
Hawaii	494.9	432.6	62.3	9.0	14.4
Idaho	256.2	224.9	31.3	8.4	26.8
Illinois	4,083.0	3,675.6	407.4	103.6	25.4
Indiana	1,674.2	1,258.4	417.8	43.3	10.4
Iowa	1,005.1	854.4	150.7	28.8	19.1
Kansas	702.7	609.7	93.0	19.7	21.2
Kentucky	1,106.1	1,020.0	86.1	38.8	45.1
Louisiana	1,319.5	1,189.4	130.1	47.6	36.6
Maine	336.3	303.6	32.7	12.6	38.5
Maryland	1,578.2	1,456.2	122.0	40.3	33.0
Massachusetts	2,204.7	2,054.1	150.6	64.8	43.0
Michigan	3,681.2	3,527.6	153.6	86.8	56.5
Minnesota	1,843.1	1,638.5	204.6	39.6	19.4
Mississippi	746.5	661.3	85.2	35.8	42.0

Missouri	1,300.4	78.7	37.8	48.0
Montana	220.0	32.8	7.9	24.1
Nebraska	405.6	30.5	12.4	40.7
Nevada	251.4	38.5	4.5	11.7
New Hampshire	165.2	9.4	4.9	52.1
New Jersey	2,056.3	136.9	63.5	46.4
New Mexico	437.7	51.0	13.3	26.1
New York	8,516.4	346.4	224.3	64.8
North Carolina	1,806.4	148.9	52.7	35.4
North Dakota	218.7	39.0	8.5	21.8
Ohio	2,788.9	112.6	80.2	71.2
Oklahoma	777.5	86.3	22.6	26.2
Oregon	701.6	105.1	21.7	20.6
Pennsylvania	4,609.1	241.7	105.9	43.8
Rhode Island	333.7	21.0	9.2	43.8
South Carolina	901.5	76.3	28.7	37.6
South Dakota	165.6	14.3	9.2	64.3
Tennessee	1,092.4	90.0	37.9	42.1
Texas	3,287.9	469.0	97.0	20.7
Utah	363.1	3.6	12.1	336.1
Vermont	179.6	4.3	5.7	132.6
Virginia	1,507.9	107.7	39.9	37.0
Washington	1,359.7	72.6	29.4	40.5
West Virginia	610.1	41.1	28.7	69.8
Wisconsin	2,032.2	164.2	51.2	31.2
Wyoming	124.2	19.0	3.3	17.4
U.S. Total	74,206.9	6,137.6	2,045.3	33.4

Source: U.S. Bureau of Census, *State Government Finances in 1973*, GF73, no. 3 (Washington, D.C.: Government Printing Office, 1974), Table 7, p. 19; U.S. Bureau of Census, *State Government Finances in 1974*, GF74, no. 3 (Washington, D.C.: Government Printing Office, 1975), Table 7, p. 19.

New York City Loan*
Appendix E

STEPS TOWARD FISCAL REFORM CITED
BY TREASURY

New York City has made considerable progress toward the objective of fiscal and financial reform. The revised financial plan, adopted by the Emergency Financial Control Board, the agreements in principle with all of the major labor unions whose contracts have expired and other factors have justified the finding required by Federal law that there is a reasonable prospect of repayment for a $500 million loan to be repaid April 15, 1977.

In making this finding, I relied on a variety of factors. New York City's actions during fiscal year 1976 were in substantial compliance with the proposals made to us last fall. Substantial reductions in expen-

---

*This is the full text of Secretary Simon's announcement of Treasury approval of a $500 million loan under the New York City Seasonal Financing Act. Source: *Treasury Papers*, 2 (July 1976): 13.

ditures have been implemented, program cuts have been made, and significant improvement in management, financial controls, and accounting and reporting systems is evident. All of these accomplishments are reflected in the fact that New York City repaid in full all Federal loans extended in fiscal year 1976.

But the loan request in question relates to fiscal year 1977, and the city's actions for this year are plainly more relevant to my decision. Given the size and duration of the new financial plan, it is likely that events now unforeseen could require even more in the way of expenditure reductions. Accordingly, it is most important that the city and the Control Board will specify $135 million of standby cuts by July 31 and will implement $50 million on these cuts by August 15.

Another key factor is the prompt and timely settlement of the major labor contracts in a manner consistent with the underlying principle of the wage freeze and the wage policy resolution. The freeze on salaries and the agreement to effect an affirmative reduction in benefits are critical to the success of the three-year plan. I share Mayor Beame's conviction that these reductions must and will occur in the fringe benefits area. We will be carefully monitoring New York City's compliance with these requirements and our action on future loan requests will implement $50 million of these cuts by August 15.

In the final analysis, however, even though the new financial plan is basically sound and the agreements announced today are consistent with the plan, it is clear that much more in the way of fundamental reform must be accomplished if New York City is to restore its fiscal and financial integrity and to regain its pre-eminence among our major cities. Specifically:

- The erosion in the real estate tax base must be addressed by forthright action to phase out rent control.
- Pension arrangements must be restructured.
- An acceptable accounting and financial control system must be implemented promptly.
- Comprehensive economic development planning must be accelerated to create an environment in which existing businesses can remain and grow and new business investment will be attracted, providing more jobs and a better standard of living.
- Consistent with such planning, the existing structure of individual and business taxation should be thoroughly reappraised.

As I have assured the Mayor and the Governor, the Treasury Department will continue to monitor closely New York City's compliance with the Financial Plan and its progress on the longer range problems as well. Without solid and consistent progress in all of these areas, the loan program will not be continued.

The New York City Seasonal Financing Act of 1975 was conceived by Congress as part of a "bridge" program to provide New York City with time to implement the fiscal and financial reforms which will enable New York City to regain access to the capital markets. I believe it to be my responsibility to leave my successor with a program consistent with this vital objective and will continue to do everything within my power to insure that the necessary steps are taken at the State and local level. New York City and New York State must continue to carry out their responsibilities as well.

Fungible Funds from Federal Grants*
Appendix F

FEDERAL JOB MONEY IS GOING AWRY

Federal funds intended to create new jobs and ease unemployment have been used instead by the North Carolina Department of Transportation to hire temporary laborers at the same time it cut back on state-paid laborers.

The practice, according to a U.S. Department of Labor official in Atlanta, defeats the purpose of the federal job program.

Earlier this year the highway division hired several hundred temporary laborers whose salaries have cost the federal government $1.6 million so far.

Several highway personnel officers said in telephone interviews this week that they hired federally paid laborers in place of state-paid laborers to save the state money.

---

*Pat Stith and Gary Pearce, *The News and Observer of Raleigh,* December 7, 1975.

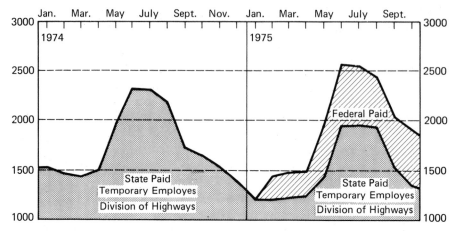

Temporary Highway Employment Month-by-Month in 1974 and 1975

After The News and Observer raised questions about the use of the money, the state office in charge of overseeing the program began an inquiry to determine whether the highway division had violated federal regulations.

The Comprehensive Employment and Training Act (CETA) requires agencies to create new jobs with CETA money—jobs that would not have existed without federal assistance.

"In the event that the regulations were violated, we would have to get the money back," said Joseph R. Balak Jr., director of the State Office of Manpower Services.

He said his office would contact highway division finance and personnel officers across the state to find out what happened.

"We'll be starting today," Balak said Friday.

Highway administrator Billy Rose and other top officials in Raleigh said they knew the $3.5 million their agency got from the Department of Labor was supposed to be used to create new jobs.

Some personnel officers in the field, however, didn't get the message.

"Whenever it has been possible for me to hire somebody as a CETA (federally-paid) employe rather than a state employe, I have done it," said James P. Bennett of Sylva, one of the highway division's 14 area personnel officers. "It has cut down considerably the number of state employes that we have had out here."

A highway accountant in another area estimated his area was getting along with 11 fewer state-paid temporary employes because federally-paid employes have been hired in their place.

He estimated his area would save about $62,000 in state money over the course of a year as a result of that practice.

James J. Stephens of Greensboro, another area personnel officer, estimated he would have hired 20 more state-paid temporary employes if his area had been given no federal job program money.

He estimated the savings in his area at over $100,000 a year.

"In some divisions that was done; in some it wasn't," said the Transportation Department personnel director, William H. Davis III. "We're trying now to determine to what extent it happened and how to correct it."

The highway division employed an average of 1,821 state-paid temporary employes in its field operations between February and October of 1974.

From February to October 1975, the division employed an average of 1,532 state-paid temporary employes, plus an average of 446 federally-paid temporary employes, a total of 1,978.

The N&O's examination of highway payroll records in Raleigh could not establish how many of the 446 federally-paid jobs are actually new jobs and how many are simply replacements for state-paid jobs.

When Highway Administrator Billy Rose was asked if his division had used all the federal money to create new jobs, he said:

"I can't answer your question. I really don't know."

Rose said there had been an effort over the last several years to "tighten up" the number of temporary laborers employed on the highways, and that effort was under way before the highway division was given the federal money to create more jobs.

Rose acknowledged however, that his division's state budget for the year beginning last July 1 indicated that it would hire as many, or more, state-paid temporary workers than it hired the previous year.

The laborers hired with the federal money at an hourly wage of $2.71 have been used to pick up litter along roadways, clear up drainage problems and patch highways. That program is to continue through next June.

The money given to the highway division is part of more than $100 million that has been funneled into North Carolina by the U.S. Department of Labor under the CETA program to fight unemployment.

STATE OFFICIALS THWART JOBS PROGRAM*

The state Transportation Department's use of federal job money to ease the pain of its budget-making defeats the purpose of the federal grants. Indeed, the practice is a cruel bureaucratic shell game for those Tar Heels who are looking for work, at last count, 7.1 per cent of the state work force.

A story in this newspaper Sunday documented how state highway personnel officers had substituted federal money for state funds to hire temporary highway workers. The practice was freely admitted. "Whenever it has been possible for me to hire somebody as a (federally paid) employe rather than a state employe, I have done it," said one officer, James P. Bennett of Sylva.

How many were hired in this way is not clear. Last year, the state hired an average of 1,821 temporary employes between February and October. This year, the state used its own money to hire only 1,532. Federal dollars were spent to hire another 446 workers.

This federal money comes to the state through the Comprehensive Employment and Training Act (CETA). Its purposes are to provide jobs for the unemployed and to stimulate the economy by putting more money in circulation. The state's misspending has thwarted both aims. The federal Office of Manpower Services says the money may have to be paid back if regulations are found to have been violated.

It is one thing to save money. It is quite another for state officials to use federal funds to make themselves look good, which is what occurred under the CETA program.

---

*The News and Observer of Raleigh, December 10, 1975.

Housing and Community Development Act* of 1974

Appendix G

The Committee of conference on the disagreeing votes of the two Houses on the amendments of the House to the bill (S. 3066) to consolidate, simplify, and improve laws relative to housing and housing assistance, to provide Federal assistance in support of community development activities, and for other purposes, having met, after full and free conference, have agreed to recommend and do recommend to their respective Houses as follows:

That the Senate recede from its disagreement to the amendment of the House to the text of the bill and agree to the same with an amendment as follows:

In lieu of the matter proposed to be inserted by the House amendment to the text of the bill insert the following:

That this Act may be cited as the "Housing and Community Development Act of 1974."

---

*Source: *Housing and Community Development Act of 1974,* Conference Report No. 93-1279, House of Representatives, 93rd Congress, 2nd Session, Washington, D.C., August 12, 1974.

TITLE I—COMMUNITY DEVELOPMENT

Findings and Purpose

SEC. 101. a. The Congress finds and declares that the Nation's cities, towns, and smaller urban communities face critical social, economic, and environmental problems arising in significant measure from—

1. the growth of population in metropolitan and other urban areas, and the concentration of persons of lower income in central cities; and
2. inadequate public and private investment and reinvestment in housing and other physical facilities, and related public and social services, resulting in the growth and persistence of urban slums and blight and the marked deterioration of the quality of the urban environment.

b. The Congress further finds and declares that the future welfare of the Nation and the well-being of its citizens depend on the establishment and maintenance of viable urban communities as social, economic, and political entities, and require—

1. systematic and sustained action by Federal, State, and local governments to eliminate blight, to conserve and renew older urban areas, to improve the living environment of low- and moderate-income families, and to develop new centers of population growth and economic activity;
2. substantial expansion of and greater continuity in the scope and level of Federal assistance, together with increased private investment in support of community development activities; and
3. continuing effort at all levels of government to streamline programs and improve the functioning of agencies responsible for planning, implementing, and evaluating community development efforts.

c. The primary objective of this title is the development of viable urban communities, by providing decent housing and a suitable living environment and expanding economic opportunities, principally for persons of low and moderate income. Consistent with this primary objective, the Federal assistance provided in this title is for the support of community development activities, which are directed toward the following specific objectives—

1. the elimination of slums and blight and the prevention of blighting influences and the deterioration of property and neighborhood and community facilities of importance to the welfare of the community, principally persons of low and moderate income;

2. the elimination of conditions which are detrimental to health, safety, and public welfare, through code enforcement, demolition, interim rehabilitation assistance, and related activities;

3. the conservation and expansion of the Nation's housing stock in order to provide a decent home and a suitable living environment for all persons, but principally those of low and moderate income;

4. the expansion and improvement of the quantity and quality of community services, principally for persons of low and moderate income, which are essential for sound community development and for the development of viable urban communities;

5. a more rational utilization of land and other natural resources and the better arrangement of residential, commercial, industrial, recreational, and other needed activity centers;

6. the reduction of the isolation of income groups within communities and geographical areas and the promotion of an increase in the diversity and vitality of neighborhoods through the spatial deconcentration of housing opportunities for persons of lower income and the revitalization of deteriorating or deteriorated neighborhoods to attract persons of higher income; and

7. the restoration and preservation of properties of special value for historic, architectural, or esthetic reasons.

It is the intent of Congress that the Federal assistance made available under this title not be utilized to reduce substantially the amount of local financial support for community development activities below the level of such support prior to the availability of such assistance.

d. It is also the purpose of this title to further the development of a national urban growth policy by consolidating a number of complex and overlapping programs of financial assistance to communities of varying sizes and needs into a consistent system of Federal aid which—

1. provides assistance on an annual basis, with maximum certainty and minimum delay, upon which communities can rely in their planning;
2. encourages community development activities which are consistent with comprehensive local and areawide development planning;
3. furthers achievement of the national housing goal of a decent home and a suitable living environment for every American family; and
4. fosters the undertaking of housing and community development activities in a coordinated and mutually supportive manner.

Comparison of State and Local Fiscal Assistance Acts of 1972 and 1976

Appendix H

Provision	Present Act (P.L. 92-512)	H.R. 13367, As Amended
Duration of Program.	5 years (through 12/31/76).	3¼ years (through 9/30/80).
Funding.	Total of $30.2 billion authorized and appropriated from a Trust Fund. Annual payments increased during the 5-year period from $5.3 billion for 1972 to $6.5 for 1976.	Total of $24.9 billion provided as an "entitlement" (as defined in Budget Control Act), at annual rate of $6.65 billion for 3¼ years. No provision for annual increases.
Allocation Formula.	States may elect either 3-factor (population, general tax effort and relative income) or the 5-factor formula (population, urbanized population, inverse per capita income, income tax collections, and general tax effort.) Funds divided between each State and its local governments on one-third, two-thirds basis, and among eligible local governments according to 3-factor formula described above. Provision for minimum and maximum local allocations.	No change.
Eligible Local Governments.	General purpose "units of local governments," (county, municipality, township) as determined by Census Bureau for general statistical purposes. Also, Indian tribes and Alaskan native villages.	Same, except that an eligible unit, effective October 1, 1977, must also impose taxes or receive intergovernmental transfers for substantial performance of at least two municipal-type services, and must spend at least 10% of its total expenditures for each of two such services; Latter requirement waived if unit performs 4 or more such services

or provided two or more such services on January 1, 1976, and continues to do so.

This restriction eliminated.

Priority Expenditures.

Expenditure of funds restricted for local units of government to 8 specified priority categories plus any necessary capital expenditures.

Citizen Participation.

No special requirements other than use of funds in accordance with State and local laws.

Strong and specific requirements for assuring that citizens (including, specifically, senior citizens and their organizations) are informed of budget proposals and are given an opportunity to participate in the budgetary process. These provisions require at least two public hearings: (a) on the preparation of a report on the proposed use of funds provided under this Act, and (b) on the proposed use of funds in relation to the entire state or local budget. Opportunity for written and oral comment by citizens must be provided. The Secretary is authorized to waive hearing requirement on the proposed use report where cost is unreasonably burdensome in relation to entitlements. The Secretary is also authorized to waive the requirement for a budget hearing if the budget process required by State or local laws assures citizens the opportunity for attendance and participation and if it includes a hearing

Source: *The Congressional Record*, June 15, 1976, pp. E3356–E3357.

Provision	Present Act (P.L. 92-512)	H.R. 13367, As Amended
Reporting Requirements.	Planned and actual use reports required for each entitlement period.	on proposed use of funds made available by this Act. Report required for each entitlement period on the proposed use of funds in comparison with current and past use, as well as a comparison of such uses in relation to the relevant functional items in official budget. Report also required on the actual use of funds in relation to relevant functional items in the official budget. The latter report must provide an explanation of any differences between proposed and actual use of funds provided under Act. The Secretary is required to provide copies of local use reports to the Governors of the respective States. Each local government within a metropolitan area must submit its proposed use report to the areawide planning organization charged with implementing provisions of certain specified Federal laws.
Publicity and Publication Requirements.	Each report must be published in a newspaper of general circulation.	(1) Public notice must be given of a public hearing to be held at least 7

News media must be advised of publication of reports.

days prior to submission of the proposed use report to the Treasury Department.

(2) Proposed use report, accompanied by a narrative summary of entire official budget proposed, must be published in a newspaper of general circulation 30 days prior to a public hearing on the budget. The proposed use report, the narrative summary, and the official budget must be available for inspection and reproduction. The budget must identify each item that will be funded in whole or in part with funds made available by this Act, and must specify the percentage of those funds in each such item.

(3) A narrative summary of official budget adopted (including an explanation of changes from the proposed budget), must be published within 30 days after adoption.

Secretary is authorized to waive publication requirements when it is impractical, infeasible, or unreasonably burdensome. The 30-day requirement in (2) above can be modified to the minimum extent necessary to comply with State or local law if the Secretary is satisfied that citizens will receive ade-

Extensions of Remarks re. State and Local Fiscal Assistance Act ("General Revenue Sharing") Comparison of Present Act with House-Passed Bill (H.R. 13367, as Amended) (continued)

Provision	Present Act (P.L. 92-512)	H.R. 13367, As Amended
Nondiscrimination Provision.	Discrimination prohibited on the ground of race, color, national origin, or sex in any program or activity funded by the Act.	quate notification of the proposed use of funds. (1) Bill extends present prohibitions to include religion, age, and handicapped status. (2) The provision prohibiting discrimination applies to all programs or activities of each State or local government, unless the government can show, by clear and convincing evidence, that funds provided under the Act were not used, directly or indirectly, in instances of alleged discrimination. (3) Specific provisions are included for the temporary suspension, resumption, termination and repayment of funds and the steps to be taken for administrative hearings and voluntary compliance. (4) Secretary is directed to promulgate regulations establishing specific time limits for investigation and determination of complaints. Regulations shall also establish specific time limits for compliance audits and reviews. (5) Aggrieved individuals must ex-

Provision		
	...haust all administrative remedies before instituting a civil action, except that administrative remedies will be deemed to be exhausted 60 days after a complaint has been filed if a determination has not been made within that time period.	No change.
Davis-Bacon Act Provision.	Prevailing area wage rate must be paid if 25% or more of a construction project's cost is financed with funds made available by this Act.	This prohibition eliminated.
Matching Prohibition.	Funds made available under the Act may not be used as a recipient's contribution in a Federal program requiring financial matching.	
Lobbying Prohibition.	None.	Funds may not be used, directly or indirectly, for lobbying or other activities intended to influence any legislation regarding the provisions of Act. However, dues paid to National or State associations are exempt from this prohibition.
Independent Audits of State and Local Governments.	No requirement.	Secretary is directed to issue regulations requiring an annual independent audit of each recipient's financial accounts in accordance with generally-accepted auditing standards. Secretary is authorized to provide for less frequent audits, or less formal reviews of financial information, when audit costs

Provision	Present Act (P.L. 92-512)	H.R. 13367, As Amended
		are unreasonably burdensome in relation to entitlements. Secretary is also directed to provide for the availability, inspection and reproduction of audit reports.
Annual Report to Congress.	Secretary is required to report by March 1 of each year on the operation and status of the trust fund during the preceding fiscal year.	In addition to reporting on the operation and status of the trust fund, the Secretary is required to make a comprehensive report by January 15 of each year on the implementation and administration of this Act.

A-95: What's It All About?*

Appendix I

This article represents an attempt to clarify present misunderstandings and misconceptions about the requirements of the OMB Circular A-95. It addresses the issue of what A-95 can and cannot do for government coordinative efforts. Some of the current problems affecting the full implementation of A-95 are discussed, and this author's view of possible solutions is presented, with the hope that the article will result in a more complete understanding of the A-95 concept on the part of those who read it.

WHAT IS A-95?

A-95 Clearinghouses exist due to passage of the *Intergovernmental Relations Act of 1968*. To implement Title IV of this Act, the U.S.

*Darryl M. Bloom, *Planning for Progress,* 7 (Winter/Spring 1975): 12-14, 25. Publication of the North Carolina Office of State Planning.

Office of Management and Budget (OMB) produced the *A-95 Circular,* which sets forth regulations involving federally funded planning, programming, and project coordination among Federal, State, and local governments. The Circular consists of four major parts, which concern:

    I. *The Project Notification and Review System*—which establishes guidelines to provide for State and local review of applications for certain federal funds. Approximately 145 of 1,000 Federal grant-in-aid programs must comply with these guidelines.

    II. *Direct Federal Projects*—establishing guidelines for State and local review of federally initiated projects within a State. (*Example:* a Corps of Engineers dredging project.)

    III. *The State Plan Review*—which establishes a process of formal review, by the Governor's Office, of federally funded State plans.

    IV. *The Coordination of Planning in Jurisdictional Areas*—establishing guidelines for the organization and utilization of multi-county planning regions.

State and regional clearinghouses are established to carry out the intent of the Circular. Each Governor creates a State Clearinghouse within State government, strategically located to best serve his administration. A State with established substate districts may locate a regional clearinghouse in each existing planning district, as designated by the Governor.

An A-95 clearinghouse is an information dissemination agency. Its purpose is to facilitate coordinated planning, assist in eliminating unnecessary duplication, and assure consistency with existing Federal, State, regional and local plans, policies, and regulations. Using the North Carolina function as an example, the mechanics of the A-95 review process are described as follows:

    A. The State Clearinghouse receives notification of an applicant's intent to apply for Federal funds, and the applicant is then acquainted with the A-95 requirement by the Federal regulations which outline the proper procedures for completion of an application.

    B. An identifying number, which assists in tracking the project throughout the review process, is assigned to the project intent, and a copy is forwarded to the appropriate regional clearinghouse for local review and comment.

C. The project intent is also referred to the appropriate State agency for its review and comment. All State agencies have been contacted by the State Clearinghouse in order to determine the types of projects each agency is interested in reviewing on a regular basis, thus expediting the referral process.

D. All comments are returned to the State Clearinghouse and are evaluated to determine whether further communication between the reviewer and the applicant is necessary.

E. The formal review statement letter is prepared, returned to the applicant, and submitted with the application to the appropriate Federal agency.

An initial period of 30 days (unless otherwise stated in the Circular) is allowed for the Clearinghouse to carry out its review and comment process. An additional 30 days may be requested, if needed.

The North Carolina State Clearinghouse has devised a form, *Notification of Intent to Apply for Federal Funds,* which when completed provides limited information about a proposed project. This form is used to initiate the review. All reviewers, however, are assured access to additional information, including the completed application or proposal, upon request. Thus, should the project intent not contain adequate information, the completed application may be requested, and an additional 30 days granted to complete the further review. This additional time may be required whether or not the actual application is submitted, depending on the problems which may be encountered during review

If a problem or conflict does arise, the reviewing agency is expected to notify the State Clearinghouse: it is also encouraged to contact the applicant in an effort to resolve the problem. Often failure to understand the total concept of a project causes a reviewer to question its intent. The Clearinghouse acts as a liaison in the resolution of such conflicts whenever possible.

There are four identifiable types of comment relating to the review of projects: 1) conditional; 2) regulatory; 3) suggestive; and 4) critical.

A conditional comment states that as long as certain directives are carried out, the Clearinghouse is in agreement with the concept of the project. For example, if an applicant's project involves retaining a large body of water, he may be directed to take the necessary precautions to avoid mosquito breeding.

A regulatory comment reminds the applicant that he must comply with certain Federal, State or local laws. For instance, the applicant must obtain a State permit when constructing sewer lines.

A suggestive comment takes the form of advice to an applicant. Such a comment is usually offered informally, and might concern alternatives available to the applicant, such as the utilization of other programs to enhance the applicant's own proposed program.

A critical comment relates to the substance of the proposal. That is, it indicates an inconsistency with established policies or procedures. Every effort is made to resolve a critical comment before submitting the formal review statement letter. Since this letter is attached to the application which goes to the Federal funding agency, it is important to reveal only those conflicts which remain unresolved and which are significant enough to be brought to the attention of the Federal agency. A critical comment, for instance, might point out the nonconformity of a proposed aging project to the regional aging plan—or the failure of a head start project to meet State requirements for a head start program.

COORDINATIVE SERVICES

These procedures indicate that the primary function of the A-95 Clearinghouse is to act as a service agency to applicants and reviewers, assisting both in improving proposed projects while providing the necessary information for proper coordination of planning efforts.

A good example of the way in which A-95 provides this service is in the implementation of the *Housing and Community Development Act of 1974.* The regulations for Community Development applications are complicated, and the U.S. Department of Housing and Urban Development has urged State and Regional agencies to assist with the development of these applications. Since the applications are subject to A-95 review, the Clearinghouse is a central collection point for receiving detailed information regarding each proposed application.

The limitations of time have made project planning a hurried process. Projects included in a Community Development proposal, for instance, might not have been planned as carefully as is necessary to determine their feasibility. A-95 review helps to assure that each application complies with various laws affecting individual projects within the proposal.

To illustrate:

- A-95 refers a sewer line extension project to State engineers in the Department of Natural and Economic Resources, thus allowing them to make sure the extension line will not overload a waste treatment plant.
- Staff of the State Department of Cultural Resources are referred projects involving the demolition of buildings which may have historical significance—or projects which involve construction site locations which may jeopardize potential archeological sites.

Regional clearinghouses also assist Community Development applicants in writing or editing their applications to reflect Federal guidelines. As local reviewers, they play a large role in making sure that Community Development applications are consistent with local plans and regulations.

While the State Clearinghouse reviews all project applications which must be submitted through the A-95 process, regional clearinghouses review only those projects which affect their specific geographic areas. In order to assure a simultaneous review of all applications, the North Carolina Clearinghouse shares administrative procedures with its 17 regional clearinghouses (each a Lead Regional Organization). Consequently, all clearinghouses are able to communicate problems which have surfaced during the review of a project, and to assist each other in resolving these problems.

Regional clearinghouses, familiar with local programs, are able to interpret the problems of a fledgling head start program, for instance, to the enlightenment of the State Clearinghouse. Through its proximity to the local scene, the regional clearinghouse has a more direct contact thereby holding an advantageous position from which to negotiate resolutions of conflict.

While most State and regional clearinghouses share their final review letters, the North Carolina Clearinghouse has established a policy of not finalizing the review of a project until the regional clearinghouse has issued its comment. Substantive comments made by the region are usually acknowledged in the formal review statement letter of State Clearinghouse.

Coordinative efforts between the State and the regions are also expanded by sharing all State plans for the information and use of the regions. Summaries of each plan under A-95 review are circulated to all 17 regions. Since many State plans have a direct effect on local planning, this procedure alerts the regions to the fact that a plan has been drafted, providing an opportunity to request the full copy for a more detailed review.

Another coordinative responsibility which has been given to the clearinghouses is the review of all draft and final environmental impact statements written in compliance with the *National Environmental Policy Act of 1969.* In North Carolina the State Clearinghouse is the central reception agency for these statements, and refers copies to the affected regional clearinghouse as well as to interested State agencies. This process is carried out in much the same way as the *Project Notification and Review System.*

The Clearinghouse, through the regulations set forth by the Council on Environmental Quality (*National Environmental Policy Act, Appendix IV*) is also called upon to provide input for environmental assessments through the review and comment process. This assessment is a preliminary procedure used to determine whether the proposed project will have sufficient environmental impact to necessitate the completion of an environmental impact statement.

ADDITIONAL SERVICES

The North Carolina Clearinghouse (as in most states) is designated the Central Information Reception Agency to receive notification of grant-in-aid action of approximately 300 programs, making it possible for the Clearinghouse to provide information regarding the funding of many Federal programs, particularly those programs which have gone through the A-95 review process. This information can contribute much toward the coordination of all comprehensive planning for the State.

Some of the services made available to State and local governments include:

- A biweekly report, which consists of three sections broken out by region and by subject area (health, education, labor, et cetera). Included in this report are: 1) notifications of intent received during a two-week period; 2) applications which have actually been submitted to a Federal funding agency for its consideration; and 3) projects which have been awarded grants by a Federal funding agency.

This mechanism alerts reviewing agencies to specific proposals in which they may be interested; saves time and effort expended in referral of individual projects; and gives the reviewer the opportunity to request a project which may concern him.

The biweekly report also serves as a followup notice of projects which have been submitted for regional clearinghouse review, providing a checklist for project intents which should have been received for review by the clearinghouses.

- A data base for analysis of the Federal dollar flow into the State is a possible derivative of Clearinghouse information, once Clearinghouse records include a majority of applications which require A-95 review. It should be kept in mind, however, that there are about 145 Federal programs out of approximately 1,000 which require an A-95 review, and about 300 of some 1,000 Federal programs which require notification of the grant-in-aid action. Data generated through A-95 should be viewed on a program-by-program basis—not as a total Federal dollar appropriation for the State.
- A valuable input to comprehensive, systematic, and coordinated planning is afforded by the A-95 process. Through its established lines of communication, the Clearinghouse systematically routes planning documents to various interested and affected agencies.

The *Vocational Education Plan* will be referred, automatically, to the Governor's Manpower Council, the Employment Security Commission, the Department of Community Colleges, the manpower planner located in the Office of State Planning, et cetera. These reviewers should compare the plan and its programs to similar programs being developed in their own planning. Perhaps the *Vocational Education Plan* will be only informative to some; in other instances it may directly affect the organization or operation of another agency.

More importantly, A-95 data can help in eliminating duplication of efforts. Often there already exist facilities or programs which can be utilized instead of organizing a new program. Sometimes State agencies have compared programs before going through the A-95 process, in which case perhaps a referral by the Clearinghouse would be unnecessary. However, it is important that these agencies be given a chance to participate in the review and comment process, even though they may be aware of existing plans.

- Assistance to gubernatorial review can be expedited through the Clearinghouse process. Special funding proposals for such Federal programs as the Coastal Plains and Appalachian Regional Commissions often require the Governor's review. The A-95 structure is designed to obtain comments of pertinent State agencies and regional clearinghouses, thus allowing the Governor access to agency assessments prior to making his own final recommendations.

The fact that a State's agencies are unable to agree on a proposed project may seriously jeopardize the funding of that project. Access to all comments and recommendations made, and the resolution of any differences in viewpoint thus revealed, avoids the presentation of conflicting and disparate opinions to the Federal funding agency.

OPERATIONAL PROBLEMS

In its attempt to operate within the guidelines of the Circular, the A-95 program has a history of aches and pains. The whole concept of "planning coordination" has been seriously questioned by all levels of government. Probably the most pressing problem is the lack of Federal commitment to A-95. The U.S. Office of Management and Budget failed in its efforts to educate Federal agencies concerning compliance with A-95 procedures.

An applicant must be told about this requirement by the Federal agency, or he will not realize he must go through the process. If he does submit his project for review, there is a good possibility the Federal funding agency will not make sure A-95 comments from both state and regional clearinghouses are attached to the application. Worse yet, the agency is likely to ignore substantive comments made, funding the project without first considering the criticism and notifying the Clearinghouse of the decision made, and the reasons behind the decision.

Some Federal agencies have used every means prossible to get out of the "red tape" process for programs which should normally come under the A-95 review. Included in this lackadaisical approach have been such programs as Family Planning, Food Stamps, and Recreation Facility Loans.

Another frustrating experience for clearinghouses is the Federal practice of establishing their own review process, such as the *State and Regional Health 1122 Procedure,* and the *Chief Elected Review and Comment Process.*

Since A-95 was originally established to carry out reviews in all areas, it would seem logical to use this mechanism for all review requirements, rather than to organize parallel procedures which only duplicate the Clearinghouse function.

The Federal Government has also been slow in making Federal funds available to State and regional clearinghouses in order that they might have adequate staff to handle the administrative details of their programs.

State governments are often as guilty as Federal agencies in not supporting the A-95 process. If the Clearinghouse is not properly staffed to carry out the administrative function as well as the educational effort, A-95 is crippled—unable to operate at a satisfactory level of efficiency.

If the Clearinghouse itself fails to take special care to inform about A-95 and its requirements, then it can little expect to build the kind of information system which will be useful to interested governmental agencies.

Reviewers on the State level need to be taken far more seriously, and comments should be significant enough to warrant the attention of the Federal funding agency. In this regard it is very important for the Governor to use the A-95 Clearinghouse for assistance in decisions about Federal grants; otherwise, Clearinghouse comments may conflict with policy decisions of the Governor, leading to much confusion.

As long as Federal and State requirements for A-95 compliance are weak, regional clearinghouses will also suffer. Their governing boards will continue to be frustrated when projects they have before them for review are funded before they have had a chance to comment upon them. Worse yet, they may discover, through their local newspapers, that projects which require an A-95 review have been funded without their knowledge or review. These situations have a direct impact on how local governments view the effectiveness of the A-95 process. Lacking a commitment to the A-95 process on the Federal,

State, and local levels of government, the real effectiveness of the program, for any purpose, is seriously jeopardized.

SOLVING THE A-95 DILEMMA

There are no quick and easy solutions for the problems discussed here. It will be a long and uphill struggle to achieve an efficiently operating clearinghouse system. In view of the Federal foot dragging on A-95 compliance, perhaps the best course of action could begin at the State level, taking the following steps:

1. A positive commitment by the State to improve A-95 compliance. State legislation or an executive order by the Governor could make the difference in gaining the attention of affected agencies. Recognizing the benefit of such action, several states—among them Georgia, Washington, South Carolina, and South Dakota—have passed laws requiring the coordinated review of all applications for Federal funds.

2. Public relations. Clearinghouses need to "talk up" the services they have to offer both applicants and reviewers. Seminars on A-95 should be held, with State, regional and local participation.

    The existence of A-95 should be made known to prospective applicants, and the proper procedures for compliance, along with the reasons for A-95 requirements, explained. Once the importance of complying with A-95, often viewed as a "red tape" process, is fully understood, participation should be voluntarily increased.

3. Clearinghouse cooperation. A real effort should be made by the State Clearinghouse to request only information that is reasonable, and not in excess of that actually necessary for review. This information should be shared with all interested parties to the greatest effect.

4. A concerted effort by State Clearinghouses to influence the participation of Federal agencies in the A-95 process. State Clearinghouses in each Federal region should demand that the Federal Regional Council study, and subsequently recommend, the inclusion of A-95 requirements (whenever applicable) in the regulations of Federal agencies. This type of

movement, in which North Carolina is participant, has been initiated in Region IV.

The Federal Regional Council, which is responsible for the administration of the A-95 Circular, is even now seeking clarification of the problems encountered by A-95. The North Carolina Clearinghouse, through sponsorship of the Council, assisted with a seminar on the A-95 Circular for regional Federal employees in Atlanta, Georgia. The results have been noticeable. Regional agencies are now more aware of A-95, and improvements have been made in methods of reporting grant-in-aid actions and informing applicants of compliance requirements.

To further lessen the gap in commitment to A-95 in Washington, the states must search out ways to let Federal agencies know that A-95 is necessary to the coordination of planning efforts. This could be done through national associations for planners, county commissioners' or mayors' associations, and other special interest groups which have an impact on Federal policies and programs.

The A-95 process can serve a useful purpose in government today. The complicated processes of Federal, State and local bureaucracies call for procedures which will help sort out and coordinate the many programs being administered by public agencies. The A-95 process can provide many of these procedures.

How You Play the Game*
Appendix J

The U.S. Conference of Mayors had a point when it complained that, while the federal government gave wealthy Palm Desert, Cal., $2 million under a public works bill designed to create jobs in areas of high unemployment, no money went to Pittsburgh (10% unemployment), Seattle (9%), Phoenix (8%), and Toledo (7%). Dozens of other disappointed communities complained of getting short-changed and several even threatened to sue for a share of the money. But not Los Angeles; L.A. made out just fine, thank you.

In its competition for a chunk of the $250 million available to California, Los Angeles received $26.7 million—more than five times the amount of any other city in the state. Of course it tried harder, submitting eight cardboard boxes filled with 400 pounds of applications—253 separate applications in all, of which 34 were approved.

According to The Los Angeles Times, the city has dethroned San Jose as West Coast king of municipal grantsmanship.

Now Los Angeles did not do anything illegal or unethical. The Commerce Department's Economic Development Administration, in charge of dispensing the $2 billion for local public works that Congress passed over President Ford's veto, has gone to great lengths to point out that grants are awarded impartially. Requests are fed into a computer, assigned a numerical score based on the area unemployment rate, total number of unemployed, per capita income and how much of the project money would be for labor. While it isn't yet clear how Palm Desert turned up a winner, Los Angeles clearly wasn't hurt any by submitting so many proposals and putting review teams to work to reshape, improve and "fine tune" its applications.

This is the way the grantsmanship game is played, of course. It's probably a vast improvement over awarding money in proportion to congressional influence. Yet this recent experience with the money available under Title I of the Public Works Employment Act of 1976 should serve to dispel some misconceptions about the way federal money is awarded for jobs or anything else.

There is a widespread assumption that the government somehow knows exactly who or what needs the money, and that omniscient public servants see to it that the money is directed impartially and scientifically. But San Diego residents might wonder about that. While San Diego's unemployment rate was at least as high as Los Angeles' at the time the awards were made, all it got for its 44 applications was one piddling grant of $1.6 million for a sludge line.

Some will no doubt conclude from all this that the solution to these disparities is to quadruple the amount of federal money so that everyone gets a cut. In fact, President Carter hopes to double the grab bag to $4 billion as part of his economic stimulus package.

But there is a great deal more to public work stimulus than this world dreams of. It is not the most equitable or efficacious way of relieving unemployment, even when approached "scientifically."

A Twenty-Year Chronology of Major Events Related to the Management of Intergovernmental Relations

Appendix K

Date	Description
1953	President Eisenhower creates the Kestnbaum Commission on Intergovernmental Relations. The Report emphasizes its study of grant-in-aid programs and recommends the establishment in the Executive Branch of "a permanent center for overall attention to the problems of inter-level relationships."
1956	President Eisenhower creates the Office of Deputy Assistant to the President for Intergovernmental Relations.
1959	The Congress establishes the Advisory Commission on Intergovernmental Relations (ACIR). Consisting of 26 members representing the various levels and branches of government in the Federal system, the ACIR has served primarily as an organization for research and policy studies. Its potential as an arm of the Federal Government for managing intergovernmental relations has not been developed.

Date	Description (continued)

1960   The Joint Federal Management Assistance Program is established under the administration leadership of GAO. In 1968-69, the JFMAP undertakes to examine problems related to intergovernmental delivery systems. As a consequence of its review of the financial administration of Federal grant-in-aid, the JFMAP finds a need for the expeditious consolidation of categorical grants, a simplification of financial reporting requirements, and a simplification of audit administration.

1964-65   President Johnson by Executive Order establishes a number of interagency coordinating committees to help manage the complexity created by the proliferation of program grants and the demands of citizens for access to the process of policy and program development and resource allocation. Among these coordinating committees are the following:

- President's Committee on Manpower (E.O. 11152, April 15, 1964)
- Development Planning Committee for Alaska (E.O. 11182, October 2, 1964)
- Federal Interagency Committee on Education (E.O. 11185, October 19, 1964)
- Federal Development Planning Committee for Appalachia (E.O. 11186, October 23, 1964)
- President's Council on Equal Employment Opportunity (E.O. 11197, February 5, 1965)

1965-74   The Office of Management and Budget issues a series of administrative directives to improve the management and facilitate the process of intergovernmental relations.

1966   President Johnson uses the Executive Order for "Convenor Orders" to broaden further the Federal government's ability to develop cross-cutting analyses of a variety of Federal Programs. The Convenor Orders were based on the urban-rural split and served to broaden the essentially programmatic focus of the coordinating committees. Included here are:

- Coordination of Federal Urban Programs. HUD played the convenor role. (E.O. 11297, August 11, 1966)
- Coordination of Federal Programs affecting agricultural and rural development. Department of Agriculture played the convenor role. (E.O. 11307, September 30, 1966)

1967   The Office of Management and Budget establishes the Joint Administration Task Force. The Task Force was chaired by HUD and charged with reducing the time required to process the variety of Federal grant-in-aid applications.

Date	Description (continued)
1968	The Intergovernmental Cooperation Act (1968). In part, this Act (1) provided for supplying grant information to governors and legislatures regarding Federal grant program activities within their States and (2) modified the "single State agency" requirement in many Federal grant statutes.
1969	The Planning Assistance and Requirement Coordinating Committee, consisting of representatives from most domestic agencies, recommends strengthened program management and support to State and local governments for strengthened functional program planning. At this point, only HUD 701 provided comprehensive planning assistance.
1969	A three-year Federal Assistance Review (FAR) program is initiated. FAR is directed by the Secretary of HEW and includes 14 major departments and agencies. Its work is guided by the Federal Assistance Review Steering Group, chaired by OMB. Its objectives included: (1) the development of standard boundaries for Federal Regions; (2) the development of ten Federal Regional Councils; (3) decentralization—which included program and administrative delegations to Federal regional (and lower level) field officials to assure decision-making closer to point of delivery of services; (4) greater reliance on State and local government in the detailed administration of Federal programs; (5) a reduction in grant application processing time and red tape cutting, by program; (6) increased consistency in Federal procedures for planning, accounting, auditing, statistical data, land appraisal practices, engineering data, and other practices that impact on the management environment of State and local governments; (7) a simplification of the procedures for joint funding and grant consolidation; and (8) the implementation of the Intergovernmental Cooperation Act.
1969	The President's Council on Executive Reorganization proposes major changes in the organization of the Executive Branch of the Federal Government. Its recommendations resulted in the President's Departmental Reorganization Program which was submitted to the Congress in 1971. The PDRP—which failed to win Congressional support —would have created four major departments. Two of these—the Department of Community Development and the Department of Human Resources—might have been expected to have major impact on management of the Federal program delivery system to State and local governments.
1970	The Intergovernmental Personnel Act (1970). In part, this Act: (1) provided grants for personnel administration improvement (2) authorized mobility assignment programs and (3) opened Federal training programs to State and local officials.

Date	Description (continued)
1972	The President's Committee on Intergovernmental Personnel Systems is established by Executive Order.
1973	The President's Advisory Committee on Management Improvement submits its report. The PACMI Report proposes, among others, the following recommendations: (1) the formulation—by the Domestic Council—of an intergovernmental management policy; (2) a review of each Federal domestic assistance program at least every five years by the Domestic Council and OMB; and (3) an assessment by OMB of the immediate and long-range fiscal impacts of Federal programs on State and local governments.
1974	Committee on Policy Management Assistance is created by the Office of Management and Budget to assess Federal-State-Local intergovernmental relationships and to formulate strategic options to improve the policy management capacity of all levels of government.
1974	Joint Funding Simplification Act is passed. This Act provides authority to expedite procedures for consideration and approval of projects drawing upon more than one Federal assistance program, and to simplify requirements for operation of those projects.

Source: Executive Office of the President, *Strengthening Public Management in the Intergovernmental System* (Washington, D.C.: Government Printing Office, 1975), pp. 59–61.

The Federal System and a Sewage System (Grantsmanship and Informal IGR)*
Appendix L

WHITE HOUSE FAVORS

Now, of all things that can sway a Republican congressman, a Republican White House is probably the greatest. The White House, however, is not one man; it is a warren, a separate culture of assistants, special assistants, counselors, and all their deputies. Their roles are unclear and their authority never exactly defined but they can be the ultimate source of favors and dispensations.

A congressman, for example, is supposed to be something of a public-relations man for his district, and Vander Jagt once worked his White House sources for five months to be allowed to present a pair of wooden shoes to President Nixon as a gift from the people of Holland, Mich., who every year hold a Tulip Festival.

*Excerpted from John Corry, "A Typical Day in the Life of Guy Vander Jagt (Rep., Mich.)," *The Washington Post*, June 20, 1971. Vander Jagt is a congressional representative from Michigan's Ninth District.

In 1969, on a trip home, Vander Jagt met with some ecologists, urban planners, and Muskegon County officials who were trying to establish a new kind of sewage system to take the sewage that was wasting Lake Michigan and divert it to fertilize barren land. It was a stunning plan with implications for every city in the country, and it was being delayed by opposition in the state capital.

When Vander Jagt returned to Washington, he met with the federal people involved, and then finally, and most importantly, with John Ehrlichman, Mr. Nixon's assistant on domestic affairs. The Ehrlichmans are friends and neighbors of the Vander Jagts. Ehrlichman's daughter is their babysitter, and from more slender circumstances than these the fate of nations, much less that of a sewage system, has been decided.

Vander Jagt and Nagelvoort (his administrative assistant) talked to Ehrlichman for two hours about the Muskegon proposal, and shortly thereafter the whole federal bureaucracy became more interested in it. Nonetheless, the state government in Michigan still was not ready to accept it until Vander Jagt carried a letter from Mr. Nixon to Gov. William Milliken at his summer home in Traverse City. The President told the governor that he was personally interested in the sewage system, and although this was unlikely—the sewage system being a highly complicated project, and Presidents generally not having the time to study such things—it was *Realpolitik*. Subsequently, Milliken visited Muskegon, the state decided it supported the sewage system and the federal government announced a $2 million grant to get it started. Vander Jagt came out ahead too, when the League of Conservation Voters, which is interested in how *effective* a politician is, named him as one of only seven congressmen it was endorsing for re-election.

Subject Index

Administrations, presidential: Carter, 278; Ford, 136, 294; Johnson, 148, 318; Nixon, 60, 147, 278, 284, 294, 318. *See also* Presidents and IGR

Administrative autonomy: effects of grants, 145-146; neutral competence, 48; state administrators, 250, 274, 280. *See also* Generalists; Program professionals

Administrative settlement: 44, 131

Administrators. *See* City/county officials; City managers; Federal administrators; Generalists; Program professionals; State administrators

Advisory Commission on Intergovernmental Relations (ACIR): 5, 7, 53-56, 73, 108, 147, 158, 176-177, 205-206, 283, 288, 294-301, 305, 312, 322; composition of, 298-299; recommendations made by, 299; record of activities, 297-298; state administrators' contacts with and evaluation of, 299-301; statutory mandates, 297

Big Seven: 61, 149, 156, 160, 226. *See also* Public Interest Groups (PIGs)

Bureau of the Budget (BOB): 289-292. *See also* Office of Management and Budget (OMB)

Cities (municipalities): 9, 10, 70-71, 183, 193-206, 320; Eisenhower's view of, 290; employment trends, 10-12, 72-74; employment variation by function, 73; expenditures, 84-86; expenditures and federal aid effects, 85-86, 97; General Revenue Sharing impacts, 87-97, 158-159; General Revenue Sharing purposes, 153-154; intergovernmental coordinator(s), 3, 7, 180-181, 200; intergovernmental revenue trends, 75-77; intergovernmental revenue variations by size, 77-80; revenue trends, 37-39, 68-71; size and success at grantsmanship, 79-80, 199-200

Citizen(s): 1-2

Council for Northeast Economic
Action: 167
Council of State Governments:
62, 248n
Counties: 6, 9, 10, 11, 12, 38,
70-71, 183, 320; employment
trends, 10-12, 74-75; intergovernmental coordinators, 8;
intergovernmental revenues
(including General Revenue
Sharing), 80-84; revenue trends,
37-39; size and success at
grantsmanship, 80-81; state-
level influence, 186
Court: *See* Supreme Court
Court cases: *Baker vs. Carr,* 204,
227, 227n; *Frothingham vs.
Mellon,* 132, 132n; *Graves vs.
New York ex rel. O'Keefe,* 43n;
Massachusetts vs. Mellon, 132,
132n; *McCulloch vs. Maryland,*
42-43, 175; *National League of
Cities vs. Usery,* 23-24, 23n,
325; *Northern States Power Co.
vs. State of Minnesota,* 45n;
*Oklahoma vs. Civil Service Com-
mission,* 295; *Steward Machine
Co., vs. Davis,* 177, 177n;
Tarbel's case, 21-22, 22n; *U.S.
vs. Butler,* 132, 132n

Democratic (Democratic Party):
134, 149, 153, 156, 270, 271,
285
Dillon's Rule: 20-21, 21n, 24, 40,
228

Education: 13, 48; city expenditures on, 84-85; General Revenue Sharing uses for, 91-92,
118. *See also* School districts;
School officials
Employment, public: by type of
government, 10-12; cities, 72-
74; counties, 74-75
Executive leadership: 61-63. *See
also* Generalists; President(s);
Program professionals

Federal administrative depart-
ments and agencies: Atomic
Energy Commission (AEC), 45;
Council of Economic Advisors,
115; Council on Intergovern-
mental Relations, 289; Defense
Department, 55; Domestic
Council, 292, 293, 294, 305,
312; Economic Development
Administration, 165, 167; Envi-
ronmental Protection Agency
(EPA), 129, 310, 317, 318; Fed-
eral Interagency Study Com-
mittee on Policy Management
Assistance, 301, 302, 312; Fed-
eral Power Commission, 44;
Federal Regional Councils
(FRCs), 288, 291, 305, 306;
Goddard Space Flight Center of
NASA, 124; Health, Education,
and Welfare (HEW), 199, 296;
Housing and Urban Develop-
ment, 1, 57, 199, 211; Law
Enforcement Assistance Admin-
istration (LEAA), 196, 197, 221;
National Resources Planning
Board, 46; National Science
Foundation, 87n, 90n, 92n, 95,
117n, 158, 158n; Office of
Economic Opportunity (OEO),
55, 95; Office of Education, 13,
199; Office of Intergovernmen-
tal Relations (OIR), 293, 294;
Office of Revenue Sharing, 152,
159; Pacific Coast Board of
Intergovernmental Relations,
289; President's Commission on

cooperative, 7, 19; creative, 19, 54, 56, 215, 318, 324; dual, 22; economic, 26; flowering, 41, 58; layer cake, 41, 45, 47, 61; marble cake, 41, 46-48; national, 25; New, 4, 7, 135, 147, 224, 265, 270-271, 278, 284-285, 318, 325; old, 325; picket fence, 41, 61-63, 66, 182, 191, 210, 237, 258; water tap, 41, 49-50. *See also* Intergovernmental Relations

Federalist (papers): 16-17, 16n, 208, 208n, 209, 209n

Fungible (fungibility): 90, 98, 143, 159

Games, intergovernmental: 191-192

Game theory: 23-24, 33

Generalists, administrative or policy: 61-63, 66; federal grant effects on, 145-146; General Revenue Sharing views, 118; intergovernmental coordinator, 237, 245; state administrators, 254, 259-260, 278-279. *See also* Program professionals; Public interest groups, specialists

General Revenue Sharing: administrative feasibility, 151-152; ACIR evaluation, 158-160; civil rights, 157, 158; citizen participation, 94-97, 98, 159; criticisms, 157-158; decision making impacts on localities, 92-94, 98; decline of party politics, 149; equalization effects, 158; extension, 156-160; fiscal impacts on localities, 88-91, 98; fiscal impacts on states, 116-121; fiscal needs of state and local governments, 153-155; impact on

socio-economic groups, 89, 92, 159; intent of Congress, 152-154; New American Revolution, 87; NSF research, 158; origins, 148-152; partisan politics, 148-149, 271; reform of categorical grants, 155-156; support by state and local officials, 149-150, 160, 218; tax effects, 88, 159

Governors: 3, 13, 46, 56, 60, 62, 210-225, 320; chief federal systems officers, 26, 211, 222, 245; consensus among, 167, 222-225; federal grants-in-aid, 51-53, 216-222, 244-245; model cities, 211-212; picket fence federalism, 210-211; policy control, 211, 244; Potomac pipelines, 212-213, 244; sensitivity to tax increases, 109-110, 121. *See also* Governors' Conference; National Governors' Conference

Governmental units: types, 8-9; number, 9-10; employees, 10-12

Grant acquisition rules: 190-191

Grant search rules: 190

Grants: *See* Federal grants-in-aid; Federal aid

Grantsmanship: 3, 56-58, 79-80, 190-191, 200-202; *Catalog of Federal Domestic Assistance,* 3, 124, 129, 190, 197

Great Society: 25, 56, 215, 224, 290, 291

Governors' Conference: 51, 211, 215, 218, 223, 224. *See also* Governors; National Governors' Conference

Home rule: 194, 195, 228-229; state administrators' views on, 261-262

Name Index

Albert, Speaker Carl: 153
Anderson, David S.: 2, 4, 12
Anderson, Congressman John: 153
Anderson, William: 5, 5n, 6, 6n, 8, 9, 9n, 27, 27n, 235n
Anton, Thomas J.: 251n
Armbrister, Trevor: 225n

Bancroft, Raymond L.: 193n, 194n
Banfield, Edward C.: 184n
Beame, Mayor Abraham: 2, 4, 12, 79, 84
Beer, Samuel H.: 63n, 149n, 153n
Bell, Michael: 127n
Beyle, Thad L.: 168n, 212n
Bingham, Richard D.: 199n
Boffey, Phillip M.: 45n
Boggs, Majority Leader Hale: 149, 150, 317
Boyles, Harlan E.: 230n
Brazer, Harvey E.: 117, 117n, 118n
Broder, David: 223, 224, 224n
Bromage, Arthur W.: 46n
Brooks, Glenn E.: 215n
Brown, Bonnie: 3, 4, 7, 12, 186
Bryant, Governor Farris: 212, 290
Bryce, Lord James: 21, 21n, 22

Burgess, Philip: 301n
Burns, John: 227n

Campbell, Richard W.: 180n, 188n, 237n
Caro, Robert A.: 184n
Carroll, James D.: 180n, 188n, 237n
Cavanaugh, Mayor Jerome: 64
Clark, Senator Joseph: 24, 25, 25n
Connally, John: 150
Connor, Edward: 187
Corwin, Edward S.: 19
Cottin, Jonathan: 63n, 213n
Crook, Stanley K.: 289n

Dahl, Robert A.: 184n
Daly, Mayor Richard J.: 184, 184n
Davis, David W.: 25n, 286n
Diamond, Martin: 17n
Dole, Senator Robert: 226
Domhoff, William: 25n
Dommel, Paul R.: 157n

Eisenhower, President Dwight D.: 51, 51n, 52, 53, 133, 136, 215, 282, 284, 289, 290, 328

Cities/States Index